NEW PERSPECTIVES
ON THE OLD TESTAMENT

EVANGELICAL THEOLOGICAL SOCIETY
SUPPLEMENTARY VOLUMES

Monograph Series:

#1. *Emil Brunner's Concept of Revelation* (1954), Paul K. Jewett
#2. *Israel and the Arameans of Damascus* (1957), Merrill F. Unger
#3. *Darius the Mede* (1959), John C. Whitcomb
#4. *Karl Barth's Theological Method* (1963), Gordon H. Clark
#5. *Paul, Apostle of Liberty* (1964), Richard N. Longenecker

Symposium Series:

#1. *Inspiration and Interpretation* (1957), John F. Walvoord, ed.
#2. *The Bible, the Living Word of Revelation* (1968), Merrill C. Tenney, ed.
#3. *New Perspectives on the Old Testament* (1970), J. Barton Payne, ed.

NEW PERSPECTIVES ON THE OLD TESTAMENT

J. Barton Payne, editor

WORD BOOKS, Publisher

Waco, Texas · London, England

NEW PERSPECTIVES ON THE OLD TESTAMENT

Library of Congress Catalog Card Number: 75–111958

CONTENTS

V. Textual Criticism

VI. Theology

PREFACE

The essays that make up the following symposium, *New Perspectives on the Old Testament,* seek to embody things both new and old. The authors come from the United States and also from abroad. Most of them are professors of Old Testament and of subjects that are related to its study. Each presents a picture of recent developments in the field of his specialization, while emphasizing certain abiding values that date back to the teachings of Scripture itself. Prominent throughout are the results, both literary and historical, of current Near Eastern archaeology, with stress falling upon those primary source-documents that illumine the ancient milieu as it actually was. The goal of each contributor, moreover, is to transcend the negative, e.g., mere refutations of the divisive criticism of the 19th (or 20th) century, and to move forward into positive syntheses and into proposed solutions for areas of Biblical discussion whose centrality may be anticipated for perhaps the next twenty years to come. Each author expresses his own creative insights, while holding to the conservative Scriptural position of the Evangelical Theological Society, for whose twentieth annual meeting these essays were prepared and whose doctrinal affirmation, that "the Bible alone, and the Bible in its entirety, is the Word of God written and therefore inerrant in the autographs," is as old as Christianity itself (cf. John 10:35, Acts 24:14).

Meeting on December 26–28, 1968, in Philadelphia, the anniversary sessions of E.T.S. centered about the theme, "An evangelical review of Old Testament studies"; and to its six areas of discussion—historiography, Pentateuch, poets, prophets, textual criticism, and Biblical theology—the divisions of the present volume correspond. The key position-papers that were there presented constitute, with minor editing, the chapters that follow.

As coordinator of the program for the meeting, I would express my special appreciation to the two other members of the planning committee, professors R. Laird Harris and Walter C. Kaiser, whose labors extend back to 1966 and brought to fruition these *New Perspectives on the*

Old Testament; to all the contributing scholars, for sharing the results of their respective research; and as coordinator of publication for the book that has resulted, to Floyd W. Thatcher, senior editor of Word Books, Inc., whose cheerful cooperation has made possible this volume, #3 in the Symposium Series of the Evangelical Theological Society.

J. BARTON PAYNE,
Wheaton, Ill.
March 1970

ABBREVIATIONS

Books of the Bible

Gen.	I Kgs.	Ecc.	Obad.	Mt.	Phil.	I Pet.
Ex.	II Kgs.	Song	Jonah	Mk.	Col.	II Pet.
Lev.	I Chr.	Isa.	Mic.	Lk.	I Thess.	I Jn.
Num.	II Chr.	Jer.	Nah.	Jn.	II Thess.	II Jn.
Deut.	Ezr.	Lam.	Hab.	Acts	I Tim.	III Jn.
Josh.	Neh.	Ezk.	Zeph.	Rom.	II Tim.	Jude
Jud.	Est.	Dan.	Hag.	I Cor.	Tit.	Rev.
Ruth	Job	Hos.	Zech.	II Cor.	Phm.	
I Sam.	Ps.	Joel	Mal.	Gal.	Heb.	
II Sam.	Prov.	Amos		Eph.	Jas.	

Apocrypha and Pseudepigrapha

I Esd. (I Esdras)
II Esd. (II Esdras)
Tob. (Tobit)
Judith
Add Est. (Rest of Esther)
Wisd. (Wisdom of Solomon)

Eccl. (Ecclesiasticus or Ben Sirach)
Bar. (Baruch, with the Epistle of Jeremiah)
Song of Three (Song of Three Holy Children)

Sus. (Susanna)
Bel (Bel and the Dragon)
Pr. of Man (Prayer of Manasses)
I Macc. (I Maccabees)
II Macc. (II Maccabees)
Bk. Jub. (Book of Jubilees)

Periodicals, reference works, dictionaries, versions

AASOR   *Annual,* American Schools of Oriental Research
ANET   *Ancient Near Eastern Texts,* ed. James Pritchard (Princeton: Princeton University Press, 1950)
ASV   American Standard Version of the Bible
BA   *Biblical Archaeologist*
BASOR   *Bulletin,* American Schools of Oriental Research
BDB   *Hebrew—English Lexicon of the Old Testament,* ed. Francis Brown, Driver, Briggs (New York: Oxford University Press)
BETS   *Bulletin,* Evangelical Theological Society
BJRL   *Bulletin,* John Rylands Library
CBQ   *Catholic Biblical Quarterly*
DOTT   *Documents from Old Testament Times,* ed. D. Winton Thomas (New York: Harper Torchbooks, 1961)
EQ   *Evangelical Quarterly*
GTT   *Gereformeerd Theologisch Tijdschrift*
HTR   *Harvard Theological Review*
HUCA   *Hebrew Union College Annual*
IB   *Interpreter's Bible,* ed. George A. Buttrick, 12 vols. (New York: Abingdon)

ICC	*International Critical Commentary*
IDB	*Interpreter's Dictionary of the Bible,* ed. George A Buttrick, 4 vols. (New York: Abingdon, 1962)
Interp	*Interpretation*
JAOS	*Journal of the American Oriental Society*
JBL	*Journal of Biblical Literature*
JCS	*Journal of Cuneiform Studies*
JJS	*Journal of Jewish Studies*
JNES	*Journal of Near Eastern Studies*
JQR	*Jewish Quarterly Review*
JSS	*Journal of Semitic Studies*
KB	Kohler, Baumgartner, *Lexicon in VT*
KD	Carl F. Keil, Franz Delitzsch, *Commentaries on the Old Testament,* 25 vols. (Grand Rapids: Wm. B. Eerdmans)
KJV	King James (Authorized) Version of the Bible
LXX	Septuagint
MT	Masoretic Text
PTR	*Princeton Theological Review*
RB	*Revue Biblique*
RSV	Revised Standard Version of the Bible
RV	English Revised Version of the Bible
TB	*Tyndale Bulletin*
TWNT	*Theologisches Wörterbuch zum Neuen Testaments,* ed. Kittel
VT	*Vetus Testamentum*
VTS	*Vetus Testamentum Supplement*
WTJ	*Westminster Theological Journal*
ZAW	Zeitschrift für alttestamentliche Wissenschaft

Others

A.D.	*anno domini*	Gr.	Greek
B.C.	before Christ	Heb.	Hebrew
ca.	*circa, about*	i.e.	that is
cen.	century	masc.	masculine
cf.	compare	mg.	margin
ch.	chapter	MS, MSS	manuscript, manuscripts
Com.	Commentary	n., nn.	note, notes
e.g.	for example	p., pp.	page, pages
et al.	and others	pl.	plural
f., ff.	following	sing.	singular
fem.	feminine	v., vv.	verse, verses

I. HISTORIOGRAPHY

—1—

ANCIENT ORIENT, "DEUTERONISM," AND THE OLD TESTAMENT

Kenneth A. Kitchen

The present paper plays the role of a provisional sketch of one limited segment ("Deuteronism") from a large topic (ancient Oriental and Old Testament historiography) only partly explored, and worthy of extended study.

Here, the term "historiography" will be used in a broad sense to cover the whole gamut of literary and allied forms utilized by the peoples of the ancient Near East to express or allude to historical events, and not solely and narrowly (or "properly") of narratives exclusively historical in their purpose, as might be true in modern times.

It is not proposed here to survey all the different kinds of such written sources so richly afforded us by the Biblical world. Suffice it to refer the reader in passing to such cross-sections of ancient Oriental sources as are offered by Pritchard, *Ancient Near Eastern Texts,* to more extensive series of texts such as the *Ancient Records* of Breasted for Egypt and Luckenbill for Assyria, and to essays and notices on historical data in symposia,[1] articles[2] and books.[3] Our purpose is to note the relevance of some phenomena from the Biblical world for consideration of just one aspect of Hebrew history and Old Testament studies, with essential, but not fullest, documentation—the aspect of Deuteronomy, Deuteronomist(s) and "Deuteronism."

I. Introductory

In recent decades, discussion of the roles of the book of Deuteronomy and of possible Deuteronomic historian(s) has received a marked impetus from Noth's *Überlieferungsgeschichtliche Studien* of 1943 (reprinted in 1957). In line with other Old Testament scholars of earlier years, Noth considered the books of Joshua-Kings to be "Deuteronomic" histories, in the sense that their authors or organizing editor(s) had given

1

to the story of Israel an interpretation tied to the religious concepts present in the book of Deuteronomy (cf. Noth, pp. 3–4).

Noth, however, took the matter some steps further. First, he took Joshua, Judges, Samuel and Kings to be not four separate works, but rather four parts of what had been one great historical work, *the* "Deuteronomic history," spanning the Hebrew story from the entry into Palestine down to the fall of Jerusalem and incidents in the Babylonian exile (cf., e.g., Noth, pp. 10–11). Secondly, Noth considered that this great "Deuteronomic work" began its story not as late as Joshua 1 (because of retrospective references to Moses and the "law"), not as far back as Genesis-Numbers, but with the book of Deuteronomy (noting its narrative elements), whose historical introduction (ch. 1–3) would preface not simply the "Deuteronomic laws" but the entire great historical work as postulated (cf. Noth, pp. 12–14, 87–90). Thus, in practice, he distinguished almost a "Tetrateuch" (Gen.–Num.),[4] plus a Deuteronomic historical work from Deuteronomy 1 (excluding 31–34) to II Kings 25.

While some scholars have preferred to follow more traditional paths in their literary criticism of a full-sized Pentateuch,[5] Noth's view has found various responsive echoes in the last twenty-five years.[6]

But this general reconstruction deserves scrutiny; and so do the supposed marks of the Deuteronomist and his theology, widely accepted also by various scholars who may not accept Noth's larger and bolder scheme. The scrutiny offered here is of necessity specifically a limited, provisional, even fragmentary one; a full-scale account of such major questions would have to be on a larger scale. Limited though this essay may be, it will at least seek to utilize the extant (as opposed to reconstructed) Biblical data—which is all that we actually have—and also to employ the direct ancient Oriental context of the Biblical world itself, a vital factor by no means sufficiently taken into account in Old Testament studies, even today.

In dealing with larger units, nowhere is this clearer than in the question of the date and nature of the book of Deuteronomy. Conventional literary criticism for the most part[7] still ties Deuteronomy in one form or another to the reform of Josiah in 622 B.C., not merely as the stimulus but also as the key date shortly before which the book was produced, and at earliest sometime within the reigns of Hezekiah, Manasseh, or Josiah.[8] Furthermore, Deuteronomy is even then subjected to schemes of partition, implying incorporation of wholly different sources (e.g., attribution of ch. 31–34 to "J–E"), and from varying and later dates ("secondary" additions).[9] Thus, Deuteronomy is considered on these views to have been originated in the later eighth or the seventh century B.C. (using older, traditional matter), and to have been crucial for Josiah's reform, before (on Noth's view) being used or adapted as preamble or first part of a larger historical opus, either of ca. 550 B.C., or of ca. 620–587 B.C., supplemented in the exile (Bright). It then received later additions and was later removed and incorporated with Genesis–Numbers in the Pentateuch.

All this speculation is, however, plausible enough *only* as long as the ancient Near Eastern cultural context of the Hebrews is firmly excluded and the Biblical data are treated in an unreal vacuum. When one compares Deuteronomy itself and the supposed distinguishing marks of the "Deuteronomic historian(s)" with external data, it is not only desirable but seems very necessary to offer an entirely different view from that conventional-critical view sketched in the preceding paragraph.

II. Deuteronomy as Renewal of the Sinai Covenant in Moab

One of the most remarkable contributions to Old Testament studies by Near Eastern sources in the last two decades has been in the field of the covenant, beginning with Mendenhall's study of 1954, comparing the covenant-features of Exodus 20 ff. and Joshua 24 with Near Eastern treaties and covenants of the fourteenth and thirteenth centuries B.C.,[10] and noting the significant differences between these covenants (both Biblical and Near Eastern) and the later treaties of the first millennium B.C.

Mendenhall and others have, however, shown notably less inclination to apply this valuable background data to the covenant in Deuteronomy. Comprehensively, this has only been done by Kline[11] and the present writer,[12] with a study of phraseology, etc., done by several others.[13] When this *is* done overall, then there can be no serious doubt (on present evidence) that the greater bulk of Deuteronomy coincides very closely indeed with the fourteenth- and thirteenth-century treaties, even more strikingly than do Exodus and Joshua.[14] The essential difference in literary nature is that the Near Eastern documents are formal legal documents of the covenants concerned, whereas Deuteronomy is cast as the report of an actual ceremony of renewing a covenant in acts and speech.

The fourteenth- and thirteenth-century documents include six main aspects in *written* form (1–6), and these could be accompanied by two or three enacted aspects (7–9).[15] We find:

Written
1. Preamble
2. Historical prologue
3. Stipulations: *a)* basic
          b) detailed[16]
4. *a)* Deposition of text in sanctuary
    b) Periodic public reading
5. Witnesses
6. *a/b* Curses and Blessings

Enacted
7/8. Oath & Solemn ceremony
(9. Formal procedure against covenant-breakers)

The text of Deuteronomy yields the following picture:

Written	*Enacted*
1. Preamble (1:1–5)	(7) /8. (Oath &) Solemn cere-
2. Historical Prologue (1:6 to	mony (27)
3:29) with attached exhorta-	(9. Formal procedure: *rib;*
tion (4:1–40, 44–49) [17]	grows from Deut. 32)
3. Stipulations: *a*) basic (5–11)	
b) detailed (12–	
26)	
4. *a*) Deposition (31:9, 24–29)	
b) Reading (31:10–13)	
5. Witnesses (Song of Moses, for	
people, 31:14–23, 30 (back-	
ground), 32:1–47 (text, etc.)	
the book itself, for Levites,	
31:26)	
6. *a/b* Blessings and Curses[18]	
(28:1–14, blessings; 28:15–64,	
curses,[19] with summarizing ex-	
hortation attached (29–30) [20]	

The present writer cannot see any legitimate way of escape from the crystal-clear evidence of the correspondence of Deuteronomy with the remarkably stable treaty or covenant form of the fourteenth-thirteenth centuries B.C. Two points follow here. First, the basic structure of Deuteronomy and much of the content that gives specific character to that structure *must* constitute a recognizable literary entity; second, this is a literary entity *not* of the eighth or seventh century B.C. but rather from ca. 1200 B.C. *at latest.*[21] Those who so choose may wish to claim that this or that individual "law" or concept appears to be of later date than the late thirteenth century B.C.; but it is no longer methodologically permissible gaily to remove essential features of the covenant-form on a mere preconception (especially if of nineteenth-century [A.D.] vintage) of what is merely thought—not proven—to be "late."

This situation brings with it a variety of consequences, which find their echo not in almost abstract theory but in the known phenomena of the Biblical world. Some affect the large-scale interpretation of Hebrew history, and others the details of critical study.

III. Some Incidental Details

Before an evaluation of the large-scale picture, one or two details may usefully be considered. Thus, in the study of Deuteronomy, much has been made of the variations in address between singular ("thou") and plural ("ye") .[22] But the variation between singular and plural in a covenant-address is not restricted to Deuteronomy: variation in number and person is securely attested in the ancient Near Eastern treaties of the first and second millennia B.C., in which documents its significance for literary prehistory is *nil*.[23] As a criterion for literary analysis of Deuteronomy, it must therefore be definitively abandoned as worthless. Nor is it the sole such item; a variety of other "criteria" must be discarded with firmness as equally worthless, seeing that the phenomena concerned recur in various Near Eastern treaty-documents wherein the kind of conclusions so beloved of *Alttestamentler* just do not work.[24]

Noth described Deuteronomy 27:1–8 as "one of the most secondary elements" in the framework of the book.[25] Yet it fits perfectly well into attested covenant-form and usage as an equivalent of aspect 8, solemn ceremony; the categorization as "secondary" rests on no controllable evidence, and hence should be discarded as unsubstantiated speculation. Similarly, the attempt to remove chapters 1–3 (or, 1–4) from its role as historical introduction to Deuteronomy (so Noth, *loc. cit.,* among others) must also itself be ruthlessly pruned away: this very section is the indispensable preamble (1:1–5) and historical prologue (1:6 to 3:29, plus dependent exhortation in 4) of a late-second-millennium B.C. treaty of covenant, as the combined evidence of some two dozen Near Eastern examples clearly illustrates. Again, Deuteronomy 5 is not to be taken as "secondarily prefaced" (Noth, p. 17) to what follows. In this covenant-renewal, it connects with the earlier Sinaitic covenant-enactment and is the most basic part of the section of "basic stipulations" (chapters 5–11), which in Deuteronomy is so largely concerned to hammer home the fundamental relationship between Israel and its divine Sovereign (illustrated from their past experiences), before turning to detailed applications (12–26) .[26]

IV. The Concept of Exile

One particular and major methodological error that insistently recurs in Old Testament studies is the assumption that any and every reference to destruction and loss of homeland with deportation to an alien land must automatically be designated a reference to the Babylonian exile (or at most, to the Assyrian deportations of ca. 734, 722 B.C.) and therefore must have been first penned in or after that particular exile. This erroneous assumption is commonly applied to such passages as Deuteronomy 28 (verses 36, 63 ff., among curses), I Kings 8:46 ff., 9:7 (Solomon's prayer and divine response), and 14:15 (against Jeroboam I). Therefore, it will be in order to reiterate here[27] that the concept and practice of exile was *always* a potential threat to the Hebrews and other politically "small" groups for most of the second and first millennia B.C., and also to outline some of the background evidence for this observation.

Thus, already as early as the first half of the second millennium B.C. (the patriarchal age), one finds evidence of deportation and resettlement[28] in the Mari archives, ca. 1800 B.C. One official writes to Iasmakh-Adad, Assyrian prince of Mari, of 1030 men designated (?) by their sovereign as a gift for the palaces in Kaḫat by the Euphrates.[29] In a damaged letter, the prince of Mari announces the capture of the town of Bakram, and the deportation of its people and dependents to Mari.[30] A later king of Mari, Zimri-lim, refers to deportation (s) in damaged contexts mentioning 30,000 men (troops ?).[31] Further letters mention deportees employed on fields of the palace of Mari,[32] land assigned to such people,[33] a census of deportees,[34] and moving some who originated in Rapiqum.[35]

In the sixteenth century B.C., the Hittite king Hattusil I in his Annals tablet mentions removing and "freeing" the servile population of two towns, and taking them off to his own land for resettlement to the benefit of the temple of the sun-goddess of Arinna.[36]

In the fifteenth century, Tuthmosis III of Egypt on the first of sixteen campaigns in Syria brought home 2,503 prisoners, some 25,000 animals and much plunder (ANET, p. 237b). His successor, Amenophis II, is credited with transplanting over 100,000 assorted Syrians to Egypt from two campaigns (ibid., p. 247 and n. 48). A small stela of the next king, Tuthmosis IV, refers to a Theban foundation as "the settlement (so-and-so) with Syrians . . . (of) the town of Gezer" (ibid., p. 248a).

In the late fourteenth century B.C., the annals of the Hittite king Mursil II offer several such allusions to transferring whole population-groups as a result of military conquest.[37] One may note in passing 15,500 people of Arzawa assigned to the Hittite royal palace alone, those taken by the king's army being "innumerable," in Mursil's third year;[38] a similar number (15,x00) thence in his fourth year;[39] and a grand total of 66,000 in his fifth year.[40] Several thousand more are recorded for a much later year,[41] and small numbers in other years.

In the thirteenth century B.C.—the latest for the pattern of Deuteronomy—we find Egyptian texts at Abu Simbel describing Ramesses II as "he who has removed Nubia to the Northland, and the Syrians to Nubia; who has placed the Shasu-Asiatics in the Westland (= Libya), and established the Libyans on the (E.) hills . . ."—i.e., the concept of transfer of peoples from S. to N., N. to S., E. to W., W. to E. After ca. 1200 B.C., Ramesses III similarly brought Libyans over the Nile from his wars there; and such settlements of Asiatics and Libyans are attested in Ramesside Egypt from ca. 1300 down to ca. 1150 B.C. (Ramesses II to VI) and beyond.[42]

In Western Asia in the thirteenth century, the same practices occur: Shalmaneser I of Assyria then carried off the youths of Urartu for service in Assyria,[43] and 14,400 prisoners from Hanigalbat.[44] His successor Tukulti-Ninurta I claimed to have brought away 28,800 Hittite warriors as captives.[45]

Thereafter, ca. 1100 B.C., Tiglath-pileser I took 4,000 men from Urumai and Abeshlai in his first year, and 20,000 men from Kumani in his fifth.[46] In 879 B.C., Assur-nasir-pal II peopled Calah with captives from all lands that he had subdued,[47] and his son Shalmaneser III during some ten years' campaigning carried off some 44,400 people into Assyria.[48] And so on, for the rest of Assyrian and Babylonian history. The Israelite deportations of ca. 734, 722 B.C., and Judean ones in 597, 586/7 B.C., etc., are merely a few more in a very long series in the ancient Near East—a perspective so easily overlooked.

In short, the concept and practice of "exile" need not wait till the eighth to the sixth centuries B.C. to appear in Hebrew literature—it is as old as the patriarchs, and can have been no mystery to a Moses, a Solomon, or a Jeroboam I, any more than to their ancestors, descendants and their contemporaries in the Levant. The concept of being removed from one's land, not to return, is already reflected directly in the Hittite treaties of the fourteenth and thirteenth centuries B.C.,[49] as well as in the Assyrian treaties of the eighth and seventh centuries[50]—a curse-tradition lasting in treaties or covenants for *at least* 800 years, and hence acceptable as a concept in Deuteronomy from before Moses, let alone Josiah. Therefore, the concept of exile cannot be used to date passages in Deuteronomy, etc., to times in or after the Assyrian and Neo-Babylonian captivities of the Hebrews.

V. Continuity of Tradition

While much can yet be done to reexamine in detail the antiquity and integrity of the contents and structure of Deuteronomy, showing that a thirteenth-twelfth-century date need yield nothing on strictest academic grounds to an eighth-seventh-century date, such a survey would go far beyond the bounds and central concerns of this limited paper, and must be relegated to some more ample occasion. Instead, it is for the present more desirable to return from individual topics and details, and look ahead to the question of how a late-thirteenth-century book of Deuteronomy would affect (i) large-scale interpretation of Hebrew history, and (ii) what one may call "Deuteronism" in Hebrew writing and religion, and thus also to the question of the modern use of the term "Deuteronomic" in relation to Hebrew history, literature and religion—all firmly in the context of the Biblical world.

If the essential book of Deuteronomy on objective form-critical grounds[51] is a report of covenant-renewal to be dated to ca. 1200 B.C. at latest, then some Old Testament scholars might well feel that this implies a long stretch of time—almost 600 years—before its celebrated impact on the reign of Josiah. One might, therefore, be tempted to raise two questions. First, is such a long continuity of distinctive concepts (ca. 600 years) a fitting and compatible thing in the Old Testament world; and secondly, is there, then, really nothing Deuteronomic between Joshua and Josiah?

A. Continuity

A continuity of concept (especially in religion) of 600 years' duration is, in fact, nothing very remarkable in the Biblical Near East. Some examples may help to make this clear.

Thus, in Egypt, one may point to the literary tradition of the triumphal speech of the god Amun of Thebes to the victorious pharaoh, current on triumphal stelae and reliefs in the New Kingdom.[52] The characteristic literary elements of the speech are first attested in the poetical stelae of Tuthmosis III (Karnak, ca. 1470 b.c.) and Amenophis III (W. Thebes, ca. 1400 b.c.). The most characteristic parts of these were combined in the speech of Amun in triumph-scenes of Sethos I (ca. 1310 b.c.), Ramesses II (ca. 1304/1290 b.c., ff.) and later kings, and recur as late as Shoshenq I (ca. 945–924 b.c.), the Biblical Shishak. The entire tradition, therefore, is attested for nearly 600 years (ca. 1470 to ca. 925 b.c.), with one significant adaptation after the first 150 years. Furthermore, one may note "gaps" in the tradition, for periods when we have no examples, of this literary entity that nevertheless continued to exist or was re(dis)coverable. More striking than the sixty years or so from Amenophis III to Sethos I is the much longer interval from Ramesses VI (ca. 1150 b.c.) —last New Kingdom example—to Shishak (ca. 925), a "gap"-period of 200 years spanned by late Dynasty XX and all of Dynasty XXI, for which no examples are so far known.

Moreover, the iconography of the triumph-scenes—graphic witness for an important segment of "pharaonic theology"—to which the above-discussed literary form was attached by the Ramessides—shows itself a sweeping continuity of usage and tradition that entirely dwarfs that of the form just referred to, or of almost anything Biblical. The traditional scene of the pharaoh smiting his foe(s) already appears full-blown at the beginning of Egyptian history, ca. 3000 b.c.,[53] and it continues throughout Egyptian history down to the temples of the Graeco-Roman epoch, to the turn of the Christian era and beyond it, appearing also on the tomb-chapels of the rulers of Meroe on into the Christian era. In other words, we here have an ideological and iconographic continuity of tradition that lasted for well over 3,000 years. Examples can be multiplied indefinitely. Suffice it to allude to the Hymn to the Uraeus (Serpent) Goddess, under Ramesses II, known 1,000 years later under the Ptolemies,[54] and to the festival-text of the god Sokar which is attested with minimal changes for at least 800 years (between ca. 1200 and ca. 300 b.c.).[55] Or to the *do ut des* concept of exchange of benefits between the king and the gods in innumerable temple-scenes—explicitly attested as early as the IIIrd Dynasty (ca. 2600 B.C.) [56] and still the underlying and essentially unchanged principle with the Graeco-Roman temples[57] up to the second Christian century; again, a vast continuity (as least 2,800 years).

Furthermore, it must be stressed that the wealth of material from Egypt is not unique in this regard. One may turn to the shorter-lived civilization of the Hittites, for example, and see the same thing. One may instance the tradition of Hittite kings extending their frontiers "to the sea" (Mediterranean) and penetrating Syria.[58] This began with Labarnas I (ca. 17th cen. B.C.), was imitated in practice by Hattusil I and Mursil I (later part of 16th cen.), and is a visible theme in the Decree of Telipinus.[59] These themes entered Hittite literature in stories in picturesque language,[60] stories of sieges and personalities in Syria,[61] and even in an ancient prayer on behalf of the monarch, that the seas (Mediterranean and Black) may be his borders on either side (i.e., N. and S.) of the realm.[62] Such texts and traditions continued down to our extant copies which date to the fourteenth and thirteenth centuries B.C., and helped to induce later Hittite kings such as Suppiluliuma I to emulate their distant predecessors. The force of Hittite religious tradition was such that Hattusil III (ca. 1260 B.C.) restored the worship of the Storm-god of Nerik when he recaptured that place, after centuries[63] of neglect that had elapsed since its capture by the Kaskeans in the days of Hantilis I.[64]

Mesopotamia, too, would yield ample evidence of continuity of tradition in religion, literature, and many other spheres of life, rivaling Egypt and surpassing the Hittites, but a passing allusion or so must suffice here. The first great age of endeavor was that of the Sumerians, in the third to early second millennium B.C.,[65] while the Semitic contribution probably reached its first peak in the Dynasty of Agade (ca. 2400–2200 B.C.), and its maturity in the second millennium, thereafter showing an impressive continuity of literary, religious, and scholarly matter for the rest of the duration of Mesopotamian civilization, from before 1000 B.C. to the Persian age at least;[66] again, we are dealing with centuries and millennia, not merely a few generations.

B. A Supposed Gap

Furthermore, in all these cultures, there can occur not only centuries-long (even millennially long) streams of consistent tradition, but also great gaps in our documentation across which these traditions evidently survived, even though the means are not visible to our eyes at present. In this context, there is nothing unwarranted in having among the Hebrews a Deuteronomy ca. 1200 B.C., and six centuries elapsing until Josiah's reform, either on grounds of length of time, or on the apparent gap between the one and the other.

But that supposed gap will bear further scrutiny. Is (or was) there a real non-Deuteronomic gulf of 600 years, if one sets Deuteronomy in ca. 1200, long before Josiah's reform? One may doubt it; and at this point, one finds oneself beset by gnawing doubts about certain habitual procedures in Old Testament studies.

First, let us consider the concept that Joshua–II Kings[67] was originally a single great work, either written ca. 550 B.C. (cf. Noth), or ca. 600 B.C. (cf. Bright) and then supplemented. This large entity is *theoretically* possible—it could conceivably be correct—but it must, physically, yet remain an unproven conjecture. Thus, one notes that Joshua has no overall framework of headings or the like, whereas much of Judges has (the Hebrews' sins, cry for help, deliverance). Samuel, again, has no patently overarching scheme, while most of Kings does exhibit definite formulae for opening and closing reigns.[68] It may be objected that the subject-matter in each case is more, or less, amenable to arrangement under explicit forms; but Joshua and Samuel could have been given a framework, while Judges and Kings need not have had such regular formulae as they in fact do.

At the same time what may look like a good reason for assuming continuity between books is not needfully so on examination. Thus, Judges 1:1 appears to follow Joshua 24:29 ff. simply enough—yet not everything in Judges 1–2 is necessarily post-Joshua.[69] Judges 1 is rather, perhaps, an introductory panorama of tribal endeavor before and after Joshua's death, followed by the so-called Deuteronomic interpretation of Israel's oscillating relationship with God and status in the land, from which the rest of the book flows by way of concrete exemplification in history.

One concludes, then, that one factor apart, there is no reason why the book of Joshua should not be dated as an entity at any time from shortly after the death of Joshua down to the early monarchy.[70] The one factor otherwise is that of the supposed Deuteronomic editing which would ostensibly set the present main presentation of this book sometime shortly before ca. 622 B.C.[71] But *this* depends (a) upon acceptance of conventional documentary analysis, now known to be invalid,[70] and (b) upon the thesis that a Deuteronomic work could not be written (nor such sentiments be conceived or expressed) before the late seventh century B.C. With Deuteronomy at ca. 1200 B.C., of course, this second thesis can be dismissed as needless. The book of Joshua would illustrate the happy consequences of obedience to the Deuteronomic (and Sinaitic) covenant—regardless of whether penned decades or centuries after Joshua's death.

Turning to Judges-Samuel, one finds that the sequence of judges in the former ends with Samson in Judges 16, which (the presence of Philistines apart) has no direct link with the episodes of Eli and Samuel in I Samuel 1 ff., and in fact is separated from the latter by the interposed stories of Judges 17–21. Thus, the much more schematic and well-ordered book of Judges[72] forms a clear entity between Joshua and Samuel. Its date, inherently, may fall within broad limits, but not before very late in the judges' period at the earliest. One also notes the repeated mention in chapters 17–21 on what happened when there was no king in Israel, with (twice) people doing right in their own eyes (i.e., what they pleased, without restraint on evil). This factor could indicate composition during the early monarchy, a time still full of promise after David's accession to overall power. Again, the only real reason for favoring a later date is the unproven assumption that the Deuteronomic formulation represents a late editing of the stories (as with Joshua); but, again, with an early Deuteronomy, the early monarchy appears quite late enough (200 years after) for any such process. Indeed, it is easier to assume one deliberate composition at this period, using extant traditions, rather than successive conflations of multiple strands centuries later.

Finally one comes to Samuel and Kings. Here again, it has become fashionable to speak of a "Succession Narrative," linking straight across from II Samuel into I Kings 1–2.[73] It is fairly generally assumed that the original narrative[74]—a court history of David, showing how the throne passed to Solomon—must have been split up by the editors of our existing Samuel and Kings, with insertion of II Samuel 21–24. While such a narrative may conceivably have once existed, yet this whole picture is merely a modern assumption[75] and pays little heed to the question of why the chapters of II Samuel 21–24 have been placed where they now are or why the assumed "court history" should eventually have been divided between two books (Sam., Kgs.). In fact, these four chapters seem simply to be a "tidying-up," pulling-in the final strands of the history and reign of David, before ending the book. On the other hand, the author or editor of Kings seems to have used the last days and death of David simply as a means of suitably beginning the reign of Solomon —particularly as Solomon was proclaimed king (hence, was briefly a co-regent) before David's death (I Kgs. 1:43–47, 53, cf. 2:1, etc.). It would, therefore, be difficult to begin Solomon's reign without appropriate reference to the aging David, up to the latter's death. That both Samuel and Kings may have been using the same source-material for what we find in II Samuel and I Kings 1–2 is probable enough; but this does not prove that Samuel and Kings are part of one book, nor can we be *sure* that modern conjectural definitions, such as a court history of David, correspond to reality. The book of I–II Samuel may well fulfil, ultimately, a dynastic role for the young Solomon, as suggested by Whybray[76] and others. Furthermore, the whole entity would well illustrate first the failure of the old usage of "judges," and then of Saul's erratic kingship, before proceeding to document the far more effective role of David as God's chosen ruler (imperfections and all).

Hence, to conclude this consideration of Joshua-Kings, we may grant that Noth's unitary thesis is a possible one; but it is nothing more than that. Instead, one can suggest that Joshua is a work illustrating the fortunate consequences of obedience to the covenant, composed (perhaps) in the early judges' period to encourage Israel to maintain such obedience. Its opening chapter would thus deliberately reecho the covenant charges of Moses in Deuteronomy.[77] Long thereafter, in the early monarchy, the book of Judges (ca. 1000 B.C.) would have painted the evils of the intervening period of frequent disobedience and in its closing narratives have hinted at the kingship as a means of focusing obedience to God's covenant (instead of a man's doing what was right in his own eyes). Then, early in Solomon's reign, ca. 970/960 B.C., the failure of previous regimes, the glory of David and legitimacy of his son and successor—on the same underlying basis of faithfulness—was gathered into the pages of the present books of Samuel, originally one. Finally, in the long history of the "divided monarchy," several kings (e.g., Asa, Jehoshaphat) sought to heed in some measure these considerations of orthodox tradition; Hezekiah attempted a reform in this light; and, after the years of reaction of Manasseh, Josiah's reform gained impetus from the rediscovery of Deuteronomy or a related document. The issues involved (fundamentally, faithful response to Israel's God and none other) found their contemporary echoes in the prophets (not least Jeremiah) and were then summed up with the lessons drawn out in the book of I–II Kings compiled or completed in the Babylonian exile (by ca. 550 B.C.), with a final ray of hope falling upon Jehoiachin.

Second, it is habitual procedure in Old Testament studies, whenever certain attitudes or topics crop up in speeches or narratives of events— coinciding with supposedly "Deuteronomic" views—to consider these occurrences spurious to the characters and situations concerned and as largely embellished, or even invented, by the Deuteronomist(s), as though it were inconceivable that such things could be thought, said, or done before the environs of 622 B.C. A classic example ca. 964 B.C.— about halfway between Deuteronomy (ca. 1200) and Josiah (622)—is the dedication of the Jerusalem temple by Solomon, where (I Kgs. 8, esp. verses 15–21, 23–53, etc.) much of his speech (esp. in its present form) is widely referred to Deuteronomic efforts in the seventh to the sixth centuries B.C.[78] But, again, this is simply begging the question. There is no material proof of any kind that such sentiments and language must be seventh century or later, no proof that it is not of the tenth century B.C., by a speaker deliberately conscious of what is religiously "right" (in his particular cultural context), and influenced by a basic covenant-document of ca. 1200 B.C. For Solomon in his dedication so to pay heed is no more remarkable than is the corresponding concern for religious propriety in the dedications of other temples by other Near Eastern kings all over the Biblical world, at all periods of its history (cf. Section VII, below). It is all too easy to assert there is no evidence for "Deuteronomic" attitudes between ca. 1200 and 622 B.C., if one has first relegated all such evidence to 622 and later on *a priori* grounds; but such a proceeding is too far-reaching to be so based, instead of being rooted in controllable facts.

VI. A Cultural Profile in Depth

One may, however, suggest that we have in the Biblical record not merely a general continuity of religious tradition extending through the centuries such as is also found elsewhere in the Biblical world. One may, with due care, go further and begin to see a *historical profile* of Hebrew history[79] within its context, giving us a far greater perspective than is possible on the "conventional" treatments of Hebrew history and religion, with their heavily foreshortened views.

A. A Formative Period

Thus, one may speak of a *formative period,* in the Hebrews' case from before the classical patriarchs through the sojourn to the Exodus. Before Terah (Gen. 11:24–32) and Abraham (Gen. 11:27 onwards), we know nothing of the immediately preceding Hebrew prehistory or "protohistory" except for a genealogy of names (Gen. 11:10–25), some of which are reminiscent of North-Mesopotamian place-names. On the other hand, the extensive narratives (Gen. 12–50) about Abraham, Isaac, Jacob and his sons show us a series of people with definite ways of life, religious beliefs and practices and social norms; and these characteristics are directly comparable with those obtaining in the Near East (especially in Mesopotamia whence the patriarchs came) in the first half of the second millennium B.C.[80] They are *not* fully identical with what can be seen from the age of the Exodus and of the Sinai/Moab covenant—these latter betray a fundamental continuity, but also changes in details of customs or emphases. They also possess a fuller range of description in our surviving traditions. During the Egyptian sojourn, in the centuries hidden from us between Genesis 50 and Exodus 1–2, there would be no lack of contact between Hebrews and other Semites in Northeast Egypt, and between Semites in Egypt and in Canaan itself.[81] As for the Hebrews in Egypt, a whole realm of continuity and development is here hidden from us, simply through lack of explicit information.

B. A Crystallizing of Forms

Then, when the Hebrews left Egypt for Sinai, an event which culminated in the Covenant made there, one comes to a *crystallizing* of cultural forms and norms (already long-evolved) that in large measure was fundamental and normative for future ages. Here, in the accepted forms of the fourteenth to thirteenth centuries B.C.,[82] a covenant was made between a people and its Great Sovereign, in this case its God—a divine sovereign—with all the appropriate features: prologue to show forth the grace of the sovereign's initiative, and stipulations (basic and detailed) by which the fitting response of a people's obedience might be defined and regulated; arrangements for retention and reading of the covenant-document, witnesses to the act, and blessings and curses for encouragement and sanctions, etc.

This particular covenant, however, was not merely another political treaty like many of its contemporaries. Its provisions centered not on payment of tribute and military service, but on the right conduct of the life of a whole people—conduct rooted in exclusive loyalty to, and worship of, one single, invisible and all-powerful God. This conduct was to be marked not only by appropriate arrangements for His cult (tabernacle, offerings, feasts), but also by relatively high moral and ethical standards, finding expression in specific laws and customs (often retained or adapted from traditional Near Eastern usage) [83] reflecting social justice and requiring that the relationships of man and man should be on the same high basis as those of God and man.

C. A Basic Tradition

This covenant finds expression in Exodus-Leviticus and, after a forty-year interval, renewal in Deuteronomy. Thereafter, it was the basis—sometimes more or less observed,[84] sometimes more or less neglected[85]—of Hebrew social and spiritual life. Much else grew up during Hebrew history in both those spheres, but largely around this nucleus. It served to crystallize attitudes toward deity and the various social norms, and so left a characteristic impress on Hebrew culture ever after. In other words, the *Leitgedanke* of the fundamental covenant henceforth influenced in varying degree those who thought or spoke or wrote in Israel, early or late. From Joshua and the judges right down to the Babylonian exile and beyond, we thus have a *basic religious viewpoint and cultural tradition* visible throughout the tapestry of ongoing history in all the undulations of its varying pattern. It is, therefore, *no* surprise to find a Joshua reechoing Deuteronomic language, and so subsequently a Solomon at his temple-dedication—other Near Easterners had *their* reechoes of concepts and literature in just this way—and no surprise to find the prophets recalling Israel to their covenant (even with heaven and earth to witness), or directly to that faithfulness to their God as required by the covenant even when unmentioned by them.

* * *

Is such a depth of perspective unparalleled and anomalous? As hinted just above, not so, and certainly not so in the Biblical world itself. Suffice it to take but one example and merely to allude to others. In Egypt, one may see to advantage the phases of a formative age, crystallization of the characteristics of a culture, and its ongoing history with variations and enrichment with the passing of time, built on basic viewpoints and attitudes. Emerging from prehistory, Egypt's *formative age* was the Ist and IInd Dynasties (ca. 3100–2700 B.C.), when the pharaonic institutions can be discerned taking their form, whether in the monarchy, in religion, in the configurations of officialdom, administration, in art and architecture and so forth. By the beginning of the "Pyramid Age" (Old Kingdom) with the IIIrd and IVth Dynasties (ca. 2700–2500 B.C.), we can witness the full and rich maturity of that civilization, the *crystallization* of its typical cultural forms and outlook. Thereafter, much that was new or variable in detail was still to come, but the *basic viewpoint and attitudes* were already established fully or in germ. What was added was on, or became in some way largely integrated with, this basis, until at last an inner loss of faith and the impact of strong, alien cultures (especially Hellenistic) speeded the dissolution of the old, traditional order of life.[86] In Egypt's case, the overall unfolding was not from (say) just ca. 2000 to ca. 400 B.C. as with the Old Testament (patriarchs to the Persians), but from ca. 3000 B.C. to 300 B.C., and in religion up to ca. A.D. 300! So, the span of time in Egypt's experience was more than a millennium longer that what we have in the Old Testament.

In other cultures, similar unfolding can be seen, but the interplay of various peoples and cultural strains in Mesopotamia and Asia Minor leads to a less clear picture than in Egypt or with the Hebrews. Thus, in Asia Minor, while the earliest history of the Hittites is far from clear, yet they are a visible element of the population by the 20th century B.C., and from such early Hittite kings and federal chiefs as Pitkhanas and Anittas (ca. 19th cen. B.C.) down to the emergence of the powerful early Hittite monarchs Labarnas and Hattusil I, one may suggest that we have the *formative period* of the Hittite kingdom, with basic *crystallization* of cultural tradition and concepts in the Old Kingdom from Labarnas to Mursil I (16th cen. B.C.). Thereafter, through thick and thin, Hittite culture largely maintained its *basic traditions,* while synthesizing with Luvian, Hattic, etc., elements, and adding new things with passing time until cut off disastrously, ca. 1200 B.C. To take but one small facet, the Deeds of Anittas give us the germ of later Hittite annalistic writing; the Deeds of Hattusil I and the Decree of Telipinus, its first flowering. In the Hittite Empire period (ca. 1400–1200), the much longer and fuller

Deeds and Annals of Suppiluliuma I, Mursil II, etc., represent the final and full-scale development of the *genre,* but add very little new in principle.

Mesopotamia would deserve full consideration on its own merits, with the rise and flowering of both Sumerian and Akkadian periods of culture, merging in Babylonian civilization. The two former had their initial developments before fusing together in a formative period down to the early second millennium B.C., and the latter crystallizing in the course of the second millennium B.C., becoming thereafter the norm in Mesopotamia for the late second and most of the first millennium B.C.

In Syria-Palestine (other than the Hebrews), the very mixed population and culture and the extremely uneven nature of our information —Ugaritic texts, Egyptian and other external allusions, late classical writers, etc.—make it currently impossible even to sketch large-scale profiles with any safety whatever. Suffice it to remark on the evident millennial continuity in Canaanite religious culture, exemplified by comparisons between data from Ugarit and from late classical/post-classical writers, up to fifteen or more centuries apart.[87]

Thus, if the existing Biblical data and their configurations be taken seriously instead of being crushed into the procrustean bed of vestigial 19th-century assumptions, one regains a full-length perspective of the rise, crystallization, and ongoing stream of tradition in Hebrew history for up to 1,600 years, from the patriarchs to the Persians. Such a view is comparable with general profiles in the Near East as a whole: in Egypt and Mesopotamia for over 3,000 years (more complex in the latter), and in Asia Minor for the Hittites during ca. 800 years (their predecessors hidden in prehistory; themselves, prematurely cut off ca. 1200 B.C.). Compared with conventional views that limit the *floruit* of a deuteronomic viewpoint to only 150 years—ca. 650–500 B.C.—the Biblical data give us a full time-depth perspective in place of a flattened out and distorted picture lacking all depth.

VII. "Deuteronism"—A Modern Myth?

In Old Testament literary and theological studies and history writing, much has been made of the "Deuteronomic" school of theology, writers, and so on. The viewpoint adopted tends to be that this is one entirely distinct outlook within Hebrew religion alongside several others (priestly, prophetic, and so forth), and that this outlook stems from Deuteronomy. In comparing Deuteronomic tenets with the rest of the Old Testament, however, and also with the wider Biblical world, one begins to wonder whether in fact the isolation of a specific Deuteronomic outlook is not somewhat overdrawn, not to say illusory, and whether the label Deuteronomic should not be dropped altogether, as being too narrow.

That there is ample comparison between supposedly Deuteronomic ideas and the rest of the Old Testament is something that can be checked by any Biblical student for himself at leisure, so brevity must rule here. Within the detailed laws of Deuteronomy itself, there is some community of matter with the so-called JE, H, and P matter.[88] Theologically, the Chronicler is a keen Deuteronomist—or, rather, Deuteronomic views on obedience to the covenant-law and against pagan practice (inevitable with an effective monotheism) are common ground between Deuteronomy, Kings etc. and Chronicles. Ezra, long after the Babylonian exile, is Deuteronomic enough to note fulfillment of prophecy (1:1)—and, surely, it is of the nature of prophecy that one should expect it to be fulfilled? In the Psalms, there is attention paid to obedience versus disobedience, to tribulation and deliverance (cf. Pss. 78, 81, 105—emphasis on covenant and obedience to it—106, and cf. 107 passim). And in Proverbs some of the same underlying basic viewpoints are to be seen, albeit in different garb and with emphasis on social justice.[89] The concern of the Hebrew prophets to recall their people to the path of faithfulness and away from paganism, etc., needs no more than mere allusion here. In fact, a careful reading of the Old Testament at large may simply indicate that much of what is attributed to the Deuteronomic viewpoint is but the common ground of Hebrew mainstream belief (orthodoxy if one will), with rather little that is absolutely distinctive. Hence, "covenantal" (or, "mainstream" rather than "orthodox"?) would be a fairer label than "Deuteronomic," if label be needed.

Not a little, however, of the realm of Deuteronomic concepts is common property far beyond Israel. The Deuteronomic concept of obedience to God and to His word has its equivalents elsewhere in the Biblical world.[90] In Egypt, the norm is not a covenant but *Ma'at,* a term covering truth, righteousness, justice, and the proper world-order. To this norm, gods, kings, and commoners *must* conform—a fact (and a Deuteronomic type of attitude) attested to satiety in Egypt for three millennia.[91] In Deuteronomy 17:19–20, obedience to God's word is enjoined upon any king that the Hebrews may elect. With a truly "Deuteronomic" spirit, a dozen Egyptian pharaohs of all periods from the Middle Kingdom to the Late Period (twelve centuries) can be cited in one breath[92] as performing "in accordance with all that the majesty of the god has commanded . . . ," ". . . according to his command . . . ," "I have not transgressed the command . . . assigned to me . . . ," "I have not acted without him" (i.e. the god), "it is he who commanded me to act"—even, with a flourish of election and predestination (Sesostris I, ca. 1950 B.C.), "he [the god] created me [the king] . . . to execute what he commanded to be done."

One may profitably return to the so-called Deuteronomic prayer of Solomon in I Kings 8. The concern with "sin and retribution"[93] is by no

means confined to Solomon among royalty, or to his supposed Deuteronomic ghost-writer. With I Kings 8:46, "there is no man that sins not,"
compare three centuries earlier (ca. 1300 B.C.) the confession by the Hittite king Mursil II in his plague-prayers (ANET, p. 395b, § 9) : "it is
only too true that man is sinful." Did he, also, have a Deuteronomic
ghost-writer? About 1,000 years earlier still (ca. 2200 B.C.), the pharaoh
Merikarē's father confesses how he sinned by violating ancient tombs,
and has suffered retribution for his transgression (ANET, pp. 416a, line
70, and 417a/b, 120).[94] In the thirteenth century B.C., one may note such
humble Egyptian Deuteronomists as the workmen Nebrē' and Nefer'abet:
"the servant ever does wrong, the Lord is ever merciful" (after deliverance of the former's son after punishment), and "when I committed
transgression against the Peak [goddess], she punished me . . . she pur-
sued him who transgressed against her . . . ; I called . . . she turned in
mercy,"[95] with a sequence worthy of Judges.

The famous prayer of Ramesses II to Amun of Thebes in the Battle
of Qadesh shows at least two aspects of Deuteronomic interest. Noth
characterizes the concept of prayer towards the Jerusalem temple (I
Kgs. 8:29, 30, 42, 44) as "Kibla," citing only late parallels.[96] But already,
in the thick of the Battle of Qadesh, Ramesses II (13th cen.) prays "at
the end of the foreign lands, and my voice re-echoes in Thebes" (Poem
120 ff.). And for obedience to his god, he is a Deuteronomist to equal his
contemporary Moses and hardly to be bettered: "Have I done any concern without thee? Did I not walk and halt at a word of thine? I have not
disobeyed a matter that thou didst command" (Poem, 95, etc.). "What
will men say, if (ever) a little thing befall him who bends himself to thy
will? Do good to him who counts on thee, then will one act for thee with
a loving heart"[97] (Poem, 108–110). "O Amun, I have not overstepped thy
will" (Poem, 120 ff.). Thereafter, the fulfillment of the prayer by Amun
is recounted with as much gusto as any Deuteronomist did over the fulfillment of prophecy.[98] And the concept of predictive prophecy as something
liable to be fulfilled is not foreign to Egypt.[99]

That cult-centralization is the great care of Deuteronomy is false; pro-
portionately little space is given to this, as can be seen on investigation.
Even in Kings, the great objection to other places of worship is their
pagan or paganizing rites. The reforms of Hezekiah and Josiah are far
more a purifying than a centralizing of cult; the latter in any case was not
new in 622 in the light of the temple existing from Solomon's time, and
the tabernacle since Sinai before that.

Then, sometimes, Old Testament scholars imagine features in their
"Deuteronomist" to be peculiar, which features are, in fact, common-
place and of no significance whatsoever. Thus, Noth seeks to play down
the role of the Jerusalem temple as such (cultically) in Solomon's prayer,
claiming that there is no reference therein to the temple's role as the

place of offering. But surely Solomon (or for Noth, "Dtr") knew this was its basic function.[100] For Noth, apparently, nothing can ever be taken for granted. In point of fact, the ritual is, of course, presupposed; what matters in the prayer is the spiritual role of the temple, the place where God's Name (or, glory) is, where He hears prayer—not the mere mechanisms of ritual. It is instructive to look not only at Solomon's dedicatory prayer, but also at the dedicatory inscriptions and addresses of other ancient Oriental kings for their temples. At Luxor, Amenophis III (ca. 1400–1360 B.C.) built a superb temple for Amun, with numerous dedicatory texts, and across the Nile his own great funerary temple with dedicatory stelae. Time and again, these texts dwell upon the splendor of the building, its role as the abode of the god, the piety of the king, etc. But in these scores of lines, there are hardly more than three or four brief and generalized references specifically to offerings and ritual![101] At the other end of the Near East, 800 years later, a series of texts of Nebuchadnezzar II of Babylon similarly concentrate on almost everything except the details of offerings and ritual.[102] So Solomon here is neither Deuteronomic nor extraordinary—just healthily normal.

Conclusion

So one might continue, with other concepts and further evidence; he need not limit himself to "Deuteronomics," the main theme of this paper. Suffice it to sum up thus. Much that is called Deuteronomic is common ground conceptually in the religions and society of the Biblical Near East at large, and not even specifically Israelite, let alone specially Deuteronomic within Israel. Such matter, therefore, should not be erected into a Deuteronomic system, and least of all dated as late as the seventh century B.C. These concepts are used in the Old Testament with a power and a truth that is without compare at the deepest level in the Near East; but they should not be forced into a straightjacket. The theory of Deuteronomist(s) and a Dtr. history reflects, undoubtedly, a segment of truth; but this theory may have refracted it needlessly in the process. Some readers may well consider the writer of this paper to have somewhat kicked over the traces; but, pray, may they first meditate upon the data offered before descending upon the culprit with Deuteronomic retribution!

Notes

1. E.g., those in Robert C. Dentan (ed.), *The Idea of History in the Ancient Near East* (New Haven & London: Yale University Press, 1955).

2. E.g., C. de Wit, "Egyptian Methods of Writing History," EQ, 28 (1956): 158–69.

3. E.g., for early Anatolia, in A. Goetze, *Kleinasien* (Munich: C. H. Beck, 1957), pp. 82–85, supplemented by (e.g.) E. Laroche, "Catalogue des Textes Hittites," I–IV, in

Revue Hittite et Asianique, 14–16 (Fascs. 58–60, 62, 1956–58), and H. Otten, "Schrift, Sprache und Literatur der Hethiter" in G. Walser (ed.), *Neuere Hethiterforschung*, "Historia, Einzelschriften," 7 (Wiesbaden: Franz Steiner, 1964), pp. 11–22.

4. A term used by others rather than by Noth himself, e.g. by John Bright in G. Ernest Wright (ed.), *The Bible and the Ancient Near East* (London: Routledge & Kegan Paul; New York: Doubleday; 1961), p. 19. Noth's Pentateuch is (roughly) Gen.-Num. plus Deut. 31–34, cf. his *Überlieferungsgeschichte des Pentateuch* (Stuttgart: Kohlhammer, 1948), pp. 5–6.

5. E.g., Harold H. Rowley, *The Growth of the Old Testament* (London: Hutchinson University Library; New York: Hillary House; 1950/64), or Otto Eissfeldt, *The Old Testament, An Introduction* (Oxford: Basil Blackwell; New York: Harper, 1965), pp. 134–6, etc.

6. At random, cf. (e.g.) George W. Anderson, *A Critical Introduction to the Old Testament* (London: Duckworth; Naperville, Ill.: Allenson, Inc., 1960; 1959), pp. 93–6, and *idem*, *The History and Religion of Israel* (Oxford: University Press, 1966), pp. 5, 49, etc.; Bright, *loc. cit.* (note 4, above), and his *A History of Israel* (Philadelphia: Westminster, 1959; London: SCM Press; 1960), pp. 118, 312, 330 (Deut.–II Kgs.), 330 (Josh.–II Kgs.). Cf. also Eissfeldt, *op. cit.* (note 5, above), 242–3.

7. For other views, cf. Eissfeldt, *op. cit.*, pp. 172–3, and Edward J. Young, *An Introduction to the Old Testament* (Grand Rapids, Mich.: Eerdmans, 1958; London: Tyndale Press; 1964), pp. 145–7.

8. Cf. (e.g.) the outline given by Eissfeldt, pp. 171–3.

9. Cf. for example, Martin Noth, *Überlieferungsgeschichtliche Studien* (Tübingen: Max Niemeyer, 1957, repr. of 1943), pp. 16–18; among older examples, Samuel R. Driver, *An Introduction to the Literature of the Old Testament*, 9th ed. (Edinburgh: Clark; Magnolia, Mass.: Peter Smith; 1913), pp. 72, 93–8.

10. G. E. Mendenhall, BA, 17 (1954), 26–46, 50–76 (esp. 53–70), reprinted as *Law and Covenant in Israel and the Ancient Near East* (Pittsburgh: Biblical Colloquium, 1955).

11. Meredith G. Kline, *Treaty of the Great King* (Grand Rapids: Eerdmans, 1963).

12. Kenneth A. Kitchen, *Ancient Orient and Old Testament* (London: Tyndale Press; Chicago: Inter-Varsity Press, 1966), pp. 90–102, with analyses (96–9), in brief form based on observations of 1955.

13. Cf. *Ibid.*, pp. 91 ff., note 15 ff.

14. The fully independent analyses by Kline and myself concord remarkably well; some minor differences arise principally from slightly different methods used of setting out the data.

15. The use of the numeral 7 to 9 does not (for 7 & 8) necessarily indicate that these features come in order of performance after 1–6.

16. A distinction usefully made by K. Baltzer, *Das Bundesformular* (Neukirchen Kreis Moers: Neukirchener Verlag, 1960), pp. 20, 22–4.

17. Deut. 4:41–43 is an incidental enactment; on ch. 4, note also Kline, *op. cit.* p. 31.

18. As already pointed out (my *Ancient Orient and Old Testament*, p. 97 and note 39), Deuteronomy contains all the essential elements of 14th–13th cen. treaties and covenants, but its order of Witnesses, Blessings, Curses exactly reverses the ancient Near Eastern order of Curses, Blessings, Witnesses; and this may be a specifically Hebrew and Old Testament variant feature. Such purely minor variations can occur, as already pointed out in *Anc. Orient & OT*, p. 93, n. 25, and that in covenants regulating a people as opposed to a vassal monarch.

19. On the preponderance of curses, cf. *ibid.*, pp. 97 f., note 41.

20. Itself following the schema of preamble, historical prologue, and stipulations (the "C" of *ibid.*, pp 96–7), passing into exhortation like ch. 4.

21. After which approximate date, the widespread upheavals (Sea Peoples, etc.)

wrought great demographic and social changes in the ancient Near East (cf. standard histories).

22. So, for example, Staerk, *Das Deuteronomium* (1894), or Steuernagel, *Deuteronomium und Josua* (1900), in earlier days. In recent times, cf. use of this criterion by Noth, *op. cit.*, pp. 16–17, also Gerhard von Rad, *Studies in Deuteronomy* (Naperville, Ill.: Allenson, Inc., 1950; London: SCM Press, 1953), p. 11, note 1, initially.

23. As already indicated by Baltzer, *Das Bundesformular*, pp. 29, n. 4, and 49, n. 2 (1st and 3rd sing.), 43, n. 1 (2nd sing. and pl.); W. L. Moran, *Biblica*, 43 (1962), 103, non-covenantal examples; and D. R. Hillers, *Treaty-Curses and the Old Testament Prophets* (Rome: Pontifical Biblical Institute, 1964), pp. 32–3, citing 2nd pers. sing. and pl. variations in the Sfiré and Assur-nirari treaties.

24. This should be perfectly plain, e.g. from the data presented by Hillers, *op. cit.*, pp. 30–5, on Deut. 28, where a whole series of misconceptions finds its answer in first-hand Near Eastern data.

25. Noth, *op. cit.*, p. 16.

26. On the distinction of basic and detailed stipulations, cf. Baltzer, in note 16, above —a distinction independently established for Deut. 5–11, 12–26, by Kline, *op. cit.*, p. 32 (but without using formal terminology as did Baltzer and I).

The main distinction in emphasis between Deuteronomy and the Near Eastern Treaties is that the former is a covenant of religious import, affecting the spiritual and daily life of a whole people far more fundamentally than the purely political treaties between rulers (affecting their people mainly in terms of tribute, troops, and diplomatic/economic relations). The *same* major means of expression is, however, being used for two parallel purposes: to regulate the relations between a divine sovereign and his people in one case, and between an earthly great king and a vassal king and state in the other case.

27. Developing the data and points briefly made by me in the *Theological Students' Bulletin,* 41 (Spring, 1965): 11–12.

28. Already in 1927, Rudolph Kittel, *Geschichte des Volkes Israel*, III/1, p. 105 f., cited military settlement of personnel under Hammurabi of Babylon, after Meissner, but failed to heed its implications, perhaps as it was not a real example of "exile."

29. G. Dossin, *Archives Royales de Mari . . . traduite (s)* (Paris: Imprimerie Nationale, 1952), V, Letter 27.

30. *Ibid.*, V, Letter 2.

31. *Ibid.*, II, Letter 67.

32. *Ibid.*, IV, Letter 4:5′ ff.; cf. IV, Letter 86, *passim.*

33. *Ibid.*, V, Letter 85; IV, Letter 4.

34. *Ibid.*, V, Letter 35.

35. *Ibid.*, V, Letter 29.

36. H. Otten, *Mitteilungen der Deutschen Orient-Gesellschaft,* 91 (1958): 83, rs. 11–17; cf. Otten, *Saeculum,* 15 (1964): 119.

37. See Albrecht Götze, *Die Annalen des Muršiliš* (Leipzig: Hinrichs, 1933).

38. *Ibid.*, pp. 56/7.

39. *Ibid.*, pp. 64/5.

40. *Ibid.*, pp. 76/7.

41. *Ibid.*, pp. 170/1.

42. For references and brief discussion, see S. Sauneron and J. Yoyotte, "Traces d'établissements asiatiques en Moyenne-Égypte sous Ramses II," *Revue d'Égyptologie,* 7 (1950): 67–70, esp. 70. Under king Ay, a "Field of the Hittites" is attested at Memphis (W. Helck, *Urkunden der 18. Dynastie* (Berlin: Akademie-Verlag, 1958), p. 2109, and *Deutsch,* 1961, p. 402.

43. Daniel D. Luckenbill, *Ancient Records of Assyria and Babylonia* (Chicago: University Press, 1926), I, § 114.

44. *Ibid.*, § 116.

45. *Ibid.*, §§ 164, 171; cf. E. F. Weidner, *Die Inschriften Tukulti-Ninurtas I und seiner Nachfolger* (Graz: Selbstverlag, 1959), p. 26.

46. Luckenbill, *op. cit.*, I, §§ 318, 321, respectively.

47. *Ibid.*, §§ 489, 511, etc.

48. *Ibid.*, § 616.

49. Cf. Weidner, *Politische Dokumente aus Kleinasien* (Leipzig: Hinrichs, 1923), pp. 54–5, lines 48, 51 (no return), noted by Hillers, *op. cit.*, p. 34.

50. Esarhaddon's treaty/ies with the Medes (Donald J. Wiseman, *Iraq*, 20 (1958): 51–2, lines 291–5 (exile), as noted by Moran, *Biblica*, 43 (1962): 103.

51. I.e., controlled by tangible, external evidence, physically open to inspection.

52. Full references for texts with publication of some, and a preliminary study of this tradition with earlier references, will be found in Kenneth A. Kitchen and G. A. Gaballa, "Ramesside Varia II," *Zeitschrift für Aegyptische Sprache*, 96 (1969).

53. On the famous palette of Narmer, founder of the 1st Dynasty.

54. Treated by Jacques Vandier, "Quatre variantes ptolémaïques d'un hymne ramesside," *Zeitschrift für Aegyptische Sprache*, 93 (1966): 132–43. A precisely similar span (or longer) is exhibited by the myth of the divine birth of Pharaoh, cf. latterly G. A. Gaballa, "New Evidence on the Birth of Pharaoh," *Orientalia*, 36 (1967): 299–304.

55. See compact but full treatment by Gaballa and Kitchen, "The Festival of Sokar," *Orientalia*, 38 (1969): 1–76.

56. Cf. Georges Posener, *De la Divinité du Pharaon* (Paris: La Societé Asiatique, 1960), p. 40.

57. E.g., P. Derchain, "Le rôle du roi d'Égypte dans le maintien de l'ordre cosmique," in *Le Pouvoir et le Sacré* (Brussels: Institut Solvay, 1962), pp. 61–73 *passim*.

58. Cf. Jaan Puhvel, "The Sea in Hittite Texts," in *Studies . . . Joshua Whatmough* (1957), pp. 225–37; on the present aspect, more briefly, Kitchen, *Suppiluliuma, I Protagonisti della Storia Universale*, I, No. 66 (Milan: C.E.I., 1966), p. 258.

59. "Proclamation of Telipinus," §§ 3, 6, 8, in (e.g.) Edgar H. Sturtevant and G. Bechtel, *A Hittite Chrestomathy* (Philadelphia: Linguistic Society of America, 1935,² 1952), pp. 182/3, 184/5.

60. Otten, *Zeitschrift für Assyriologie*, 55/NF.21 (1963): 156–68, and *Saeculum*, 15 (1964), 117 n. 10, 118.

61. *Ibid.*, pp. 120–1 and references.

62. *Ibid.*, p. 117 and n. 8.

63. In the Hittite text (KUB, XXV:21) put at "500 years," but in fact nearer to 350 years; cf. A. Goetze, BASOR, No. 122 (1951): 24–5 (the mention is by Hattusil III's son and successor Tudkhalia IV).

64. Reserves about this datum by E. von Schuler, *Die Kaškäer* (Berlin: de Gruyter, 1965), pp. 22–5, rest perhaps too heavily on negative evidence.

65. I.e., in the historical period as determined by the emergence of clear written records, without prejudice to the notable achievements in the pre-literate periods.

66. Cf. (e.g.) the sketch of Sumerian and Akkadian traditions into and from the second millennium B.C. given by Wilfrid G. Lambert, *Babylonian Wisdom Literature* (Oxford: University Press, 1960), pp. 1–20; and cf. A. Leo Oppenheim, *Ancient Mesopotamia* (Chicago: University Press, 1964), pp. 255 ff. (some texts, 400 and more years; Old-Babylonian/early Kassite coming down to Neo-Babylonian).

67. Omitting Deuteronomy here, not accepted as part of the unit by some.

68. An observation also made long ago by Kittel, *Geschichte des Volkes Israel*, III/1 (1927): 196.

69. Cf. briefly my *Ancient Orient & OT*, p. 66.

70. The conventional documentary analyses of Joshua, precisely as of the Penta-

teuchal books, is unacceptable *not* simply for dogmatic reasons but because its methods and results are alike absurd in the light of what can be known of actual literary usage in the Biblical world; cf. my *Ancient Orient & OT*, pp. 112–38, for a compact outline of this matter in relation to the Pentateuch (but not irrelevant to Joshua).

71. E.g., Eissfeldt, *op. cit.*, p. 255 (who, of course, would also add his "P" passages later than this).

72. Ch. 1 to 3:6, Introduction; 3:7 to 16, main survey; 17–21, supplements, possibly to point a further lesson on lawless life without kingship.

73. On which see latterly Roger N. Whybray, *The Succession Narrative* (London: SCM Press, 1968).

74. Substantially II Sam. 9–20 plus I Kgs. 1–2, with minor omissions.

75. While his work raises various points of interest, Whybray's interpretation of the "Narrative" as a historical novel finds very little echo in the known categories of *ancient* literature and is too directly the imposition of a relatively modern concept.

76. Whybray, *op. cit.*, pp. 51–5.

77. Note that Kittel, *op. cit.*, III/I (1927) : 197, considers the outlook of Judges and Kings as the same, yet (p. 196), considers the material differences enough to preclude that the editing was done by the same hands. Hence, where greater degrees of difference exist (as between Deuteronomy and Joshua, and Joshua, Samuel, Judges, and Kings) it would seem still less wise to assume one work, without other cause.

78. Cf. by way of random example, Driver, *op. cit.*, p. 191, John Gray, *Kings I and II* (London: SCM Press; Philadelphia: Westminster; 1963), pp. 189, 197, or Martin Noth, *Könige* (Neukirchener Verlag, 1967), pp. 173 ff., *passim*.

79. Following out observations made in *Christianity Today*, 12/No. 19 (June 21, 1968) : 10 (922).

80. In this day and age, I make no apology for treating the patriarchs as essentially historical people, and the traditions concerning them in Gen. 12–50 as a long-transmitted, genuinely early source of data. On the question of approach to the patriarchs and methodology, cf. my paper, "Historical Method and Early Hebrew Tradition," *Tyndale Bulletin* 17 (1966) : 63–97.

81. On Semites in Egypt, cf. references in J. D. Douglas *et al.* (eds.), *New Bible Dictionary* (London: Inter-Varsity Fellowship; Grand Rapids: Eerdmans; 1962), pp. 343–4, and 844–5. On movement in and out of Egypt, cf. the texts (Papyri Anastasi III and VI) cited in ANET, pp. 258–9.

82. On which cf. above, pp. 3–4, with references.

83. When considering the legal matter in the Pentateuch, especially in comparison with collections of laws in the ancient Near East, the striking thing is that, even if one credits pentateuchal matter with a 14th–13th cen. date, the comparative material is in most cases not of "Mosaic" but of *"patriarchal"* age or earlier—thus, Ur-Nammu, "Bilalama," Lipit-Ishtar, Hammurapi, and the Old-Hittite origin and versions of the Hittite laws; hence my not so flippant term "patriarchal core," *Christianity Today*, 12/No. 19 (1968) : 921. Note further, the observations by William F. Albright, *Yahweh and the Gods of Canaan* (London: Athlone Press, 1968), pp. 88–92.

84. E.g., covenant-renewal by Joshua (Josh. 24); the pieties of David and Solomon; reforming moves by such as Asa or Jehoshaphat, and by Hezekiah and of course Josiah; covenant-renewal by Ezra and Nehemiah.

85. E.g., much of the period of the judges, or of the divided monarchy.

86. One cannot even begin to document here three millennia of Egypt's immensely rich and varied culture. In the realm of religion, cf. S. Morenz, *Ägyptische Religion* (Stuttgart: Kohlhammer, 1960), his *Die Heraufkunft des transzendenten Gottes in Ägypten* (Berlin: Akademie-Verlag, 1964, Leipzig Sitzungsberichte, 109/2), and *Gott und Mensch im alten Ägypten* (Leipzig & Heidelberg: Koehler-Amelang & Schneider, 1965), for ably drawn perspectives.

87. Well visible in the versatile treatment of West Semitic mythology by Albright, *op. cit.,* pp. 193–6, 207–9, 212–19, etc.

88. Cf. (e.g.) the convenient tables in G. T. Manley, *The Book of the Law* (London: Tyndale Press, 1957), pp. 77 (A), 85 (C), 88 (D), and 90 (E).

89. Cf. classified references to relevant passages, Kitchen in Carl F. H. Henry (ed.), *The Biblical Expositor* (Philadelphia: Holman, 1960), II: 79–83 *passim,* for convenience.

90. Obedience to God is, surely, a generality in most religions; I know of none that enjoin *dis*obedience.

91. E.g., Morenz, *op. cit.,* pp. 118–26. On a famous stela (ca. 1170 B.C.) when addressing Osiris, Ramesses IV says "For thou art he that made all, and thou canst not forsake them to carry out other designs with them, (for) that would not be right" *(ma'at),* line 20, cf. Breasted, *Ancient Records of Egypt,* IV, § 470.

92. References are in Posener, *op. cit.,* (1960), pp. 32–5.

93. E.g., Gray, *op. cit.,* pp. 189, 197.

94. Cf. also ANET, p. 415b, line 50, for the god condemning a seditious person's sins in blood.

95. Cf. ANET, p. 380b, end, and 381b.

96. Noth, *op. cit.,* p. 105.

97. Cf. the love of God in Deuteronomic theology, e.g. Walther Eichrodt, *Theology of the Old Testament* (London: SCM Press; Philadelphia: Westminster; 1967), II:335.

98. On which theme cf. G. von Rad, *op. cit.* (see note 22 above), pp. 78–81.

99. Kitchen, *Tyndale House Bulletin,* Nos. 5–6 (1960) : 6–7.

100. Noth, *op. cit.,* pp. 104–5.

101. Texts in Helck, *Urkunden der 18. Dynastie,* pp. 1648–55, 1667–74, 1682–1712, and *Deutsch,* pp. 195 ff.

102. E.g., in S. Langdon, *Building Inscriptions of the Neo-Babylonian Empire* (Paris: Leroux, 1905), I, Nebuchadnezzar Texts 1–3, 6–7, 10–13, 15–17; contrast the Texts 9, 19, where offerings are an important topic.

2

THE BEARING OF CURRENT EGYPTIAN STUDIES ON THE OLD TESTAMENT

Carl E. DeVries

Egyptian studies are herein defined as researches and publications by scholars academically trained in the field of Egyptology or otherwise recognized as competent in the area of ancient Egyptian language, history, and culture. It is desirable to place "current" studies as close as possible to the present, though it is convenient to extend the term to cover about twenty years, a period coinciding with the existence of this society; for since 1947 the Egyptologist has had a useful tool, the *Annual Egyptological Bibliography*, first compiled by Jozef M. A. Janssen. This bibliography provides a listing, often with summary and sometimes with evaluation, of practically everything published which relates to ancient Egypt, whether by non-specialists and popularizers or by experts in the most technical aspects of Egyptology. Among the *Indexes 1947–1956* there is a section entitled "Biblical References and Hebrew Words," which Old Testament scholars may find of assistance in researches relating to their field of specialization.[1]

I. Relationships Between the Two Disciplines

Before surveying the relevant studies which have been, or presently are, in progress, it will be helpful to look at the history of the relationships of Egyptological and Old Testament studies.

At the beginning of archaeological excavation in the Near East, the study of the Bible was the stimulus for much of the investigation. Not only were names, places, and artifacts related to the Bible, but the Scriptures themselves often provided the key for the interpretation of the materials unearthed. As the number of excavations increased and as knowledge of Near Eastern history and culture expanded, it became necessary for scholars in the general field to concentrate on ever smaller areas of specialization and to acquaint themselves with a burgeoning technical literature. Taking Egyptology as an example, one may note that in recent years it has been remarked that the volume of written material concerning ancient Egypt has become so great that no one who attempts seriously to keep up with the current publications can expect to make a significant contribution of his own. In 1961 the eminent English Egyptologist, Sir Alan H. Gardiner, writing of the development of Egyptological studies from the mid-eighteenth century onwards, commented: "The rivulet of Egyptological research was gradually swelling into the mighty stream which now makes it impossible for any student to keep abreast of all that is written save at the cost of abandoning all hope of personal contributions."[2]

In the light of such specialization it is not surprising that few Egyptologists have found time to devote to the study of the relationships between Egypt and the Bible. To most of them, the Bible is of little interest; for they have no personal involvement in its message and no professional concern for its contents, except in those relatively infrequent instances in which Biblical references may concern Egyptology. Undoubtedly, some Egyptologists are afraid of contact with subject matter involving Christian theology; but this attitude is understandable. Theological debate has a reputation for being especially acrimonious; consequently, many Egyptologists have been reluctant to expose themselves to the theological crossfire on the Old Testament battleground. Finally, it is felt that there are definite professional risks in bridging the areas of Old Testament and Egyptology. There is the danger of being charged with impiety on one hand and with religious bias on the other. In any case, there is the possibility of experiencing criticism based on prejudice, ridicule because of nonconformity, and academic or religious ostracism.

It must be admitted that Bible study is a particularly democratic undertaking, ranging from the practical and devotional to the academic and theoretical. Between these there often is a great gulf fixed. The various aspects of Bible study also run the gamut of theological convictions, with proponents of conflicting theological positions mutually suspicious of each other. Even in the so-called objective climate of the academic world there is little opportunity for sober discussion of common interests by such groups, usually because their basic assumptions are so much at variance. It is little wonder that most Egyptologists, especially on the American scene, having enough chronological and other problems in their own province, have not ventured into the larger scene which appears so charged with emotion.

On the other hand, writers concerned with popularizing archaeology for the sake of Bible students have not hesitated to plunge into the discussion of Egypt and the Bible. Though some of these publications perform an admirable service, often they overextend their authors' abilities. When noticed by the professional Egyptologist, publications of this kind have characteristically been greeted with disdain, frequently well-deserved. An older example of qualified, fair reproof is provided by T. Eric Peet, the author of the well-known *Egypt and the Old Testament* (1923) and for a number of years editor of the *Journal of Egyptian*

Archaeology. In the JEA for 1923, Peet reviewed a book on the exodus and labeled it a "typical example" of how Old Testament problems "should not be treated."[3] He condemns the author's lack of attention to Egyptological fact and concludes with a forthright summary, worthy of being quoted in its entirety:

> This book is intended to vindicate the Old Testament narrative. It fails in its task, and it fails not because the Old Testament narrative is false, but because the evidence which would prove it correct is not at present forthcoming in Egypt. This being so the only honest procedure is to admit it, and not to bodge up a vindication by elevating mere guesses into the region of established facts and by quietly suppressing or distorting such ascertained facts as prove recalcitrant. He who does this merely damages in the eyes of the intelligent the cause which he sets out to defend.[4]

This statement by Prof. Peet is elaborated in the preface to his *Egypt and the Old Testament*.[5] Though he made these observations more than forty years ago the principles enunciated are still valid and pertinent.

Prof. Peet has been referred to here not only because of the current applicability of the quoted comment but also because another and different statement by him points to a hazard for the non-Biblical specialist who dares to discuss subjects relating to the Bible. In his review of A. S. Yahuda's *Die Sprache des Pentateuch in ihren Beziehungen zum Aegyptischen,* Peet concludes: "For most of us the archaeological evidence seems to fit the conclusions of the Higher Criticism remarkably well."[6] This view is now traditional among Old Testament scholars and the Documentary Hypothesis has become nearly sacrosanct. Unquestioning mouthing of the doctrine has become the shibboleth by which certain academicians test what they regard as authentic scholarship. To depart from the establishment is to invite possible academic banishment, just as the speaking of heresy may result in excommunication.

Be that as it may, several Egyptologists have recently engaged in the study of Egyptian–Old Testament relationships and have found that applying to the Old Testament the principles used in the investigation of other ancient texts from the Near East has brought them to the conclusion that the theory of the documentary origin of the Pentateuch is an artificial device which does not fit the Old Testament data.[7]

The experience of Prof. J. Vergote of the University of Louvain is of particular interest. At meetings of the Near Eastern society "Ex Oriente Lux" in 1947–48, he presented some lectures relating to Joseph. When he later decided to publish this material in popular form, it was suggested to him by J. Coppens, Professor of Old Testament Exegesis at Louvain, that a book of this kind should take into account the documentary theory.[8] The result of a diligent accounting was the conclusion that the original of the history of Joseph was best explained as the work of Moses.

K. A. Kitchen agrees with this conclusion and in his review of Vergote's book devotes nearly two pages to the documentary hypothesis.[9] He briefly sketches the principles of the theory for Egyptologist readers unacquainted with Old Testament studies and then spells out six criteria of composite authorship which Egyptian documents demonstrate to be normal Near Eastern literary practice. These include multiple terms for deity, personal names, group names, names of places, common nouns, and personal pronouns.

It should be encouraging to conservative Old Testament scholars to see philologists and historians from the field of Egyptology publishing evidence which controverts the traditional documentary views. It is also refreshing to observe that the material is presented in positive terms, not in the defensive, negative, or offensive manner which often typifies the approach of the evangelical scholar. If the views of these Egyptologists were to have widespread acceptance, a most drastic change in Old Testament criticism would be forthcoming. A candid observer of human nature, however, may clearly predict the more probable result. If there should appear an appreciable affirmative response to the conclusions advanced by these two scholars, there will certainly also be a reaction from those opposed to these views. In the case of these Egyptologists one may well expect this opposition to come also from Egyptologists who hold other theological and critical positions. Already the rumbling has been heard in the distance.

II. Problematic Areas

In order to end on a somewhat positive note, it is best to look first at some of the less certain results of the study of Biblical and Egyptian relationships during this period of two decades. The evaluations are liable to some degree of subjectivism, for surely not all would place the same estimate on the present state of our knowledge of Egypt and the Bible.

A. Chronology

Chronology is still a thorny problem. In the more limited area of Egyptian chronology there are yet many questions, and during the past few years much ink has been spilled in an inconclusive debate concerning the possibility of a coregency of Amenhotep III and Amenhotep IV (Akhenaton).[10] In this case there is not just the involvement of harmonizing a few years, or the fixing of a kind of historical peg, but there are also complicated issues of relationships in art, religion, and government administration.

In terms of absolute dates for the period of the New Kingdom, chronologists operate within a margin of some fourteen years and often are at variance among themselves and subject to changing their own views.

A few years ago, the matter of chronology, both Egyptian and Western Asiatic, was given an Egyptologist's summary by Prof. Keith C. Seele in the second edition of *When Egypt Ruled the East*: "Most dates in Egyptian chronology are approximate. Fixed dates for the period covered by this book depend on synchronization with western Asia, but the Assyriologists are at present in sharp disagreement over matters of chronology."[11] More recently, there have been attempts to clear up the difficulties in the chronologies of the various geographic or national areas and to bring them into practical harmony; but problems of synchronization still exist, and certainty of dating continues to elude the best efforts.[12] It seems improbable that absolute dates can reach any final state, surely not within the near future, though we may expect refinements and greater exactitude as additional information comes to light and further studies are made.

B. The Exodus

Questions of chronology relating to Egypt and the Old Testament center around the date of the Israelite exodus from Egypt.[13] On this subject the Egyptian sources have contributed relatively little, and nothing of primary importance has been discovered during the last twenty years. Previously known monuments and inscriptions have been interpreted variously by proponents of differing views. Though the majority of scholars and the most prolific writers among them appear now to favor a late (13th cen.) as opposed to an early (15th cen.) date for this event, there are a number who support the earlier one. Those who argue for the late date do so primarily on the basis of the evidence from Palestinian archaeology, but it is my understanding that the author of the article on the exodus in the revised *International Standard Bible Encyclopedia* will use that source in support of the other position.

In 1960 Shemuel Yeivin published a short article on the exodus in which he proposed that Amenhotep III was the Pharaoh of the Oppression and Akhenaton the Pharaoh of the Exodus.[14] The condensed statement given in the 1961 *Egyptological Bibliography*[15] shows that the author exercises some degree of imagination and that he makes certain assumptions for which there is little historical evidence. This view has not attracted much attention, but it does illustrate an exception to a trend toward the later date.

Vergote, who decided that the basic account of the life of Joseph was best explained as written by Moses, also came to the decision that this account dated to the Ramesside period, and particularly the XIXth Dynasty; so one must grant that the evidence from Egypt may be interpreted as favoring a thirteenth-century date for the exodus.[16]

Obviously, conclusions relating to chronology cannot be reached by listing the names of those who hold to various views, but it is impossible, and undesirable, in a short generalized paper to rehash the essential facts and reasonings that have led to the present state of chronological study. At best, concerning the date of the exodus, one must judge that we have not yet reached certainty on this focal point of Old Testament chronology. The writer's own inclination is still toward the early date, essentially because the relevant chronological notes of the Biblical narrative consistently point in that direction and, secondarily, because the combined archaeological and historical data from other sources do not appear to have produced a date for the exodus so definite and certain as to require reinterpretation of the Biblical statements to fit it. One may remark, however, that if the secular evidence eventually establishes the later date of the exodus, Old Testament scholars presently convinced of the validity of this dating have already proposed interpretations of varying degrees of possibility and ingenuity in order to permit the harmonizing of this date with the Biblical passages which appear to conflict with it.

Similarly, matters of Egyptian geography relating to the exodus have been the subject of much discussion over a period of many years; and the debate will undoubtedly continue for some time.[17] There is at present no near unanimity of opinion as to the identity of the store cities, Pithom and Raamses. Here we can only remark on the fact that again we have no final archaeological answers to a problem of identification. It was hoped that the revived interest in archaeological excavation in the Delta following the intensive Nubian campaigns would result in our learning more about this section of Egypt and the cities which were anciently situated there. This hope has diminished with the crisis in international relations which has forced the postponement or reconsideration of plans to dig in this part of Egypt.

C. Wisdom Literature

Another area of continued and varied discussion is the relationship between the wisdom literature of Egypt and the book of Proverbs. Though there is a wealth of proverbial wisdom, often called "instruction," from ancient Egypt, ranging from the Old Kingdom onwards, there is one work in particular, "the Wisdom of Amenemope," whose proverbial sayings are so strikingly similar to part of Proverbs that many have sought to explain the likenesses.[18] The British Museum manuscript of Amenemope was published by E. A. W. Budge in 1923.[19] The following year Budge produced a book entitled *The Teaching of Amen-em-apt,* in which he stated that he could not believe that certain of the teachings could be of native Egyptian origin; he referred to the possibility of Asiatic influence during the Middle Kingdom or under the Hyksos.[20] Also in 1924 there appeared a short study by Adolf Erman, who concluded that Proverbs was dependent on Amenemope and that Jews living in

Egypt during Saite or Persian times became acquainted with Amenemope and adapted its sayings for Jewish use, translating them into Hebrew, or possibly into Aramaic.[21] Erman's view of borrowing on the part of the Hebrew book was soon generally accepted by the majority of Old Testament experts, as well as by most Egyptologists.

In 1926, D. C. Simpson wrote that the resemblances between Amenemope and Proverbs were so great that one must conclude either that the Hebrews borrowed from the Egyptian work or that Proverbs and Amenemope were dependent upon a common source. Expanding on the latter alternative, he suggested that there was an international proverbial literature of the Near East.[22]

Robert O. Kevin argued that the Egyptian author borrowed from Proverbs,[23] but this thesis was largely rejected. In the judgment of Ronald J. Williams, this view failed to gain support because Kevin's "superficial knowledge of Egyptian rendered his arguments valueless,"[24] but other reasons may be cited, among them the eminence of Erman, whose conclusions on the subject had found wide acceptance in a very short time.

Discussion of these relationships lagged a bit until 1957, when Etienne Drioton proposed that Amenemope was an Egyptian translation of a Hebrew original written by Jews in Egypt.[25] Kitchen states that Drioton has shown "weighty reasons" for his view, mainly "un-Egyptian usages in grammar, syntax, and vocabulary." Kitchen enthusiastically endorses Drioton's argument and declares that "Drioton's thesis will be difficult to controvert and if it wins acceptance will be of the greatest importance for Old Testament studies."[26]

Williams does not concur with Kitchen's evaluation. In a well-written article in the *Journal of Egyptian Archaeology,*[27] he assails Drioton's arguments and attacks his position on the basis of misinterpretation of the Egyptian text, mistaken understanding of the syntactic construction, and misidentification as Semitic certain words or concepts of which there are good Egyptian examples. Williams goes on to reason that there is "strong support for an original Egyptian text" in "the fact that paronomasia occurs at least three times in *Amenemope,* involving words which are not amenable to word-plays in Semitic."[28] He also feels that the language of Amenemope resembles that of the Wisdom of Ani, which probably dates to the latter half of the XVIIIth Dynasty. This is part of the argument which Williams advances for a possible XIXth Dynasty date for Amenemope.

Drioton also championed the Persian period as the time of the origin of Amenemope. Various previously proposed dates mentioned by Williams[29] range from the XXth Dynasty to the reign of Darius, but the later dates are no longer possible, for Williams points out that a broken, unpublished Cairo Museum ostracon bearing parts of Amenemope has been definitely assigned to the XXIst Dynasty by Prof. Jarolav Černy.[30] Williams reasons that use of the text for school purposes shows that Amenemope had been known for some time; he suggests that the original composition may date as early as the XIXth Dynasty.

Establishing a comparatively early date for the writing of the Wisdom of Amenemope is an important contribution to our knowledge of ancient Egyptian wisdom literature, but it does not settle the question of the direction of the theoretical relationship between Amenemope and Proverbs; indeed, in spite of the "striking similarities" to which allusion is often made, the existence of historical literary connection between the two cannot be demonstrated, though it often is assumed. There remains a possibility that the section of Proverbs most immediately involved (22:17–23:14) may have had an earlier Hebrew history, but this suggestion is unduly speculative and certainly springs from silence.[31]

One cannot, however, escape wondering about Israelite contributions to the culture of Egypt during the long period of Egyptian sojourn; and one would expect this influence to have been most pronounced during the Second Intermediate and New Kingdom periods. Little or no evidence of such influence has been forthcoming from Egypt, and on the surface this may appear strikingly strange.[32] It may well be that with respect to possible connections between Amenemope and Proverbs the relationships are neither as many nor as close as has been thought. It has been hinted that a prospective publication will set forth arguments showing that the likelihood of such relationships has been overstated.[33]

In closing these comments on wisdom literature in Egypt and the Old Testament, one must conclude that at present there is apparently still wide disagreement among scholars who hold differing views of theology and of the history of Near Eastern literature. No doubt there will be more discussion of Amenemope and Proverbs in the near future.

III. Areas of Egyptian Contribution

Thus far we have considered subjects of longstanding debate and problems not yet fully solved in spite of increasing information. Let us turn now to matters which are not so productive of disagreement but which may be of more importance, for they do give us light on the Old Testament and its background.

A. Social Life

From Egyptian literature and especially from the art associated with Egyptian funerary beliefs has come a wealth of information concerning the daily life of ancient times. The Egyptian contribution to knowledge of this background of the Bible is great, and it is probably the highest value that Egyptian studies provide for the understanding and appreciation of the Old Testament. Much of this material has been repeatedly and widely discussed in a variety of publications, and many of the subjects have recently been capably treated by K. A. Kitchen in *Egypt and the Bible: Some Recent Advances* and in *Ancient Orient and Old Testament*.[34] I am happy to recommend these works and I feel that it would be mere redundancy to go over many items already so excellently presented by Kitchen. Passing by the plagues and those other subjects of interest which usually appear in writings about Egypt and the Old Testament, I would comment briefly on several less generally known contributions to our understanding of the Old Testament and Egypt.

Interesting light on the background of several events in the life of Joseph has been provided by the publication of a Brooklyn Museum papyrus by William C. Hayes.[35] The recto of this papyrus dates mostly from the XIIth Dynasty and deals with orders given to the Great Prison at Thebes concerning residents of Upper Egypt who have failed to perform government services required of them. Previous writers have commented on the information up to then available concerning prisons and imprisonment in ancient Egypt and have related this material to the Joseph narrative.[36]

On the verso of this papyrus is a list of household servants whose ownership is being transferred by an official to his wife. More than half of the servants bear West Semitic names, and it appears that these persons were slaves from Syria or Palestine. Hayes concluded: "We must, it would seem, postulate the existence at the time—as later, in the New Kingdom—of a brisk trade in Asiatic slaves carried on by the Asiatics themselves, with Egypt, still one of the richest nations in the Near East, providing the principal market for this class of merchandise."[37] He then cites Genesis 37:28 and 36 as affording "a somewhat unusual example of the type of transaction I had in mind."

B. King "So"

Much later in Bible history there is in our English Bibles an apparent reference to an Egyptian king named So, whose identity has been puzzling.[38] II Kings 17:4 states that king Hoshea "had sent messengers to So king of Egypt" (RSV). It appears now that Hans Goedicke has made a significant contribution to Old Testament study by eliminating this royal name altogether.[39] W. F. Albright has received Goedicke's conclusions favorably and has added some helpful comments.[40] The proposed reading is: "to Sais, to the king of Egypt," the king of Egypt being Tefnakhte and Sais his residence city.

A paper of this length cannot even list the varied subjects of Egyptological origin which focus in some way on the Old Testament, but in conclusion I should like to mention a facet of Egyptology which has enjoyed widespread and effective use. There are many Biblically oriented books which are well illustrated by photographs of ancient Egyptian matters, whether large constructions like pyramids or small items of jewelry. Among the ironies of the present Near Eastern international situation one may remark that the two-volume publication by Major-General Professor Yigael Yadin, *The Art of Warfare in Biblical Lands in the Light of Archaeological Study*,[41] contains many fine plates showing ancient Egyptian wall paintings and objects excavated in Egypt. Relationships in scholarly areas may lead one to hope for more. Here is a reminder to pray that the modern nations of the Near East may soon be able to lay down their arms and that the predicted peace of the Old Testament prophecies may finally be realized.

Egypt, the land of the Nile, the country to which God sent Joseph to preserve a people, the nation to which in New Testament times another Joseph was directed to find a family refuge from a cruel king, has played an important role in the understanding of the Bible; and Egyptian studies will continue to add much to our knowledge of the Old Testament, its background, and its environment.

Notes

1. Jozef M. A. Janssen, *Annual Egyptological Bibliography. Indexes 1947–1956* (Leiden: E. J. Brill, 1960), pp. 433–4.
2. Alan H. Gardiner, *Egypt of the Pharaohs* (Oxford: Clarendon Press; New York: Oxford University Press, Inc.; 1961), p. 16.
3. T. Eric Peet, *Journal of Egyptian Archaeology*, 9 (1923): 256–7. (Hereafter referred to as *JEA*.)
4. *Ibid.*, p. 257.
5. T. Eric Peet, *Egypt and the Old Testament*, (Liverpool: University Press of Liverpool, 1923), pp. 5–7.
6. T. Eric Peet, "A. S. Yahuda's *Die Sprache des Pentateuch in ihren Beziehungen zum Aegyptischen*," *JEA*, 16 (1930): 159.
7. For the documentary hypothesis and the Joseph account, see J. Vergote, *Joseph en Égypte* (Louvain: Publications Universitaires, 1959), esp. pp. v–vi and 3–7; reviewed by Kenneth A. Kitchen in *JEA*, 47 (1961): 158–64. See also Kitchen, *Egypt and the Bible: Some Recent Advances*, offprint from *Faith and Thought*, 91 (1959–60): 177–97, and Kitchen, *Ancient Orient and Old Testament* (London: Tyndale Press; Chicago: Inter-Varsity Press; 1966), pp. 18–20, 112–38.
8. *Op. cit.*, p. v.
9. Kenneth A. Kitchen, "J. Vergote's *Joseph en Égypte*," *JEA*, 47 (1961): 162–3.
10. For discussion of Egyptian chronology, see, for example, E. Hornung, *Untersuchungen zur Chronologie und Geschichte des Neuen Reiches* (Wiesbaden: Otto Harrassowitz, 1964), reviewed by Kitchen in *Chronique d'Égypte*, 40 (1965): 310–22. See also Donald B. Redford, *Studies in the History and Chronology of the Eighteenth Egyptian Dynasty* (Toronto: University of Toronto Press, 1967) and Edward F. Campbell, *The Chronology of the Amarna Letters* (Baltimore: Johns Hopkins Press, 1964).
11. Keith C. Seele, *When Egypt Ruled the East* (Chicago: University of Chicago Press, 1956), p. 274.
12. In addition to the sources named in Note 10, above, see Kitchen, *Suppiluliuma and the Amarna Pharaohs* (Liverpool: Liverpool University Press, 1962).

13. For a convenient source of current information concerning the date of the exodus, see Kitchen, *Ancient Orient and Old Testament,* pp. 57–75, where numerous bibliographical references are given.

14. Shemuel Yeivin, *Tarbiz: A Quarterly for Jewish Studies* (Oct. 1960) : pp. 1–7.

15. *1961 Egyptological Bibliography* (Leiden: E. J. Brill, 1963), pp. 261–2.

16. Vergote, *op. cit.,* pp. 203–13.

17. Cf. C. de Wit, *The Date and Route of the Exodus* (London: Tyndale Press, 1960) ; Pierre Montet, *Géographie de l'Égyptienne ancienne* (Paris: Imprimerie Nationale, 1957), I: 218–19; and *L'Égypte et la Bible* (Neuchatel: Delachaux and Niestlé, 1959), pp. 59–64.

18. An extensive bibliography relating to Amenemope has appeared, so the following documentation is only representative. For the text of Amenemope, see E. A. Wallis Budge (cf. Note 19) and H. O. Lange, *Das Weisheitsbuch des Amenemope aus dem Papyrus 10.474 des British Museum* (Copenhagen: A. F. Høst and Son, 1925). The history of the papyrus and its interpretation is given in some detail by Robert O. Kevin, "The Wisdom of Amen-Em-Apt and Its Possible Dependence Upon the Hebrew Book of Proverbs," *Journal of the Society of Oriental Research,* 14 (1930) : 115–16. See also K. A. Kitchen, *Egypt and the Bible, op. cit.,* pp. 192–3, and Ronald J. Williams, "The Alleged Semitic Original of the Wisdom of Amenemope," *JEA,* 47 (1961) : 100. For a discussion of the extant texts of Amenemope, see Bengt Julius Peterson, "A New Fragment of the Wisdom of Amenemope," *JEA,* 52 (1966) : 120. Jean Leclant has compiled a bibliography of wisdom literature, published in conjunction with his "Documents nouveaux et points de vue recents sur les sagesses de l'Égypte ancienne," *Les sagesses du Proche-Orient ancienne* (Paris: Presses Universitaires de France, 1963), pp. 18–26, esp. pp. 23–4, 25–6.

19. E. A. Wallis Budge, *Facsimiles of Egyptian Hieratic Papyri in the British Museum,* 2nd Series (London: British Museum, 1923), 9–18, 39–51, Plates I–XIV.

20. E. A. Wallis Budge, *The Teaching of Amen-em-apt, Son of Kanekht* (London: Martin Hopkinson, 1924), pp. xv, 103.

21. Adolf Erman, "Eine ägyptische Quelle der 'Sprüche Salomos,' " *Sitzungsberichte der Preussischen Akademie der Wissenschaften* XV (1924) : 92.

22. D. C. Simpson, "The Hebrew Book of Proverbs and the Teaching of Amenophis," *JEA,* 12 (1962) : 232.

23. Kevin, *op. cit.,* esp. pp. 154–7.

24. Williams, *op. cit.,* p. 100.

25. Etienne Drioton, "Sur la Sagesse d'Aménemopé, in *Mélanges bibliques André Robert* (Paris, 1957), pp. 254–80; "Le Livre des Proverbes et la Sagesse d'Aménemopé," in *Sacra Pagina, Miscellanea Biblica,* I (Louvain, 1959) : 229–41: "Un livre hebreu sous couverture égyptienne," in *La Table Ronde,* No. 154 (Oct. 1960) : 81–91; "L'Apologue des deux arbres," Melanges V. V. Struve (Moscow: 1962), pp. 76–80.

26. Kitchen, *Egypt and the Bible, op. cit.,* p. 193.

27. Williams, *op. cit.,* pp. 100–6.

28. *Ibid.,* p. 106.

29. *Ibid.,* p. 106, text and note 1.

30. See also Peterson, *op. cit.,* p. 120, text and note 4.

31. It must be remembered that Williams has presented a strong case not only against Amenemope's dependence upon a Semitic source but also for an original text of Amenemope in Egyptian; Williams, *op. cit.,* p. 106.

32. Certainly the Israelites were neither a subservient nor insignificant element of the population during all of their stay in Egypt. It seems highly probable that a capable people should have contributed something meaningful to the land of their sojourn, particularly during the time in which Joseph and his family enjoyed royal favor. It is nearly incredible that a sizable and well-placed family, an incipient nation, could have

left no record of its achievements or even of its presence. Was this evidence destroyed anciently, has our sampling of ancient times been so accidentally selective as to have missed it, or have we incorrectly observed the known materials and misinterpreted this influence?

33. J. Ruffle, unpublished M.A. thesis, Liverpool University, 1964. Of the research of J. Ruffle there is only a reference in Peterson, *op. cit.*, p. 121 (text and note 3) and a comment by Kitchen: "careful study of both books *in their full Near Eastern context* (instead of in isolation, as is commonly done) has shown how inadequate are the grounds for relationship offered hitherto" (*Ancient Orient and Old Testament*, p. 88, n. 3).

34. See Note 7, above.

35. William C. Hayes, *A Papyrus of the Late Middle Kingdom in the Brooklyn Museum (Papyrus Brooklyn 35.1446)* (Brooklyn: The Brooklyn Museum, 1955).

36. Cf. Jozef M. A. Janssen, "Egyptological Remarks on the Story of Joseph in Genesis," *Jaarbericht Ex Oriente Lux*, 14 (1955–1956) : 64; Kitchen, *Egypt and the Bible*, pp. 180–2.

37. Hayes, *op. cit.*, p. 99.

38. Cf. Kitchen, *Egypt and the Bible, op. cit.*, pp. 194–5.

39. Hans Goedicke, "The End of 'So, King of Egypt,' " BASOR, 171 (Oct. 1963) : 64–6.

40. William F. Albright, "The Elimination of King 'So,' BASOR, 171 (Oct. 1963) : 66.

41. Yigael Yadin, *The Art of Warfare in Biblical Lands in the Light of Archaeological Study*, 2 vols. (New York: McGraw-Hill Book Co., Inc., 1963).

—3—

THE HISTORICITY OF THE BOOK
OF ESTHER

J. Stafford Wright

Most commentators on the Book of Esther agree that the author, wherever he lived, had an unusual knowledge of the Persian area of which he writes.[1] With a few exceptions,[2] however, they dismiss the idea that the book contains serious history, even though it professes to be an accurate record.

In the present paper it is not possible to argue every point. It is my intention, therefore, to take some things briefly and to expand other points that have been overlooked; but this paper cannot be regarded as a complete introduction to Esther.

The action of the book takes place in the reign of Ahasuerus. This name is the equivalent of Xerxes (485–465 B.C.), although both the Septuagint and Josephus regard him as Artaxerxes I (464–424 B.C.) In recent years two writers who take the book seriously have argued for Artaxerxes II (404–359). They are Jacob Hoschander and A. T. Olmstead.[3] I believe that etymologically the equation of the names is against them. The equation normally is *khshayarsha* (Persian) = *akhashwerosh* (Hebrew) = *xerxes* (Greek) = *ahasuerus* (English) as compared with *artakhshatra* (Persian) = *artaksatsu* (Babylonian) = *artakhshasta* (Hebrew) = *artaxerxes* (Greek) = *artaxerxes* (English).

What Hoschander and Olmstead write about Persian customs and the palace at Susa is valuable, but if the events of Esther can be shown to fit the reign of Xerxes then there is no need to look elsewhere. Hence this paper will concentrate on the time of Xerxes.

I. Some Agreed Points of Accuracy

The following are points which commentators accept as significantly accurate when compared with what is otherwise known about Persia.[4]

A. The extent of Xerxes' empire, India to Ethiopia, 1:1.

B. The banquet in the third year corresponds to the great council to plan for the invasion of Greece, 1:3; Herodotus vii.8.

C. The strange gap of four years between 1:3 and 2:16 would represent the period when Xerxes was occupied with the Greek campaign.

D. The allusions to the layout and fittings of the palace correspond to the excavated palace of Artaxerxes II at Susa. This was a restoration of the palace built by Darius and used by Xerxes.

E. L. B. Paton in his introduction to Esther summarizes additional minor points:

> The arrangement of the banquet (i.6–8), the seven princes who formed a council of state (i.14), obeisance before the king and his favorites (iii.2), belief in lucky and unlucky days (iii.7), exclusion of mourning garb from the palace (iv.2), hanging as the death penalty (v.14), dressing a royal benefactor in the king's robes (vi), the dispatching of couriers with royal messages (iii.13 and viii.10).[5]

We will not stay to amplify these points, since they are generally admitted, but might add that Herodotus viii, 85, 90 confirms that there were royal records of benefactors (2:23; 6:1–3).

II. Alleged Inaccuracies

We must look at what have been alleged as inaccuracies in Esther in greater detail than we considered the points of agreement, leaving the identity of Esther, Vashti, and Mordecai for separate treatment.

A. "According to i.1 and viii.9 the Persian empire was divided into 127 satrapies, but Herodotus iii.89 knows only 20."[6] But the satrapies were divided into smaller units, and the word used in 1:1 (*medinah*) is used in Ezra 5:8 and Nehemiah 1:3, etc., of the province of Judah which formed part of the larger satrapy (Ezra 5:3).

B. "In ii.5 Mordecai is one of the captives carried away with Jehoiachin in 596 B.C., but he becomes prime minister in 474 B.C., i.e. 122 years later."[7] But if the relative pronoun applies to the last name in the genealogy (as in II Chronicles 22:9 and Ezra 2:61), it was Kish, Mordecai's great-grandfather, who was taken with Jehoiachin. In Esther 2:5, 6, there are three relative pronouns, and each refers to the name that immediately precedes.

C. Commentaries unite in saying that Esther, a Jewess, could not have been chosen as queen, since Herodotus iii.84 states that the king must choose his wife from one of seven families. The seven families are the six, plus Darius, who together overthrew the usurper, Gaumata.

It is a pity, however, that one commentator copies another without checking the facts for himself. Certainly Darius married other wives besides one from the Seven;[8] and his son, Xerxes, who succeeded him, was not the son of this wife. Xerxes' wife, Amestris, was the daughter of Otanes; but this Otanes was the son of a certain Sisamnes,[9] while the Otanes who was one of the Seven was the son of Pharnaspes.[10] Ctesias xiii.51, moreover, says that she was the daughter of Onophas; and he was not one of the Seven.

D. If the Feast of Purim was instituted in the time of Xerxes, it would surely have been mentioned again before II Maccabees 15:36, where the victory of Judas Maccabaeus in 161 B.C. is on "the day before Mordecai's day." Yet where could it have been mentioned in extant literature? The Books of Ezra and Nehemiah do not mention even all of the festivals of the Law, far less a new festival that would have been slow to gain a footing among a well-established cycle of feasts.

The worth of this objection can be judged by the scant number of references to the festival even after it had certainly been established. The LXX translation of Esther and its additions are likely to have been made in the first century B.C. II Maccabees 15:36, also written in the first century B.C., uses "Mordecai's Day" as a well-known date. Josephus at the end of the 1st Christian century says that the festival was kept by Jews throughout the world.[11] Yet it is not mentioned in the New Testament, with the unlikely exception of the unknown feast of John 5:1, and only rarely in Jewish writings in the first few Christian centuries.

E. Objection is raised to the enormous size of the gallows (over 80 feet) in 5:14 and 7:9, built in an hour or two (5:14). The word translated as *gallows* need mean no more than *tree,* and some have interpreted the punishment as impaling on a stake, which was then suspended at a great height. But it may well have been a high gallows, though not necessarily fifty cubits. This figure occurs only on the lips of two people, and it is not so set down in the actual history. It belongs to the language of popular exaggeration, as when an exasperated mother says to her child, "I've told you fifty times already not to do that!" or when a teenager accuses a parent of being fifty years behind the times, or when Nebuchadnezzar orders the furnace to be heated seven times more than usual (Dan. 3:19). If there were various heights or grades of gallows, this might simply have been the highest.

F. It is strange that neither Mordecai nor Esther is mentioned in the list of famous people in Ecclesiasticus 44–49. But even Ezra does not occur in this list, and Ben Sirach may not have approved of Esther's marriage to a pagan king.

G. "The statement in i.19 and viii.8 that the laws of Persia were unalterable is also found in Dan. vi.9, 13. It is not attested by any other early evidence, and seems most unlikely."[12] However, H. H. Rowley quotes, without comment or translation, a sentence from Diodorus Siculus: *all' ou gar ēn dunaton to gegonos dia tēs basilikēs exousias agenēton kataskeuasai.*[13] Taken in isolation this appears to mean, "It was not possible for what was done by the royal authority to be undone." I think it does mean this; but, to be fair, one must grant that the context offers the possibility of a different translation. The comment concludes the story of how Darius III in a rage ordered the execution of a certain Charidemus. After Charidemus has been led away, we are told, "When the King's anger abated, he at once repented and blamed himself for having made the greatest mistake, but . . ." and then follows the above sentence. Diodorus may therefore mean that it was too late now, because Charidemus was dead, and the sentence could be differently divided: "But what was done could not be undone by the royal authority."

On the whole I think the previous translation is the better. The latter is a piece of sententious moralizing and is not improved by adding "by the royal authority." The translation by Bradford Welles in the Loeb Classical Library is a little too colorful: "But all his royal power was not able to undo what was done." I cannot find that Diodorus is given to rhetorical pathos of this kind.

Also noteworthy is his choice of words. If a Greek writer wanted to convey, "It was impossible that this particular event could be undone by Darius's authority," he is likely to have used the aorist (to genomenon) and the personal genitive (tou basileōs). The use here of the perfect participle and the adjective (basilikēs) makes the statement a general comment on Persian law.

There is a further pointer toward this understanding a few sentences earlier, where Darius arrests Charidemus. "Having laid hold of the girdle of Charidemus according to the law of the Persians he handed him over to the attendants and ordered his execution." I have reproduced the order of the Greek words without punctuation, but whether "according to the law of the Persians" is attached to the preceding or to the following words, it is significant that Diodorus mentions this law in conjunction with a probable statement that Darius could not reverse his command.

If we regard these as the main difficulties of historicity, apart from one's subjective feelings of what is "likely," we can see that these are trivial, and at times based on false deductions. We may, therefore, proceed to a fuller treatment of the identity of the three main characters, Vashti, Esther, and Mordecai.

IV. Vashti, Amestris, and Esther

According to the Book of Esther, Vashti was Xerxes' queen until she was deposed in 484–3 B.C. as recorded in chapter 1. After a gap of four years Esther becomes queen and is still queen at the end of the book, about 473 B.C.

On the other hand both Herodotus and Ctesias speak of Amēstris[14] as queen. Since the third son of Xerxes and Amestris, Artaxerxes I, was born about 483, Amestris cannot be identified with Esther who was not yet married. She accompanied Xerxes during part at least of his Greek campaign, ending with the battle of Salamis in 480 B.C., and she had considerable power as queen-mother (i.e. the widow of the former king) during the reign of Artaxerxes I. This at first sight makes it impossible to identify her with Vashti.

Nevertheless I believe that she can be. There are two points of difficulty, linguistic and historical.

A. Linguistic

Can the two names, Vashti and Amestris, be equated? If one were to use an *argumentum ad hominem,* he could point out that those who interpret the story mythologically of a battle between the Babylonian deities Marduk and Ishtar with two Elamite gods, identify the latter with Humman and Mashti. If the initial M can be interchanged with V (W) in the Old Persian, then there is no great difference between Mashti and Amestris. Students of Old Persian, however, find no apparent interchange of M and V (W) in this script.[15] In Babylonian of the fifth century B.C. there is a tendency for B, M, and V (W) to be confused, but not usually in the initial position.

Yet we are not actually concerned with Old Persian or Babylonian mutations, though this seems to have escaped general notice. We are concerned with matching a Hebrew rendering of a Persian name (Vashti) with a Greek rendering of possibly the same name (Amestris). We have no independent Persian record of the name of Xerxes' queen but are dependent on Herodotus and Ctesias, who wrote in Greek.

Occasionally today we are aware of the difficulty of rendering a foreign name into English. When a new Russian or African name leaps into the public eye, there is at first some difference over its spelling in the newspapers and over its pronunciation on radio and television. The Greeks had a similar difficulty with Babylonian and Persian names. Thus one would hardly recognize the Persian Khshayarsha as Xerxes, which became the standard Greek transliteration, or as Akhashwerosh which is the Hebrew form and is Anglicized as Ahasuerus.

The Greek had trouble over the letter W. This in Hebrew is the letter that our Bible translators render as V, because this is how it was then pronounced by Western Jews and how it is still pronounced in modern Hebrew. Western students of Biblical Hebrew today learn it as W, which corresponds to its sound in ancient Semitic languages. For a time the Greek alphabet, which is based on the Semitic letters, used a letter known as *digamma* with the W sound; but it was dropped because there was no W sound in normal Greek words. Correspondingly, certain present-day visitors to Britain and America from overseas countries fail to pronounce the W. Thus we hear "Vhy are ve vaiting?" or "Fhy are fe faiting?" Others have difficulty with *th,* and put *zee* or *see* for *the.* W is, as its name suggests, a double vowel sound, and is still used as a vowel in Welsh, both long and short, e.g. Gwlad (country).

One can see how the Greek LXX translators handle Hebrew words with the initial W (v) : *Vashti* becomes *Astin; Vashni* (II Chron. 6:28) becomes *Sani; Vophsi* (Num. 13:14) becomes *Sabi; Vaniah* (Ezra 10:36) becomes *Ououania,* which is the nearest attempt at rendering the W.

If the original Persian name of the queen was Vashti, or something approaching this, Herodotus was faced with a double difficulty. He had no W and no Sh in Greek. He had to find a word that would look and sound right to a Greek reader. We have already seen that there was a certain affinity in Babylonian between W and M; and, if the reader says *Ooashti* quickly, he will find that he is on the way to forming an initial M, N, F, or V. Obviously Herodotus did not detect an F or V or he would have used the Greek letter PHI. Having chosen M as most suitable, he may well have put a short A in front of it to bring it a little nearer to the original opening vowel sound. The Sh had to become a simple S. Did Herodotus then add the R, perhaps to make a still clearer distinction between Amestris and Xerxes' daughter, whose name is rendered as Amutis? Or was the R in the Persian original, but omitted by the Hebrew, which does not use a TR sequence?

Without any sleight of hand we have been able to show a possible linguistic link between Vashti and Amestris.

B. Historical Difficulty

The Book of Esther does not mention Xerxes' absence on the campaign against Greece, but it records an otherwise inexplicable gap of four years between the deposition of Vashti and the taking of Esther as queen (1:3 and 2:16). Note also that in Ezra 4:6 the opponents of the Jews in Palestine write a letter of complaint to Xerxes "in the beginning of his reign," but evidently get no reply.

Herodotus records a singularly unpleasant incident at Sardis while Xerxes was returning from Greece. Amestris gave Xerxes a specially fine robe, which she had woven herself. Xerxes was having an affair with his brother's wife and her daughter, and he was tricked, as Herod was later, into giving her daughter whatever she asked. She chose the robe. Amestris was furious, but blamed the mother, and had her horribly mutilated and her tongue torn out.[16]

Obviously therefore Amestris, or Vashti, was still acting as queen. Here one must consider not only the Book of Esther but also the habits of Persian kings and queens. One does not get rid of the mother of royal children during a drunken dinner party, nor does a powerful queen submit to be put away. Once Xerxes and his lord had "let off steam" in a childish passion, Xerxes had to accept the status quo for the time being. The new queen, if there was to be one, would have to wait. He had the Greek campaign to see to, and Amestris-Vashti would accompany him part of the way at least.

If she had played her cards properly, we might never have heard of Esther. But when she mutilated Xerxes' mistress, and in consequence almost caused a revolution which would have brought his brother to the throne, she must have fallen into disfavor; and Xerxes on his return to Susa would have been ready for his new queen. We notice the rather strange wording of Esther 2:1 which implies some lapse of time: "After these things, when the anger of King Ahasuerus had abated, he remembered Vashti and what she had done and what had been decreed against her." This would not make sense on the day after the feast, or even six months after the feast; but on his return from the Greek campaign Xerxes remembers that he has an excuse handy for getting rid of Vashti.

No one appears to have checked the evidence for the dates when Amestris's children were born. Ctesias xiii.51 gives some useful information. "Xerxes married Amestris the daughter of Onophas, and a son Dareiaios [sic] was born to him: and a second, Hystaspes, was born after two years, and then Artaxerxes, and two daughters, of whom one was called Amytis after her grandmother, and the other Rodogoune." Artaxerxes was eighteen when he came to the throne in 465, so he must have been born about 483; and Amestris-Vashti's refusal to appear in Esther may well have been because she was pregnant. Although the Greek might mean that the daughters were born after the sons, their place at the end of the list may merely be because sons were felt more important than daughters. I think Amytis was born before Artaxerxes, since before the death of Xerxes in 465 she was already not only married, but accused of adultery.[17] But even if she and her sister were born after 483, no children were born to Amestris-Vashti after the time when the Bible says that Esther became queen.

There is no record of Esther's bearing a child, and she may well have died soon after the close of the Book in 473 B.C. We have little information about the second part of Xerxes' life. The history of Herodotus ends shortly after 480 B.C.; and Ctesias has only two brief incidents, of about ten lines in all, between that date and the murder of Xerxes in 465 B.C.

Amestris's son, Artaxerxes I, succeeded Xerxes on the throne. This is Artaxerxes of Ezra and Nehemiah. Amestris as queen mother now came into prominence once more and continued to exert her power until her death in about 424 B.C. Ctesias records her pressure on Artaxerxes for the beheading of fifty Greek prisoners and her crucifixion of a man who killed her grandson in battle.

By accepting the strong-willed Vashti as identical with Amestris, we are not doing violence to the record of Esther as queen.

V. Mordecai

Whether or not the names of Mordecai and Esther have any connection with Marduk and Ishtar is not of great importance in view of the names known to have been adopted by Daniel and his three friends in Daniel 1:7. We cannot here discuss the theory that the story is based on a myth of the conquest by Marduk and Ishtar of the Edomite deities, Humman and Mashti. Commentators who are subject to cult-identifications seem to lose all sense of proportion, not only here but in their interpretation of the Song of Songs, e.g., as Canaanite fertility cult songs. These two Books had a struggle to maintain their place in the canon: it seems unlikely that they could even have competed for a place if they had originated in polytheism and sensualism.

To the best of my knowledge we have no Persian or Greek references to any vizier or prime minister in Susa during the period when Haman and Mordecai are said to have held this office. There is thus no external confirmation or disproof of what Esther says about them.

There may, however, be some confirmation of Mordecai as an historical character, both in the Greek and in a Persian writing.

Ctesias xiii.51, lists three men who had great influence in the early part of Xerxes' reign. Among them is Matakas who "was the most influential of the eunuchs." Ctesias subsequently relates that, on his way home from Greece, Xerxes told Megabazus to plunder the shrine of Apollo at Delphi. On his refusal, Xerxes sent Matakas "to insult Apollo and plunder everything. He did this, and returned to Xerxes."[18] It seems unlikely that, after the recent defeat of the Persians, an individual could have made a raid of this sort on Delphi; but Strabo XIV, i,5, relates that Xerxes destroyed the shrine of Apollo at Miletus, and Ctesias may have confused this with the more famous shrine at Delphi.

This identification of Mordecai and Matakas goes back into the last century, but more recently claims have been made for a Persian equivalent. In 1941 Professor A. Ungnad of Berlin published a tablet in ZAW with the twofold mention of a certain Marduka as a high official at Susa during the early years of Xerxes, or possibly the last years of Darius. According to Professor Ungnad his title indicates that he was an accountant or privy counsellor. A full discussion of the evidence in English is given by Siegfried H. Horn.[19]

I believe that one can make a good case for equating both of these men with Mordecai. I cannot understand Horn's reasoning when he rejects Ctesias's Matacas on the ground that his spoilage of Delphi took place before the events of the Book of Esther, and yet accepts Marduka although he is mentioned before the same events.

The picture unfolds in a fascinating way. When Xerxes came to the throne he seems to have taken Matakas/Marduka/Mordecai into his confidence. If Mordecai were not already in office as privy counsellor, Xerxes may have appointed him as such. Mordecai was a eunuch, as the Bible indicates when it presents him without any mention of wife and family (2:7), and with access to the women's quarters (2:11).

Mordecai could have traveled in the personal retinue of Xerxes on his campaign. As a eunuch he was probably in charge of Vashti and the other women. Xerxes was a staunch Zoroastrian, and in an inscription discovered at Persepolis he declares his devotion to Ahuramazda. He tells how he destroyed the temples of the evil gods in various countries and performed a proper religious service on the sites. One may suggest that he was thus able to rationalize his pillaging of the shrine of Apollo. Mordecai, the Jew, was a congenial accessory. He also had no use for pagan gods and may have delighted to help Xerxes in insulting Apollo.

Yet something must have happened on the way home which partially set him back. As keeper of the women he may have taken sides with Vashti-Amestris in her conflict with Xerxes' mistresses; and, when Vashti was discredited, Mordecai seems to have withdrawn. He may have planned to get back into favor by means of Esther. It is difficult to see how Esther could have been selected among the potential candidates unless she had had some influence behind her.

In reading Esther 2–4 one gains the impression that Mordecai was a man of influence, even though his fortunes were temporarily at a low ebb: he can communicate freely with the palace; he is on sufficiently close terms with the king's eunuchs to discover their plot against the king (2:21, 22). Could they have assumed that he would join them as a fallen favorite? Also he is sufficiently powerful to refuse to acknowledge Haman, and Haman can do nothing about it. How ludicrous if Mordecai were but an ordinary Jew! Haman knew the ups-and-downs of court favoritism. So when the latter's own downfall came, Mordecai was ready to step back into his old influential position (8:1, 2).

The Christian judgment of the Book of Esther has been unnecessarily cramped through our feeling that because Mordecai is a Bible character, he must be a good man. Yet, like Samson and Jehu he may have been little more than a time-server. The Bible makes no moral judgment upon him, but it expects us to use our Christian sense. He was raised up by God, but he was not necessarily a godly man.

We note how he first forces Esther to conceal her Jewish ancestry (2:20), and then almost blackmails her on the ground that she is a Jewess (4:13, 14). We commend his astuteness in getting around the laws that could not be changed (8:11); but we condemn Esther's encouragement of the Jews in Susa to go beyond what they needed for self-defense, although we cannot say how far Mordecai advised her in this.

If Mordecai was a racist, without too much devotion to Yahweh, we can suggest that in the book of Esther he wrote the records of the events in a suitable form for Persian consumption. He would not offend Xerxes, with his zeal for Ahuramazda, by mentioning the God of Israel by name.

I do not see any other reasonable explanation of the total omission of the Name of God. If, as is often supposed, the book had been written in the Maccabaean period to encourage Jewish resistance, the enthusiastic author could not have omitted Yahweh's name. The LXX takes appropriate action by inserting additions into the Hebrew version to introduce God into the story.

The idea of Mordecai's authorship used to be widely held, though it has been generally abandoned today because of the theory of a late date for the book. But if we consider this idea as a possibility, there is some significance in the statements that Mordecai "recorded these things" (9:20). If Mordecai was Marduka, the accountant, he would be able to write and to dictate and would have put his version of the story in the court records mentioned in 10:2 and 6:1. At what point the story was transcribed into Hebrew we cannot say, but we are at liberty to accept any date that the style of Hebrew demands.[20]

Some have supposed that the Mordecai of Ezra 2:2, who is listed among important people who returned at various times to Jerusalem, is our Mordecai. This is possible, if Esther died and if the royal favor swung away to another vizier. Ctesias and Diodorus Siculus describe how Artabanus, captain of the royal bodyguard plotted with Aspamitros the eunuch, a man of great influence (so Ctesias), or, according to Diodorus, with Mithridates, the eunuch, who was the king's chamberlain and enjoyed his supreme confidence; and they murdered Xerxes.[21] How long before this Aspamitros or Mithridates had been in Mordecai's place, we cannot say. There was room for only one at the top; and Mordecai, reading the signs of the times, may have felt it wise to join the next train of returning exiles to Judah.

Conclusion

If the presentation in this paper is approximately correct, there is obviously a need to take the book of Esther seriously as a first-hand historical document. We have been able to show, not merely how the story can be fitted into a gap in the secular records, but how it may be linked to those very people and events in the story of Xerxes of which we have independent knowledge.

Notes

1. In English, in addition to the standard commentaries and dictionaries, there are excellent treatments of the period in Arthur T. Olmstead's two books, *The History of*

Palestine and Syria (New York: Scribner, 1931; Grand Rapids: Baker Book House; 1965) and *The History of the Persian Empire* (Chicago: University of Chicago and Cambridge: Cambridge University Press; 1948).

2. Two important articles are by Siegfried H. Horn, "Mordecai, A Historical Problem," *Biblical Research* 9 (1964) and by A. Ungnad, "Keilinschriftliche Beitrage zum Buch Esra und Esther," ZAW 58 (1940, 1941) and 59 (1942, 1943).

3. Jacob Hoschander, *The Book of Esther in the Light of History* (Philadelphia: 1923); Olmstead, *History of Palestine and Syria*, op. cit., pp. 612–14.

4. The two main sources for Persian history are Herodotus' *History of the Persian Wars* and Ctesias' *History of Persia*. Herodotus (ca. 484–424 B.C.) was a contemporary of Xerxes, and Ctesias completed his history about 398 B.C. Both had some access to original sources, and Ctesias was physician at the Persian court from about 412 B.C. onwards. For the part of the history with which we are concerned, he claims to have used written records and the testimony of eyewitnesses. There are many editions of Herodotus, but, so far as I know, the only edition of the Fragments of the Persika of Ctesias is that edited by John Gilmore in 1888, and this has not been translated.

Diodorus Siculus, writing a long history shortly before the time of Christ, uses Ctesias and other sources. Plutarch's Life of Artaxerxes II is relevant for the Persian background, although not for the special period of Esther. I have not found anything of importance in Thucydides, Xenophon, or in Aeschylus's *Persae*.

5. ICC., *Esther*, p. 65.

6. *Ibid.*, p. 72.

7. *Ibid.*, p. 73.

8. Herodotus, iii. 87.

9. Herodotus, v. 25, vii. 61.

10. Herodotus, iii. 67.

11. *Antiquities*, XI. vi. 13.

12. Ed. L. E. Browne and A. S. Peake, *A Commentary on the Bible* (London: T. Nelson, 1936), p. 381; similarly B. W. Anderson in the IB claims that there is no extra-biblical evidence for this.

13. Harold H. Rowley, *Men of God* (London: Nelson, 1963) p. 238, note. The sentence is from Diodorus Siculus xvii. 30 (incorrectly given as xviii.30).

14. N.B. The e is long.

15. Cf. R. G. Kent, *Old Persian Grammar* (New Haven: American Oriental Society, 1953).

16. Herodotus ix, 108 f.

17. Ctesias xiii, 59.

18. xiii, 58.

19. *Biblical Research*, 9 (1964).

20. ICC (p. 62) lists certain late words.

21. Ctesias, xiii. 60; Diodorus Siculus, xi. 69.

II. PENTATEUCH

—4—

THE LITERARY FORM OF GENESIS 1–11

Walter C. Kaiser, Jr.

The primary task of the Biblical scholar is to unfold the meaning of the text of Scripture as it was originally intended to be understood by the writer of that text. Those ideas, meanings, and truth-intentions which he had in mind are the first order of business. Further, if the concept of Biblical authority is to be introduced into the discussion, it will only heighten rather than decrease the intensity of the search to get back to that original writer's thought; for he is the man who claims to have heard the revelation of God.

Nowhere is this task filled with more difficulties for the modern Biblical scholar than in the first eleven chapters of Genesis. Indeed the very subjects contained in these chapters and the admittedly long interval of time that separates the writer from the topics he is writing about are enough to keep the researcher busy.

But with the advent of modern destructive higher criticism following Astruc's "clue" in 1753, a new problem was added to the two already mentioned: the alleged variations and repetitions within the narratives themselves. Now it was not the discipline of higher criticism which was the new feature; but the new and objectionable feature was the introduction of a philosophical and historical grid, borrowed from Hegel (the dialectic) and Darwin (evolution applied to religious history) which was laid over the Biblical corpus so as to control its "true" sequence, order, and development.

This fallacy has since been corrected and for the most part retracted.[1] Unfortunately it was the Wellhausen foundation stone and the first floor of a house upon which had been built a second floor of the various source-documents distinguished by the criteria of doublets, style, and lexicography. While many contemporary Old Testament scholars agree that the foundation and first story of this house, built by J. Wellhausen, K. H. Graf, and A. Kuenen, has fallen, only a few Jewish and evangelical scholars have investigated the situation to see if the second story with its J, E, D, P, L, K, S source documents has actually remained intact despite the collapse of the foundation. Umberto Cassuto and now Kenneth A. Kitchen are two of these who have documented the fact that the source documents did not survive the crash.[2] It is beyond the limits of this paper to trace this development, but students of the Scriptures are urged to acquaint themselves with the dispassionate presentation of contemporary Near Eastern materials by Kitchen in order to avoid the bottomless pit of subjectivism in this important area of higher criticism.

While source criticism was emerging, another challenge was being prepared as a result of a collection of tablets uncovered in the 1850's by the British Museum. In 1872, George Smith began to publish the contents of a flood story which he found on one of these tablets which had been excavated from the Ashurbanipal library in Nineveh. This was followed in 1876 with a publication entitled: *The Chaldean Account of Creation*. The next contribution seems to have been a paper which a young American scholar named George A. Barton read in 1890 and later published in 1893, where he connected the Old Testament passages concerning Rahab, Leviathan, Lotan, and the Dragon in the Revelation of John with the materials in these Babylonian myths. It would appear that George Barton's work was influential in the thinking of the German scholar Hermann Gunkel, for in 1895 Gunkel continued this line of thought by pointing to a series of poetic texts in the Old Testament where he found a battle between Yahweh and the various sea monsters named above. This tradition, he affirmed, was the background for the creation story of Genesis, though it had been purged by a monotheistic faith.

Here we were introduced to our fourth problem, the alleged similarities between the literary form and content of Genesis and the ancient Near Eastern mythologies—particularly the Babylonian mythologies. From these early contributions up to our present day, very few scholars have found it necessary to challenge the validity of these results as a basis for understanding these chapters in Genesis.

S. R. Driver, in his commentary on Genesis, did squirm a little; but he settled his fears by saying that any "antecedent difficulty" which he may have felt in tracing the Genesis material on creation to a Babylonian source was "considerably lessened" when he put alongside this the Babylonian similarities to the Genesis flood which seemed to be so obviously borrowed.[3]

These were not the only challenges; several have been added by our own century: the semantical problem as evidenced in all language which describes the action of God (particularly now in light of the revolt against metaphysical discussions), and the historical problem as seen in the difficulty of historiography to define its task and to validate its material. If these areas are staggering in their implications for current speech and history, surely the task does not become less difficult when it turns to the early chapters of Genesis.

In part these last two issues in their Biblical application await the results of the first four problems posed above. All too often it has been possible to slide back and forth in the argument, e.g. to go from the literary form to the documents and from there to some conclusion about the level of truth or type of historiography that one could expect from these chapters in Genesis. To be sure, the questions all play their part, but an orderly discussion dictates that we must take one area at a time. Since we believe that the challenge of source criticism has been met, or at least is well on the road to being effectively met, this chapter proposes to investigate the alleged parallels from the ancient Near Eastern mythologies as to their relevance for the type of literary form and content to be gleaned from the first eleven chapters of Genesis.

One is fully aware that a number of disciplines stand off in the wings awaiting both the opportunity for an exchange of materials and the results of our investigations—not the least are the two mentioned above (semantics and history) and the sciences.

It is with the name and results of Hermann Gunkel that any researcher in Genesis must reckon. As early as 1895[4] Gunkel began to draw the contrasts between history and the contents of Genesis 1–11. In 1901 he introduced his famous Genesis commentary with these words: "Are the narratives of Genesis history or legend? For the modern historian this is no longer an open question. . . ."[5] And so it was. Skinner repeated this controlling thesis in his *ICC* Commentary saying:

"We are not entitled to assume *a priori:* That Israel is an exception to the general rule that a legendary age forms the ideal background of history."[6]

Thus Genesis 1–11, it was assumed, reflected "a pre-literary and uncritical stage of society."[7] The difference between what these chapters reflected and real history could be put into six points. According to Gunkel they were the following:

1. Gen. 1–11 originates in oral tradition while history is found in literate societies and in written documents of actual events.
2. Gen. 1–11 deals with personal and family stories while history concerns itself with great events of public interest.
3. Gen. 1–11 depends on the imagination of the raconteurs while history must be traced back to first-hand evidence.
4. Gen. 1–11 (and this is the "most significant" criterion) narrates the impossible (origin of stars after the planets, derivation of all the streams of the earth from a single source, a chronology of 2666 years from creation to the Exodus, all the animals in the ark, Ararat the highest mountain) whereas history narrates the possible.

5. Gen. 1–11 is poetic by nature and intends to delight, inspire, and elevate while history is prose which seeks to inform.
6. Gen. 1–11 is different in form from the classical example of true Hebrew historiography in I Samuel 9–20 whereas history is identical in form and style to those searching, uncomplimentary documents of David's Court in I Samuel 9–20.[8]

Gunkel, of course, did not limit these observations to Genesis 1–11 as we have here, but he certainly meant that they should apply here.

Therefore, under the heavy pressure of the prestigious scholarship of the late nineteenth and the present twentieth century, the approach has become all but unanimous by now: Genesis 1–11 is primaeval history reflecting its Near Eastern origins (mainly Babylonian) from which it was borrowed. Any modern appraisal of this section of Scripture must thereby reflect these philological and mythological connections.

I. The Subject Content

What are those elements in the Genesis narratives which suggest a connection with the mythology of the ancient Near East and Babylon in particular? Principally, the subjects discussed are common to the literature and culture of both groups. They are as follows:

1. The so-called four accounts of creation[9]
   a. Gen. 1:1–2:4a
   b. Gen. 2:4b–2:25
   c. Prov. 8:22–31
   d. Allusions found in prophetic and poetical books of O. T.
2. The Serpent and the Garden of Eden, Gen. 3 (Ezk. 28:12–19)
3. The Cain and Abel conflict, Gen. 4
4. The Genealogies of Gen. 5 and 11:10–22
5. The Sons of god marrying the daughters of men, Gen. 6:1–4
6. The Flood, Gen. 6:5–9:19
7. The Curse of Canaan, Gen. 9:20–29
8. The Table of Nations, Gen. 10
9. The Tower of Babel, Gen. 11:1–9

For each of these subjects or topics there are parallels to a greater or lesser degree. The two most famous are the *Gilgamesh Epic* (Babylonian flood) and the *Enuma Elish* (Babylonian Genesis). For the Garden of Eden there is the Sumerian Dilmun Poem, the myth of Enki and Ninhursag, and the Akkadian myth of Adapa. The Cain and Abel story is seen in the contest of Dumuzi, shepherd-god, and Enkimdu, the farmer-god. The Weld-Blundell prism or the Sumerian king list is said to reflect our genealogical list; while the themes of the sons of god, the ethnological details on Canaan and the seventy nations, and finally the tower of Babel are all seen as being authentically Babylonian or at least Near Eastern in their origin.

The scholarly community is beholden to W. G. Lambert for his masterful article on the Babylonian background to Genesis. Noting how important the Gilgamesh Epic is, with its striking examples of parallelism to the Genesis flood story (the episode of the sending out of the birds being one of the most impressive of those parallels), he begins by re-evaluating the dates of our alleged protoypes in Sumer and Babylon. Here is the interesting development: The Sumerian prototype dates from 1800 B.C., but makes no mention of the birds. The incomplete copy for the earliest known Babylonian text (1600 B.C.) also, to date, lacks any reference to the birds. "Thus the only surviving testimony to the most telling parallel happens to be later than the Biblical account, but nevertheless," continues W. G. Lambert, "I hold that there is a certain dependence of the Hebrew writers on a Mesopotamian tradition."[10] Apparently, no copies earlier than 750 B.C. contain this reference in Tablet XI which is parallel to Genesis 8:6–12! This might have stirred up S. R. Driver[11] sufficiently to retain his "antecedent difficulty."

If this bird episode in the 750 B.C. copies of the Gilgamesh Epic represents the best example of parallelism, there are other examples which rate as a mere superficial comparison. An illustration of this type can be seen in the Cain and Abel comparison with Enkimdu and Dumuzi. The parallel is said to reflect the ancient feud between the pastoral nomad (here the shepherd-god Dumuzi) and the farmer (farmer-god Enkimdu).

This identification is "extremely flimsy."[12] The Sumerian story has Inanna (same goddess as Ishtar) preferring the hand of the farmer-god, Enkimdu, in marriage rather than that of Dumuzi. Inanna's brother, the son-god Utu, prefers the latter, but Inanna holds firm and Enkimdu appeases the loser, Dumuzi, with all kinds of gifts.[13]

How can this be the background for the Genesis 4 narrative? As Sarna points out, never does the Biblical text disparage the occupation of the farmer, let alone evaluate and compare the two occupations. The contrast is on the quality of the men in their heart attitudes and not on their occupations. Nor is anything said of a marriage or of appeasing a loser in Genesis. Indeed, the chapter does go on, as Sarna observes, to enumerate just those skills which are generally connected with a pastoral and nomadic culture and places them in the line of Cain, the farmer, viz. cattle-rearing, music and metallurgy.

II. The Philological Parallels

Another approach to the relationship of Genesis 1–11 with other Near Eastern accounts involves the philological aspect. Nowhere is this illustrated better than in the much discussed word *tᵉhôm,* "the deep" in Genesis 1:2. Typical of the canonical status[14] this discussion has reached is the statement of S. H. Hooke:

> The Hebrew word used for the chaos of waters, "the deep" is *tehom,* a word which is generally acknowledged to be a Hebrew corruption of the name of the chaos-dragon slain by Marduk before he proceeded to create order out of chaos.[15]

Even though Alexander Heidel dealt with the basic philological facts as long ago as 1942, Old Testament scholarship has been exceedingly slow in facing up to the realities he presented there.[16]

The difficulty of borrowing a feminine Babylonian word and bringing it over into Hebrew unaugmented by any sufformative elements, and locating a guttural letter "h" in the middle of the word has never been adequately explained. This observation by Heidel is generally by-passed with some remark about his orthodox motives for observing this feature.[17] Kitchen also calls the identification a "complete fallacy" and points to the fact that *tᵉhôm* is common Semitic as shown now by the Ugaritic *thm,* which was known in the early second millennium B.C.[18] Moreover, he faults the whole assumption of Hebrew dependence on the Babylonian myths on methodological grounds as well. "In the Ancient Near East, the rule is that simple accounts or traditions may give rise (by accretion and embellishment) to elaborate legends, but not vice versa."

Recently Thorkild Jacobsen has made an excellent case for the fact that Marduk means "son of the storm" and therefore his conflict with Tiamat is a battle of the elements: the god of storm, rain, lightning, and thunder versus the goddess of the sea. This same motif occurs at the same time (middle of the 2nd millennium) in the Ugaritic myth of Baal versus Yam. This immediately raises the question of dependence and the direction of the borrowing. Since Canaan supplies the environmental context, because of its proximity to the Mediterranean Sea, whereas Babylon was somewhat removed, Jacobsen concludes that the myth comes from Ugarit and the possibility that the borrowing of the term for "sea" could be just the reverse of that pictured heretofore by orientalists, i.e. *tiamat* comes from *tihāmatum.*[19]

Now if this identification of Tehom with Tiamat has run on to hard times with morphological differences and methodological problems, then the final blow, so it would seem, is again given in W. G. Lambert's recent study. Not only is a watery beginning only *one* Mesopotamian notion among others, but it is not as commonly attested as is the notion that the earth came first. Neither is it the earliest cosmological idea known to us from the Babylonian sources. The primacy of the earth is known first around 2600 B.C.; then sometime after 2000 B.C. the primacy of water is known, followed by the primacy of time about 1700 B.C. Lambert concludes that the "watery beginning of Genesis in itself is no evidence of Mesopotamian influence."[20]

Another example of the results yielded by philological studies is to be found in the word taken to mean "to brood" in Genesis 1:2. This word, Gunkel felt, lent support to a connection with the Phoenician cosmic world-egg theory. Now it turns out that this very *rhp*, does occur in Ugaritic and has the same meaning there as it does in Deuteronomy 32:11, where the eagles are said "to hover, flutter or coast" in the air.[21] The imagery here is one of God caring for the forming of the earth just as the young eaglets are dependent on their parent's attention while they soar over them until they are able to fly and fend for themselves.

III. The Mythological Motif

Recently some have acknowledged the point just made concerning "the deep" and "to flutter" in Genesis 1:2 and have moved on to discuss the conflict of Yahweh versus the chaos monster. Brevard S. Childs puts it this way, "Although the present usage of the word in Genesis 1:2 has little in common with Tiamat, Gunkel has shown convincingly that the Old Testament does possess traditions in which the *tĕhôm* is connected with a primeval battle which initiates the creation (cf. Isa. 51:9, 10)."[22]

Here again Lambert gathers together the Near Eastern materials and the result is that "the case for a battle as a prelude to God's dividing of the cosmic waters is unproven."[23] While the *Enuma Elish* does have a battle which precedes the division and separation of the waters, the problem is to locate such a battle in Genesis, or even in the poetry of the Old Testament. The reference in Isaiah 51:9–10 clearly alludes to a request that God act in the historic present like He acted in the historic past, when the Red Sea opened up and "the redeemed passed over." The only other convincing example one could suggest is in Psalm 74:13: "Thou didst crush or divide sea by thy strength"; even here, however, there is a lexicographical dispute and Lambert[24] advises us to translate it: "Thou didst set the sea in commotion." The separation does not necessarily imply a conflict in the Near Eastern mythology, for the three Sumerian accounts do it peacefully, as do the Hittites, Egyptians, and Phoenicians.[25] Childs had used just such a conflict as his basis for concluding that "the material found in Gen. 1:2 has its roots ultimately in myth."[26]

The search for the mythological background to the Hebrew creation narratives does not seem to be any more successful when it turns to the figure of wisdom in the book of Proverbs, particularly in Proverbs 8.22–31. A recent examination of this theory by R. N. Whybray[27] concludes that mythology is "notably absent" in the wisdom literature of Egypt and Mesopotamia. Indeed, the very name "wisdom" was never used as a name for any of the gods or goddesses. Although W. F. Albright had suggested a Canaanite goddess of wisdom, principally on the basis of four short passages in the Ugaritic corpus where *ḥkm* occurs six times, Whybray complains that every one is a reference to the wisdom of the high god El. On examination, the alleged mythological features, such as the famous statement that wisdom built her house on seven pillars (9:1), also fails to yield the expected results. In the example just cited, it turns out that "remains of Phoenician houses from the late third millennium did have roofs supported by seven interior pillars."[28] The detail is not mythological but rather concrete. Whybray concludes by observing that "the terms used to describe wisdom's origin are metaphorical, not mythological."[29]

The conclusion seems to be building that neither the subject material with its apparent, but unfulfilled, parallelism to ancient Near Eastern mythologies nor the initial lexicographical studies involving words like "the deep" and "to brood" will serve as guides in leading us to the conclusion that the literary genus (*Gattung*) of these chapters is the category of myth.

IV. The Scientifically Impossible

But let us turn to Gunkel's fourth category; the one he finds to be the "most significant." What about those things in Genesis 1–11 which are clearly impossible? To begin with a fairly concrete example, one could point to the obvious reference to iron in Genesis 4:22, well in advance to the iron age, which is usually placed around 1200 B.C.

Without pretending to be able to date this incident to lives of Cain's descendants, one may remark that the knowledge of working iron is clearly much earlier than 1200 B.C. The very Hebrew word (*barzel*) appears to be a loan word from the Sumerian *parzillum*.[30] Several finds have added to the importance of this observation. At Tel Asmar,[31] at Dorah in N. W. Turkey,[32] and at Catal Hüyük,[33] evidence has been uncovered for working in terrestrial iron (as opposed to meteorite iron, which has a different nickel content) as early as 2500 B.C. for the first two sites and 6500–5800 B.C. in the last case. Apparently arts and crafts can be mastered and then lost only to reappear again in another age. One should be hesitant to declare an "impossibility" here.

The genealogies of chapters five and eleven have often been paraded as prime examples of chronological impossibilities. The remedy, however, for this difficulty is to be found in the type of exposure to the Biblical genealogies given almost a century ago in William Henry Green's epochal article.[34] Green reminds us that these numbers are never totaled and are apparently in a symmetrical form of ten names each, with three sons climaxing each list. He points to the parallel lists in the Bible where obvious omissions can be demonstrated, e.g. in I Chronicles 6:3–14 and Ezra 7:1–5. Further, when we consider the range of meanings of Old Testament terms such as "generation" (which can equal 80 plus years) [35] "begat," "son of," "father of," "she bore [yālaḏ] a son,"[36] both in the Bible and now in the ancient Near East,[37] we are delivered from making some foolish occidental mistakes. The most instructive lesson of all can be gleaned from Kohath's descent into Egypt (Gen. 46:6–11), 480 years (Ex. 12:40) before the Exodus.[38] Now if Moses was 80 years old at the time of the Exodus (Ex. 7:7), and no gap is understood (as we believe the evidence above now forces us to conclude), then the "grandfather" of Moses had in Moses' lifetime 8,600 descendants, 2,750 of which were males between the ages of 30 and 50 alone! (Num. 3:19, 27, 28, 34–36). Certainly the writers of the Bible are not that naïve!

The only new feature one meets in the Genesis 5 and 11 lists is the inclusion of the number of years A lived before he begat B and the total number of years A lived. The solution to the question concerning the function of these numbers was suggested as far back as 1906 by John H. Raven.[39] Observing, correctly, that Zilpah was credited with "bearing" (yālaḏ) her great-grandchildren (Gen. 46:18), while Bilhah "bore" her grandchildren (46:25), and Canaan "bore" whole nations (10:15–18), Raven allows that the first number in the formula may mean that B literally "was born" to A or that B was a distant descendant "born" to A. If it is the latter case, then "the age of A is his age at the birth of that child from whom B (eventually) descended."[40]

Many have seized upon the Genesis 6:1–4 incident, with the "sons of god" and the daughters of men in cohabitation, as one of the clearest examples of an impossibility in the natural realm leading to the category of myth. We believe this analysis fails to investigate the original meanings signified by the writer's use of the terms "sons of god" and "nᵉpîlîm gibbôrîm," i.e. the so-called "giants." The most adequate treatment and solution known to us is that article which calls upon an exegesis of the text in light of the cognate materials from the Near East by Meredith Kline.[41] To equate "sons of god" with angels does not tally with the divine response given in v. 3, viz., God's displeasure with the sin of man. The situation is not relieved by seeing in the "sons of god" a reference to a godly Sethite line as opposed to an ungodly Cainite line in the daughters of men; for while it meets the test of v. 3, it must equivocate on the meaning of "men" in vv. 1 and 2, i.e. "mankind" generically in v. 1 and "Cainites" specifically in v. 2. Further, why do we find the kind of offspring mentioned in v. 4 if these are just religiously mixed marriages? Kline's solution is to interpret "sons of god" (bn il) in its Near Eastern setting as a title for nobles, aristocrats and kings. These sociologically mixed marriages lusted after power and wealth (the gibbôrîm as seen in 6:4 = Gen. 10:8–10 and 4:19–24), i.e. they desired to become "men of a name"—somebodies (cf. 11:4)! This structure of events, coming as it does before the flood narrative, agrees with the Sumerian Nippur fragment where the flood narrative is also immediately preceded by the lowering of kingship from heaven, and thus it suggests that both could be an historical reflex of the same event in time and space.

Of course, common to all these "impossibilities" is the underlying supposition that the world view resident in Genesis 1–11 is pre-scientific and primaeval. Nowhere can one find a greater unanimity on this point than in those discussions which point, with elaborately labeled diagrams, to a three-storied universe.[42] A flat earth (Isa. 11:12, Rev. 20:8) is capped with a solid firmament (Gen. 1:7, 8, *et passim*) appropriately outfitted with windows (Gen. 7:11; 8:12; II Kgs. 7:2; Isa. 24:18, *et passim*) and supported by pillars (I Sam. 2:8; Job 9:6; etc.), stretching upward past Sheol and "The Deep."

Laird Harris[43] has shown each step of this diagram depends more on the ingenuity of the modern scholar than it does upon the imagination of the original raconteurs. Nowhere does the text state or imply that the *raqî*, better translated "expanse," is solid or firm. This latter idea of "firmness" is derived from the Vulgate *firmamentum* and the Septuagint *stereōma*. S. R. Driver tries to document the dome or canopy effect in his commentary on Genesis 1:6; but he fails to explain the Ezekiel 1 and 10 references, where the word clearly refers to an "extended" platform on which the throne of Ezekiel's vision rests. As R. Laird Harris observes, the heavens are also likened to a curtain or a scroll which could be rolled up (Isa. 34:4; 40:22).[44] As for those windows in this vault which are alleged to let the starlight and rains in, we need only to see what is said to come in through these windows: barley in II Kings 7:2, trouble and anguish in Isaiah 24:18, and blessings in Malachi 3:10! Actually, in the II Kings passage God had to *make* the windows (not just *open* them) before he could send down the barley! (Note also the distinct Hebrew word used for window *'rubbā* vs. the more common *ḥallôn*.[45]

The subterranean features, including the pillars, sheol, and "the waters under the earth," on examination also fail to uphold the triple-decked or three-storied universe. The "waters under the earth" easily qualify as waters below the shore line where the fish dwell (Deut. 4:18), and sheol is the poetic word for the usual prose word "the grave." While some poetic passages describe the "foundations" of the earth as resting on "pillars," we may note that both words are used metaphorically (one even continues today); and Job 26:7 even has the earth resting upon nothing![45]

The primitive view turns out to be an assigned interpretation and not one which was derived from the texts themselves. Nor does it help the case if one alludes to additional examples of alleged naïveté in these chapters—for example, the wet cosmology of Genesis 1:1 vs. the dry cosmology of Genesis 2:4b ff.;[46] the animal fable of Genesis 3, where the snake talks;[47] the tree of the knowledge of good and evil and the tree of life as containing, so to speak, some sort of mysterious enzymes;[48] and the origin of Eve from the rib of man or man from the dust of the earth.[49]

Even the Tower of Babel incident is yielding to investigation. Samuel Noah Kramer[50] has recently found a tablet which completes the earlier "Golden Age" passage, and in its completed form it turns out to be a Sumerian story which recalls a time when all men spoke the same tongue. "While the confounding of tongues came about," says Kramer, "as the result of rivalry, . . . in the Sumerian case this was between god and god, and in the Hebrew, between god and man." Everything that can be tested in this eleventh chapter (e.g. the type of mortar and the type of architecture) leads us to conclude that the chapter has a genuine setting in Babylon.

V. The Literary Style

Now if subject matter, content, philological connections, and so-called "impossibilities" do not furnish us with either the rationale, the occasion, nor the literary form (Gattung), will not the style and literary form of these units when compared to the ancient Near Eastern epics, provide the key for identifying the type of literature?

W. F. Albright provided just such an example when he pointed to the "when . . . then . . ." translation for Genesis 1:1–3 as a definite borrowing of the Sumero-Babylonian style from the Enuma Elish.[51] Even this proposal, which makes the first two verses dependent statements, with the main verb coming in verse three, while being in and of itself based upon a grammatical phenomena which can be illustrated elsewhere in the Hebrew scriptures, does not meet all the demands of the text, as E. J. Young has pointed out.[52] Genesis 1:1 is an independent statement as indicated by: the disjunctive accent used by the Massoretes (thereby showing their early understanding), the ancient versions, the context, the position of the subject in verse 2, and the syntax of the three circumstantial clauses in verse 2 anticipating the main verb in verse 3.

Conclusion

Therefore we conclude that the suggested literary type (Gattung) of myth fails to establish itself because it cannot be validated in content subject matter, individual words chosen, pre-scientific views of the world, style, or form. This is not to say that all modern scholars have chosen this form as the only possibility; but it does point out that almost all of the modern discussion borrows some or all of this form when it chooses to classify this section of Scripture; e.g. Alan Richardship labels these chapters as "parables" because of the undesirable associations of our word "myth" but appeals to the same type of evidence we have been discussing in this paper.

The writer's intention must be the first order of business if we are going to make any progress in locating the literary form for this section. We believe such an indicator is given to us by the recurring heading, "These are the generations of."[53] In Genesis 12–50, the author used this device four (or five) times to introduce each new Patriarch, and in these chapters we have been experiencing a growing confirmation of the reliability of the record due to unprecedented archaeological finds relating to Patriarchal customs, names, places, and times.[54] Is it not worth noting that the writer (or at least in the view of some—the editor (s)) also used this same device six times to introduce blocks of material in chapters 1–11?

The opening chapters of Genesis are just as vulnerable and just as exposed to the searching eye of the scholar in those tangible ways as Genesis 12–50. While the job is fantastically more difficult, the point is clear: there are 64 geographical terms, 88 personal names, 48 generic names and at least 21 identifiable cultural items (such as gold, bdellium, onyx, brass, iron, gopher wood, bitumen, mortar, brick, stone, harp, pipe, cities, towers) in these opening chapters.[55] The significance of this list may be seen by comparing it, for example, with "the paucity of references in the Koran. The single tenth chapter of Genesis has five times more geographical data of importance than the whole of the Koran."[56] Every one of these items presents us with the possibility of establishing the reliability of our author.[57] The content runs head on into a description of the real world rather than recounting events belonging to another world or level of reality.

Of course this does not exclude figures of speech and figurative language. E. W. Bullinger[58] can list approximately 150 different items in these eleven chapters alone illustrating one figure of speech or another: the point being that this is all controlled objectively as a science. Further, to say something is a figure of speech is only to begin the problem; for we must say which figure it is, supply other examples as a comparative exegetical control, and then go on to assign a meaning which is in keeping with this figure of speech.

Neither are we left to our own devices when it comes to talking about such forms as poetry, parable, allegory, or apocalyptic-like literature. Each of these has its own control. Basically, there are two broad categories for arranging the material: poetry or prose. The decision is easy: Genesis 1–11 is prose and not poetry. The use of the *waw* consecutive with the verb to describe sequential acts, the frequent use of the direct object sign and the so-called relative pronoun, the stress on definitions, and the spreading out of these events in a sequential order indicates that we are in prose and not in poetry. Say what *we* will, the author plainly intends to be doing the same thing in these chapters that he is doing in chapters 12–50. If we want a sample of what the author's poetry, with its Hebrew parallelism and fixed pairs, would look like, Genesis 4:23–24 will serve as an illustration.[59]

Unfortunately, the decision that we are dealing with prose is not the end of the discussion. Eissfeld teaches us that there are three subgroups of prose forms: speeches, records, and narratives.[60]

While there seems to be very little to represent the sub-category of speeches and prayers, there are large sections in Genesis illustrating the second area called records. Included in this category are contracts, letters, lists, laws, and the two genealogical lists (5 and 11). It should be especially noted that Genesis 5:1 makes reference to a "letter" or "scroll" as a source for the list which has the same formula that the writer uses elsewhere some ten times, i.e. "the generations of." This could well indicate the author's free admission of his dependence upon sources and lists, just as the writers of the Old Testament historical books give us a veritable string of sources which they consulted as they moved from one historical period to another. Particularly instructive is the appearance of this identical formula at the end of the book of Ruth, which also gives us a list of ten generations and brings the reader down to the writer's own day, i.e. the Davidic era. One should compare Luke's historical and literary methodology as he began to write his Gospel under the revelation and inspiration of the Triune God (Lk. 1:1–4).

With large sections of the text of Genesis 1–11 still unmatched in form, we turn finally to the last subcategory of prose: narrative; but we are surprised to find two kinds of narrative prose: poetic narratives and prose narratives. Since the poetic narratives include myth, fairy tales, sagas, legends, anecdotes, and tales, the preceding discussion is all the more important. How shall we decide between historic and poetic narrative? The approach should be uniform for all Biblical scholarship. But indeed let the hallmark of evangelical Old Testament research be the primacy of the author's own truth intention, the full utilization of all tools of exegesis, and the constant reference to all the advantages available in the plethora of ancient Near Eastern materials. The difference in our results will mainly come in two areas: the alleged inviolability of the causal continuum of a space-time world in all instances, and the consistent restriction of mythological values to certain semantical terms on the part of some Biblical scholars.

Happily, some have felt obliged to go on beyond the acknowledged "Continental Divide" in Biblical scholarship to show that these things need not be so. Langdon B. Gilkey has written an article which must already be recognized as one of the greatest religious articles of our times.[61] He confesses that his stance and that of most modern scholarship is "half liberal and modern on the one hand, and half Biblical and orthodox on the other, i.e. its world view or cosmology is modern while its theological language is Biblical and orthodox."[62] He writes "what has happened is clear: because of our modern cosmology, we have stripped what we regard as 'the Biblical point of view' of all its wonders and voices . . . we have rejected as invalid all the innumerable cases of God's acting and speaking."[63] We agree not only with Langdon's self-analysis, but also with his solution; for he goes on to write, "first there is the job of stating what the Biblical writers meant to say, a statement couched in the Bible's own terms, cosmological, historical, and theological."[64]

Now the way back to the author's intention is through the words he uses. We believe along with J. Stafford Wright that the metaphorical use of words might relieve many of the semantical difficulties which we might otherwise instinctively class as mythological clues.[65] He illustrates our present heavy use of metaphors in such scientific terminology as used by psychoanalysis and analytical philosophy, e.g. the subconscious, the superego, the depths of the psyche, the threshold of consciousness, etc. He warns, "a critical reader a thousand years hence might well think that the twentieth century held the idea of a three-story solid mind, with doors and gates. We know how wrong he would be; but we would still maintain that these phrases are legitimate metaphors, and indeed almost essential metaphors, to translate non-spatial and comprehensible language."[66] How shall we communicate spiritual realities into spatial terms? He even suggests that we ought to press behind the stories of such dragons as Tiamat, Leviathan, Lotan, and Rahab, which are common coin to the ancient Near Eastern writer and the Bible, "and ask whether the pagan religions may not themselves be preserving a primeval truth that underlies the Biblical conception of the fall of Satan and the warfare between Satan and God."[67] At any rate, the proximity in time when these terms are used does not necessarily imply similarity in meaning for all the authors.

If we do not insist upon injecting these two *a prioris* into our exegesis, we believe the arguments illustrated above will yield the conclusion that we are dealing with the genera of historical narrative-prose, interspersed with some lists, sources, sayings, and poetical lines. The real key to the literary genus of this difficult section of Scripture is found in the author's recurring formula "the generations of" which demonstrates *his* organization and *his* understanding of the materials.

Notes

1. George E. Wright, ed., *The Bible and the Ancient Near East* (Garden City: Doubleday & Co., 1961). See especially the article by John Bright, "Modern Study of

the Old Testament Literature," pp. 13–31. Compare the criticisms of J. Coppens *The Old Testament and the Critics* (Paterson: St. Anthony Guild Press, 1952), pp. 52–79; and Moses H. Segal, *The Pentateuch: Its Composition and Its Authorship,* 1968.

2. Umberto Cassuto, *The Documentary Hypothesis* (Jerusalem: Magnes Press, 1961); and Kenneth A. Kitchen, *Ancient Orient and the Old Testament* (Chicago: Inter-Varsity Press, London: Tyndale Press; 1966), pp. 112–38; also Edwin E. Yamauchi, *Composition and Corroboration in Classical and Biblical Studies* (Philadelphia: Presbyterian and Reformed Publishing Co., 1966), pp. 7–38; and J. A. Motyer, *The Revelation of the Divine Name* (London: Tyndale Press, 1955). See also the standard evangelical O.T. Introductions by M. Unger, E. J. Young, G. Archer, and R. K. Harrison.

3. Samuel R. Driver, the *Book of Genesis*, 11th ed. (London: Methuen & Co. Ltd., 1920), p. 30. See Wilfred G. Lambert, "A New Look at the Babylonian Background of Genesis," *Journal of Theological Studies*, New Series, 16 (1965) : 288.

4. Hermann Gunkel, *Schoepfung und Chaos in Urzeit und Endzeit* (1895). A preface to his famous commentary on Genesis is translated into English as *The Legends of Genesis* (New York: Schocken Books, 1964), pp. 1–12.

5. *Ibid.*, p. 1.

6. John Skinner, *A Critical and Exegetical Commentary on Genesis,* 2nd ed. (Edinburgh: T. & T. Clark; Naperville, Ill.: Allenson, Inc.; 1963), p. v.

7. *Ibid.*

8. Hermann Gunkel, *Das Buch Genesis* (1922), pp. viii–xiv; cf. John L. McKenzie, "The Literary Characteristics of Gen. 2–3," *Theological Studies* 15 (1954) : pp. 541–72.

9. Theodore H. Gaster, "Cosmogony," in IDB, 1:702.

10. Lambert, *op. cit.,* p. 292.

11. Driver, *op. cit.,* p. 30. See Lambert, *op. cit.,* p. 288.

12. Nahum M. Sarna, *Understanding Genesis* (New York: McGraw-Hill, 1966), p. 28.

13. Samuel Noah Kramer, *Sumerian Mythology,* rev. ed. (New York: Harper Torchbooks, 1961), pp. 101–3.

14. Bernard W. Anderson, *Understanding the Old Testament* (New York: Prentice-Hall, 1957), p. 385, n. 11; "The Hebrew word for 'deep' (*tehom*) is equivalent to the Babylonian word for Tiamat; here we have a distant echo of the mythology of the ancient world." Also, Norman Gottwald, *A Light to the Nations* (New York: Harper, 1959), p. 457, "The priestly term *tehom*, 'the deep' is linguistically related to the Babylonian Tiamat, goddess of the chaotic deep." And B. Davie Napier, *Song of the Vineyard* (New York: Harper & Row, 1962), pp. 48–9, "Here [*Enuma Elish*] chaos is represented in the goddess Tiamat, a name perhaps echoed in the Hebrew word for 'deep,' *tehom.*"

15. Sidney H. Hooke, *Middle Eastern Mythology* (Baltimore: Penguin Books, 1963), p. 119.

16. Alexander Heidel, *Babylonian Genesis,* 2nd ed. (Chicago: Phoenix Books, 1963), pp. 98–101.

17. Sarna, *op. cit.,* p. 22, does call to our attention three facts: (a) while *tehom* is not feminine by grammatical form, it does frequently employ a feminine verb or adjective; (b) *tehom* has the characteristics of a proper name since it is used without the definite article and (c) in Gen. 19:25; Deut. 33:13; and Hab. 3:10 we have in poetic address, "*tehom* that crouches below" and "*tehom* crying out."

J. Skinner, *op. cit.,* p. 17, note 2, answered these three arguments by observing that *tehom* is "confined to poetry (except Gen. 1:2; 7:11; 8:2; Deut. 8:7; Amos 7:4) . . . . The invariable absence of the article (except with pl. in Ps. 106:9; Isa. 63:13) proves that it is a proper name, but *not* that it is a personification." The admittedly clear references to personification are in the poetic passages of Gen. 49:25 and Deut. 33:13.

18. Kitchen, *op. cit.*, pp. 89–90; also see J. V. Kinnier Wilson, in DOTT, p. 14: "The theory that the Hebrew Genesis is genetically related to the Babylonian has long been held . . . and has relied to a large extent on the much publicized equation of Tiamat with the Hebrew *tehōm* 'the deep.' It is now, however, recognized that since the two words have different meanings . . . it is of no importance whether they are etymologically connected or not . . . and that the epic has no connections of any kind at any point with Genesis."

19. Thorkild Jacobsen, "The Battle Between Marduk and Tiamat," JAOS, 88 (1968) : 104–8. Also Laird Harris, "The Bible and Cosmology," BETS, 5 (1962) : 14.

20. Lambert, *op. cit.*, p. 293.

21. The Ugaritic texts are the Story of Aqhat or Dan'el, Tablet I:32 ff.; III: i, 20–21 and 31–32. Note the similarity of subjects for this verb in Deut. 32:11 and Ugaritic: The *nšr* or plural *nšrm*, "eagles."

22. Brevard S. Childs, *Myth and Reality in the Old Testament*, 2nd ed. (Naperville, Ill.: Allenson, Inc., 1960; London: S.C.M. Press: 1962) , p. 37.

23. Lambert, *op. cit.*, p. 294.

24. *Ibid.*

25. *Ibid.*, p. 294 and n. 2.

26. Childs, *op. cit.*, p. 37. Also see the acknowledgment that in the Canaanite mythology "the battle is not connected with the original creation" and his, "Nevertheless," on p. 38, n. 3.

27. Roger N. Whybray, *Wisdom in Proverbs* (Naperville, Ill.: Allenson, Inc.; London: S.C.M. Press; 1965) , pp. 82–92, 99–104.

28. *Ibid.*, p. 90.

29. *Ibid.*, p. 103.

30. See Deimel's *Sumerisches Lexikon*, Heft 2, where he quotes an inscription from Ebeling's KAR I, 185, 3, 1.

31. *Oriental Institute Communications*, No. 17, pp. 59–61.

32. *Illustrated London News* (Nov. 28, 1959) , p. 754.

33. Kitchen, *op. cit.*, p. 37, n. 10, where he refers to *Anatolian Studies* 14 (1962–4) : 111–114.

34. William H. Green, "Primeval Chronology," *Bibliotheca Sacra* (1890) , pp. 285–303. Also see Appendix II in John Whitcomb, *Genesis Flood* (Philadelphia: Presbyterian & Reformed, 1966) , pp. 474–89.

35. William F. Albright, *The Biblical Period From Abraham to Ezra* (New York: Harper Torchbooks, 1963) , p. 9 and n. 26.

36. Gen. 46:18, 25; Ex. 6:20; Ruth 4:17.

37. Kitchen, *op. cit.*, pp. 36–41 and the fine documentation. Also Abraham Malamat, "King Lists of the Old Babylonian Period and Biblical Genealogies," JAOS, 88 (1968) : 163–73. See the remarks of David N. Freedman in *The Bible and the Ancient Near East*, *op. cit.*, pp. 206 f.

38. Green, *loc. cit.*

39. John H. Raven, *Old Testament Introduction* (New York: Fleming Revell, 1906) , pp. 134–5.

40. *Ibid.*, p. 135. Malamat, *op. cit.*, pp. 170–1, illustrates this telescoping effect of some 20 generations from Levi to Samuel in the genealogy of Heman in I Chr. 6:33–38 (18–23 Hebrew) down to David's genealogy of the Hammurabi dynasty (J. J. Finkelstein, "The Genealogy of the Hammurapi Dynasty," JCS, 20 (1966) : 95–118) and the upper portion of the Assyrian King List.

41. Meredith G. Kline, "Divine Kingship and Genesis 6:1–4," WTJ, 24 (1962) : 187–204.

42. T. H. Gaster, "Cosmogony," IDB, I:702. The same illustration is repeated in

Sarna, *op. cit.*, p. 5; S. H. Hooke, *In the Beginning*, Vol. VI of the *Clarendon Bible* (Oxford: Clarendon Press, 1947) , p. 20; Skinner, *op. cit.*, pp. 21–2; and Driver, *op. cit.*, pp. 6–7.

43. R. Laird Harris, "Bible and Cosmology," BETS, 5 (1962) : 11–17; "The Meaning of the Word Sheol as Shown by Parallels in Poetic Texts," *ibid.*, 4 (1961) : 129–35; "The Mist, the Canopy, and the Rivers of Eden," *ibid.*, 11 (1968) : 177–9.

44. Harris, "Bible and Cosmology," p. 12; Gaster, *op. cit.*, p. 704, translates *raqiaʿ* as a "strip of metal"—mentioning Ex. 39:3, Jer. 10:9; but no such meaning can be attested from these ideas of stretching, hammering, or extending.

45. For supporting evidence, see Harris, *ibid.*

46. Umberto Cassuto, *A Commentary on the Book of Genesis*, Part I (Jerusalem: Magnes Press, 1961) , pp. 101–4, and by the same author *The Documentary Hypothesis*, p. 74–8; Derek Kidner, "Genesis 2:5, 6: Wet or Dry?" TB 17 (1966) : 109–14. See above n. 43.

47. J. Oliver Buswell, *A Systematic Theology of the Christian Religion*, Vol. I (Grand Rapids: Zondervan, 1962) , pp. 264–5, 279–82, where he argues that the grammar supports in the rendering, not of a biological reptile (which does not eat dirt and is not the object of the enmity in 3:14) , but the Serpent, the Devil. Creepers are already created in Gen. 1 and declared to be good.

48. *Ibid.*, pp. 272–9; Geerhardus Vos, *Biblical Theology* (Grand Rapids: Wm. B. Eerdmans, 1954) , pp. 37–51; and Arthur H. Lewis "The Localization of the Garden of Eden," BETS, 11 (1968) : 169–75.

49. Gaster, *op. cit.*, p. 705, notes that this connection of woman with the flesh of man cannot be limited to the connection observed by Samuel N. Kramer, BASOR (Supplem. Studies No. 1, 1945) , p. 9, in the Enki and Ninhursag epic (TI = "rib" and "life" with NIN.TI "lady of the rib") . Many other peoples witness the same general connection where the influence of missionaries and the philological similarities "can be reasonably discounted." See also the magnificent demonstration of R. A. Martin, "The Earliest Messianic Interpretation of Gen. 3:15," JBL, 84 (1965) : 425–7.

50. Samuel N. Kramer, "The Babel of Tongues: A Sumerian Version," JAOS, 88 (1968) : 108–11. See Sarna, *op. cit.*, pp. 63–80.

51. William F. Albright, "Review of Heidel, *The Babylonian Genesis . . . : The Story of Creation*," JBL, 62 (1943) : 366–70.

52. Edward J. Young, "The Relation of the First Two Verses of Genesis One to Verses Two and Three," WTJ, 21 (1959) : 133–46. Also by the same author "The Interpretation of Genesis 1:2," *ibid.*, 23 (1961) : 151–78; cf. Heidel, *op. cit.*, pp. 95 ff. Also Walther Eichrodt, "In the Beginning," in *Israel's Prophetic Heritage: Essays in Honor of James Muilenburg*, ed. B. W. Anderson and W. Harrelson (New York: Harper & Row, 1962) , pp. 1–10.

53. Gen. 2:4, 5:1, 6:9, 10:1, 11:10, 27, 25:12, 19, 36:1, (36:9) , 37:2. Note also Num. 3:1, Ruth 4:18, Mt. 1:1. Malamat, *op. cit.*, pp. 164–5, 170–1, compares the *tôleḏôt* of Perez (Ruth 4:18) , for example, with the three *palûs* ("eras," or "dynasties") of the Genealogy of the Hammurabi dynasty and guesses that the implication is that these terms indicate earlier genealogical documents which were used as sources for the present compositions.

54. Recently there seems to be a growing undercurrent of rejecting the conclusion that the Patriarchal names, customs, geography and laws fit perfectly within the early second millennium as witnessed by such sites as Nuzu, Mari and Alalakh. Illustrative of this point of view are Gene M. Tucker, "The Legal Background of Gen. 23," JBL, 85 (1966) : 77–84, and John Van Seters, "The Problem of Childlessness in New Eastern Law and the Patriarchs of Israel," JBL, 87 (1968) : 401–8; cf. a partial response of Kitchen, *op. cit.*, pp. 154–5.

55. I am indebted to my assistant Arnold Conrad for supplying and documenting this list.

56. Wilbur N. Smith, *Egypt in Prophecy* (Boston: Wilde Co., 1957), pp. 13–23, especially pp. 21–2, n. 2.

57. Some preliminary work has begun, e.g. T. C. Mitchell, "Archaeology and Genesis i–xi," *Faith and Thought,* 91 (1959): 28–49. Also on Gen. 10: Donald J. Wiseman, "Genesis 10: Some Archaeological Considerations," *Journal of Transactions of Victorian Institute,* 87 (1955): 14–24, 113–18.

58. E. W. Bullinger, *Figures of Speech* (1898; r.p. Grand Rapids: Baker Book House, 1968), pp. 1032–3.

59. Mitchell, *op. cit.,* p. 48 ". . . There is no plain indication that these chapters are couched in other than plain narrative prose."

60. Otto Eissfeldt, *The Old Testament: An Introduction,* trans. Peter R. Ackroyd (New York: Harper & Row, 1965), p. 11 ff.

61. Langdon B. Gilkey, "Cosmology, Ontology, and The Travail of Biblical Language," *Concordia Theological Monthly,* 33 (1962): 143–54 (reprinted from *Journal of Religion,* 1961, pp. 194–205).

62. *Ibid.,* p. 143.

63. *Ibid.,* p. 152.

64. *Ibid.,* p. 153.

65. J. Stafford Wright, "The Place of Myth in the Interpretation of the Bible," *Journal of the Transactions of the Victorian Institute,* 88 (1956): 18–30.

66. *Ibid.,* p. 23.

67. *Ibid.,* p. 27.

DATE OF THE EXODUS

Leon T. Wood

Few historical questions relating to the Old Testament have been discussed as frequently during the past half century as the date of the exodus. Yet the need for consideration continues. Archaeological research repeatedly brings new evidence to light which requires evaluation, and recurring suggestions as to interpretation of both new and old evidence call for examination.

Not many years ago, most scholars believed that evidence pointed to a date in the fifteenth century B.C., the so-called early date. Now a majority of liberal scholars have taken more recent discoveries to favor a date in the thirteenth century, the so-called late date. Most conservatives continue to accept the early date, believing that Biblical evidence allows for this date alone, though recently a few representatives have turned to the later time.[1] That these few have so turned gives further reason for this treatment. What is the nature of recent discoveries which has persuaded these men to make such a change? And can one make the change and still be true to the Biblical materials?

This paper seeks to survey and evaluate evidence, with some attention to interpretations of it, laying stress on matters of greatest and more recent significance. First the Biblical factors are reviewed briefly, with attention to making judgment whether these can be interpreted in keeping with the late date position. Then extra-Biblical matters are discussed more at length, considering whether they may fairly be interpreted in keeping with the early date.

I. Biblical Evidence

A. I Kings 6:1

A direct statement is made in I Kings 6:1 that the exodus preceded the time when Solomon began to build the Temple (ca. 966 B.C.) by 480 years. Adding 480 years to 966 B.C. gives the mid-fifteenth century date of 1446 B.C. To offset this evidence, adherents of the late date assert that the number 480, being the twelfth multiple of 40 (40 being said to represent a generation[2]) is indicative only of twelve generations.[3] It is pointed out further that, since a generation was really much less than 40 years, one is justified in reducing 480 by as much as 200 years,[4] bringing the actual number of years signified into agreement with the late date.

In evaluation, it must be said that this explanation is not in keeping with the view of Biblical inspiration traditionally held by conservatives. The text in no way states or implies the thought of twelve generations, but mentions only the definite number 480. More seriously, the reduction of a number to nearly half its size, by whatever means of analysis employed, must be considered a denial of its original accuracy and so of Biblical inerrancy.

B. Jephthah's Statement

Jephthah, eighth Judge of Israel, spoke of Israel as having possessed the land of Palestine by his day for a period of 300 years (Jud. 11:26).[5] Jephthah's own date may be figured approximately by totaling the years which elapsed after him[6] until Solomon began the Temple ca. 966 B.C. The date which results is ca. 1100 B.C., just 300 years after 1400 B.C., the time of the conquest on the basis of the early date. There is no way to harmonize Jephthah's statement with the late date except to deny its historical accuracy. It is argued that Jephthah could have simply been mistaken in his knowledge of history, but, if so, one wonders at the propriety of the inspired Scriptures including the error, especially when spoken by a leader in Israel. It would also be highly coincidental that this error should figure exactly to a time in keeping with the early date.

C. The Length of the Judges Period

An analysis of the length of the Judges Period requires a total time much longer than possible with the late date. The Judges Period occupied a major portion of the time between the exodus and the establishment of Israel's monarchy in ca. 1050 B.C., but not all. Not included were the wilderness journey of forty years, Joshua's headship of perhaps twenty years, and the approximate twenty years of Samuel's leadership prior to Saul, a total of approximately eighty years. So then between the date of the exodus and 1050 B.C. enough time must be allowed for these eighty years in addition to the Judges Period. On the basis of the early date, just over three centuries result for the length of the Judges Period,[7] but with the late date less than a century and a half. Admittedly, some overlapping of judgeships and times of rest existed in the period, but only enough to suit the three-century allotted time of the early date.[8] There is no way to compress the period to a century and a half, apart from seriously reworking its historical structure, which, again, would be out of keeping with the conservative view of inspiration.

D. Historical Correlations

A much better correlation between the events of Scripture and Egyptian history can be made on the basis of the early date. The Biblical story of the exodus fits Egyptian history well if the exodus transpired in the fifteenth century, but not if in the thirteenth. Two aspects of the story call for particular notice.

One concerns the order by an Egyptian Pharaoh for the building of Pithom and Raamses (Ex. 1:11) by enslaved Israelites. Late date adherents commonly identify Rameses II (1304–1238)[9] as both the one who gave the order[10] and the Pharaoh of the exodus. But if he were, then the order could not have preceded the exodus by more than a few years, thirty at the most.[11] The Biblical account, however, implies a much longer time. The mention of the order falls in a context which suggests that it was a part of already initiated afflictions[12] imposed by the Egyptians on the Israelites in an endeavor to curtail their population growth. It was after this, then, that more direct methods for curtailment were employed, first ordering Hebrew midwives to kill all Hebrew male babies (Ex. 1:15–21) and later issuing a blanket decree that all Hebrew male children be cast into the Nile (Ex. 1:22). Then to the years for these measures must be added eighty more, for Moses was only born at the time of the last order and he was that old by the time of the exodus. This means that the ruler who directed Pithom and Raamses to be built must have lived more than a century prior to the exodus, and probably much more, and so could not have been the same as the Pharaoh of the exodus. Late date adherents find difficulty in allowing this much time, because a principal argument for their overall position is found in identifying Rameses II as the one who ordered the city of his name, Raamses, as well as Pithom, built, of which matter we shall see more later. Early date adherents, on the other hand, have no difficulty in placing this Pharaoh wherever the evidence best indicates.[13]

The other aspect concerns the identity of the king who died while Moses was in Midian (Ex. 2:23–25). The implied rationale for the mention of this king's death in the Biblical record is that his decease made possible Moses' return to Egypt, which suggests that the one who died was the same as the one from whom Moses fled forty years before (Ex. 2:15). Whenever the exodus occurred, then, a Pharaoh who ruled at least forty years must have just died. On the basis of the early date, such a death had just occurred; namely, of Thutmose III who died ca. 1450 B.C., shortly before our accepted date for the exodus of 1446 B.C. Also he had ruled alone for the prior thirty-two years, and before this jointly with his famous aunt-stepmother, Hatshepsut (1504–1482), long enough to be the one from whom Moses had fled. For the late date, however, there is no death of a long-ruling Pharaoh which fits. Seti I (1316–1304) was the ruler who immediately preceded Rameses II, but he reigned only twelve years. Furthermore, late date adherents normally place the exodus well into the reign of Rameses II,[14] which locates the death of Seti I too many years prior to the exodus to suit the rationale for the mention of death in Exodus 2:23. At one time, late date adherents commonly identified the successor of Rameses II, Merneptah (1238–1228), as the exodus Pharaoh, thus making Rameses II as the one who died, permitting Moses to return to Egypt; and Rameses II did rule long enough to qualify as the one from whom Moses could have fled. Few, however, make this identification today, due to the discovery of the so-called "Israel Stele" written by this same Merneptah. On it he commemorates his victory over listed peoples of Canaan and among these includes Israel.[15] If Israel was defeated by Merneptah in Canaan, she must have left Egypt at least forty years before (time of the wilderness journey), long before he began to rule.[16]

E. Evaluation

Each of the above areas of evidence prohibits the acceptance of the late date for the exodus. There is no way to harmonize any one of them with this viewpoint and at the same time maintain the view of Biblical inspiration traditionally held by conservatives.

We move on now to consider extra-Biblical matters at somewhat greater length, to determine if they may be fairly interpreted in keeping with the early date. These matters may be divided into three groups: those which concern, first, the time of the conquest of Canaan, second, the time of the wilderness journey, and third, the time of the departure from Egypt.

II. Evidence for the Time of the Conquest

A. Jericho

One of the more controversial areas of evidence concerns the ancient city of Jericho, modern Tell es-Sultan. Following excavations there by John Garstang during the years 1930–36, a majority of scholars accepted the evidence he presented as favoring the early date. Garstang himself declared that the city fell in conquest to Joshua "between 1400 and 1385 B.C."[17] During the years 1952–58, however, Miss Kathleen Kenyon worked further at Jericho and concluded that the city fell in "the third quarter of the fourteenth century."[18] This variant viewpoint contributed to a change by many scholars away from the early date view; and, though her conclusion did not fit the late date either, most believed that other areas of evidence were sufficiently clear in favor of that position to take these as determinative rather than Jericho. They sought warrant for this thinking in Miss Kenyon's repeated observation that Jericho was severely denuded of evidence, which made conclusion regarding it appear minimal in value. As a result, little notice is taken today of the evidence and position presented by Garstang. It may be, however, that his view has been set aside too easily in an effort to make the Jericho evidence agree with what is believed convincing from other sources. For this reason it is worthwhile to review his evidence in view of the conclusions more recently presented by Miss Kenyon.

1. *Garstang's evidence.* Garstang's evidence may be summarized under four heads: (a) that both on the city mound and in the tombs he found "an abundant and parallel series of pottery and scarabs covering the reigns of the Pharaohs from Thothmes III to Amenhotep III"; (b) that neither on the city mound nor in the tombs did he find "any objects datable to the reign of Akhenaton," the successor of Amenhotep III, "though on other sites in Palestine" the distinctive art from his time "is presented in abundance"; (c) that a few pottery pieces dating to Late Bronze II, "from the reign of Seti I onwards" were found associated with one building only (his so-called "Middle Building"), which appears to have stood quite alone at its time of existence; and (d) that in two tombs (nos. 4 and 13) of forty-three examined, a few pieces of later pottery (including imitation Mycenaean) were found dating to Late Bronze II.[19]

Garstang concluded from the first two items that Jericho fell to Joshua sometime during the reign of Amenhotep III (1414–1378), since both pottery and scarabs still existed for his time but none for his successor, Akhenaton. The small amount of pottery of the third item found in the lone "Middle Building" was believed to represent the brief occupation of Jericho by Eglon, King of Moab (Jud. 3:12–14). Garstang believed this conclusion was substantiated by the absence of similar pottery in the tombs, showing that whoever lived there at the time did not bury in Jericho's cemetery. And the pottery of the fourth item he concluded was from yet later dwellers, few in number, who sporadically took up residence, as evidenced by the fewness of the pieces found, their intrusive nature, and their appearance in only two tombs, with none at all found on the mound.

2. *Miss Kenyon's conclusions.* Miss Kenyon's conclusions which bear on the matter may be summarized in the following points. (a) Garstang's well-known "double-wall,"[20] which he believed was the wall which fell before Joshua, was not a double wall at all, but two separate walls, dating from different times and both more than 500 years before Joshua.[21] (b) The city mound was severely denuded of all remains of Late Bronze occupancy (i.e. after 1500 B.C.) except on the mound "above the spring," which minimizes all the evidence regarding such occupancy.[22] (c) The pottery found by Garstang either on this portion of the mound or else in tombs, which he said was continuous into the reign of Amenhotep III

at 1400 B.C., actually ceased with Middle Bronze II, probably about 1550 B.C. This means that a layer of ash found by Garstang in connection with this pottery does not represent Joshua's destruction, as Garstang held, but probably one effected by Egyptians shortly after the Hyksos expulsion.[23] (d) The few pottery pieces Garstang found in the lone building above the spring,[24] which he ascribed to the occupation of Eglon, King of Moab, are actually the only evidence of the city Joshua destroyed. That city, then, was apparently small and was destroyed ca. 1325 B.C. And (e) the few pottery pieces Garstang found in two tombs are of the same date as the pottery of the city Joshua destroyed and so the destruction was not of Late Bronze II as Garstang thought.

3. *Evaluation.* With the evidence and conclusions of both archaeologists before us, an evaluation is possible. First, as to items (a) and (b) of Miss Kenyon's conclusions, she is certainly correct. The evidence she gathered regarding the "double wall" is convincing that Garstang was wrong. It is true also that the city mound was severely denuded. Neither item, however, makes any difference as to Garstang's real evidence. The section of the wrongly dated wall found is far removed from the area where he located his significant material, the evidence from which has no necessary connection with the wall and is not lessened in value because of its redating. Also, Garstang realized too, as did Miss Kenyon, that the city mound was denuded, though he did not make as much of it. Both based their conclusions on materials found on the mound above the spring.

As to item (e), Miss Kenyon really conflicts with late date adherents more than with Garstang. Garstang held that a few pottery pieces, found in only two of forty-three tombs, were from the thirteenth century and represented unimportant, sporadic habitation. Miss Kenyon took them as contemporary with the pottery Garstang found in the lone "Middle Building" of the fourteenth century. Late date adherents, however, prefer to think of them as did Garstang, for they see them as some evidence at least of a thirteenth-century city which they believe must have been the one Joshua destroyed.[25]

Coming now to items (c) and (d) we find the areas of significant difference between Garstang and Miss Kenyon. Whether the conquest of Jericho dates near 1400 B.C. or not depends on these two matters.

Speaking first of item (d), it may be fairly stated that the explanation of Garstang fits the evidence measurably better than that of Miss Kenyon. This item concerns the several pottery pieces found by Garstang in or near the lone "Middle Building" above the spring. Both Garstang and Miss Kenyon date these pieces to the latter half of the fourteenth century,[26] but Miss Kenyon believes they represent the city of Joshua's destruction while Garstang attributes them to the temporary occupancy of Eglon, King of Moab. Miss Kenyon's reason is only that this is the one occupancy that can date to Joshua's time, the former one having closed at ca. 1550 B.C., with a long gap intervening. She admits that the evidence points to only a small unwalled city for the time, which is entirely out of keeping with the Biblical story; but she suggests that evidence for the city having been larger and walled may have completely washed away. Garstang's explanation, in contrast, fits very well. That the city was small suits, for certainly Eglon, occupying Jericho only temporarily, would not have rebuilt extensively. And that none of the pottery found in the city was found duplicated in the tombs suits; for surely Eglon, being King of Moab, would not have buried at Jericho but returned any who died to the home country.

We come now to item (c) which is the most pivotal of all. This concerns the extensive pottery found on both the mound above the spring and in the tombs which Garstang contends represents occupancy until ca. 1400 B.C., but which Miss Kenyon says terminated before 1500 B.C. A thick burned layer of ash lies below this pottery, representing a major destruction, which Garstang takes as the destruction of Joshua, while Miss Kenyon ascribes it to Egyptians.

Admittedly, fair judgment here can be passed only by those expert in pottery analysis. Both Miss Kenyon and Garstang, however, hold the distinction of being experts, and they disagree. Miss Kenyon contends that her conclusions are warranted because pottery of Late Bronze I is now better known than when Garstang made his evaluation, particularly in view of the Megiddo excavations.[27] Garstang, however, writing a preface to a second edition of his book *The Story of Jericho* in 1947, eight years after completion of work at Megiddo, still stated that his earlier conclusions were valid, being based on "material evidence which the reader may examine for himself."[28]

The "material evidence" which Garstang[29] seems mainly to have had in mind is of two kinds. One is the number of scarabs found, which constituted a long series ending exactly with the reign of Amenhotep III at ca. 1400 B.C. Of these Miss Kenyon only remarks that scarabs are not safe as evidence for dating, for they "are the sort of thing liable to be heirlooms."[30] One would not disagree with this generally speaking, but here at Jericho these "heirlooms" are continuous until the very time of the early date conquest when they significantly cease. This coincidence, convincing as it was to Garstang, still remains as factual as ever.

The other matter concerns imported Cypriot pottery, especially well-known wishbone milk bowls and pipe-necked bilbils.[31] Garstang found these as part of the pottery here concerned. At Megiddo, the site Miss Kenyon believes is determinative, the same were found in Levels X to VII, with the major number in Levels VIII and VII which date 1479 to 1150 B.C.[32] Since Jericho was well inland, in contrast to Megiddo, it is to be expected that this imported ware would have reached Jericho later than Megiddo and quite possibly only after it had become plentiful there, which means after 1479 B.C.[33] If so, this pottery constitutes good evidence in favor of Garstang's position.

The particular type of pottery which is lacking at Jericho, that gives reason for Miss Kenyon to assert that the city was destroyed in the sixteenth century, is a bichrome ware using red and black geometric lines enclosing stylized figures of fish, birds, and animals.[34] The pottery is attractive, distinctive, and attributed by some to the genius of an itinerant artist.[35] Found in both north and south Palestine, it is commonly taken as marking the transition point between Middle and Late Bronze for the land generally.

Reason exists, however, to doubt that its absence at sites in all parts of the land, including the Jordan Valley, is an adequate criterion for abandonment. For what has been found of the pottery to date shows its employment really was quite limited. As to the duration of its use, it is generally agreed not to have exceeded a century, ca. 1575 to 1475 B.C. And as to the area over which it has been found, it appears to have spread out from two basic centers, Megiddo in the north and Tell el-'Ajjul near the coast in the south, but not extensively. From Megiddo it moved east in the Esdraelon Valley to Ta'anach and north above the Sea of Galilee to Hazor; and from Tell el-'Ajjul it spread to numerous sites but only as far east as the foothills of Judah. It has not been found in the mountain region of central Palestine nor in the Jordan Valley.[36]

These limitations give reason to doubt that bichrome pottery ever came to the region of Jericho. Some have said, in support of the common viewpoint, that sites in the mountain and Jordan areas of Palestine have not been adequately excavated to provide a fair test for the presence there of the ware. However, numerous sites have been worked on as extensively as several which have shown it, which causes one to wonder why no places at all have revealed it if it was used. The observation seems more warranted that this rather specialized pottery simply never penetrated the less accessible and more removed mountain and Jordan areas. Even Bethshan, located on the quite accessible crossroad of the Esdraelon and Jordan Valleys, though still fifty miles north of Jericho, has revealed no bichrome pottery proper, though enough that was contemporary to demonstrate the uninterrupted occupancy of the site during the time concerned.[37]

B. Lachish, Debir, and Hazor

One of the more significant reasons why scholars have come to reject the ca. 1400 B.C. time for Jericho's fall is the fact that certain other cities captured by Joshua show a layer of destruction dating more in keeping with the late date. Three cities are mainly involved: Lachish, Debir, and Hazor.[38] Lachish and Debir were captured by Joshua in his southern

campaign (Josh. 10:32, 38, 39) and Hazor in his northern (Josh. 11:10).
It is important to notice and evaluate this source of evidence.

1. *Destruction in the thirteenth century.* Lachish has been successfully
identified with modern Tell ed-Duweir.[39] Besides scarabs from Amenhotep III and Rameses II, a broken bowl, generally accepted as dating to
the "year four" of Merneptah (1238–1228), was found here. The fragments of the bowl were discovered in a burned layer of destruction and
serve particularly to date this layer to the latter half of the thirteenth
century.[40] Debir (Kiriath-Sepher, Josh. 15:15) is thought to be Tell Beit
Mirsim,[41] though with less convincing reasons.[42] A burned layer of destruction was found also here and it is dated to the same general time by its
location at the cessation point of Late Bronze Age material.[43] Neither
Tell ed-Duweir nor Tell Beit Mirsim show a similar burned layer for a
ca. 1400 B.C. date.[44]

Hazor has been well identified with Tell el-Qeday, nine miles north of
the Sea of Galilee.[45] The site boasts an oval-shaped tell of about twenty-
five acres and a much larger plateau next to it of about one hundred
seventy-five acres, indicating that Hazor was by far the largest city of
ancient Palestine.[46] There is evidence of violent destruction sometime in
the thirteenth century, so that nearly all habitation ceased on the plateau,[47] and life on the main tell was able to continue only in a poor and
modest way. Such a change in living pattern speaks of a major defeat;
and late date adherents take the enemy to have been Israel, thus linking
the date of Hazor's destruction with that of Lachish and Debir. Again,
an exact time in the thirteenth century for this destruction cannot be
determined; but a date is assumed which fits the Lachish information.
Some observations regarding this evidence are pertinent.

2. *Earlier burning at Hazor.* First, concerning Hazor, Yadin found no
indication of burning in connection with the destruction of the thirteenth
century (Stratum I on the plateau), whereas Joshua 11:11 states definitely that the city destroyed by Joshua was burned. At Stratum III below, however, Yadin did find evidence of burning, stating that this level
"was effectively destroyed by fire, most probably by one of the Egyptian
pharaohs of the New Kingdom, Amenophis II or more probably Thutmose III."[48] Since it is at this level where burning is indicated, and since
a destruction by Amenhotep II or Thutmose III, as suggested by Yadin,
would be only something less than half a century prior to the early date
time for Joshua's destruction, it may very well be that the city of Stratum
III was really the one Joshua destroyed and not that of thirteenth-century
Stratum I. In keeping too, is the fact that Hazor still appears strong at
the time of Deborah and Barak, later in the Judges Period. Though
Deborah and Barak fought their battle with Sisera, this man was only
a military underling of "Jabin, king of Canaan, that reigned in Hazor"
(Jud. 4:2, 17), which means that Hazor was still the leading city of the
north. If so, the time for Joshua's destruction belongs well before the

thirteenth century and the condition of semi-demise for Hazor appears more suitable after Deborah.[49]

3. *Lachish and Debir not burned by Joshua.* Concerning Lachish and Debir, two observations are pertinent. The first is that, contrary to what we have seen relative to Hazor, the Bible does not say that these cities were burned. This omission cannot be considered insignificant, either; for when Joshua did burn cities, as Jericho (Josh. 6:21) and Ai (Josh. 8:28), the fact is mentioned. Further, Joshua 11:13 states specifically that the cities that "stood on their mounds, Israel burned none of these, save Hazor only, that did Joshua burn." Admittedly the primary reference in this last passage is to cities of northern Palestine; but there is no reason to think that the general practice differed greatly in the south, and both Lachish and Debir did stand on "mounds."[50] Regarding these cities, the Biblical record states only that Joshua "took" (*lāqad*) them, smiting them with "the edge of the sword," which could well refer only to a thorough defeat, without doing extensive harm to buildings. After all, Israel could use the buildings, which would give reason not to destroy them. The point to notice is that, if Joshua did not burn Lachish and Debir, then the burned layers found must represent a destruction by another foe; and the fact that no such layer is found for ca. 1400 B.C. is only what might have been expected on the early date basis.

The second observation is that other enemies to cause these burned layers did exist in the thirteenth century. That is, if Israel is removed as the foe involved, other possible causes for the destructions are not difficult to find. One is simply inter-city warfare, known to have been frequent in all these centuries. Another is the inroad into Canaan by Merneptah, known to have transpired 1234 B.C. Still another, and perhaps the most likely, is the invasion of the Sea Peoples, when many sites along the eastern Mediterranean suffered similar fate. These warlike groups swept down the coast and spread havoc all the way to Egypt.[51] At Egypt they were finally repulsed, one group by Merneptah in his fifth year and another by Rameses III from his fifth to his eleventh years (ca. 1190–1184).[52] If these migrating peoples destroyed other coastal cities, why not Lachish and Debir? Indeed, why not thirteenth-century Hazor?[53]

C. The Amarna Tablets

A third area of evidence as to the date of Joshua's conquest concerns the Amarna Tablets[54] and their mention of Habiru invading Canaan. This is admittedly a complex question. At one time it was commonly believed that these Tablets held good evidence for the early date of the exodus, but the opinion of many scholars has changed in recent years.

1. *The evidence.* The Tablets are letters written between ca. 1400 and 1367 B.C. to the Egyptian courts of Amenhotep III and Akenaton, mostly by Canaanite city-kings. The letters reveal a chaotic condition of plot,

counterplot, and contradictory accusations among these Canaanite rulers. Particularly pertinent is the frequent mention of trouble from a people called Habiru.[55] Since there is possible equivalency in name between "Habiru" and "Hebrew" ('*ibri*),[56] and since the disturbances wrought by these people are approximately at the time of the Israelite conquest on the early date basis, attraction exists for identifying the Habiru with Joshua's invading forces.

In recent years, however, this attraction has been measurably lessened by the discovery that Habiru are mentioned also in many other texts, found as far distant as Boghazkoi, Mari, Nuzi, and Babylon, and dating back as early as the Third Dynasty of Ur. Also, scholars have come to recognize more fully that the letters speak of Habiru causing trouble in northern Canaanite cities (where Joshua did not campaign) as well as southern. And still further, it has been learned that the term "Habiru" carried a social and descriptive connotation rather than ethnical. Habiru were thought of as migrants, people without citizenship, undesirables, even bandits and raiders. As a result, many late date adherents today believe that there is no connection between the Habiru of the Tablets and the Hebrews of Joshua, and so no bearing of the letters on the date of the Exodus.[57]

2. *One explanation: Hebrews were Habiru.* Many early date adherents, however, believe the Amarna letters still do carry evidential value. Most of these scholars directly identify the Habiru with the Hebrews, as formerly held.[58] That is, they identify those Habiru involved in southern Canaan with the Hebrews. Other Habiru in other places and at other times obviously were not, but those who invaded southern Canaan could have been. The disturbed city-kings of that area could have classed Joshua's forces as Habiru in type, since they were without country and trying to seize Canaanite land. This view considers the Canaanites to have used the name quite as an epithet, a derogatory term, at least at first.[59] Supporting this view is the fact that the southern Canaanite Amarna letters were written only from cities late in being captured by Israel, among them Megiddo, Gezer, Ashkelon, and Acco, which fits the fact that all letters would have been written after the time of Joshua's first victories.

3. *Another explanation: Hebrews preceded Habiru.* There is also a second viewpoint as to a relation between the Habiru and the Hebrews, which is forcefully espoused by Meredith Kline.[60] He does not identify the two, but places the conquest of Joshua shortly before the Habiru notices.[61]

Kline argues against identification by showing first that the term "Hebrew" is not used in the Old Testament with a social connotation (true for the term "Habiru"), but with an ethnic, harking back to Eber, ancestor of Abraham; second, that there is difficulty in exactly equating the two terms "Habiru" and "Hebrew" etymologically (asserted also by some late-date adherents) ; and third, that there is conflict historically when one compares the activities and manners of the Habiru in the Amarna letters with those of the Hebrews in Joshua's conquest.

Then to show that the conquest preceded the Habiru references, Kline develops a historical reconstruction which he believes best harmonizes all given factors. He states that Joshua's main campaigns had been completed by the time that certain Habiru raiders entered southern Canaan. He states further that these southern raiders probably were sent by a larger group of Habiru already established in northern Canaan, and that coming into the south where Joshua's people had recently arrived, they did not at first take notice of them, since they were new and not yet settled. But later, upon becoming stronger themselves, they did recognize them and proceeded to force them into subjection, which occasion Kline identifies with Israel's oppression at the hands of Cushan-rishathaim of Mesopotamia (Jud. 3:8–10). This last point lends credence to Kline's view, for otherwise there is real problem in harmonizing this first oppression of Israel with the Amarna tablets' mention of the Habiru, for they date at the same general time.[62]

It is unnecessary to choose which of these two views is better. Perhaps there is more to commend the second at the present time, but it may be that further discovery and study will bring favor to the first. What is significant here is that either view gives satisfactory explanation for harmonizing the Amarna evidence with the early date position.

D. *Military Campaigns of Seti I and Rameses II*

The last area of evidence to be noticed as to the date of Joshua's conquest concerns the military campaigns through Palestine undertaken by the Egyptian Pharoahs Seti I and Rameses II. Late date adherents argue that if Israel were in Palestine at the time of these campaigns, which would have been true on the early date basis, the campaigns of each should be mentioned in the book of Judges, a book given largely to military activities. Since they are not, Israel must not yet have been there.

1. *The evidence.* Seti I campaigned northward already in his first year (1316 B.C.), encountering enemy forces in northern Palestine and slightly beyond. In a later campaign he pressed as far as Kadesh on the Orontes River, where he made a treaty with the Hittite King, Muwatallis.[63] Rameses II followed with other campaigns, notably in his fifth and twenty-first years, in the last of which he made his famous treaty with the Hittite, Hattusilis III (1283 B.C.).[64] In each of these campaigns, the Egyptian army had to march through the length of Palestine, certainly coming in contact with Israelites, if indeed they were there. Then further, both Seti I and Rameses II appear to have engaged in actual warfare in Palestine itself. At least both left a stele at Bethshan,[65] and Seti I tells on his

of clashing with 'Apiru near that city, a reference conceivably to the Hebrews, in which the term "Habiru-'Apiru" is again used. These Palestinian activities do make the question pertinent as to why, if Israel was in the land at the time, the book of Judges gives no record of them.

2. *The explanation.* Two observations may be made in giving answer. The first is a negative one, that the later military inroads into Palestine of Merneptah (1238–1228) and Rameses III (ca. 1195–1164) are not mentioned in the book of Judges either; and the campaigns of each did follow the time of Israel's entrance into Canaan, even on, the late date basis. Merneptah, as noticed earlier, claims to have wrought extensive havoc in Palestine, writing, "Israel is laid waste, his seed is not; Hurru is become a widow for Egypt."[66] Rameses III of the XXth Dynasty boasts of having reduced both the "Tjeker and the Philistines" to ashes.[67] He even had scenes of his campaign into Palestine depicted on the walls of the famous temple of Medinet Habu. He seems to have been interested mainly in the Bethshan area, even as Seti I and Rameses II had been, for he rebuilt the city, including a fine temple, and made the city a type of frontier post.[68] It is clear that both later Pharaohs centered attacks on the Palestine sector for itself and did not merely pass through, as had been mainly true for Seti I and Rameses II. But the book of Judges omits their activities too. One may conclude from this that, if their campaigns are not mentioned, when Israel surely was in the land, then that the earlier campaigns are not mentioned need not be evidence that Israel was not in the land at that time.

The other observation concerns the reason for this omission in the book of Judges, whether of the earlier or of the later campaigns. The book does not constitute a history as such of the period of time covered. It is rather an accounting of Israel's deviant behavior and corresponding punishments. Accordingly, those military encounters which served as means of punishment or correction are mentioned, and those which did not are omitted. An outside power would strike, Israel would be defeated and then suffer a period of oppression, and finally a delivering Judge would arise to bring relief. Several outside powers were so involved,[69] but Egypt was not among them. Her military encounters did not lead to servitude and punishment on Israel's part. Therefore, that all Egyptian inroads into Palestine are omitted in the record of Judges in no way gives evidence that Israel was not in the land at the time.

III. Evidence for the Time of the Wilderness Journey

We come now to evidence relative to the time when Israel experienced her forty years in the wilderness on the way from Egypt to Canaan. Here late date adherents rely on one main argument. It is that both Transjordan and the Negeb show an alleged absence of sedentary occupation between ca. 1900 and ca. 1300 B.C.[70] Nelson Glueck's presentation of evidence to this effect is well known.[71] Yet the Biblical story tells of Israel being refused a travel route through the land of Edom by her King (Num. 20:14–21); of defeating great nations east of the Jordan ruled by the Kings Sihon and Og (Num. 21:21–35); and of being the object of a plot by Balak, King of Moab, who called for a prophet Balaam to "curse" Israel (Num. 22–25). All these occasions transpired in the Trans-jordan-Negeb region, which suggests that there was a sedentary habitation in this area at the time of Israel's wilderness experiences. Late date adherents argue from this that Israel, therefore, must have traveled through this region sometime after 1300 B.C. when sedentary occupation did exist.

Some scholars of note, however, have recently been challenging Glueck's conclusions. Some have refused full acceptance at any time because his work necessarily dealt almost solely with surface exploration; but now other discoveries have prompted some openly to challenge the idea of the extended gap in occupation that he has set forth. Lancaster Harding, for instance, points out that in the district of Ammon at least, sedentary occupation existed during the Hyksos period, because tombs found there from that time have been found well stocked with burial objects.[72] He asserts that such tombs "are not the work of nomads." He speaks also of a small temple, found while the Amman airport was being built, which held considerable pottery and Egyptian stone vases, which are typical of the period 1600 to 1399 B.C." Lastly he notes a large tomb found at Madaba dating from the "end of the Late Bronze to the Early Iron periods." In the light of these items, and others which can be anticipated to be found of a similar nature, Harding suggests that the sherds found in the surface exploration be reexamined, particularly since it is now known that Transjordanian pottery differed somewhat from that in Palestine proper during these "empty" centuries.

IV. Evidence for the Time of the Departure from Egypt

Late date adherents point to two arguments relative to the time when Israel left Egypt.

A. Pithom and Raamses

One concerns the building of the cities Pithom and Raamses by enslaved Israelites. It is pointed out that at Pithom, generally identified with Tell er-Retabeh,[73] the oldest royal building uncovered was a temple claimed to have been built by Rameses II. Hence if Israelites built for royalty in this city, it could not have been earlier than his time. Then it is argued that it was this same ruler who gave the name Pi-Ramesse (House of Rameses) to the old Hyksos' capital Avaris; and so, since

Exodus 1:11 uses the name Raamses for the city ordered built by the Pharaoh, this Pharaoh must have been Rameses II.

This is impressive evidence, not so much respecting Pithom, the identification of which with Tell er-Retabeh is not certain, but with Raamses. For whatever the modern site of ancient Avaris may be,[74] Rameses II seems to be the first to name it Pi-Ramesse, and at present there does not appear to be any other old Egyptian city called Raamses to correspond to the mention of Exodus 1:11.

M. Unger, arguing for the early date position, accounts for this evidence in terms of what he calls "a modernization of an archaic place name" by a later writer.[75] This explanation is possible, but it can explain Exodus 1:11 better than it can a similar use of the name in Genesis 47:11, where the phrase "land of Raamses" is used to designate the area still better known as Goshen and called Goshen elsewhere.

A more likely explanation is suggested by John Rea[76] followed by Gleason Archer.[77] This concerns the possibility that the name Raamses had already been used by the Hyksos' kings many years before the XIXth Dynasty. Rea first gives convincing reasons that the Pharaoh who began the Israelite oppression was the first of the Hyksos, and he then shows that this ruler and his successors may well have used the name Raamses. It is known for instance, that the XIXth Dynasty traced its ancestry back to the Hyksos line.[78] Then the XIXth Dynasty, in keeping with this fact, once again made the old Hyksos city of Avaris their northern capital. Further, Rameses II built there a temple to the Hyksos deity Seth, a deity adopted earlier by the Hyksos from the Egyptians. And still further, the father of Rameses II took his official name from this Hyksos deity, calling himself Seti I. It is noteworthy too, that the name Raamses (Egyptian, *Ra amessu*), meaning "Begotten of Ra," was a suitable Hyksos name, since the Hyksos venerated the god Ra as well as Seth, as is evidenced by the occurrence of the element Ra in various Hyksos personal names.[79] If one of the XIXth Dynasty Pharaohs took his name from the Hyksos god, Seth, then another might have taken his from the god, Ra; and, more significant here, the name Raamses might have been used for the capital city at the earlier time as well as later.

B. Egyptian Capital Location

The second argument cited relative to the date of Israel's departure from Egypt concerns the location of the Egyptian capital. During the period of the XVIIIth Dynasty, ruling at the time of the exodus on the early date basis, the capital was located at Thebes, nearly 400 miles south of the Delta. But during the reign of the XIXth Dynasty, involved with the late date, a northern capital was established once more at the old Hyksos site, Avaris. Since the Biblical story implies that the Pharaoh concerned was near the northern area of Goshen when Moses made frequent contacts with him during the period of the plagues, it is argued that the capital can only have been in the north at the time and so the general date must have been that of the XIXth Dynasty.

Good evidence exists, however that although the XVIIIth Dynasty did maintain its capital in the south, still some of the rulers, particularly Thutmose III and his son, Amenhotep II, the two most concerned in the early date position, did conduct extensive operations in the north and even resided there for substantial periods of time.

Speaking first of the father, Thutmose appointed a vizier for northern Egypt at Heliopolis in addition to the vizier at Thebes. This can only mean that he had unusually important interests there. Further, this man had himself named "Lord of Heliopolis" on two red granite obelisks erected in the city,[80] indicating particular attachment to this northern center of Ra worship. A scarab was found stating that Thutmose' son Amenhotep II was born at Memphis, the ancient northern capital. This is especially significant, for the mother at least must have resided there a few months, and likely the father too, being interested in the birth of the crown prince. Indeed, that he wanted his son born in the ancient capital carries important implications. Lastly, Thutmose III campaigned extensively against the Hittites and Mitanni far to the north,[81] and so must have maintained substantial supply bases in northern Egypt to make this possible. These military forays could hardly have left from Thebes, as far south as it was. In fact, they probably constituted a prime cause for the other matters noted.

As for Amenhotep II, the son, pertinent discoveries were made at Tell Basta, the ancient city of Bubastis (Pi-beseth of Ezek. 20:17) by the Swiss archaelogist Naville, as early as 1887–89. On a red granite slab of two carved panels, this king is shown in worship before Amon-Ra, "he who dwells in Perunefer."[82] Amenhotep II had been appointed as a youth to serve as commandant at Perunefer, a dockyard near Memphis, and evidence shows that he spent much time there. W. Hayes even states that he "seems to have maintained large estates" in the vicinity of Perunefer, where not only he but "his successors appear to have resided for extended periods of time."[83] This is substantiated further by the discovery of a temple which his grandson Amenhotep III had erected at the same site. All of this indicates that Amenhotep II, the Pharaoh of the Exodus on the early date basis, could well have been residing in the north at the time Moses needed to contact him relative to the plagues.

Conclusion

In conclusion it seems fair to say that of the seven total areas of extra-Biblical evidence considered, only four carry a measure of strength for the late date position. These concern Jericho, non-sedentary occupation in Transjordan and the Negeb, the building of Pithom and Raamses, and the location of Egypt's capital. If these, especially the last three, were the only areas of evidence to consider, a person would choose for the late-date view. This, however, is not the case. The Biblical evidence is clear in favor of the early date and it is decisive. Also, it has been shown that even these three strongest arguments for the late date are subject to satisfactory explanations in keeping with the early date. For this reason we may be sure that Israel left Egypt at approximately the midpoint of the fifteenth century.

Notes

1. Notably, Frederick F. Bruce, *Israel and the Nations* (Grand Rapids: Eerdmans, 1963), pp. 13–14; Charles F. Pfeiffer, *Egypt and the Exodus* (Grand Rapids: Baker Book House, 1964), pp. 84–8; or Kenneth A. Kitchen, *Ancient Orient and Old Testament* (Chicago: Inter-Varsity Press; London: Tyndale Press; 1966), pp. 57–75.

2. This is argued from the many times the number 40 is used in the O.T. For instance, Israel was 40 years in the wilderness; Moses was 40 years old when he fled to Midian and there remained for 40 more; Saul ruled 40 years, and so did both David and Solomon. Many other numbers, however, appear along with these and in parallel with them, which argues that these too must be taken as exact numbers.

3. Cf. Jack Finegan, *Light from the Ancient Past*, 2nd ed. (Princeton: Princeton University Press, 1959), p. 121; G. Ernest Wright, *Biblical Archaeology*, Rev. ed. (Philadelphia: The Westminster Press, 1962), pp. 84–5.

4. The exact amount of reduction varies with the date for the Exodus respectively favored. Most late date scholars favor a time in the early reign of Rameses II (1304–1238), but Harold H. Rowley, "Israel's Sojourn in Egypt," BJRL, 22 (1938) : 263, for instance, favors ca. 1225 B.C.

5. His words are: "While Israel dwelt in Heshbon and its towns, and in Aroer and its towns, and in all the cities that are along by the side of the Arnon, three hundred years."

6. Following him came four other judges (Ibzan for 7 years, Elon 10 years, Abdon 8 years, and Samson 20 years; cf. Jud. 12:8–15; 16:31), Samuel's time of leadership, the kingships of Saul and David, and four years of Solomon's reign. The years for the kings total 84, Samuel's time may be figured about 20 years, and though the times of the four preceding judges may overlap so that a definite figure cannot be given, their years plus those of Samson, who also overlapped Samuel, would be at least 20, making a grand total of no less than 124.

7. From 1446 B.C. to 1050 B.C. is 396 years, less 80 leaves 316.

8. When added together, all the judgeships and periods of rest of the Judges Period total 410 years, which is 94 more than the 316 available even on the early date basis. The Book of Judges itself, however, contains hints that overlapping did exist; as, for instance, 10:7, which suggests that the oppression of the Ammonites, whom Jephthah defeated, and the oppression of the Philistines, whom Samson encountered, were contemporary. Cf. J. Barton Payne, *An Outline of Hebrew History* (Grand Rapids: Baker Book House, 1954), p. 79, for discussion.

9. The date of Rameses II is determinative for the XVIIIth and XIXth dynasties. From the mention of a new moon in his 52nd year, astronomical calculations make his accession year either 1304 or 1290 B.C. In an article, "Comparative Chronology at the

Time of Dynasty XIX," JNES, 19 (Jan., 1960) : 15–22, M. B. Rowton reverses his former position in favor of the earlier year. E. Hornung, *Untersuchungen zur Chronologie und Geschichte des Neuen Reiches*, 1964, however, still argues for the later. Herein, dates in keeping with the earlier year are followed.

10. Sometimes Seti I (1316–1304), predecessor of Rameses II, is suggested as the one who gave the order; but still this does not allow enough time.

11. Most late date adherents place the exodus no later than ca. 1275 B.C. Merneptah (1238–1228), successor of Rameses II, defeated Israelites in Canaan (cf. footnote 15), which means the exodus had to precede this time by at least the 40 years of the wilderness wanderings.

12. Kitchen, *op. cit.*, p. 57, n. 3, defending the late date, argues that Ex. 1:7–14 is merely a general summary of Egypt's total oppression of Israel, so that events listed later need not be taken as having followed chronologically. He believes the fact that the Pithom and Raamses matter is mentioned at all argues that it came last when it would have been best remembered. Two questions, however, come quickly to mind on this basis. Why, if Ex. 1:7–14 is such a general summary, was the specific matter of Pithom and Raamses mentioned in it when other events are listed later? And why, if the Pithom and Raamses matter came last in the overall story, was its mention made rather early in the summary rather than last where one would expect it?

13. Some identify him with Ahmose (1584–1560), the first of the XVIIIth Dynasty who expelled the Hyksos from Egypt, and others with the first of the Hyksos rulers about 1730 B.C. This latter view is admirably set forth by John Rea, "The Time of the Oppression and the Exodus," BETS, 3 (Summer, 1960) : 58–9, who is followed by Gleason Archer, Jr., *A Survey of Old Testament Introduction* (Chicago: Moody Press, 1964), pp. 205–8.

14. If Rameses II was the one who gave the order for Pithom and Raamses to be built, as is commonly held, there is need to put several years between this order and the actual exodus.

15. The stele, with 28 lines of closely spaced writing, was found in Merneptah's mortuary temple at Thebes. On it he commemorates his victory over the Libyans as well as various peoples of Canaan. Cf. Kitchen, *op. cit.*, pp. 59–60, for good discussion of evidence concerning it.

16. Most scholars agree on this, but Harold H. Rowley still finds place for the exodus under Merneptah by greatly shortening the wilderness journey time; *From Joseph to Joshua* (London and New York: Oxford University Press, 1950), pp. 133 f. Few follow his suggestion, however.

17. John Garstang and J. B. E. Garstang, *The Story of Jericho*, 2nd ed. (London: Marshall, Morgan & Scott, Ltd., 1948), see especially pp. 125–30.

18. Kathleen Kenyon, *Digging Up Jericho* (New York: Frederick A. Praeger, 1957), p. 262.

19. Garstang, *op. cit.*, pp. 120–9; 177–80.

20. Garstang believed he had located a double wall as that which fell when Joshua destroyed the city. Though this wall really did not enter into his evidence as to the date Jericho fell, he made quite a little of it; and accordingly Miss Kenyon reacts in stressing his apparent error regarding it.

21. *Ibid.*, pp. 112–14; Kenyon, *op. cit.*, pp. 45–6.

22. Kenyon, *op. cit.*, pp. 44–7; 261–2. This denudation was due to the mound lying unoccupied from Joshua's destruction to the time of Ahab (I Kgs. 16:34; cf. Josh. 6:26).

23. *Ibid.*, p. 229.

24. Kenyon found one more in the room of a house nearby; cf. *ibid.*, p. 261.

25. Kitchen, for instance, does, following William F. Albright (*The Biblical Period from Abraham to Ezra* (New York: Harper Torchbooks, 1963), p. 100, n. 59) in saying, "Positive evidence that a settlement existed in the thirteenth century BC comes

from the tombs, these yielding Mycenaean pottery and imitations of such"; *op. cit.*, p. 63, n. 22.

26. Kenyon, *op. cit.*, pp. 261–2. Both Albright and Wright agree with this dating; cf. Wright, *op. cit.*, p. 79.

27. Kenyon, *op. cit.*, p. 260; cf. her *Archaeology in the Holy Land* (New York: Frederick A. Praeger, 1960), p. 198.

28. Garstang, *op. cit.*, pp. xiv–xv; cf. pp. 120–2.

29. *Ibid.*, p. xiv.

30. Kenyon, *Digging Up Jericho, op. cit.*, p. 260.

31. Garstang includes a picture of the 4 principal types in his book: *op. cit.*, p. 121.

32. Cf. Gordon Loud, *Megiddo II: Seasons of 1935–39*, Vol. Plates (Chicago: University of Chicago Press, 1948), plates 45, 54, 58, 61, 65, 69, 72, 130, 133–4, 137–41.

33. Kenyon herself states: "Cypriot imports during the Middle Bronze Age are rare. . . . But in the transitional period covered by Megiddo IX they become much more numerous, until during the Late Bronze Age almost as much pottery of Cypriot connections is found as that in the native tradition"; *Archaeology in the Holy Land*, p. 200.

34. For fullest treatment, cf. C. Epstein, *Palestinian Bichrome Ware* (Leiden: E. J. Brill, 1966).

35. Kenyon, *op. cit.*, p. 200; D. W. Thomas, *Archaeology and Old Testament Study* (Oxford: Clarendon Press, 1967), p. 317. Epstein, however, argues for its introduction to Palestine by the Hurrian migration.

36. Cf. map of all sites where it has been found in Epstein, *op. cit.*, facing p. 188.

37. Epstein, *ibid.*, p. 118.

38. Bethel and Eglon are sometimes included in this list; cf. Wright, *op. cit.*, pp. 80–5. Evidence respecting Bethel, however, is largely dependent on identifying it as the city captured by Joshua in Josh. 8, rather than Ai. But this is doubtful (as an answer to the problem of Ai) if only because Josh. 7:2 says specifically that Ai, as attacked by Israel, lay "on the east side of Bethel." Thus the burned layer at Bethel, dating to the 13th century, could well represent only its capture by the "house of Joseph" (Jud. 1:22–25). Also, Bethel's pottery, being superior to that of Lachish and Debir at the time of destruction, suggests a different date for Bethel's fall. Eglon suffers in evidential value both because its identification with Tell el Hesy is quite uncertain and because the evidence for the date of destruction of this tell, excavated in the last century by Petrie and Bliss, is not clearly determinative.

39. Excavated 1932–38 by Wellcome-Marston Archaeological Expedition led by J. L. Starkey. Lachish was formerly thought to be Tell el Hesy. Cf. H. Torczyner, Lachish I: *The Lachish Letters*, 1935; O. Tuffnel, et al., Lachish II: *The Fosse Temple*, 1940; Lachish III: *The Iron Age*, 1953; Lachish IV: *The Bronze Age*, 1957.

40. Cf. Finegan, *op. cit.*, pp. 161–3. A scarab of Rameses III (1195–1164) found there, however, has suggested a date even in the 12th century which does not fit the late date view; cf. O. Tuffnell, Lachish IV, p. 97, and her article, "Lachish," in Thomas, *op. cit.*, p. 302.

41. Excavated in 1926 and following years by a joint effort of the American School of Oriental Research and the Pittsburgh-Xenia Theological Seminary, William F. Albright and M. G. Kyle directors. It is located 12 miles southwest of Hebron. Cf. Kyle, *Excavating Kiriath-Sepher's Ten Cities*, 1934; Albright, AASOR, 12 (1930–31); 17 (1936–37); 21–22 (1941–43); and Albright, "Debir," in Thomas, *op. cit.*, pp. 207–19, for recent treatment.

42. The identification is challenged, for instance, by Martin Noth, *Journal of the Palestine Oriental Society*, 15 (1935): 48.

43. The Late Bronze Age closes ca. 1200 B.C. This city, however, may have lain waste

for several years after its fall so that one cannot date its fall as precisely as Lachish.

44. Thomas, *op. cit.*, p. 215, believes a non-occupancy period which began ca. 1564 B.C. at Tell Beit Mirsim continued after 1400. However, the following C1 level probably began already at 1475 B.C. (cf. Epstein, *op. tit.*, p. 185). Even if not, it is very possible that Tell Beit Mirsim is not ancient Debir (cf. Simons, GTT, p. 282).

45. Excavation began in 1955 under direction of Yigael Yadin who gives summaries in BA, 19–22 (1956–59). As many as 200 laborers and 45 technicians worked on this major project.

46. This size of some 200 acres compares with Lachish at 18 acres, Megiddo at 14, and Jericho at 8.

47. Thirteenth-century Mycenaean pottery is found just under the surface of the plateau.

48. Yadin, BA, 20 (1957): 44.

49. Kitchen, *op. cit.*, pp. 67, 68, argues against this conclusion, stating that the stress in the Biblical account of Deborah and Barak's battle is elsewhere than on Hazor. This, however, is because the battle took place elsewhere, farther south toward Megiddo.

50. The Hebrew word used is the very word "tell" which has come to be employed as the technical designation for such mounds. O. Tuffnell agrees that Israel did not cause the burned layer at Lachish; cf. "Lachish," in Thomas, op. cit., p. 302.

51. Cf. Albright, AASOR, 12 (1934): 53–8; Wright, *op. cit.*, pp. 87–8; D. N. Freedman, BA, 26 (Dec., 1963): 134–9 for significant discussions.

52. The dates of Rameses III are uncertain. William F. Albright, *From the Stone Age to Christianity*, 2nd ed. (Garden City: Doubleday Anchor Books, 1957), p. 289, prefers 1175 B.C. as his accession year.

53. Martin Noth, *The History of Israel*, 2d ed. (London: A. & C. Black, 1958; New York: Harper, 1960), p. 82, favors this explanation, saying, "These destructions were more probably due . . . to the warlike emergence of the 'Sea Peoples.' "

54. The first of these were found by an Egyptian peasant woman in 1887 at Tell el-Amarna, Akhenaton's capital. Total collection now numbers 378, of which about 300 were written by Canaanite scribes in Palestine, Phoenicia, and southern Syria. Cf. Samuel, A. B. Mercer's two-volume work, *The Tell el-Amarna Tablets* (Toronto, 1939) for full treatment; ANET, pp. 483–90 for translation by Albright and Mendenhall of 28 representative letters; or F. F. Bruce, "Tell el-Amarna," in Thomas, *op. cit.*, pp. 3–20, for recent brief discussion.

55. Also called 'Apiru, especially in Canaan, the frequently occurring idiogram, SA. GAZ being used interchangeably.

56. For discussion of name equivalency and other matters, as well as listing of significant works, cf. M. Greenberg, *The Hab/piru* (New Haven: American Oriental Society, 1955). Cf. also Rowley, *From Joseph to Joshua, op. cit.*, pp. 46–56 for good discussion and references.

57. Some scholars even argue for evidence in the letters against the early date: cf. Wright, *op. cit.*, p. 75, and Finegan, *op. cit.*, p. 118. These arguments, however, can be adequately answered on the basis of either of the two viewpoints set forth in the text following, especially the second.

58. For instance, Merrill F. Unger, *Archaeology and the Old Testament* (Grand Rapids: Zondervan, 1954), pp. 124–5, 145–6; also Archer, *op. cit.*, pp. 164, 214, 253–9.

59. The term was not always used derogatorily, however; at Alalakh, for instance, Habiru held official positions in the city government and were among the chariot owning *maryannu* (highest warrior caste). Abraham was already called a Hebrew (Gen. 14:13) and certainly not derogatorily. Abraham may have been given this term because he too was a foreigner when he entered Canaan years earlier, and the term then came to be retained and transmuted in time into an ethnic designation. The name

continued after the conquest too (I Sam. 4:6, 9; 13:3, 7; 29:3, etc.; though never used frequently) and not with the derogatory connotation. Yet the Canaanites could have so used it in the process of being divested of their land.

60. Kline, "The Ha-Bi-Ru—Kin or Foe of Israel?—III," WTJ, 20 (Nov., 1957): 54–61.

61. If the conquest began in 1406 B.C. (40 years after 1446), it likely was completed in its initial stages before 1400 B.C., the date of the first of the Amarna letters. The letters indicate that the main Habiru threat came about two decades later.

62. The first oppression lasted 8 years and is best dated ca. 1375–67 B.C., exactly during the years of Akhenaton (1384–1367) when the Habiru seem to have been the most active.

63. Cf. William C. Hayes, *The Scepter of Egypt* (Cambridge: Harvard University Press, 1959), II:327. This agreement continued to place all Palestine under Egyptian control. The main intention of both Seti I and Rameses II was to restore the northern borders of empire days, but in this they did not succeed.

64. Copies of this treaty have been found both in cuneiform and hieroglyphic writing, respectively at Boghazkoi and Karnak. Cordial relations followed this treaty, with Rameses II even marrying the eldest daughter of Hattusilis in Rameses' 34th year of reign. Cf. Hayes, *op. cit.*, II:344–5; and ANET, pp. 201–3, for copy of the treaty.

65. Cf. ANET, p. 255 for text of each. Cf. G. M. Fitzgerald, "Beth-Shean," in Thomas, *op. cit.*, pp. 185–96, for recent brief treatment of discoveries at Bethshan.

66. Cf. ANET, pp. 376–8 for text. "Hurru" is Syria, here no doubt including Palestine.

67. Cf. ANET, p. 262 for text. "Tjeker" (*tkr*) is the name of one of the Sea Peoples who in part, along with the Philistines (*prst*) took up residence in Palestine. The Egyptian Wen-Amon (1100 B.C.) speaks of the (*tkr*) occupying the coastal town of Dor, just south of Mt. Carmel; cf. ANET, p. 262, n. 21.

68. Cf. Wright, *Biblical Archaeology, op. cit.*, p. 95; and ANET, p. 262, n. 21.

69. Mesopotamians (Jud. 3:8), Moabites (Jud. 3:12), Canaanites (Jud. 4:2), Midianites (Jud. 6:1), Ammonites (Jud. 10:7), and Philistines (Jud. 10:7).

70. Nelson Glueck states that occupation of Transjordan did not start again until "the beginning of Iron Age I"; BA, 18 (Feb., 1955): 9. Now Iron I is normally dated as beginning 1200 B.C., not 1300, but Glueck here uses 1300 B.C. for the renewal of occupation, no doubt to fit the exodus late date position, which must have Israel making her journey well before 1200 B.C. But one wonders if he is not forcing the archaeological evidence here a little.

71. Glueck, *ibid.*, pp. 8–9; BA, 10 (1947): 77–84; also *The Other Side of the Jordan* (New Haven: American School of Oriental Research, 1940), pp. 125–47.

72. Lancaster Harding, *The Antiquities of Jordan* (New York: Thomas Y. Crowell Co., 1959), p. 17. In defense of his position, Glueck has stated recently that these tombs could still be the work of "nomads and semi-nomads"; "Transjordan," Thomas, *op. cit.*, p. 444.

73. In 1883 the Swiss archaeologist Naville suggested that Tell el-Mashkuta (also in wadi Tumelat, 6 miles east of Tell er-Retabeh) was Pithom. He found the word, *Pi-Tum* meaning "House of the god" there inscribed. Most prefer Tell er-Retabeh today, however.

74. Most commonly identified with old Tanis (cf. Wright, *op. cit.*, p. 60), but some favor Qantir (cf. Hayes, *op. cit.*, II: 339 and John Van Seters, *The Hyksos* (New Haven: Yale University Press, 1966), pp. 128–49.)

75. Unger, *op. cit.*, p. 149.

76. John Rea, "The Time of the Oppression and the Exodus," BETS, 3 (Summer, 1960): 63.

77. Archer, *op. cit.*, pp. 207–8.

78. Cf. Albright, *From the Stone Age to Christianity*, p. 223.

79. For a discussion of Hyksos religion, cf. Van Seters, *op. cit.*, pp. 171–80. Van Seters believes that the Hyksos identified old Canaanite deities with Egyptian; e.g. Baal with Seth and El with Ra.

80. Cf. Hayes, *op. cit.*, II:118, and Rea, *op. cit.*, p. 65. One of these obelisks now stands in Central Park, New York City and the other on the Thames embankment in London.

81. Commonly considered the greatest of the Egyptian pharaohs. In 16 campaigns during 18 summers he pushed the Egyptian boundary even across the Euphrates and some distance beyond, thus fashioning the Egyptian Empire.

82. Rea, *op. cit.*, p. 65, who refers to Naville, *Bubastis* (London: Kegan Paul, Trench, Trubner & Co., 1891), p. 30.

83. Hayes, *op. cit.*, II:141.

—6—

THE TABERNACLE IN BIBLICAL-THEOLOGICAL PERSPECTIVE

Marten H. Woudstra

The topic of this chapter, "The Tabernacle," can be thought of as fitting under the general heading of "Theology." Yet it appears in the section of the book entitled "Pentateuch." Both classifications make perfect sense, neither is the one necessarily opposed to the other. Pentateuchal studies deal with far more than the nomenclature of certain supposed documents.[1] They touch on the fundamental understanding of the Old Testament revelation; and, in their own way, they show a strong concern for a certain kind of "theology."

In a recent book by R. E. Clements, entitled *God and Temple*,[2] the "theology" of the Priestly document receives very ample attention. Yet on the other hand Geerhardus Vos has correctly observed that one of the practical uses of the study of Biblical Theology is that it supplies us with a useful antidote against the teachings of rationalistic higher criticism.[3] This it does in the following way: The Bible exhibits an organism of its own; this organism, inborn in the Bible itself, the critical hypothesis destroys, and that not only upon a conservative view, but as freely acknowledged by negative critics on the ground of its being an artificial organism foisted upon the Bible, and for which a newly discovered better organism should be substituted. Vos urges his readers to make themselves thoroughly conversant with the Biblical consciousness of its own revelation structure. Thus doing, so he rightly observes, one should be able to perceive how radically criticism destroys this, and that, so far from being a mere question of dates and compositions of books, it involves a choice between two widely divergent, nay, antagonistic conceptions of the Scripture and of religion.

Vos's words still possess relevance today. For while Wellhausenism has been modified at various points,[4] its basic structure is as widely accepted by critical scholarship as it ever was. At no point is this more evident than in the treatment of the tabernacle materials. He who says tabernacle says cultus, and Wellhausen's reconstruction of Israel's religious history hinged on the cultus. This reconstruction still is generally accepted today, although various changes have had to be made in it. Nicolaas H. Ridderbos observed some years ago that the position of orthodoxy in Biblical scholarship is as isolated as it ever was, if not more so.[5] Surveying some of the pertinent materials dealing with the tabernacle the present writer has become convinced that this assessment of the present situation is not a bit too pessimistic.

I. Survey of Current Positions

A. The Position of Julius Wellhausen

According to Wellhausen the legislation concerning the tabernacle as found in Exodus 25 ff., was the product of the fancy of the post-exilic priestly writers; or, more precisely, it was the description of the temple in flimsy desert disguise.[6] While admitting, on the basis of Exodus 33:7–11, that there might have been some sort of primitive tent-shelter for the ark in the desert, Wellhausen regarded the description of the priestly tabernacle to be a pious fraud. Hartmann, a Wellhausen disciple, speaks of *"das monströse Gebilde des PC, die Stiftshütte."*[7] Martin Noth, writing at a much later time, describes the tabernacle as "an astonishing construction for which there is no analogy anywhere in cultic history."[8]

B. Modified Wellhausenism[9]

Under the impact of archaeology and philology Wellhausenism has been revised at many a point. Due to new discoveries in the Near East the horizon of Biblical history has been widened. The patriarchal narratives have received confirmation from outside sources.[10] Proponents of the theory that Israel's religious and political organization may rightfully be compared with an amphictyony structure have shown a greater readiness to look for the fundamental tenets of Israel's faith, including that of the covenant, at a relatively early time in Israel's religious history. Albright's early dating of passages such as Exodus 15 (the song of Moses), Deuteronomy 33 (the blessing of Moses), Judges 5 (the song of Deborah), and other portions (such as Gen. 49, Ps. 68, etc.), have prompted Old Testament scholars to conclude that the basic beliefs of prophetic religion are already found in the earlier, pre-prophetic strands. Wellhausen admittedly had considerable difficulty in explaining the historical roots of the prophetic movement. Today scholars are more ready to point to certain lofty conceptions, such as that of God as cosmic Judge and Lord of nature and history, as already present in the time preceding the prophets.

Along with this more positive evaluation of the pre-prophetic religion of Israel comes a more positive attitude toward the so-called priestly tradition as a reliable witness to the Mosaic Age. While scholars continue to maintain that the priestly account is schematized and idealized,[11] and while they also continue to maintain that the priestly writers read the theological interpretations and historical developments of later ages into their system, the modified Wellhausenists now point to such things as the lists and genealogies of P as containing information that cannot be passed over lightly.

Since so much of the tabernacle materials according to the adherents of the documentary hypothesis belongs to the priestly document, it will be understood that the tabernacle institution has shared in this positive reappraisal of pre-prophetic religion. In the following section of this paper a brief review will be presented of some of the opinions with respect to the tabernacle as currently held by modified Wellhausenism.

C. The Tabernacle in Current Old Testament Study

As a result of further investigation and of archaeological data, current Old Testament scholarship is now more disposed toward assuming the existence of a desert-shrine during the Mosaic period than was previously the case. Eichrodt, e.g., believes that there was such a tent-shrine but that it was not used merely as a covering for the ark.[12] While Wellhausen had stressed the inseparability of tent and ark and had declared both of them to be late, Eichrodt believes that the tent is a shrine in its own right. The constructive element which the priestly writers introduced into their description of the desert situation is not, according to Eichrodt, the tent-shrine as such but rather the unbreakable association between tent and ark.

One of the reasons why Old Testament scholarship today is more will-ing to speak of a desert-shrine going back to Moses' days is the archaeo-logical evidence concerning the existence of tent-shrines among the Arabs of Islamic and pre-Islamic times.[13] Roland de Vaux in the light of these archaeological data, decides in favor of the Mosaic origin of the taber-nacle, while at the same time considering much of the priestly tradition to be due to idealization.

The Arab tent-shrines to which frequent reference is made in current literature are called by the following names: utfah, mahmal, and qubbah. The utfah, also called merkab or abu dhur, is a little tent, a sort of palanquin, or litter, which the tribe, when moving camp, took with them. It takes the form of a camel saddle in modern times, is made of a wooden framework and decorated with ostrich feathers. It is considered to have supernatural power. Sacrifices are sometimes brought to it, because it is thought that the deity is residing in it. These sacrifices include the sprin-kling of blood.

The mahmal likewise looks like a tent. Like the utfah it was carried on camel back, and was regarded as having some kind of supernatural power. It was thought to be able to guide caravans through the desert by exercising its sway over the camel on whose back it was carried.

An institution even more ancient than those just described was that of the *qubbah.* It goes back to pre-Islamic times and is regarded as the ancestor of the *mahmal* and the *utfah.* It was a sacred tent made of red leather. Some *qubbahs* were suitable for mounting on camel back; others were larger. These *qubbahs* generally contained the tribal idols. In camp the *qubbah* was set beside the sheikh's tent, and men came there to seek oracles.

A special point has been drawn from the fact that the *qubbah* was made of red leather. This differs from ordinary tents, which are usually made of a black substance. The redness of the *qubbah,* which would expose to danger both it and the camp in which it was housed, is believed to argue for a strong conservative religious tradition underlying this tent-shrine. At the same time, it is pointed out that the Biblical tabernacle had a covering of ram's skin, dyed red. Thus it is argued that the *qubbah* institution sheds light on the origin of the tabernacle. The portable red leather tent, so it is held, is one of the oldest motifs in Semitic religion. Both tabernacle and ark are believed to have historical connections with their Semitic past. But scholars have been careful to point out that one may not push the parallels so hard as to obliterate the uniqueness of Israel's desert institutions, as has been done, e.g., by Julian Morgenstern.

As to the existence of two more or less independent shrines, one the tent-shrine and the other the ark-sanctuary, de Vaux is of a different opinion than Eichrodt. De Vaux thinks that we may not have all the traditions concerning the original connection between these two preserved for us. As to the much discussed passage, Exodus 33:17, de Vaux believes that the expression *lô* ("for him," or "for it") may contain a cryptic reference to the ark of the covenant. But even if this could not be proven, de Vaux nevertheless believes that if there was a tent-shrine in the desert this shrine must have been used to cover something, just as the *qubbah* was used to cover divine symbols.[14]

The review presented thus far indicates that current Old Testament scholarship is willing to hold to the existence of a tent-shrine in the wilderness period but that opinions differ as to the original connection between the ark and the tent. A middle position with respect to this latter question is taken by R. E. Clements. Clements observes that the whole question of the original relationship between the ark and the tent is "a very vexed one, in which absolute conclusions are not possible." Admitting that the ark and the tent were united during the time of the sanctuary at Shiloh, Clements leaves undecided the question of whether they were united before that time. Having come to that point, he then observes that both tent and ark witnessed to a similar view of the divine presence and that together they formed the foremost sanctuary of Yahweh.[15]

II. The Tabernacle in Biblical-Theological Perspective

A. Old Testament Cultus in General

The background to this discussion concerns the role which the cultus was intended to play in the development of God's self-revelation. The tabernacle and ark were the foremost expressions of the cultus of the theocratic community. They embodied, no matter how one may wish to read the "documents" which testify to the existence of this sanctuary, everything that Yahweh had revealed to Israel concerning the way in which He was to be worshiped.

Traditionally, evangelical Protestantism has made an ample use of the symbolism and the typology which the various cultic institutions of the Old Testament convey. We should be the last to repudiate such use, although, as is the case with all typology, a word of caution concerning the way this is done is definitely in order.[16] But the question must nevertheless be asked whether, along with the typology of the tabernacle, enough attention has been paid to the role which the cultus as such was meant to play within the unfolding of God's self-revelation to man.[17] It is more than obvious that religious life in Israel expressed itself in cultus. Cultic thinking, cultic acts, and cultic expressions permeated its entire life. The bulk of the Mosaic legislation concerns itself with the cultus. Arvid S. Kapelrud states with some justification: "If we cut out the cult, we cut out the covenant, and in cutting out the covenant we also take the ground away from under Israelite morality."[18]

B. Current Definitions of Cultus

A number of definitions of "cultus" are currently held, since the subject of cultus is not always as clear as it might be. Scholars such as G. E. Wright[19] and H. J. Kraus[20] have therefore called attention to the confusion which at times seems to prevail when this matter is discussed.

According to Paul Tillich "all religious acting is cultic acting,"[21] and offerings are thus "the central, cultic symbol." Kapelrud, while admitting that this definition appears to be very wide, observes that a wide definition is preferable, if our picture of Israel's religion is to be a right one. Vriezen defines cultus as "that complex of external forms and actions, through which the intercourse between God and man takes place."[22] In this definition the emphasis has been placed on the externality of certain actions and forms. This is done in contrast to those who would wish to use the word cultus also for the inner attitudes of religion.

S. Mowinckel declares, "Cult or worship may be generally defined as the socially established and regulated holy acts and words, through which the encounter and communion of God with the congregation is established."[23] Kapelrud describes cult in the following manner: "Cult is religious life in certain regulated forms, expressing the relationship between God and man and intended for use in a society."[24]

According to Walther Eichrodt cultus "is the expression of religion in concrete external actions performed within the congregation or community, preferably by officially appointed exponents and in set forms."[25] In contrast to the more immediate human experience in which it is rooted, cultus must be considered secondary, says Eichrodt. Furthermore, there is in cultus an element of "limitation and restraint." Under this limitation and restraint the personal and spontaneous feelings of piety are bound to suffer. The limitations of which Eichrodt speaks are twofold: (1) material, because of the stress which the cultus puts on sacred places, seasons, and rites; (2) sociological, because in the cultus the determining factor is the community as a whole.

Nevertheless, Eichrodt correctly points out that cultus is not opposed to a truly religious concern. Cultus is not fundamentally different from a spiritual intercourse with God. It is not on an inferior plane. Rather, it is the genuine expression of living religion, seeking to penetrate the whole of human life. This it does by making not only the spiritual and the personal but also the physical side of life into an agent and medium of its activities. Thus viewed cultus is indispensable to genuine religion.

One of the major deficiencies in the current definitions lies in the fact that cultus is defined in almost exclusively phenomenological terms. The element of revelation does not significantly enter into the definition. Mowinckel's discussion of this point might seem to be an exception to what has just been said:

> It may often look as though the initiative lies with the congregation, on the human side. But seen from the point of view of cult and religion it is rather the other way around; the initiative lies with God. True enough, it is man that "searches for God," "seeks God," but he can, and does so, because the deity has first "revealed himself" and taught man where and when and how to seek him.[26]

Here, it would seem, one finds a helpful emphasis on revelation as lying behind cultus. But it should not be overlooked that Mowinckel's assertion that revelation precedes cultus is itself a purely comparative statement. For Mowinckel makes it quite clear that not *only* Israel has a God who has "revealed" Himself as to where He may be found, but that this idea is "a fundamental idea in all religion." In other words, we are not face to face with revelation. All that we do confront is the claim to having received revelation, and this claim is fundamental to all religions. Hence we are not yet beyond the phenomenological and the comparative. In this respect the term "cultus" has undergone a radical transformation when it is compared with earlier usages in medieval and early Reformation theology.[27]

C. The Role of the Cultus in Biblical Religion

As has been pointed out by Vriezen[28] and others, within the sphere of Old Testament revelation the cultus never was intended to play as predominant a role as was the case in other religions of the ancient Near East. Thorkild Jacobsen observes that according to the Babylonian creation legend the very purpose of man's creation is that through man the cultus of the gods may be maintained. This latter attitude is also reflected in the organization of the early city-states of the Sumerians. Jacobsen thus describes this city-state complex:

> By upholding a great god, by providing the economic basis, which permits the god to enjoy full and free self-expression, the city-state is upholding some great power of the universe and assuring its freedom to function as it should. And this is the function of the human city-state within the cosmos. In this manner it contributes to maintaining and perpetuating the ordered cosmos and its powers.[29]

Thus viewed, cultus is the service to and for the gods, in order that the world of which one is a part, and the state which is connected with a particular set of gods, may continue to exist. Cultus ensures the existence of the gods of the cosmos as well as of the state. It becomes the all-dominating means for the preservation of God, man, and the world. It is totalitarian in character.

In contrast to the picture just presented, the Biblical account of creation is silent on the subject of the cultus.[30] Man's chief task is not to "maintain" the gods. This task is largely cultural in nature. Ludwig Koehler correctly states that according to the Old Testament account of creation the purpose for all of human life is its shalom (Heb. šālôm).[31] Koehler mentions in this connection Genesis 1:28 and refers in the same context to Numbers 6:26 (see D below). The shalom which the Creator has in store for man consists of man's comprehensive well-being. Pedersen defines it as "all the harmony and happiness which anyone can take."[32] Shalom signifies anything but a retreat from life; it does not suggest some quiet corner away from the places where the world makes its demands upon man. Shalom is closely allied to covenant. The two are each other's supplements. He who says shalom says covenant and he who says covenant says shalom. This, then, is God's destiny for man.[33]

It has been argued by Herman Bavinck that the creation account is not entirely culture-centered but that in the institution of the Sabbath (Gen. 2:3) there is some indication that life before the fall "demanded a form and a service and a day of its own next to the life of culture."[34]

The scope of the present investigation does not permit a review of everything that has been said and written about the question of the institution of the sabbath. What should be noted is that outside of the

Genesis account of creation, the book of Genesis contains no further reference to the sabbath anywhere. Even in Genesis 2:3 the noun "sabbath" is not used, though the verb šābat does occur. All that the verse says is that God set apart this day for a special purpose by sanctifying it. Nahum Sarna, correctly so we believe, calls the sabbath "part of the divinely ordained cosmic order."[35] It is quite clear, of course, that the fourth commandment connects the sabbath with the fact that God rested from His creative work on the seventh day. Attention may also be called to the fact that the fourth commandment uses the word "remember" (zākar) for what must be done concerning the day. In this connection one may also recall that according to Exodus 16:23–29 the sabbath was already something that the people of Israel should observe. The present writer considers the suggestion unsuitable that in this passage one finds the actual promulgation of the command to keep the sabbath day holy.[36] Not the institution of the sabbath day, but its proper observance, is the purpose of the legislator at this point.

Of great value for a proper understanding of the sabbath is what Geerhardus Vos writes in his comments on the fourth commandment. Vos points out the positive import which this day was meant to have. The "rest" of the sabbath, according to Vos, resembles the word "peace" in this respect that it has a positive rather than a negative import. It stands for consummation of a work accomplished and the joy and satisfaction attendant upon this.[37]

Whatever one may say about the role which the sabbath may or may not have had in paradise as a cultic element next to the life of culture, it is clear from Genesis 4:26 that the cultus began to play a more prominent role in the days of Enosh. "Calling upon the name of the Lord" is an expression denoting the public proclamation of that Name in worship.[38] This preoccupation with the worship of God on the part of the people of Enosh's day stands in apparent contrast to what we read concerning the cultural inventions made by the descendants of Cain. It almost seems as if the latter, not the former, were seeking to capture something of the shalom-ideal which God had ordained for man when he blessed him in paradise. But this attempt ends with Lamech's titanic song of defiance.

There is not enough information in the early chapters of Genesis to state with certainty the manner in which the cultus, as practiced by those of Seth's line, was intended to further the shalom of God. A look at the patriarchal narratives does not directly provide an answer either. To be sure, the cultus is widely attested to in the patriarchal narratives; in fact, the patriarchs took no definite steps in their lives without cultic acts. Sanctuaries were erected, principally in places where God had shown himself in a theophany. Kapelrud goes so far as to argue that the patriarchs, if they would survive and not be submerged by the Canaanite religion, would have had to master the power of the cult. The decisive fact, so Kapelrud contends, was that the cult had to be performed because it was necessary for a continued life in the new country.[39]

Though the connection between the cultic acts which the patriarchs performed and the shalom of Yahweh which had been promised mankind in paradise may not have been explicit, there are some instances where the blessing of Yahweh attaches itself meaningfully to the sacrificial act of a given patriarch (Gen. 22:17; 26:24). This blessing, as has been pointed out, may be summed up in terms of shalom.[40]

D. Tabernacle and Shalom

The following passages will here be treated. (1) Numbers 6:26; this passage contains the formula of blessing which Aaron and his sons were to put upon the waiting congregation of Israel, which in turn constituted the epitome of the tabernacle service. (2) Jeremiah 3:16, 17, which deals with the ark of the covenant, the tabernacle's most sacred piece of cult-furniture. (3) Ezekiel 37:26–28, in which some of the most commonly used designations for the tabernacle, those of *miškān* and *miqdāš* will be examined. (4) Isaiah 4:5, 6, a passage that deals with another of the significant features pertaining to the tabernacle, namely the appearance of the theophanic cloud. (5) Zechariah 14:20, at which point the distinction of the "clean and unclean" will be examined.

1. *Shalom and the high-priestly blessing.* Earlier reference was made to the fact that according to L. Koehler both Genesis 1:28 and Numbers 6:26 speak of essentially the same thing. Koehler's suggestion of a direct connection between paradise and tabernacle is further enhanced by E. Jacob's observation to the effect that the very structure of the tabernacle, with its motifs of palm trees and cherubim, may have been calculated to evoke memories of the shalom of paradise.[41]

The significance of the high-priestly blessing in respect to the total tabernacle service can hardly be overestimated. Mowinckel correctly observes that "the entire content of the cultic celebration was finally summed up in the solemn intoning of the blessing of the priest from the altar." This "blessing" which the priest was to put on the people occurs in close parallelism with "salvation."[42] (Cf. Ps. 3:9: "Salvation belongeth to Yahweh. Thy blessing be upon thy people.") To "bless" the people was tantamount to putting the Lord's "Name" on the people. This "Name" had been "called upon" in the cultic celebration. The Lord now promised that He would bless His people when the priests put His Name on them; and the final word of that blessing would be the word "shalom."

The inference seems warranted that the tabernacle with its cumbersome holiness, its inaccessible mysteries, and its priestly ministrations was nevertheless Yahweh's intended instrument for effecting the theocratic shalom. It was at the tabernacle that this shalom was dispensed, so that it might work itself out in the life of every worshiper.

2. *The ark becomes superfluous.* The ark was the most important piece of cult-furniture which tabernacle and temple possessed. Yet Jeremiah 3:16–17 deals with the future loss of function of the ark in the situation of the end time. The setting of this prophecy is one of a promised return to Jerusalem by the exiled people of God. Not only Judah but also Israel is portrayed as journeying to the sacred city. The blessings concomitant with this joyful return are reminiscent of the shalom of paradise. The people will multiply and increase in the land. At that distinctive juncture, still in the distant future, the ark will no longer be the central element of the cultic worship of God. It will have lost its *raison d'être.* It will not be remembered, neither will it be missed.

Many interpreters have understood this future eclipse of the ark in negative terms only. Some hold that Jeremiah, being a prophet, is here introducing to us a more "spiritual" type of worship, in which material objects will have less of a role to play. This point of view may imply that the more external notions of holiness, which attach themselves to the ark in passages such as I Samuel 6:20 and II Samuel 6:10, are less than spiritual.[43] Hentschke speaks in this connection of a *"gegenstaendliche Bindung Jahwes"* (a material binding of Yahweh).[44] Jeremiah's polemic, according to Hentschke, is aimed at this kind of material binding of Yahweh. But Hentschke fails to point out that there is a kind of "binding" which is explicitly willed by Yahweh and meets with His approval. Other expositors have observed that Jeremiah wishes to emphasize the dispensability of the most sacred cult-symbol of ancient Israel.[45] But as Buber has correctly pointed out,[46] this lesson had already been taught quite effectively at the time of the ark's capture by the Philistines and its subsequent storage in the house of Abinadab.

The real import of this Jeremiah passage can best be grasped if it is observed that immediately following the prediction of the ark's loss of function we read of Jerusalem becoming the throne of Yahweh. Stating things in terms of what we have discovered so far concerning the role of the cultus in the furtherance of Yahweh's shalom, we may say that the ark's loss of function, far from being purely negative in its import, has a strongly positive side. In due time the cultic establishment, of which the ark is the center and the epitome, will impart its sanctity to the city of Zion.[47] This is already the case in the earlier writing prophets. But this will be even more so in the eschatological future which Jeremiah is here depicting. All the city will have become throne, and hence there will be no further need for a separate throne. The cultic symbol is in no way depreciated. On the contrary, its positive, world-affirming function is properly grasped.

3. *The tabernacle "over" the people.* Two of the names most frequently used to designate the tabernacle are *miqdāš* and *miškān*. In Exodus 25:8–9 they are used side by side: "And let them make me a sanctuary (*miqdāš*), that I may dwell among them. According to all that I show thee, the pattern of the tabernacle (*miškān*), and the pattern of all the furniture thereof, even so shall ye make it" (ASV).

Significantly enough, these two names of the tabernacle also occur side by side in Ezekiel 37:26–28. This passage deals with the covenant which Yahweh will yet make with Israel. This covenant will be a covenant of shalom: it will consist of shalom, shalom will be the substance of it. We note, moreover, that the prophecy again hints at a return of the blessings of paradise: God will bless and multiply the people of Israel.

It is in this connection that the words *miškān* and *miqdāš* occur. Their simultaneous use should not, however, becloud the important distinction which the prophet is making between them at this point. The *miqdāš*, so he informs us, will be in the midst of Israel, but the *miškān* will be "over" (prep. *'al*) them. This particular clause has been correctly paraphrased as follows: "God's presence extends itself protectingly over his people." The RSV translates the word *miškān* as "dwelling place." This is a proper rendering of the word, but what should be kept in mind is that the word *miškān* is also the *terminus technicus* for what has come to be known as the tabernacle.

This Ezekiel passage makes it once again clear that in the great future the tabernacle of God will extend itself over the dwelling place of man. The two will become coextensive. The purpose of the cultus, prior to that point in time, is therefore to bring this great reality into being. Far from being a "withering away" of the cultic institution, as is often suggested in current anti-"establishment" discussions,[48] the opposite actually is the case. The cultic establishment makes itself superfluous as a separate institution by extending itself over the whole city area. The prospect to which the eschatology of this passage points is not a city without a church, but a city which will be all church. At the same time this will be a realization of the *berit šalôm*, which is the situation God intended for man in paradise.

4. *The theophanic cloud and redeemed Zion.* An important feature of the tabernacle was the periodic appearance of the theophanic cloud (Ex. 16:7, 10; 24:16; 29:43; 40:34 ff.; Lev. 9:6, 23; Num. 14:10; 16:19). Yahweh comes down from heaven in a cloud which contains His "glory." This glory in the cloud is the vehicle and mode of the divine presence within Israel. According to Isaiah 4:5–6 this same manifestation of God's indwelling, but this time city-wide, will be experienced by redeemed Zion. It will be at the time when the branch of the Lord shall be beautiful and glorious, and when those left in mount Zion shall be called holy. Though the translations of this passage vary somewhat, for which the

reader is advised to consult one or more commentaries, the basic idea expressed at this point is not affected. The cloud and the fire, two manifestations of Yahweh's presence in the tabernacle, will characterize the whole habitation of mount Zion. Some commentators make too exclusive a reference at this point to the phenomena accompanying the exodus.[49] Though such a reference need not be denied altogether, it would seem more natural to think of a passage such as Numbers 9:15, 16, which speaks of the cloud and the fire as covering the tabernacle, as being the primary point of reference.

Here again, the emphasis is similar to what was noted earlier. At the time of Zion's future happiness and bliss the separateness of the sanctuary will have ceased to exist, simply because the city in its entirety will have become "sanctuary." The separateness of the cultus, although assiduously practiced throughout the old dispensation (and rightly so), will cease to be, simply because God always intended the cultus to extend its categories on to the life of the ordinary citizen. Again we note that the emphasis is not on the withering away of the cultic establishment but on its fulfillment, on its accomplishment in becoming the city-wide refuge that it was intended to be.

5. *Holiness everywhere.* One of the best-known passages illustrating the principle being investigated in this essay is Zechariah 14:20. The passage concerns still another aspect of the tabernacle and its service: it refers to the inscription which the high priest was to carry on his headband, *Holy unto the Lord.* It also refers to the utensils used for sacrifice. In "that day" of which the prophet is speaking, the inscription which otherwise occurs only on the headband of the high priest will appear on the bells of the horses. Horses in Israel never enjoyed full approval.[50] Yet the time will come when their bells will be as holy as the high priest's headband. Likewise the distinction between the clean and the unclean, that cumbersome concomitant of the tabernacle service which barred from or admitted to the service within the sacred precincts, will have ceased to operate. Every pot in Jerusalem and in Judah will be holy unto Yahweh of hosts, and everyone who sacrifices can take one of them to boil in.

6. *Summary.* The cultus is not intended to be practiced by itself, it is meant to do its work so effectively that it will make itself superfluous by becoming coextensive with the life of the restored people of God. Though much in the Mosaic economy is transient because it is ceremonial, and though other parts of it point forward typically to the New Testament realities they foreshadow, there is something in the cultus that is of permanent validity, something that becomes a constant element in the stream of God's self-revelation. That element has to do with that which constitutes the cultic establishment as such. This cultic establishment, this sacred place, is meant to be the concentration point and

the starting point of the shalom which God had intended for man from the beginning. The cultus is the means whereby this shalom will extend itself over all of the life of God's people.

E. The New Testament Evidence

The question may be raised whether this consistent Old Testament teaching is perhaps so characteristically Old Testament that one may not and cannot use it during the New Testament dispensation. The answer to this question, within the scope of the present essay, must be brief.

By the time of Christ's death the tabernacle and the temple as such had served their God-appointed purpose. The temple continued to function for a while, but then it ceased to play a role in the Christian faith. Ceremonial and typical features no longer function the way they did under the old dispensation. Only the Roman Catholic church, as Vos and Patrick Fairbairn have pointed out, perpetuates in its forms of worship something of the Old Testament ceremonies without perceiving that these have been lifted to their plane of fulfillment.[51]

Nevertheless, the cultus does continue to play a part in Christianity. No Protestant sect, however informal and low church it may be, is completely without it. Christ himself, who is our peace (*šālôm, eirēnē*, Eph. 2:14) and on whom the chastisement of our peace has fallen (Isa. 53:5; RSV translates it "the chastisement that made us whole"), does not brush aside the cultus, not even in His answer to the Samaritan woman (John 4:24). The woman's question as well as the Lord's answer must be seen in the light of the Biblical-theological perspective in which they occur. Jesus' remark that "salvation is from the Jews" is indicative of His awareness of the progress of God's self-revelation. It is within that context that the woman's question must be evaluated. Note should also be taken of the phrase, "the hour cometh and now is," which again indicates an awareness of the movement of redemptive history. Neither does the substance of Christ's answer take issue with the continuation of the cultic worship of God, but only with a cultic worship that fails to see the movement of God through redemptive history.

The continued importance of the cultus for the new dispensation may also be indicated, though in a negative way, by the manner in which the anti-Christ is described, as one who exalts himself against all that is called God or that is worshiped so that he sits in the temple of God (I Thess. 2:4). It appears that the anti-Christian spirit will want to make use of the powerful motif of the cultus in order thereby to influence culture in an apostate manner and to bring about a counterfeit shalom.

The tabernacle's highest realization is depicted in Revelation 21:3, which describes the eschatological stage of the history of redemption. In dependence on Isaiah 4:5 and 6, the area of the temple is widened so as to become coextensive with the entire city of Jerusalem. The very form of the sacred city, with its length and breadth and height equal (Rev. 21:16), suggests that the new Jerusalem will have become one giant holy of holies. At the same time the city also symbolizes the shalom of paradise, with its river, and with the tree of life. Again the tent of God is referred to as being with man (Rev. 21:3), while in 7:15 we read that He who sits on the throne will spread His tent over them. This, then, is the establishment brought to its ultimate realization.

F. Epilogue

The practical implications of this Biblical-theological perspective, in which the tabernacle and cultus must be viewed, are significant. The church, which is the divinely willed New Testament expression of cultus, may be confident that in God's good time and through the faithful application to its God-prescribed task it will serve the full-orbed shalom with which the cultus has been concerned "from the beginning." Instead of the withering away of the church we may look forward to the expansion of the church to include all of life and all of human endeavor; not, to be sure, in the sense of the apostate cultures of the Sumerian city-states, but in the sense of the city foursquare, whose twelve gates are permanently open, a perfect symbol of God's realized and undisturbed shalom.

Notes

1. Cf. Christopher R. North, "Pentateuchal Criticism," in *The Old Testament and Modern Study,* ed. Harold H. Rowley (Oxford: Clarendon Press, 1951; New York: Oxford University Press, 1952), p. 74.

2. Ronald E. Clements, *God and Temple* (Oxford: Basil Blackwell, 1965).

3. Cf. Geerhardus Vos, *Biblical Theology* (Grand Rapids: Eerdmans, 1948), p. 26.

4. For a useful survey of the various causes for this modification see Frank Moore Cross, Jr., "The Priestly Tabernacle," in *The Biblical Archaeologist Reader,* ed. G. Ernest Wright and David Noel Freedman (Garden City, New York: Doubleday Anchor, 1961), pp. 201–12.

5. Cf. Nicolaas H. Ridderbos, "Reversals of Old Testament Criticism," in *Revelation and the Bible,* ed. Carl F. H. Henry (Grand Rapids: Baker Book House), p. 349.

6. Julius Wellhausen, *Prolegomena zur Geschichte Israels* (Berlin: 1883), p. 41. [Engl. translation: *Prolegomena to the History of Ancient Israel* (Magnolia, Mass.: Peter Smith), p. 39.]

7. R. Hartmann, "Zelt und Lade," ZAW, 37 (1917–18): 225.

8. Martin Noth, *Exodus,* (Philadelphia: The Westminster Press, 1962), p. 211.

9. For the following survey cf. Cross, *op. cit.*

10. Not all Old Testament scholars agree concerning this point. For a discussion of the questions involved cf. Roland de Vaux, "Method in the Study of Early Hebrew History," *The Bible in Modern Scholarship,* ed. J. Philip Hyatt (Nashville: Abingdon Press, 1965), p. 26. For a rather skeptical approach toward the question of the "historicity" of the patriarchs cf. Martin Noth, *Geschichte Israels* (Göttingen: Vanden Hoeck & Ruprecht, 1954), pp. 114–20.

11. Cf. Roland de Vaux, *Ancient Israel* (New York: McGraw-Hill Book Company, 1961) , p. 296: "It is only too obvious that much of this description is merely an idealization."

12. Walther Eichrodt, *Theology of the Old Testament*, by J. A. Baker, (Philadelphia: The Westminster Press, 1961) , I:109.

13. For an extreme utilization of this Arab material in understanding the ark and the tent, cf. Julian Morgenstern, "The Ark, the Ephod and the Tent of Meeting," HUCA, XVII:153–264; XVIII:1–52.

14. De Vaux, "Method," *loc. cit.*

15. *Ibid.*, p. 38.

16. Cf. D. W. Gooding's balanced approach to this matter, "Tabernacle," *The New Bible Dictionary*, ed. J. D. Douglas (Grand Rapids: Eerdmans, 1962) .

17. Cf. Harold H. Rowley's considerations concerning the interest shown by non-liturgical churches in the cultus: *Worship in Ancient Israel* (Philadelphia: Fortress Press, 1967) , p. 2, n. 3: "I can say that the church to which I belong is one of the least liturgical . . . churches. Yet for many years I have shared this interest in the Israelite cultus. . . ."

18. Cf. Arvid S. Kapelrud, "The Role of the Cult in Old Israel," *The Bible in Modern Scholarship, op. cit.,* p. 45.

19. Cf. G. Ernest Wright, "The Nations in Hebrew Prophecy," *Encounter,* 26 (1965) : 229.

20. H. J. Kraus, *Gottesdienst in Israel* (Munich: Chr. Kaiser Verlag, 1962) , p. 31.

21. Quoted by Kapelrud, *loc. cit.*

22. Theodorus C. Vriezen, *An Outline of Old Testament Theology*, trans. from the 2nd Dutch ed. (Newton, Mass.: Chas. T. Branford Company, 1958) , p. 282.

23. Cf. Sigmund Mowinckel, *The Psalms in Israel's Worship*, trans. D. R. Ap-Thomas (Nashville: Abingdon Press, 1962) , p. 15.

24. Kapelrud, *loc. cit.*

25. Cf. Eichrodt, *op. cit.,* p. 98.

26. Cf. Mowinckel, *op. cit.,* pp. 16 f.

27. For a discussion of medieval and Reformation use of the relation between religion and cultus cf. Herman Bavinck, *Gereformeerde Dogmatiek* (Kampen: Bos, 1906) , I:241 ff. Thomas defined religion as the *virtus per quam homines Deo debitum cultum et reverentiam exhibent.* The Reformers distinguished between *pietas* as the principle, and *cultus* as the *actio* of religion. They also distinguished between *cultus internus* and *externus.*

28. Vriezen, *op. cit.,* pp. 279 ff.

29. Henri Frankfort, *et al.,* eds., *Before Philosophy* (Harmondsworth: Penguin Books, 1946) , p. 207. Also published as *The Intellectual Adventure of Ancient Man,* (Chicago: U. of Chicago Press, 1946) .

30. On the limited role of the cultus in Biblical religion compared with non-Biblical religion cf. also K. J. Popma, *Inleiding in de Wijsbegeerte* (Kampen: J. H. Kok, 1956) , p. 40.

31. Cf. Ludwig Koehler, *Old Testament Theology*, trans. A. S. Todd (Philadelphia: The Westminster Press, 1957) , p. 203.

32. Cf. Johannes Pedersen, *Israel: Its Life and Culture* (London and New York: Oxford University Press, 1926) , I, II, p. 311; cf. also G. Ernest Wright, *The Challenge of Israel's Faith* (Chicago: U. of Chicago Press, 1944) , p. 77.

33. For further discussion on the Hebrew word šālôm and its New Testament counterpart cf. also *"Eirēnē,"* TWNT, II:398 ff.

34. Cf. Bavinck, *op. cit.,* II:618.

35. Nahum M. Sarna, *Understanding Genesis* (New York: McGraw-Hill, 1966) , p. 21. For a further discussion of the origin of the Sabbath cf. also A. R. Hulst, "Bemer-

kungen zum Sabbatgebot," in *Studia Biblica et Semitica* (Wageningen: H. Veenman, 1966), pp. 152–65.

36. The position here criticized may be found in Merrill F. Unger, *Unger's Bible Dictionary* (Chicago: Moody Press, c. 1961), p. 940.

37. Cf. Vos, *op. cit.*, p. 156.

38. According to BDB, p. 895, this phrase means to use the name in invocation.

39. Kapelrud, *op. cit.*, pp. 47 ff.

40. Cf. *"Eulogeō,"* TWNT; cf. also J. L. Koole, *Het laatste woord* (Kampen: J. H. Kok, 1967), pp. 4–9.

41. "It was at the temple and the temple alone that it was possible to see the face of God and to realize that fullness of strength and joy expressed by the word *shalom"*; Ed. Jacob, *Theology of the Old Testament,* trans. A. W. Heathcote and P. J. Allcock (New York: Harper, 1958), p. 259.

42. The centrality of the notion of "blessing" may also be seen in Acts 3:26, where all of Jesus' redemptive work is summed up in that one word "bless."

43. So e.g. R. H. Kennett, "Ark," in *Encyclopedia of Religion and Ethics* (New York: Scribner's, 1913).

44. Cf. R. Hentschke, *Die Stellung der vor-exilischen Schriftpropheten zum Kultus,* Beihefte zur ZAW, (Berlin: Alfred Topelman, 1957), p. 71.

45. So e.g. G. Ch. Aalders, "Jeremia en de Ark," *Gereformeerd Theologisch Tijdschrift* (1921–22): 275.

46. Martin Buber, *Der Glaube der Propheten* (Zurich: Manesse Verlag, 1950), p. 92.

47. For the transfer of the ark's holiness to the city, cf. also Martin Noth, "Jerusalem und die Israelitische Tradition," in *Gesammelte Studien zum Alten Testament* (Munich: 1957), p. 185. For a fuller discussion of Jeremiah 3:16, cf. also Marten H. Woudstra, *The Ark of the Covenant From Conquest to Kingship* (Philadelphia: Presbyterian and Reformed Publishing House, 1965), pp. 33–7.

48. Cf. Colin W. Williams, *What in the World* (New York: National Council of the Churches of Christ in the U.S.A., 1964), p. 40.

49. This is done by George Buchanan Gray, *Isaiah I–XXVII* (ICC), *ad loc.* and by Emil G. Kraeling, *Commentary on the Prophets,* Vol. I, (Camden, N.J.: Thomas Nelson and Sons, 1966), *ad loc.*

50. Cf. Deut. 17:16; and compare I Kgs. 1:5 with 1:33.

51. Cf. Patrick Fairbairn, *The Interpretation of Prophecy* (London: The Banner of Truth Trust, 1964; first publ. 1856), p. 236, where Fairbairn speaks of the "Christianized Judaism of popery," and Vos, *op. cit.*, p. 164.

III. POETRY

—7—

UGARITIC AND THE THEOLOGY OF THE PSALMS

Elmer B. Smick

The publication of Psalms I and II in the Anchor Bible has inflamed a smoldering fire of diverse opinion among modern Hebraists. The argument centers around the question, How shall the newer materials such as Ugaritic be used in Biblical studies? The traditional school opposes the northwest Semitic school with shades of opinion between. Extremists in the former school hold tenaciously to the explanations of Gesenius-Kautsch and the medieval grammarians, usually because they have had little exposure to the northwest Semitic documents. In the latter school Mitchell Dahood, the author of the *Anchor Bible Psalms* volumes has been accused of such things as poor methodology in his use of the source materials.

There can be no doubt that Dahood has done some brainstorming, some of which, as he admits, may not stand the test of scholarly scrutiny. We may, however, be grateful to Dahood for providing a compendium of references where the northwest Semitic grammatical and lexical data may illuminate the Psalms. The result is a breath of fresh air in Psalms studies. Those Ugaritic scholars who decry Dahood's efforts do so because as specialists they disagree with this or that detail of matter or method, not because they want to accept Gesenius-Kautsch uncritically. There are those like R. Tournay who maintain that the Ugaritic of the second millenium can have little bearing on the Hebrew of the first. Dahood points to the number of Ugaritic texts discovered in Palestine at Beth Shemesh, Mount Tabor, Tell Taanach, etc., which show that the Canaanite of Late Bronze and Early Iron Age Palestine was similar to the northwest Semitic of Ugarit.[1] Tournay represents a dying viewpoint which would rather emend a text than use such available Ugaritic data as results in a reading which opposes "modern" theory.[2] James Barr's book *Comparative Philology and the Text of the Old Testament*, Oxford, 1968, is highly critical of the present use of comparative philology. Some of his strictures are needed but he fails to offer much that is positive and constructive. He deals largely with examples that suit his apparent negative purpose.

Such is the state of affairs in one phase of Old Testament textual studies. As may be gathered, the writer is in favor of the northwest Semitic school, for it has given fresh hope to understanding the idiom of Old Testament poetry. The Hebrews, the Phoenicians, and the Ugaritians were not only of the same Semitic language branch but they also shared the same cultural background before the upheavals which most radically affected Hebrew language and culture, namely the Exile and Hellenization. Even following these upheavals it is amazing how sometimes the Septuagint preserves a rare meaning in keeping with the Canaanite texts but unknown to the Masoretes.

Continued study in the northwest Semitic sources is leading to some far-reaching possibilities in Old Testament theology. Some of these possibilities run counter to the accepted axioms of critical scholarship. Some appear to make the Biblical writers quite dependent on Canaanite religious conceptions. With a proper approach, the New Testament view of the Old Testament fares much better from this evidence than does orthodox higher criticism. As a Hebraist who believes that the New Testament is a divine commentary on the Old, the writer will now try to evaluate some of this newer evidence for the light it may shed on the theology of the Psalms.

Without committing ourselves to all of Dahood's conclusions, our indebtedness to him is fully acknowledged. Some of Dahood's conclusions are interesting. For example, with reference to the dating of the Psalms he maintains that the old methods, still being used, of seeking alleged literary dependence and historical allusions, can no longer be considered valid, because the psalmists and prophets were indebted to an ancient literary tradition that went deep into the second millenium. An examination of the vocabulary of Psalms 2 and 110, says Dahood, "reveals that virtually every word, image and parallelism are now reported in Bronze Age Canaanite texts."[3] He therefore tentatively dates these psalms to the tenth century.

I. Immortality and Resurrection

The consensus of critical opinion still insists that emergent belief in the resurrection of the dead was a thing unattested in the literature of pre-exilic Israel. John Bright, a conservative among critics, says, "The idea of a resurrection begins to appear sporadically and tentatively in later Biblical literature, and by the second century was a well-established belief."[4]

H. H. Rowley admits that resurrection may be in view in Job 19:26 and 27 but only as a "momentary resurrection to witness his (Job's) vindication."[5] Daniel 12:2 is taken by many to be the only verse anywhere in the Old Testament which deals with resurrection of the body, and it is attributed to the second century B.C. As for immortality, Rowley sees "no uniform or sure faith in the afterlife that is meaningful, but there are . . . reachings-out after such a faith"[6] in certain Psalms.

But now *Anchor Bible 16* proposes that the Psalms are full of expressions of hope for immortality and resurrection. Dahood studiously avoids references to the New Testament use of the Psalms. From his viewpoint this would amount to reading later notions into the Psalms, while he proposes to convince the reader that his conclusions are based solely on evidence from the world of the Old Testament.

That concepts of immortality and resurrection are present to any extended degree in the Psalter is called by D. A. Robertson one of Dahood's wild interpretations which should not be presented to the general public.[7] The following statement in the Introduction to *Anchor Bible 16*, Volume I, was bound to draw fire.

> Perhaps the most significant contribution to Biblical theology that flows from the translations based on the new philological principles concerns the subject of resurrection and immortality. If the translations and exegesis propounded . . . bear up under criticism, then the treatment of these topics in standard Biblical theologies will need drastic revision. The mythological motif of the Elysian Fields that stands forth from the translations offered . . . is the clearest example of a theological verity finding expression in the idiom of mythological poetry; the opinion of Sigmund Mowinckel that "neither Israel nor early Judaism knew of a faith in any resurrection nor is such a faith represented in the psalms" will not survive serious scrutiny.[8]

Along this line let us briefly review Dahood's handling of some relevant passages. He renders the *crux interpretum,* Psalm 16:9–11, as follows:

> 9. And so my heart rejoices,
>   my liver leaps with joy,
>   and my body dwells at ease,
> 10. Since you will not put me in Sheol,
>   nor allow your devoted one to see the Pit.
> 11. You will make me know the path of life eternal,
>   filling me with happiness before you,
>   with pleasures at your right hand forever.

Because of the peculiar Phoenician style and language, Dahood considers the psalmist here to be a Canaanite convert to Yahwism who gives his profession of faith in verse two. "O Yahweh, you are my Lord, there is none above you." This is followed by an abjuration of the false

Canaanite gods, the "holy ones" *q⁰dōšim* and the "mighty ones" *'⁰dîrîm* (typical epithets for Phoenician gods). Finally the psalmist enumerates the joys and blessings of the newly found faith with a final statement of the poet's belief in an afterlife of eternal happiness.[9]

Ignoring Acts 2 and 13 Dahood maintains that the psalmist expects to experience assumption like Enoch or Elijah. This position of bodily assumption rather than bodily resurrection hinges on his translation of verse 10 as teaching deliverance from death rather than being "put in Sheol" or "seeing the pit." The New Testament, following LXX uses *diaphthora* "corruption" instead of "pit" and lays stress on the last line of verse nine, "My flesh will lie down in hope." The New Testament also uses the common meaning of *'āzab*, "to forsake," rather than the rarer meaning "to put." "I will not be forsaken in Sheol" nor "see corruption"; that is, though I die my body will not decompose. This the apostles knew could be said only of Jesus Christ (Acts 13:34–38).

Psalms 49 and 73 are likewise said to express the conviction that the psalmist will be assumed like Enoch and Elijah. Thus Dahood translates Psalm 73:24:

> Into your council you will lead me
> And with glory you will receive me.

And Psalm 49:16:

> But God will ransom me,
> from the hand of Sheol
> Will he surely snatch me.

Bodily assumption is derived by Dahood from the use of *lāqah* "to take" as it is used with reference to Enoch and Elijah, which is a valid point, but it needs to be qualified by the fact that neither of these were snatched from Sheol.

It is curious that Dahood sees no resurrection (though he does see eternal afterlife) in Psalm 16, despite the New Testament commentary, while in Psalm 17:15, which is not quoted in the New Testament, he finds both resurrection and final judgment. He renders Psalm 17:15:

> At my vindication
> I will gaze upon your face
> At the resurrection
> I will be saturated with your being.

"At the resurrection," comments Dahood, "seems to be the plain sense of *b⁰hāqîṣ* [in Ps. 17:15] when one compares it with the eschatological passages Isaiah 26:19, 'But your dead will live, their bodies will rise. Arise (*hāqîṣû*) and sing, ye who dwell in the slime!' and Daniel 12:2, 'And many of those who sleep in the land of slime will arise' (*yāqîṣû*)." Dahood maintains that "the archaic language throughout the psalm [17] suggests that the Israelite belief in the beatific vision was very ancient indeed."[10]

The references to "dwelling in the house of the Lord all the days" in Psalms 23:6 and 27:4 also speak to Dahood of this "beatific vision." Psalm 27:13 is even clearer to him:

> In the Victor[11] do I trust,
>   to behold the beauty of Yahweh
>   in the land of life eternal.

Though Daniel 12:2 is often given in the lexicons as the only place where *ḥayyîm* means eternal life, Dahood sees it in many places and more than once refers to the Ugaritic antecedent in 2 Aqht VI 27–29.[12]

> Ask for eternal life (*ḥym*)
>   And I will give it to you,
> Immortality (*bl·mt*)
>   And I will bestow it on you.
> I will make you number years with Baal,
>   With gods you will number months.

Proverbs 12:28 uses *'al-māwet* (no death) as the parallel of *ḥayyîm* (life). The Ugaritic *bl·mt* translated "immortality" above is an equivalent expression. The RSV says the Hebrew is uncertain and proceeds to give a translation based on an emended text. But Ewald, Bertheau, Franz Delitzsch, and even the Judeo-Arabist Saadia in the Middle Ages said *'al-māwet* means "immortality." The KJV wisely translated it "no death." They have all been proved correct by the Ugaritic *bl·mt* as used in the above citation. Dahood translates the verse.

> In the path of virtue is eternal life,
>   And the treading of her way is immortality.

Marvin Pope in an article entitled "Marginalia to M. Dahood's Ugaritic Hebrew Philology"[13] objects to this translation on the basis that such synonymous parallelism goes against the larger context which consists of a series of couplets in antithetical parallelism, and "therefore death not immortality is the proper antithesis."[14] But is there here a larger context? Are not these proverbs a list of independent thoughts? Indeed it is typical of the proverbs to list antithetical sayings with one or two synonymous parallelisms sandwiched in.[15]

Pope states that *ḥayyîm* as eternal life is not justified by the parallelism of *ḥym* and *bl·mt* in Ugaritic, because Aqhat's reply shows he did not believe immortality could be had by a mortal and he therefore accuses the goddess Anat of lying to him. The implication is that since the Ugaritic hero did not believe humans could have immortality, the writers of the Old Testament must share the same skepticism. The point is not what the Ugaritians believed but that they used the word *ḥym*

for eternal life, whereas the Hebrew lexicons generally list only Daniel
12:2 as using *ḥayyîm* distinctively to denote eternal life because of Daniel's alleged Maccabean origin.[16]

Dahood looks on Psalm 1:5, 6 as future.

> And so the wicked shall not stand
>   in the place of judgment,
> Nor sinners in the congregation of the just,
> But Yahweh shall safekeep
>   the assembly of the just,
> While the assembly of the wicked shall perish.

He argues from Ugaritic that *derek*[17] can mean "assembly" and from
Hebrew usage, that *mišpāt* can mean "place of judgment." Here the
wicked shall not stand on Judgment Day while the Lord safekeeps
yôḏēaʿ the assembly of the just. All this, says Dahood, assumes an advanced concept of resurrection and immortality.

The New Testament employs the word "paradise" (II Cor. 12:4, Rev.
2:7, Luke 23:43), a Persian root which originally meant "a park" (Neh.
2:8, etc.) much as Dahood views the Old Testament use of the two
words *ṣᵉḏāqā* and *'ûr*. Psalm 5:9 he translates, "Lead me into your
meadow. . . ." The word *ṣᵉḏāqā*, usually "righteousness," is rendered
"paradise" or "meadow" here and elsewhere, as a poetic term similar to
the Homeric use of the Elysian fields. That notions of abundance and
luxuriance are resident in the root *ṣdq* seems clear. Students of Hebrew
will call to mind Joel 2:23, "For he shall give to you the former rain in
abundance (*liṣᵉḏāqā*). Similarly in Psalm 23:3 *maʿgᵉlê ṣeḏeq* is taken as
"luxuriant pastures" paralleling "green meadows" in verse 2.[18] Thus
the comfort of paradise is mentioned here in verses 2 and 3 and returned
to again in verse 6, "I shall dwell in the house of the Lord forever."

Dahood claims that the eschatological context in Psalm 69:28, 29
makes "meadow" a better translation for *ṣᵉḏāqā*. He translates this passage:

> Add punishment to their punishment.
> Let them not enter your meadow,
> And let them not be enrolled among the just.

Taking Psalm 143:10b–11 as a couplet Dahood also renders *ṣᵉḏāqā*
"meadow":

> With your good spirit lead me into the level land,
> For your name's sake, O Yahweh, grant me life in your meadow.

The Elysian field or paradise motif is considered strong in Psalm 36.
Here Dahood develops it from the root *'wr*, whose common meaning
"light" has obscured the rarer root meaning "field." Thus Psalm 36:10
says:

> Truly with you is the fountain of life,
> In your field we shall see the light.

Isaiah 26:19 is rendered smoother with this meaning:

> Your dead shall live, their bodies will rise;
> Those who dwell in the dust will awake and sing for joy:
> For your dew is the dew of the fields (*'ûrôt*)
> But the land of the Shades will be parched.

The familiar terms "the light of life" and "the land of the living" are shown to be two ways of saying the same thing. So Psalm 56:14 reads, ". . . to walk before God in the field of life *b⁰'ûr haḥayyîm*";[19] and Psalm 116:9, "I shall walk before the Lord in the fields of life *b⁰'arṣôt haḥayyîm.*" Also Psalm 97:11 is translated:

> A sown field awaits the just, *'ûr zārûa' laṣṣaddîq*
> And happiness the upright in heart.[20]

II. Messianism and Divine Sovereignty

The second half of Psalm 22 (vv. 23–31) usually receives little attention.[21] Hebrews 2:12 quotes the opening words of this section to show that the Lord was not ashamed to call those whom He had sanctified brothers: "Saying, I will declare your name (O God) unto my brothers, I will sing praise to you in the midst of the church." On this authority Christians have considered these the words of the resurrected Messiah, though few have seen here the message of resurrection itself. This message is clearer than most have imagined, but it can be appreciated only with the help of Ugaritic lexicography.

The voice of the great Elder Brother continues. We render Psalm 22:26–32:

> I (give) Thee my praise a hundred times in the great congregation;
> My vows I pay before those who fear (worship) Him.
> Let the afflicted eat and be satisfied,
> Let those who seek Yahweh praise Him,
> Let their hearts live forever.
> For all the ends of the earth shall remember and turn to the Yahweh,
> Yea, all the families of the nations shall worship before Thee,
> Because verily Yahweh is the Ruler,
> A Suzerain among the nations.

> Surely to Him all those who sleep in the earth shall bow down,
> And before Him shall crouch all who have descended to the dust.
> And the Victor himself shall give life.
> A posterity (who) shall serve Him,
> Will tell about the Lord,
> To a generation that shall come.

They will declare his righteousness,
To a people yet to be born,
That He has acted.

Verse 26 (25) : "I (give) Thee my praise a hundred times in the great congregation."

The use of a denominative verb from the word *mē'ā,* "a hundred," meaning "to do or say a hundred times," is not used elsewhere in Old Testament denominatively; but other numbers are so used. Ezekiel 39:2 *šeš* (six) seems to be used with the same pronoun object. Furthermore in Ugaritic, Aramaic, and Assyrian the number "two" is consistently used meaning "to say a second time, to repeat."

Verse 27 (26) :

> Let the afflicted eat and be satisfied,
> Let those who seek the Lord praise him,
> Let *their* hearts live forever."

Following the Septuagint and internal evidence, we choose "their hearts" for "your hearts," *hē* for *kaph,* which in paleo-hebrew script would look somewhat alike.

Verse 29 (28) : "Because, verily Yahweh is the Ruler."
"Verily" stands for emphatic *lamed,* attested in Ugaritic and many other Old Testament passages.

Hammᵉlûkā does not mean "kingdom," which would be *malkût* or *mamlākût;* here the meaning is either "royal office" or a title "The Royal One" or "Ruler," having the feminine ending of such titles as *haqqōhelet* "the preacher."

Verse 30 (29) : "Surely to Him shall bow down all those who sleep in the earth." The rsv saw that *'ākᵉlû* does not mean "they shall eat." The reading "The fat ones of the earth shall eat and worship" is not convincing, and here it destroys the parallelism. It is rather *'ak + lô:* "Surely to him they shall bow down." Ugaritic has taught us that the conjunction *waw,* like *gar* in Greek, need not begin a clause.

Verse 30 (29) : *Dišnê 'ereṣ* might mean "the fat ones of the earth," but *dešen* (fatness) is simply not used in this way in the Bible. While rsv starts out as an improvement over kjv, it also misses the force of the synonymous parallelism by translating *dišnê 'ereṣ,* "all the proud of the earth." This phrase, however, is obviously parallel to "all those descending to the dust." In *dišnê 'ereṣ* the *d* might be a relative pronoun, as in Ugaritic and Aramaic, and *šᵉnê* might be a syncopated form of *yāšēn* (sleep) as in Daniel 12:2, *miyyᵉšēnê 'admat 'āpār*—"from those who sleep in the dust of the earth." So here "all who sleep in the earth" would parallel "all who descend to the dust."

Verse 30 (29) : "And the Victor himself shall give life." This third line in the tristich has been badly obscured in the translations: rsv, "And he who cannot keep himself alive"; KJV, "And none can keep alive his own soul."

The MT reads *w*ʿnapšô lōʾ hiyyâ*. *Napšô, napšekā*, commonly means "himself," "thyself," etc. If we take the *lōʾ* to be the negative "not," we can conceivably arrive at the innocuous truism "that he who descends to the dust cannot keep himself alive." But what has that to do with his worshiping the Lord? If, however, we see here the divine epithet *lēʾ* or *lēʾōn* as it appears in Ugaritic in the honorific name of Baal as *aliyn·bʿl* (Victorious Baal) from the root *lʾy* "to prevail," then this passage springs to life:

> "Those who sleep in the earth . . .
> "Those who descend to the dust . . .
> "Do worship before him
> "For the Victor himself gives life."

This then becomes the key to numerous other passages, such as I Samuel 2:3 where the Massoretic text reads:

> *kî ʾel deʿôṯ yhwh*
> *wʿlōʾ niṯkʿnû ʿ°lîlōṯ*

The English versions follow the Qere, changing *lʾ* to *lw* and reading, "For the Lord is a God of knowledge and by him actions are weighed."

The LXX vorlage reads *wʿēl tōkēn* [*kai theos hetoimazōn*]—"and a God who weighs." Neither reversal of the consonants *lʾ* to *ʾl* nor the Qere which deletes the aleph is necessary, because the very same adjectival form of the divine epithet is attested in Ugaritic text 127:13–14:

mt dm ḥt/šʾtqt dm lan, "Mot (death) is stilled/Shaʿtaqat is Victor." So we should read Hannah's prayer:

> The Lord is a God of knowledge;
> Yea, the Victor is a weigher of actions. *wʿlēʾōn tōkēn ʿ°lîlōṯ*

The very same form is found in Habakkuk 1:12 where *lōʾ nāmûṯ*, "we shall not die," is an intrusion into a series of epithets. This should read *lēʾ ōn māweṯ, which makes the verse read smoothly,*

> Are you not from everlasting, O Yahweh, O my God,
> My Holy One, Victor over death?[22]

Another great expression of confidence in the Lord and in hope beyond the grave appears in Psalm 27:13. The verse begins with the word *lûlēʾ*, "unless," which hangs unattached syntactically. Feeling this difficulty, a few manuscripts omit it. The RSV, taking the easy way out, also omits it. The KJV simply adds the clause "I had fainted" in italics, followed by "unless I had believed." Dahood takes the consonants just as they are *l + lʾ*, preposition + the divine epithet, the preposition *l* going with the verb *ʾāman* as usual. Thus we arrive at the translation:

In the Victor do I trust,
to behold the beauty of the Lord
in the land of life (eternal) .

As we have seen in some cases where *l'* is used, the LXX sensed the need for something like *'ēl* and, assuming the consonants were switched, translated *theos* which made good sense. But in Malachi 2:15 *Biblia Hebraica 3* felt the need for such an emendation and suggests making *lō' 'eḥād* read *'ēl 'eḥād*. This fits the context well; Malachi says earlier (v. 10) : "Has not one God (*'ēl 'eḥād*) created us?" So it is suggested this verse read: "and one God made and sustains life (*rûaḥ*) for himself." But it is unnecessary to switch the consonants, especially since all the external evidence including the LXX witness to *l'*, if we understand *lē'* as an epithet for God. Thus Malachi 2:15 reads, "The One Victor has made and sustains life for himself."

In some Psalms, titles for God seem to have been confused with common words which threw the translators off. Psalm 7:11 (10) reads,

> *māginnî 'al "lōhîm*
> *môsîa' yišrê lēḇ.*

The KJV translates it "My defence is of God, which saveth the upright in heart." The RSV makes the first phrase read, "My shield is with God." In neither of these translations does the first clause correspond realistically to the Hebrew, where *'al* can hardly mean "with" or "of."

Evidence from both Ugaritic and the Samaritan Ostraca witness to *'al* as a shortened form of *'ēlî* or *'alyôn*.[23] The latter appears in verse 9 of this Psalm:

> Judge me, O Lord, according to my righteousness,
> According to my integrity, O most High.

Again Hannah's song in I Samuel 2:10 affords a striking example of this title:

The adversaries of the Lord will be broken in pieces;
The Almighty shall thunder from the heavens (*'ālāw baššāmayim yar-'ēm*) ;
Yahweh will judge the ends of the earth.

In Psalm 7, another title for God is used which clarifies this and a number of other contexts. It is the term *māgēn* (shield) . This common meaning may have hidden the Canaanite word *māgān*, which means Suzerain or Sovereign. So in the familiar Psalm 84:12 (11) "The Lord is a Sun and a Sovereign" (not shield) .

Psalm 47:9 takes on sparkling clarity when understood in this light. Both KJV and RSV say, "The shields of the earth belong to God." But the context, beginning in verse 7, says:

For God is the King of all the earth . . .
God reigneth over the nations . . .

Thus the end of verse 9 should read:

For verily [emphatic *lamed*] God is the Suzerain of the earth,
He is to be greatly exalted.

Returning again to Psalm 7:11 (10):

My Sovereign is the Almighty God (*māgānî 'ēl 'elōhîm*),
Who saves the upright in heart.

* * *

Theological verity must find expression in terms that are available in the language used. The Old Testament employs the same Northwest Semitic idiom common to the mythology of Canaanite poetry. Though the Hebrews in the Old Testament were expressing an emphatic reaction to polytheism, it must be borne in mind that they were not literary iconoclasts as were the Jews of a later date. Many graphic phrases, especially those which expressed the highly personal nature of the deity, were used to enhance Hebrew monotheism.

That the Lord is called "the rider on the clouds" (Psalm 68:5), a frequently used epithet for Baal, may suggest an early date but not necessarily a primitive stage of Hebrew religion. It marks a time of religious vitality and verbal fluency. Such an epithet would have been impossible in the Maccabean period when Hebrew was wooden and Hebrew scholars were given to the use of anti-anthropomorphisms. The poet of Psalm 68 expressed God's control over nature in artful poetic idiom without necessarily a thought of the polytheistic usage. The Canaanite substratum was a readily available vehicle through which the prophets and poets could communicate the truth, whether of the character of their only God or theological verities such as immortality and resurrection. Though the idiom was freely used, it was not carelessly used, so that only theologically acceptable concepts were communicated. For example, the common semitic word *ilt,* meaning "goddess," was rejected by all Old Testament writers of all periods. Female deities like Asherah were referred to by the proper names given to their images but were never called goddesses, simply because the Hebrews had no mythology in which such a concept would have meaning.

That certain valid theological concepts are not late in human history still does not answer the question of when and where they originated. According to the Bible, man originally had a true concept of deity which he proceeded to distort. The Hebrew prophets rejected these distorted notions and progressively revealed the truth of God. But some of this truth was, and is, always mingled in all religions. The polytheistic antecedents to the Old Testament had one truth emphatically in common with Biblical revelation. That was the personality of deity. Likewise a distorted concept of immortality antedates the Bible in written records of the Egyptians and Babylonians, and some notion of resurrection from the dead was a part of Sumerian mythology. Ancient law codes often provide for reprobate practices like bestiality, but here and there may be found some higher principles such as care for the widow and orphan. Yet the Decalogue of Moses is a crowning glory and a completely unique expression in the ancient world. Although the Old Testament was in one sense a product of its time, its own claim to be the product of the Holy Spirit of God is enhanced by its just reaction to the base practices and beliefs of surrounding religions, withal not rejecting those elements which were part of that vestige of truth still remaining in a corrupt world.

Notes

1. Mitchell Dahood, tr., *Psalms Two, Fifty One to One Hundred, Anchor Bible 17* (New York: Doubleday & Co., 1968), p. xv.

2. *Ibid.*, p. xxvii, n. 17.

3. Mitchell Dahood, tr., *Psalms One, One to Fifty, Anchor Bible 16* (New York: Doubleday & Co., 1966).

4. John Bright, *History of Israel* (Philadelphia: Westminster, 1959), p. 438.

5. Harold H. Rowley, *The Faith of Israel* (Philadelphia: Westminster, 1957), p. 170.

6. *Ibid.*, p. 175.

7. JBL, 85 (196): 484.

8. Dahood, *Psalms One*, p. xxxvi.

9. *Ibid.*, pp. 87, 88.

10. *Ibid.*, pp. 99, 100.

11. MT *lûlē'* is taken to be *l°lē'*. The word *lē'*, translated "Victor," is derived from the common Ugaritic-Phoenician root *l'y* "to prevail," as is explained later in this article.

12. Dahood, *Psalms One*, pp. 91, 170, etc.

13. Marvin Pope, "Marginalia to M. Dahood's Ugaritic Philology," JBL, 85 (196): 455–66.

14. *Ibid.*, p. 462.

15. Prov. 15:23 is unquestionably synonymous in the midst of a long list of antithetical statements. See BDB, p. 313.

16. Prov. 15:24 puts *ḥayyîm* and *š°'ôl* in antithesis as follows:

> The path of life above belongs to the wise,
> Because he turns away from Sheol below.

If Sheol here, as in some contexts, means only "grave," then *ḥayyîm* means only "this life." If Sheol can mean "netherworld," then *ḥayyîm* can mean "life after death." Proverbs repeats the concept that *māwet* and *š°'ôl* involve more than the grave. So Prov. 2:18, 19 parallels death with "the place of the shades," just as Prov. 9:18 parallels *š°'ôl* with "the place of the shades." Therefore, "the path of life above" can mean eternal life above in heaven, as contrasted with Sheol below, where dwell the shades.

17. In addition to Dahood's aligning *derek* with Ugaritic *drkt* "dominion," *derek* commonly means "manner or custom" just as *mišpāṭ* means "justice" but also means "custom or way." His argument for *derek* to mean "assembly" proceeds from

mišpāṭ meaning "court of justice"; so *derek* "dominion" can mean "place of dominion." On this basis Dahood translates *derek* "throne" in Ps. 110:7. He also notes the synonymous parallelism in Ps. 1 between *derek ṣaddîqîm* (v. 6) and *ʿadat ṣaddîqîm* (v. 5) and that *ʿēṣā* (v. 1) which can mean "council" as well as "counsel" (Ps. 14:6) is parallel with *derek*.

18. That *maʿgāl* can mean "pasture" is conclusive from Ps. 65:12, 13:

> May your pastures drip with fatness,
> May the meadows of the wilderness drip.

19. Cf. Job 33:30. rsv's translation "that he might see the light of life" puts the meaning "see" into *ʾwr* which it cannot bear. The translation with Dahood is:

> To turn back his soul from the pit,
> That he might be resplendent in the field of life.

20. kjv has the anomalous "light is sown." rsv follows the versions reading "light dawns" with a footnote saying the Hebrew reads "is sown."

21. The Messianic elements in the Psalms generally suffer from the treatment received by Dahood and others. The New Testament application of Pss. 2, 16, 22, 45, and 110 is ignored in an attempt to understand them in the light of Canaanite culture. One should not, of course, deny the presence of Canaanisms nor the unique applications made by the Hebrews. The question is whether the New Testament in its *dᵉrāšâ* (interpretive) and *pᵉšāṭâ* (plain meaning) usages of the Old Testament has correctly understood Messianic hopes in the Psalms or has forced meaning which was completely foreign to the original text.

22. Another place where *lʾ* is to be changed to *lw* in order for the text to make sense is Job 13:15:

> *hēn yiqtelēnî lōʾ ʾᵃyaḥēl*
> *ʾak dᵃrākay ʾel pānāyw ʾôkîaḥ*

kjv: Though he slay me, yet will I trust in him.
But I will maintain mine own ways before him.

The rsv refuses to follow the Qere in changing *lʾ* to *lw:*

> Behold, he will slay me, I have no hope;
> Yet I will defend my ways to his face.

Marvin H. Pope, translator of *Job* in the *Anchor Bible* (15), says: "This utterance has been hailed as the quintessence of the Hebrew spirit of faith as contrasted with the sullen acquiescence of the pagan philosophers . . . but there is no real basis for it in these words of Job. This interpretation derives from an ingenious emendation by the Masoretes who suggested that the reading should be *lô* spelled with the vocalic consonant *waw* rather than *ʾālep* which stands in the text" (p. 96).

By taking *lʾ* as *lē* "Victor" we may translate:

> Though the Victor slay me, I will still hope,
> Indeed I will (then) defend my ways to his face.

Here Job's words do fit the immediate context because Job is not simply expressing hopelessness but is more concerned with his own vindication, even after death if necessary (Job 13:2, 3, 22).

23. Dahood, *Psalms One*, p. 45.

WISDOM LITERATURE OF THE
OLD TESTAMENT

Derek Kidner

I. Wisdom at Large

The wisdom literature is the Old Testament's antidote to one of the diseases of religion: unreality. There is a tendency in most faiths to retire indoors, into a private world that has its own language and is half contemptuous, half afraid, of what goes on outside. These writings take us out into the open. Wisdom belongs there: "In the markets she raises her voice" (Prov. 1:20), and the whole of creation is claimed for her province.

The Biblical material itself carries us outside Israel by its interest in foreign *savants*,[1] by its Edomite setting for the book of Job, and by its inclusion of (apparently) Gentile converts among the authors of Proverbs.[2] It also tells of the international reputation which Solomon acquired in his lifetime, whereby Jerusalem became, for a while, a center which attracted the intellectuals of many nations.[3]

But this element of Israel's life is older than Solomon (though he gave it its greatest stimulus)[4] and wider than the books we classify as wisdom. In the book of Judges, Jotham and Samson speak its language (9:7 ff.; 14:14), and its presence is obvious in the Psalter (e.g. Pss. 1, 19, 37 . . . 119) and in the parables and aphorisms of the prophets (e.g. Isa. 28:23 ff.; Hos. 14:9). There is some ground also for calling Apocalyptic the child of Wisdom as well as of Prophecy.[5] But what is of particular interest to certain scholars is that some of the favorite wisdom concepts are in the Pentateuch, which opens with the themes of creation, knowledge, and life, and closes in Deuteronomy with fatherly exhortations not unlike those of Proverbs 1–9. This has given rise to various theories.

In the realm of narrative, von Rad treats the Joseph story as a wisdom writing[6]—not in the sense merely that Joseph *displays* certain qualities commended in Proverbs, but that the qualities have shaped the narrative, which, in its finished form, he regards as a piece of didactic writing from the early monarchy. In the realm of Law, E. Gerstenberger[7] argues that the so-called apodictic commands, such as those of the Decalogue, have their original setting in the family or tribe (cf. the little clusters of prohibitions found in, e.g., Prov. 3:27–30; Jer. 35:6 f.), where they were handed down in teachings akin to those of Egypt and Mesopotamia and were only later given a cultic setting and put into the mouth of God. E. Nielsen, approaching the Decalogue from another angle, seeks to account for the positive form of the fifth commandment (which he conceives to have been originally negative) by ascribing the change to the influence of the moral fervor engendered by Proverbs 1–9 —an enthusiasm for the law which is seen at its height in the wisdom psalms.[8]

But it is important to recognize that these reconstructions, and others like them, arise out of the complexities of pentateuchal criticism rather than any inherent difficulty of relating wisdom to the narratives or laws. Joseph can be intelligibly explained as a man whose character was shaped by the same Spirit of God who inspired the Proverbs. In purely literary terms, as well, this is the more convincing assessment, since such a portrait as his is more easily analyzed into virtues than constructed out of maxims. The relation of Proverbs to the Decalogue and Deuteronomy is similarly straightforward by Scripture's own account of itself; for it is seen as the relation between the commending and the commanding of truth—a relation already established by Deuteronomy itself, with its preaching of the law. Even the similarity of tone and approach between Deuteronomy and Proverbs 1–9 is hardly surprising if the law was indeed preached at festivals from time to time (cf. Deut. 31:10 f.) in the Deuteronomic style.

The harmony between these two parts of Scripture is expressed in the saying of Deuteronomy 6:24: "The Lord commanded us to do all these statutes . . . for our good always, that he might preserve us alive." Here is the union of right and good, of obligation and satisfaction. Centered upon God's will, Wisdom unites with Law, and indeed with all the diversity of voices, whether prophecy, poetry, history or apocalyptic, which make up the Old Testament.

II. The Canonical Wisdom Books

A. Proverbs

Having approached Proverbs (in the foregoing remarks) by way of the Law, we are in little danger of reading it as mere worldly wisdom; and its opening discourses make doubly sure of this. For all its interest in what pays and what will work, its god is not success. By its faith in Yahweh it is sure that for the God-fearing "there is a future" (23:17, 18), while "the evil man has no future" (24:20), but its values are independent of the fact. Come what may, it is simply "better" to be poor and honest than rich and crooked (28:6), "better" to rule one's spirit than to capture a city (16:32). Some of its sayings, notably those that speak of generosity to an enemy (24:17; 25:21) and succor for the weak (e.g. 24:11 f.), go far beyond this, to a level of self-sacrifice which leaves little if anything for the New Testament to add.

Yet even these moral heights are approached, at times, in the writings of Israel's contemporaries, and most of the favorite subjects of Proverbs (e.g. teachability, friendship, chastity, the use of words) are treated by them in similar and sometimes identical terms. Certainly Proverbs maintains a higher level—above all, it knows the living God—but it inhabits the same world as these others and invites comparative study.

It has certainly not lacked it. Out of a great quantity of material we shall choose samples of recent discussion of three areas of the book.

1. The Discourses. This section of Proverbs (chs. 1–9) has attracted special attention in the last two or three decades. In 1945 C. I. K. Story pointed out the presence of considerable Canaanite literary influence on Proverbs, especially on chapters 8 and 9.[9] This was wholeheartedly endorsed by Albright, who stated in a characteristic phrase that this section "swarms with words and expressions otherwise found only in such Canaanite texts as the Ugaritic tablets and the Phoenician inscriptions."[10] Albright himself went on to postulate a distinct Canaanite document and an early Canaanite wisdom-goddess, *ḥokmôt,* underlying these two chapters.

These claims have been strongly criticized by R. N. Whybray,[11] who holds that Albright's Canaanite "swarm" can be reduced to a single example (the rest being Hebraisms to which Ugaritic has merely opened our eyes), and points out that such statements as "the wise El has attributed to thee (O Baal) wisdom . . ."[12] fall far short of making *ḥokmôt* (wisdom) a distinct personal being. We may add that some of Story's examples, too, lack cogency. Most of his paired expressions common to Ugaritic literature and Proverbs are too universal to prove his point,[13] and one of his strongest poetic examples (a Ugaritic parallel to the form of Prov. 10:26 and 25:20)[14] is now seen to have been a not unusual proverbial form.[15]

For all this, quite enough remains to link the language of Proverbs with the early literature of Canaan, which is found to illuminate both its modes of expression (to which we return below, in considering numerical sayings) and its vocabulary and syntax.[16]

Even more than Canaan, however, Egypt has increasingly claimed attention in relation to the first nine chapters. Solomon's leanings in this direction, and the new necessity of training a diplomatic staff, suggest the possibility that Egyptian instruction manuals for officials might have come into use in Israel in his reign and so left their mark on the teaching style of these chapters of Proverbs, different though the purpose of the latter was. Whybray would go further than this, to argue that the discourses here are Egyptian also in basic outlook, appealing to no wisdom higher than the teacher's own, and reducing Yahweh to a mere executive of "the inflexible rules which govern the world."[17] But this assertion rests on a text from which all references to Wisdom as personified have first been excised as secondary, and all statements that wisdom is God-given excised as tertiary, on no better grounds than the "wearisomely" repetitive style of the writing and the assumption that the teacher's appeal to his own authority in some passages is incompatible with his appeal elsewhere to that of God.[18] Such a sequence of primary, secondary, and tertiary matter convinces the author of a three-stage development of the concept of wisdom in Israel. With so arbitrary a method, however, one tends to find what one is looking for,[19] and the high-handedness of the whole procedure betrays itself in the significant word "wearisomely," which judges the eloquence of one age by the impatience of another.

A more objective approach is used in a recent study which also compares these chapters with Egyptian writings, namely *Studien in Proverbien 1–9*, by Christa Kayatz.[20] This examines the text without conjectural changes or evolutionary preconceptions. As to the latter (and particularly Gunkel's method of dating sayings by their length and religious content), this author points out that the oldest Egyptian teachings known to us are in a connected, flowing style suited to the intellectuals who were training for public office, whereas the teaching of 'Onchsheshonqy,[21] some two thousand years younger, chiefly consists of short (and we might add, earthy) sayings matched to the outlook of the peasant farmers for whom they were intended.[22] Style, in fact, is more an index of function than of date, and there is no reason why distinct types of wisdom writing should not have arisen simultaneously in a given period.

What is true of form is no less true of content. Christa Kayatz does not belittle the distinctive emphases of Proverbs 1–9, its more explicit religious teaching[23] and its personifying of Wisdom; yet these differences, she contends, great as they are, decide nothing in the area of chronology. There is no reason why theologically didactic wisdom circles could not have coexisted with others of a more practical bias, still less why they must necessarily be thought postexilic. If the influence that gave rise to the personification of Wisdom was foreign, there was no lack of it, to be sure, during the monarchy.

But the bulk of this monograph is a rigorous form- and theme-study of certain Egyptian texts, with a corresponding scrutiny of Proverbs 1–9. From her analysis of these formal characteristics (e.g. if-clauses, imperatives, series of infinitives, etc.) this author finds the Biblical material indebted in this respect to the Teachings, except in so far as its unique content modifies its structure. In her study of the subject-matter, however, she goes further afield, to find the background of personified Wisdom mainly in Egyptian magical and mythological texts, where various deities offer life or safety to their protégés and speak of their pre-cosmic origin, and where, in particular, Ma'at (justice, fair dealing) is portrayed as the darling child[24] of her creator, the comrade and confidant of those who love her,[25] who dispenses life and safety,[26] and is the ornament of the just[27] and the guide of kings.[28] On the other hand the same writer argues that in Proverbs 1.20 ff. the oration of Wisdom is as strongly Israelite in its coloring as that of chapter 8 is Egyptian; and she concludes that together these passages show the authors of this collection to be theologians in the mainstream of Israelite faith, who are yet sufficiently at home in Egyptian thought-forms to make creative use of them to the glory of Yahweh. No period would be more fitting, in her view, than that of the Solomonic Enlightenment.[29]

Whether future debate confirms or refutes this hypothesis, it should be borne in mind that it has no necessary bearing on the authority of these passages as Scripture. It may be paradoxical to speak of contact between the word of God and the literature of magic or mythology, and indeed the theory may be ill-founded. But to purge heathen thought-forms and fill them with truth is what Scripture regularly does in the realm of human words and expressions. In this sphere, as in others, former enemies can make good apostles.

2. *The Words of the Wise* (Prov. 22:17–24:22). In this section too, since the publication in 1923 of the *Teaching of Amenemope,* the presence of Egyptian influence has come to be generally accepted, especially since it was recognized that the Cairo ostracon[30] indicates a date for this writer prior to the age of Solomon. But the majority view has not gone altogether unchallenged. E. Drioton produced linguistic arguments in 1957 and 1959[31] (which have been answered, however, point for point by R. J. Williams)[32] for a joint dependence of Amenemope and the relevant part of Proverbs on a Hebrew or Aramaic source. More recently J. Ruffle, in an M.A. thesis for Liverpool University, as yet unpublished, has argued that many of the resemblances between Amenemope and Proverbs rest on mistranslations of the former and emendations of the latter, while others could well be fortuitous, arising out of universal human situations. According to this thesis, this section of Proverbs is nourished by Old Testament forms and concepts, is shaped by the common tendencies and forms of proverbial sayings and didactic utterances, and has no special ties with Amenemope.

This is a salutary check to any careless acceptance of a prevailing opinion, and it very properly reopens a question which may have been prematurely closed. At the same time it should be recognized that it raises no dogmatic issues and needs no defense on such grounds—as if it were more fitting that Scripture should handle anonymous wisdom material than a named collection. Either way, revelation transfigures what it touches. Meanwhile, the publication of this thesis, with its new translation of Amenemope, will be awaited with interest.

3. *Numerical Sayings*. Comparative study is hampered here by the scarcity of Canaanite proverbial material so far published;[33] but the numerical series emerges as an ancient and favorite device, especially in Ugaritic narrative poetry, and therefore must no longer be thought a late development[34] when it appears in Proverbs 6:16 ff. and Proverbs 30. G. Sauer, in his study of Proverbs 30, *Die Sprüche Agurs*,[35] discusses particularly its aesthetic aspect, which he finds a means of fixing a relationship in the mind without tedium—a device however which would appeal neither to a very primitive nor to a mathematically sophisticated culture. He argues that Israel was ripe for this kind of thinking when she encountered it in the Canaanite milieu[36] but had outgrown it by the end of the Old Testament period. Another angle of approach is taken by W. M. W. Roth,[37] who distrusts such an emphasis as Sauer's on cultural development, and sets himself to analyze the use of numerical sayings in narrative, reflection, and exhortation. He concludes that their main function was to bring a degree of order into the mass of diverse information and obligation which confronts man in the realms of both nature and religion—thereby fulfilling in these spheres a purpose somewhat analogous to that of decalogues and dodecalogues within the Torah.[38]

It is appropriate to return to the subject of order, so characteristic of Proverbs, before passing to the book of Job. Proverbs itself concludes on such a note, in describing the ménage of the perfect wife, whose spotless house, a hive of industry and a boon to the poor (31:20), is the well-ordered world of this book in miniature. It is not the part of Proverbs to speak of the storm which could at any moment smite "the four corners of the house" (as Job's messenger was to put it) and bring it down. Yet this is a possibility which it would be anything but wisdom to ignore, and which the wisdom writings resolutely face. It is our next theme.

B. Job

Here, as in studies of Proverbs, recent years have brought a quantity of Near Eastern literature within general reach, notably the very ancient Sumerian poem, "Man and His God"[39] (edited by S. N. Kramer, who pieced together three fragments in Philadelphia (U.S.A.) with two in Istanbul), which shows that the problem of the innocent sufferer was already a live issue to the contemporaries of Abraham. This well-constructed poem, and the still more elaborate works, *Ludlul Bēl Nēmeqi* and the Babylonian Theodicy,[40] have some general resemblances to Job, with their descriptions of the victims' plight, and (in the Theodicy) the persistent dialogue between the orthodox friend and the outspoken sufferer.

For all this, it is the distinctiveness of Job that stands out from the comparison; and this is apparent not only in the central poem but in the prologue and epilogue. We shall look at the three sections in turn.

1. The Prologue. In passing, it is worth noting that this prose narrative is, to quote N. M. Sarna,[41] "saturated with poeticisms" and cast in an ancient epic style which convinces the same writer that "the detailed and consistent patriarchal setting must be regarded as genuine."[42] But the immediate concern is with its function in the book as a whole, where it establishes the fact that the suffering of Job—whatever may be the rationale of other cases—is neither random nor punitive nor purgative. As H. H. Rowley[43] has pointed out, to insist that "there is such a thing as innocent suffering," and that it can be even an honor and a service, is to remove the cruelest sting of such an experience. There are no such certainties in the Babylonian poems.

2. The Dialogue. The outstanding difference between Job and the non-biblical sufferers lies in his love for God. Admittedly he heaps reproaches on Him as his enemy and tormentor; but the pain of it is that he has once known Him as friend: "Thou hast *turned* cruel to me" (30:21) . Further, against all his immediate impressions, the deeper conviction of God's integrity keeps asserting itself unawares,[44] so that it is as unthinkable for him to buy back his prosperity with a false confession (27:2–6) —even if his own honesty had allowed it—as to throw up everything and trample on his religion (as the sufferer in the Theodicy threatened to do) .[45] The supreme blessing of his former days had been that, as he put it, "The friendship of God was upon my tent; . . . the Almighty was yet with me" (29:5, 4) . And this was not merely a religious way of saying that things had gone well for him, for he had known trouble even then; but "by his light I walked through darkness"—that was the difference. It is also the crucial difference between his "redeemer" saying (19:25–27) and the affirmation in *Ludlul* II: 119 f. which runs: "But I know the day . . . when among my friends, their Sun-god will have mercy."[46] To Job, the climax would be no less than to "see God." "My own eyes will see him unestranged."[47] It was to be granted sooner and more shatteringly than he expected (42:5, 6) , but it would fulfil all his desire.

3. The Epilogue. The Epilogue, often characterized as a misfit which shares the reward-and-punishment philosophy of Job's comforters, drives home in fact the lesson of the dialogue. Other tales of sufferers beside Job have happy endings; what is unique is God's commission to the

victim to intercede for his accusers, which highlights the spiritual issue
once more, and finally refutes their accusations. Vindicated, Job is given
back his wealth; but this is the overflowing of a cup already full.

Some attempt, finally, must be made to suggest the function of Job
within Scripture as a whole. In brief, Job can be seen as a preparation
for the gospel and a standing corrective to human complacency and
pride.

As preparation, Job emphasizes the darkness to be dispelled by the
New Testament and so presents the gospel in its true character as news
badly needed. It does this by asking some of the questions which could
receive only provisional answers before the Incarnation. The bitter out-
burst of 7:13, "What is man, that thou dost make so much of him?" and
the recurrent perplexity over God's sensitivity to human sin (7:20, "If
I sin, what do I do to thee?"; cf. 10:6; 13:26) are unresolved discords
until God *becomes* man and *bears* sin. It is the same with His disconcerting otherness—"He is not a man . . . ; there is no umpire between
us . . . " (9:32, 33) ; "Dost thou see as man sees?" (10:4)—and His
enigmatic foreknowledge (10:13). Even the question, "If a man die,
shall he live again?" (14:14), which Job comes to the brink of answering,
will have no resounding reply until the first Easter.

Secondly, as a corrective to complacency and pride, Job makes its
point partly by its vehement presentation of human misery, which is
still with us, and partly by its exposure of glib rationalizations. The fact
that God listened to Job and his friends in context and in depth, attend-
ing to the heartlessness behind the pious words, and the desperation behind Job's near-blasphemies, seems to have some bearing on the presence
of certain other violent passages in the Old Testament. If God could
take note of the passion for justice and the hunger for Himself which
created the pressure behind Job's invective, and treat them as ingredients
in a totality which was "right," we may infer that He will have made a
similar judgment of such a cry as that of Ps. 137:8 f. or 109:10 ff. Such
language has, by analogy with Job's, something of the function in a discussion of theodicy that hyperbole has in the realm of description: to be
not definitive but evocative.

So its exaggerations are not blemishes but necessary means of communicating the agony of the situation, to make it in some degree felt as well
as stated. Otherwise, any argument about suffering will be as much an
impertinence as was that of Job's comforters.

But Job was rebuked as well as praised. His demands that God should
explain Himself were "words without knowledge." Even the prologue
makes that point, in showing that a vital part of his own story was inaccessible to him; and the Lord's torrent of questions in the final chapters makes it clear that even the observable world is a masterpiece which

we can only peer at, never comprehend. It is significant that Job cries out in the end, not "I understand!" but "I repent." This is not to belittle rationality but to give it its proper sphere and God His proper honor—"that no flesh should glory in his presence."[48]

So the book of Job enforces the old lesson of Deuteronomy,[49] that "the secret things belong to God; but the things which are revealed belong to us . . . that we may do all the words of this law." It is not for God, in fact, to be called to account. It is for God to will, and for man to worship.

C. Ecclesiastes

Study of this book has been beset for a long time by the temptation to force it into categories which are foreign to it. There is now, however, a more general readiness to accept it on its own terms, without pruning away its paradoxes as the work of interpolators and correctors,[50] or classifying its author as sceptic, pessimist, or another of our familiar types. But there is still a tendency to relate the book to a supposed stage in Israel's religious evolution at which, as von Rad puts it, "belief in Jahweh's action in history grew weak" and Ecclesiastes "fell back on the cyclical way of thinking common to the East."[51] This rests on precarious assumptions. Even the date of the book is still an open question, to which current answers range over a large part of the Persian and Greek periods. Zimmerli, for example, inclines to the mid-third century, Dahood to the late fourth, and Albright now[52] to the fifth (preferring the second half but not ruling out the first). With so wide a spread of possibilities the attempt to match it to a passing phase of Israel's development (a doubtful procedure in any case) is hard to justify. It is also questionable whether the thinking of the ancient Near East was indeed cyclical. The idea largely rests on an etymology which connected the Hebrew *dwr* and the Akkadian *dūru* and *dāru* with an Arabic root for what is circular; and this is by no means proved.[53]

The remainder of this section will therefore be an attempt to expound what Qoheleth is saying and so to arrive at some understanding of his place in Scripture.

At the base of his thought is a quite uncompromising belief in God: a God who is not to be trifled with ("let your words be few," 5:2); a Creator (12:1) whose world has its own obstinate shape which we cannot iron out to our liking (7:13), and its own inexorable rhythm in which we find ourselves caught up (3:1 ff.).

A consequence of this is that we cannot extrapolate from the present. The pattern will change and go on changing, "so that man may not find out anything that will be after him" (7:14). What is more disturbing is that the present itself eludes us. "Man cannot find out the work that is done under the sun" (8:17)—cannot fathom, that is, the ordinary happenings around him; though he constructs his philosophies they will always be inadequate. "Even though a wise man claims to know, he cannot find it out" (8:17). It is poignantly expressed in 7:23 f.: "I said, 'I will be wise'; but it was far from me. That which is, is far off, and deep, very deep; who can find it out?"

This obscurity is intellectually teasing, but one can enjoy a good problem if little hangs on it. It is quite another matter if we are left to guess whether we are ultimately in the hands of friend or foe; and that is what we cannot by ourselves find out or take steps to control. This seems to be the sense of 9:1, in the light of its context and its own last phrase. To be "in the hand of God" has a reassuring ring to the man who knows Him; but to one who is groping for the meaning of life, uncertain "whether it is love or hate," it is daunting. We are anything but masters of our fate, and God has decreed it so.

This last point is emphatic. The treadmill which opens the book and expounds the refrain, "Vanity of vanities," is God's ordinance, "an unhappy business that God has *given* to the sons of men to be busy with" (1:13).[54] At times His decree will make sense to us—for the sinner, on the whole, gets an extra share of disappointment, as 2:28 points out; but in the end no one is exempt. The more one has, the more one has to lose (6:2); and lose it he will.

Much of the haunting quality of the book lies in its tireless search for some point of rest. But three things make the world a quicksand. The uncertainty of "time and chance" (9:11 f.) undermines all our maxims for success (and these are "as dear to the typical modern as they were to the writer of Proverbs").[55] Worse than this, wickedness is endemic and incurable (7:20; cf. 9:3): there can be no rest of heart while injustice (3:16; 4:1; 5:8; 7:7) and all the lesser scandals of public life are thriving. Worst of all, death has the last word in every human enterprise.

If there is nothing left after this analysis, it is precisely what the writer intends. His task has been to hold the reader to the fact that man is neither sovereign nor immortal, and that life is beyond his unaided power to make secure or even meaningful.

These negatives, even if they had stood alone, would have given the book a crucial role in Scripture as destroyer of illusions. But Qoheleth is no sceptic; he demolishes in order to build. His "vanity of vanities" is (to quote G. S. Hendry)[56] "not his verdict upon life in general, but only upon the . . . endeavour to treat the created world as an end in itself." So the final chapters, displaying a faith already glimpsed, e.g. in 3:17,[57] 8:12 f., challenge the reader to redeem the time: not paralyzed but stimulated by the uncertainties of life (11:1–6); not depressed by its shortness but gratefully enjoying its blessings, which are beautiful in their time (11:9 f.; cf. 2:24 ff.; 3:11 ff.; 5:18 ff.; etc.); above all, remembering, reverencing and serving God while he still has opportunity (12:1–14).

The somber colors are still the background to this final scene, which makes explicit what has been implied throughout: that the world has nothing permanent to offer, and God alone endures.

Even now there is no concession to self-seeking. God is not presented as man's haven or his prize, only as his proper Sovereign. It would be but a step beyond Qoheleth's affirmations of what is everlasting—the permanence of what God does (3:14) and the inklings of eternity He has implanted (3:11)—to the corollary that He will satisfy the thirst for immortality that He has given. But the step is not taken. If it had been, perhaps a trace of self-interest, of making use of God, could have edged its way into the picture. No Christian, for example, can be utterly sure, with everything to gain, how pure his love is. Qoheleth, with this truth in eclipse, can show us godliness disinterested, undazzled by reward. The fear of God in this book, like the obedience of Abraham on mount Moriah, has a quality only possible in the dark.

III. Wisdom and Revelation

It remains to draw together some of the threads we have already noticed running through the separate books, to gain some idea of the contribution of wisdom to Scripture as a whole.

First, there is its witness to the oneness of all God's works, from the universe itself to the smallest creature and the humblest activity. "In wisdom hast thou made them all." This brings into relation with a single Mind the multiplicity of people and things which seem unrelated and are at present divided. Its thrust is towards the gospel's announcement of the breaking down of barriers in Christ, and towards the climax when God will be all in all.

Secondly it establishes that the world is meaningful. "The works of the Lord" (as a wisdom Psalm declares) are not only "great"; they can be "*studied* by all those who have pleasure in them."[58] Admittedly our mental arrogance must be rebuked, as Job's was; and our inability to "find out" the scheme of things is tirelessly reiterated in Qoheleth.[59] But there is no retreat into irrationality. The pattern of the world is beyond us, but pattern it is. "Can you lead forth Mazzaroth *in their season?* . . . Do you know the *ordinances* of the heavens? . . . Who has put *wisdom* in the clouds?" (Job 38:32, 33, 36). In Qoheleth's words, again, God "has made everything beautiful in its time" (Eccl. 3:11); and man, with eternity in his mind, can stand clear enough of the process to recognize the presence of design, even while its totality escapes him.

Thirdly, this very emphasis on a meaningful world sharpens the problem of suffering. Here the role of wisdom is to teach us proper attitudes, rather than provide the answers—for this sphere remains among the "secret things" that "belong to the Lord."[60] So the teaching method in

Job is discussion, not pronouncement; and even when the Lord inter-
venes, it is to rain questions, not explanations, on the sufferer. To get
rid of glibness and half-truths is the task of this book, as much as to
inspire humility and faith.

Finally, the figure of personified Wisdom paves the way for the New
Testament's proclamation of the personal Word and Wisdom of God.
Wisdom is in any case a term which throws the emphasis on the one who
exercises it; and the use of such a word, rather than an impersonal term,
such as "order" or "law," for the principle that runs through all things,
carries the implication that God's active thought sustains the world. The
further step of portraying Wisdom personified, though only a poetic
device, strengthens this emphasis, and provides the New Testament with
part of the language it will need for its Christology.

To quote in conclusion what I have written elsewhere, "While the
New Testament took up the language of the Law and the Prophets to
describe [our Lord's] office among His people as Prophet, Priest and
King, it turned to . . . the thought-forms of the wise for terms to express
His relation to the universe and His one-ness with the Father, as the
One in whom all things were created and consist, in whom lie all the
treasures of wisdom and knowledge; Christ, in fact . . . the Wisdom of
God."[61]

Notes

1. E.g. 1 Kgs. 4:30 ff. (Heb. 5:10 ff.) ; Ezk. 28:2 ff.; Obad. 8.

2. Prov. 30:1; 31:1.

3. 1 Kgs. 4:34 (Heb. 5:14) ; 10:1 ff.

4. Solomon's cultural initiative is disputed by R. B. Y. Scott, "Solomon and the
Beginnings of Wisdom in Israel," VTS 3 (1955) : 262–79. Scott's arguments against accepting the testimony of I Kgs. 4:29–34 (Heb. 5:9–14) are briefly but effectively
criticized by W. M. W. Roth, Numerical Sayings in the Old Testament (Leiden: Brill,
1965), p. 24.

5. Cf. Eric W. Heaton, Daniel (London: SCM Press, 1956; Naperville, Ill.: Allenson,
Inc., 1966), p. 33.

6. Gerhard von Rad, "The Joseph Narrative and Ancient Wisdom," VTS 1 (1953) :
120–7 = von Rad, The Problem of the Hexateuch (New York: McGraw Hill: Edinburgh: Oliver and Boyd, 1966), pp. 292–300. Cf. the same author's Genesis (London:
SCM Press, 1961) and Old Testament Theology I (Edinburgh: Oliver and Boyd; New
York: Harper and Row, 1962), p. 432.

7. E. Gerstenberger, Wesen und Herkunft des "Apodiktischen Rechts," Wissenschaftliche Monographien zum Alten und Neuen Testament, 20 (Neukirchener Verlag, 1965),
pp. 110 ff.; cf. "Covenant and Commandment," JBL 84 (1965) : 38–51.

8. E. Nielsen, The Ten Commandments in New Perspective, Studies in Biblical
Theology ii, 7 (London: SCM Press, 1968), pp. 116 ff.

9. C. I. K. Story, "The Book of Proverbs and Northwest-Semitic Literature," JBL 64
(1945) : 319–37.

10. William F. Albright, From the Stone Age to Christianity, 2nd. ed. (New York:
Doubleday, 1957), p. 368. Cf. VTS 3 (1955) : 7 ff.

11. Roger N. Whybray, *Wisdom in Proverbs*, Studies in Biblical Theology 45 (London: SCM Press; Naperville, Ill.: A. R. Allenson; 1965), pp. 83 ff.

12. Albright, *op. cit.*, pp. 368 f.

13. E.g. "silver and gold," "hungry and thirsty," "left and right": *ibid.*, p. 326 ff.

14. *Ibid.*, p. 322.

15. Cf. E. I. Gordon, *Sumerian Proverbs* (Philadelphia: University of Pennsylvania, 1959), p. 16.

16. Cf. Mitchell J. Dahood, *Proverbs and Northwest Semitic Philology* (Rome: Pontifical Biblical Institute, 1964).

17. Whybray, *op. cit.*, p. 64.

18. By analogy with this, Paul would mean by his expression "my gospel" a gospel other than Christ's.

19. Cf. mention of the "fascinating possibility" of discovering some such development, Whybray, p. 31.

20. Christa Kayatz, *Studien in Proverbien 1–9*, Wissenschaftliche Monographien zum Alten und Neuen Testament, 22 (Neukirchener Verlag, 1966).

21. Text in Stephen R. K. Glanville, *Catalogue of Demotic Papyri*, II (London: British Museum, 1955).

22. Kayatz, *op. cit.*, p. 24; cf. Glanville, *op. cit.*, pp. xiv f.

23. Present indeed, but mostly implicit, in chapters 10 ff. Cf. Kayatz, *op. cit.*, pp. 7 ff.

24. Cf. Prov. 8:30, Aq., KJV; see however RV, RSV.

25. Cf. Prov. 7:4; 8:17.

26. Cf. Prov. 3:16.

27. Cf. Prov. 3:22.

28. Cf. Prov. 8:15 f.

29. Kayatz, *op. cit.*, p. 135.

30. See e.g., VTS 3 (1955) : 13; DOTT p. 173.

31. Etienne Drioton, *Mélanges Bibliques* (Paris: Bloud et Gay, 1957), pp. 254 ff.; *Sacra Pagina* (Paris: Gabalda, 1959), pp. 229 ff.

32. R. J. Williams, Journal of Egyptian Archaeology 47 (1961) : 100 ff.

33. Only one didactic "graded" numerical saying is known from Ugarit, and one (through Aḥikar) from Mesopotamia. Both use the form "two . . . (yea) three . . .": see ANET, 2nd ed., pp. 132 (iii. 17–21), 428 (vi, end).

34. So, e.g., H. Ranston, *The Old Testament Wisdom Books and Their Teaching* (London: Epworth Press, 1930), p. 57.

35. G. Sauer, *Die Sprüche Agurs*, Beiträge zur Wissenschaft vom Alten und Neuen Testament 84, (Stuttgart: Kohlhammer, 1963).

36. Sauer, *op. cit.*, p. 77.

37. W. M. W. Roth, *Numerical Sayings in the Old Testament*, VTS 13 (1965).

38. On the *form* of "graded" sayings (e.g. "three things . . . yea four . . .") see further Roth, "The Numerical Sequence $x/x + 1$ in the Old Testament," VT 12 (1962) : 300–11. Cf. R. B. Y. Scott, ed., *Proverbs, Ecclesiastes* in the *Anchor Bible* (New York: Doubleday, 1965), p. 59.

39. S. N. Kramer, ed., VTS 3 (1955) : 170–82.

40. Texts in Wilfrid G. Lambert, *Babylonian Wisdom Literature* (New York: Oxford University Press; Oxford: Clarendon; 1960) pp. 32 ff., 70 ff. Also in ANET pp. 434 ff., 439 f.

41. Nahum M. Sarna, "Epic Substratum in the Prose of Job," JBL 76 (1957) : 13–25. Agreeing with Sarna as to the "poeticisms," Marvin H. Pope, *Job* in the *Anchor Bible* (New York: Doubleday, 1965) sets out most of chapters 1 and 2 (all the speeches) as verse.

42. Sarna, *op. cit.*, p. 25.

43. Harold H. Rowley, "The Book of Job and Its Meaning," BJRL 41 (1958–9) :

167–207, reprinted in *From Moses to Qumran* (London: Lutterworth; New York; Association Press, 1963), pp. 141–83.

44. E.g. Job 13:7,10; 16:19–21; 31:13–15.

45. Lambert, *op. cit.*, p. 79 (1.135); ANET p. 440.

46. Lambert, *op. cit.*, p. 46; cf. a slightly different translation in ANET p. 436a.

47. Job 19:27, Pope, *loc. cit.*

48. I Cor. 1:29, KJV.

49. Deut. 29:29.

50. But see O. S. Rankin (IB, 5, 1956) and E. Jones in the Torch Commentary (London: SCM Press, 1961).

51. Von Rad, *Old Testament Theology*, p. 454.

52. William F. Albright, *Yahweh and the Gods of Canaan* (London: Athlone, 1968), p. 227.

53. See the careful discussion in O. Loretz, *Qohelet und der Alte Orient* (Freiburg: Herder, 1964), pp. 248 ff. Loretz rejects this etymology, as does the University of Chicago *Assyrian Dictionary* (D, p. 108) in respect of the Akkadian. For a more recent discussion see P. R. Ackroyd in JSS 13 (1968): 3–10.

54. Eccl. 7:29 makes it clear that this is not comparable with the Babylonian Theodicy's doctrine of an arbitrary handicap: "With lies, not truth (the gods) endowed them for ever" (1.280); DOTT p. 102; cf. ANET p. 440.

55. J. C. Rylaarsdam, *Proverbs to Song of Solomon* (London: SCM, Layman's Bible Commentaries, 1964), p. 125.

56. G. S. Hendry, "Ecclesiastes," *New Bible Commentary*, ed., Francis Davidson (London: Inter-Varsity Fellowship; Grand Rapids: Eerdmans; 1953), p. 538.

57. But possibly judgment in this book means no more than death, cutting short all human enterprises; Loretz, *op. cit.*, pp. 291 f.

58. Ps. 111:2.

59. Eccl. 3:11; 7:14; 8:17; 9:1; 11:5.

60. Deut. 29:29.

61. Derek Kidner, *Proverbs* (London: Tyndale Press; Chicago: Inter-Varsity Press; 1964), p. 16.

IV. PROPHETS

—9—

STUDY OF THE PROPHETS SINCE WORLD WAR II

Robert L. Alden

The guidelines that characterize the most popular evaluations of the Biblical prophets came into being generations before the present day. It is nearly impossible to find a genuinely new view of interpretation in the past twenty-five years. The negative nature of higher criticism that characterized the study of the prophets at the turn of the century still characterizes that study today. Of course, this indictment is a sweeping one and does not refer to those pockets of evangelical resistance. Confessedly, evangelicals have not produced much that is genuinely novel either, but at least their contributions are less discouraging.

Names such as H. W. Robinson and T. H. Robinson, Gunkel, Holscher, W. Robertson Smith, Duhm, Skinner, and Eissfeldt are still the most quoted and revered. All of these wrote before World War II. In evangelical circles men such as Calvin, Hengstenberg, Keil, Delitzsch, Green, and Alexander are the opinion formers. These men wrote even earlier.

Nevertheless our generation has not been altogether bereft of brilliant minds and devoted scholars who have spent their energies in pursuit of those elusive answers to some ever-present and ever-pressing questions regarding the prophets of the Old Testament. If the books and commentaries produced have been many, the articles in periodicals have been numberless. To list them would require a volume in itself. It is the intent of this paper, therefore, to list only the major contributions representing the various opinions.

There has been no giving of ground on the part of those whose basic presupposition is that the Bible is solely a human production and is therefore not necessarily true, accurate, or without error. Hence, despite archaeological advances and refinements of many uncertainties, the majority of those who produce books about the Bible do not believe it to be the infallible Word of God. Some of the tenets of negative Biblical criticism have been altered but not denied. As an example, although Wellhausen is now criticized or ignored, his basic thesis that the Pentateuch is a compilation centuries later than Moses still has the greatest following. The debate today is on the nature of the transmission of the information, whether orally or in writing. Assumed as inherent in this question is the "fact" of alteration, addition, or subtraction during transmission.

For the evangelical scholar who believes in an inerrant God-breathed autograph, the matter of compilation is less significant a question. He also believes in the divine superintendence of the Holy Spirit over the writings He inspired, so the question of transmission is of less moment for him. This presupposition still provides the watershed for Biblical scholarship. Although it sounds harsh, it can rather accurately be said that from the negative critical camp little of positive, constructive understanding of the texts has been offered. It is true that many new and novel ways of dissecting the prophets have been suggested; a few new identifications for the "Servant of the Lord" have been made, and we have new answers to the question of the compilation of the older Biblical books. But the more perplexing questions still remain unanswered. Some of these are: What was the relationship between the prophets and the monarchy and the established religion? Who exactly penned the first copies of the written prophecies and when? As they were uttered, were they taken by dictation by a disciple, digested and condensed? Or were they, perhaps, expanded by the prophet himself after he had spoken them? Were some of them ever given orally? These are questions of initial criticism. We also have questions of deeper criticism: What is the significance of Ezekiel's temple? What is the change of attitude at Isaiah 40? What is the meaning of some of those enigmatic creatures in Daniel's book?

The past twenty-five years of study in the prophets have produced few answers to questions of this sort. Probably ninety-eight percent of what we know about the prophets, their times, and their message was already written in some commentary in the nineteenth century and probably ninety percent was known to the Reformers.

Yet of the production of books there has been no dearth. Let us begin this catalog and commentary of the most important contributions since World War II by noting new Bible translations which include the prophets.

I. Translations

The best known new translation is the Revised Standard Version (New York: Nelson) which was completed in 1952. Apart from several now famous inadvisable renderings in the prophets it is not as different from the Authorized Version as many people think. It is not as novel as the Berkeley Version (Grand Rapids: Zondervan, 1959), for instance, which was produced partly to answer the RSV. A Catholic version of the RSV has been produced, but there are no significant changes in the prophets (New York: Nelson, 1966). The Roman Church's imprimatur also appears on the Confraternity translations that are slowly replacing the Douay Version (New York: Catholic Book, 1962). The prophets have been translated afresh. But what may be more popular than this rather standard version is *The Jerusalem Bible* (Garden City, N.Y.: Doubleday, 1966), which is the English Bible based on the work behind, but not translated from, *La Bible de Jerusalem* (Paris: Les Éditions du Cerf, 1961). This work of fine Catholic scholars is more of a paraphrase than a literal translation. Even a hasty investigation will show this. For this reason it reads easily and understandably. The problem is that it may not necessarily represent what the Biblical author was saying.

Two other translations are enjoying popularity among Protestants and evangelicals in particular: *The Amplified Bible* (Grand Rapids: Zondervan, 1965) and Kenneth Taylor's *Living Prophecies* (Wheaton: Tyndale, 1965). Actually this latter contains only the minor prophets, Daniel, and Revelation. The major prophets are included in his *Living Psalms and Proverbs* (Wheaton: Tyndale, 1967). While *The Amplified Bible* is laborious to read because of the piling up of synonyms and synonymous phrases, it is in itself a handy commentary. What was said regarding *The Jerusalem Bible* is also true of the Taylor's series. One ought not to replace his standard translation with it. Another translation which must be mentioned is *Four Prophets* (New York: Macmillan, 1963) by J. B. Phillips, translator of the *New Testament in Modern English*. This is his first Old Testament translation and includes Amos, Hosea, Micah, and Isaiah 1–35.

To this point I have said nothing of the Dead Sea Scrolls, which are indeed the most significant discoveries of our generation. The later editions of Kittel's *Biblica Hebraica* (Stuttgart: Privileg. Württ. Bibelanstalt) have footnotes to some of the prophets regarding alternate readings found in the Dead Sea Scrolls. The world still waits for a complete critical text compiled of all the scrolls, to compare with the generally accepted Masoretic text. It is assumed that the newer translations of the Old Testament have made use of what Qumran material was available to each although some do not state it.

It is proper to include here mention of the *New Scofield Reference Bible* (New York: Oxford, 1967). Although a few changes have been made in the translations, it is basically the Authorized Version (KJV) that is used with archaisms replaced. The notes, although altered in places in the light of long-standing criticism, still represent the dispensational theology of the Plymouth Brethren, Darby, and Scofield himself.

Oxford also produced the *Oxford Annotated Bible* (eds., H. G. May and B. Metzger, New York: 1962) which has brief introductory articles and comments on the RSV text.

II. General Publications

Two noteworthy periodicals have commenced publication in the period of our consideration. First is *Interpretation: A Journal of Bible and Theology* and second is *Vetus Testamentum*. The former is a quarterly begun in 1946 by members of the faculty of Union Theological Seminary in Richmond, Virginia. It enjoys a degree of popularity among preachers as well as teachers. The latter, founded in 1950, contains articles of a more technical nature in English, German, and French. The old standard periodical is still the *Journal of Biblical Literature*.

Sets of commentaries contain much of the scholarship of any generation. At the beginning of the list there stands the monument to liberal scholarship, *The Interpreter's Bible* (New York: Abingdon-Cokesbury, 1951–57). This twelve-volume set contains, besides general articles on the whole Bible, Dead Sea Scrolls, etc., a kind of three-layer text. On top is the Scripture text itself, both KJV and RSV; in the middle is the exegesis; and on the bottom the exposition. The format is commendable. The exposition and exegesis to one book may be by different men. R. B. Y. Scott wrote on Isaiah 1–39 and James Muilenburg on chapters 40–66. Other significant authors are: J. P. Hyatt, H. G. May, Arthur Jeffrey, D. W. Thomas, R. C. Dentan, and J. D. Smart. Volumes of the *Soncino Bible* (London: Soncino) began appearing in 1945. These contain the Hebrew text, an English translation, and selected comments from ancient Jewish rabbis translated into English.

There were also parts of complete sets of commentaries produced in our period as well as some smaller sets which deserve mention. Carl F. H. Henry edited a three-volume set, *The Biblical Expositor* (Philadelphia: Holman, 1960). Recently the *Wesleyan Bible Commentary* (Grand Rapids: Eerdmans, 1964) has appeared, its six volumes edited by C. W. Carter. As the above two represent an evangelical opinion, so does the *Beacon Bible Commentary* (Kansas City, Mo.: Nazarene, 1965) produced by Nazarene and Holiness scholarship. Although the *New International Commentary* is well on its way in the New Testament, the Old Testament readers have so far received only Edward J. Young's three volumes on Isaiah (Grand Rapids: Eerdmans, 1965–68). If the other books continue to be of such high and commendable value, this commentary will become the outstanding contribution of evangelical scholarship for the century.

Zondervan Publishing House has produced a number of reprints such as Alexander on Isaiah (1953) and Fairbairn on Ezekiel (1960); but their most popular offering has been the one-volume condensed commentary of Matthew Henry (1960). Though old, this monumental work is still wholesome milk and solid meat for the Bible student. Eerdmans has published Keil and Delitzsch in English (1949) as well as Calvin (1960). These are considered by many to be the best conservative commentary sets on the Old Testament. J. Sidlow Baxter's more popular commentary on the entire Bible, *Explore the Book* (Grand Rapids: Zondervan, 1960) is also widely used.

III. Commentaries on Individual Books

A. Isaiah

The listing and discussion of commentaries on individual books begins with those on the prophecy of Isaiah. J. Yeoman Muckle who published *Isaiah 1–39* (Naperville, Ill.: Allenson Inc., 1959) represents a sadly typical attempt at understanding the greatest prophet of the Old Testament without seeing Christ therein. Elmer A. Leslie, along with Duhm (*Das Buch Jesaja,* 2nd ed., Göttingen: Vandenhoeck und Ruprecht, 1902) of the preceding generation, advocated three Isaiahs in his well-received work, *Isaiah: Chronologically Arranged, Translated, and Interpreted* (New York: Abingdon, 1963). The title alone is enough to inform the reader of the number of Isaiahs held by G. A. F. Knight: his *Deutero-Isaiah: A Theological Commentary on Isaiah 40–55* was published in 1965 by Abingdon. J. D. Smart, on the other hand, holds to the unity of Isaiah 40–66, albeit of the exilic period, in his *History and Theology in Second Isaiah: A Commentary on Isaiah 35, 40–66* (Philadelphia: Westminster, 1966). In the same vein is S. Paul Schilling's *Isaiah Speaks,* published in 1959 (New York: Crowell). In 1953 U. E. Simon wrote *A Theology of Salvation: A Commentary on Isaiah xl-lv* (New York: Macmillan).

In addition to his three-volume commentary on Isaiah mentioned above, the late Dr. E. J. Young also produced two special studies on the same prophet. In 1954 there appeared *Studies in Isaiah* (Grand Rapids: Eerdmans). The largest part of that book deals with "The Study of Isaiah since the time of Joseph Addison Alexander" and "The Immanuel Prophecy." In 1958 there appeared *Who Wrote Isaiah?* (Grand Rapids: Eerdmans). Obviously this book deals with the question of authorship; throughout, the unity and the eighth century B.C. authorship of the prophecy is claimed and defended. A similar work by Young's predecessor appeared in 1950 when Oswald T. Allis wrote *The Unity of Isaiah* (Philadelphia: Presbyterian and Reformed).

Among other noteworthy special studies on Isaiah is C. R. North's *The Suffering Servant in Deutero-Isaiah* (London: Oxford; New York:

Oxford University Press; 1948), which is now a standard work on this subject with over three hundred entries in the bibliography. Incidentally, North also produced a short commentary on *Isaiah 40–55* (Oxford: Clarendon; Naperville, Ill.: Allenson, Inc.; 1949). In 1949 Ivar Engnell made a study on *The Call of Isaiah*. (Uppsala: Uppsala Universitets årsskrift, 1949). Sigmund Mowinckel did a brief personality study of the great prophet titled simply *Jesaja* (Oslo: Gyldendal Norsk, 1949). The latest contribution is John L. McKenzie's *Second Isaiah* in the *Anchor Bible* (New York: Doubleday, 1968).

Directly opposite to conservatism is the work by Sheldon H. Blank. His *Prophetic Faith in Isaiah* (New York: Harper, 1958) is a typical example of the liberal scholarship which holds that Isaiah, the son of Amoz of Jerusalem, did not write the entire book and that no man before Christ could speak of Him since there is no such thing as predictive prophecy. Hence he sees, with most Jewish interpreters, the nation as the suffering servant and, with many non-evangelical scholars, not only a duality or a triplicity of authorship but also many fragments from an unknown number of appenders, emendators, editors, and redactors. Back on the conservative side we might mention Harry Ironside's commentary *Expository Notes on the Prophet Isaiah* (New York: Loizeaux, 1952), as well as G. L. Robinson's *The Book of Isaiah in Fifteen Studies* (Grand Rapids: Baker, 1954).

B. Jeremiah

The material produced on Jeremiah is not as voluminous as that on Isaiah but is nevertheless considerable. The following are a few of the more noteworthy representatives of various points of view. Elmer A. Leslie wrote *Jeremiah* in 1954 (New York: Abingdon) and it is a thorough piece of work reflecting the opinions of negative criticism. Also from Abingdon comes J. Philip Hyatt's *Jeremiah, Prophet of Courage and Hope* (1958), a non-technical investigation into the content of the book. Although this volume can prove an aid to the understanding of Jeremiah's prophecy, the author's unorthodox theology eventuates in unorthodox conclusions, such as his belittling of the doctrine of human depravity. In the series *Handbuch zum Alten Testament* edited by Otto Eissfeldt, W. Rudolph produced the commentary on Jeremiah in 1947 (Tübingen: Mohr). He has a unique division of the material into stratas A, B, and C, following a kind of Mowinckel motif. Naturally this novel view is not well received, but it should not detract from the otherwise high quality of this scholarly work. A. Weiser has produced a two-volume commentary, *Das Buch der Prophet Jeremia* (Göttingen: Vandenhoeck und Ruprecht, 1952, 1955) for the German series, *Das Alte Testament Deutsch*. He provides the reader with rhythmical translations of the poetic sections of the prophet and also incorporates an interpretation which makes much of the cult as over against politics. The second volume contains the introductory essays. Professor Blank has also written on this prophet: *Jeremiah: Man and Prophet* (Cincinnati: Hebrew Union College Press, 1961).

A series of translations with commentaries under the name *The Anchor Bible* began to be published by Doubleday in 1964. The only prophet, other than Isaiah 40–66, to be written on up to this time is Jeremiah, by John Bright. As with the other contributors, Bright makes much use of our expanded knowledge of the ancient Near East through archaeology. He has been accused of conservatism.

On the conservative side, Theodore F. K. Laetsch produced *Jeremiah* (St. Louis: Concordia) in 1952. He maintains the unity of the book and with a certain warmth comments on the noncontroversial elements of this great prophecy.

By way of special studies which have to do with Jeremiah one must note Ivar P. Seierstad's *Die Offenbarungserlebnisse der Propheten Amos, Jesaja und Jeremia* (Oslo: Dybwad, 1946). As a study of revelation it complements Mowinckel's *Die Erkenntnis Gottes bei den Alttestament-lichen Profeten* which came out a few years earlier (Oslo: Norsk Teologisk Tidsskrift, 1941).

C. Ezekiel

The struggle to solve the time-space problem of Ezekiel continues. W. A. Irwin, in 1943, set out to answer the question in an objective way in his book, *The Problem of Ezekiel* (Chicago: Univ. of Chicago). He was not successful. In 1945 appeared the Norwegian scholar Messel's work, *Ezechielfragen,* which explains Ezekiel as having never left Palestine. According to Messel, the prophecy has been heavily glossed. Carl G. Howie put his hand to the problem in his work, *The Date and Composition of Ezekiel* (Philadelphia: Society of Biblical Literature, 1950) with more conservative conclusions. Van den Born changed his mind between the time he wrote *De historische situatie van Ezechiels prophetic* (Paris: Desclée de Brouwer, 1947) and *Ezechieluit de grondtekst vertaald en uitgelegd* (Roermond: Romen und Zonen, 1954). In the earlier work he agreed with Auvray who held in *Ezéchiel* (Paris: Éditions du Cerf, 1947) that Ezekiel started in Jerusalem but had a second inaugural vision in Babylon after the thirteenth year of Jehoiachin's captivity. Van den Born's later work maintains the possibility that the main part of the book is a product of the post-exilic period.

Holding to the traditional opinion is Georg Fohrer. In 1952 he wrote *Die Hauptprobleme des Buches Ezechiel* (Berlin: Topelmann), and in 1955 he shared with Kurt Galling in the production of *Ezechiel* for the *Handbuch zum Alten Testament* (Tübingen: Mohr, 1955). In 1953 Harold H. Rowley produced a study of Ezekiel which is both rich in bibliography as well as valuable in its own right, as contributing to the answers regarding this prophecy. A relatively conservative viewpoint appears in his *The Book of Ezekiel in Modern Study* (Manchester: John Rylands Library, 1953). Numbers 8 and 9 in *Harper's Annotated Bible* is J. A. Bewer's two-volume work, *The Book of Ezekiel* (New York: Harper, 1954). This relatively popular commentary presents the traditional view of Ezekiel's two loci of operation, but the author does not maintain that Ezekiel is responsible for the entire book as we now have it. H. L. Ellison's commendable work, *Ezekiel, The Man and His Message* (Grand Rapids: Eerdmans, 1956), although it pleases neither the dispensationalist nor the amillennialist, is written from a conservative viewpoint. In the year of 1955 appeared Aalders' *Ezechiel verklaard* (Kampen: Lok) which presents the view that maintains the historicity, integrity, authenticity, and accuracy of Ezekiel. Then there is Neil's *Jeremiah and Ezekiel* (London: Lutterworth, 1964). From a homiletical perspective we have Andrew W. Blackwood's *Ezekiel: Prophecy of Hope,* published in 1965 (Grand Rapids: Baker).

D. Daniel

Apart from Isaiah, perhaps no Old Testament book, certainly no prophet, has been subjected to more varied and drastic theories than has the book of Daniel. Not only do the well-known visions perpetually plague Daniel's interpreters but the dates for both him and his book are set at widely divergent points. Since World War II no new interpretations or novel solutions have come to light. Basically the conservatives contend for the authenticity of the book. They believe Daniel the Jew really existed in the court of Nebuchadnezzar and Belshazzar; they believe in the miracles recorded in the book, and they believe in true predictive prophecy, "pre-eventum."

To begin this abridged list of authors who chose to write on the prophet-statesman we have H. L. Ginsberg of the Jewish Theological Seminary who in 1948 produced *Studies in Daniel* (New York: J. T. S. of America). He discovers the work of six Aramaic authors and glossators who produced the book between 300 and 150 B.C. In the next year, 1949, two other works on Daniel appeared. Herbert C. Leupold wrote *Exposition of Daniel* (Columbus, Ohio: Wartburg, now Augsburg Press in Minneapolis) and Edward J. Young wrote *The Prophecy of Daniel* (Grand Rapids: Eerdmans). Young makes a strong case for the sixth century B.C. origin of the book. Concerning the visions of the four kingdoms—another watershed of interpretation—Young identifies the last as Rome, not Greece or the Seleucids as most liberal commentators maintain. He does not postpone the seventieth week as dispensationalists do. Young was unable to identify Darius the Mede, but ten years later John C. Whitcomb wrote a commendable monograph on that elusive monarch (*Darius the Mede,* Grand Rapids: Eerdmans, 1959). His identification of Darius with "Gubaru" is cogently presented and substantially documented. Young wrote two smaller books entitled *The Messianic Prophecies of Daniel* (Grand Rapids: Eerdmans, 1955) and *Daniel's Vision of the Son of Man* (London: Tyndale, 1958). Of similar orientation is Robert D. Culver and his *Daniel and the Latter Days* (Old Tappan, N.J.: Revell, 1954) and Philip R. Newell, *Daniel the Man Greatly Beloved and His Prophecies* (Chicago: Moody, 1951).

On the liberal side with its widely varying opinions, we have Aage Bentzen, who in 1952 produced a second edition of his commentary for the series *Handbuch zum Alten Testament* (Tübingen: Mohr, first edition, 1937). It is a thorough work which takes account of all opinions regarding Daniel. Bentzen believes that Daniel was written ca. 165 B.C. Two others who share this common critical view are J. A. Bewer, *The Book of Daniel* (New York: Harper, 1955) and E. W. Heaton, whose 1956 effort bears the same title (New York: Macmillan).

In this decade we have a collection by Donald J. Wiseman and others, *Notes on Some Problems in the Book of Daniel,* published by Tyndale (1965). Kenneth A. Kitchen uses half of the pages to argue for a sixth century B.C. date for the Aramaic of Daniel. Lastly, in N. W. Porteous' *Daniel, A Commentary* (Philadelphia: Westminster, 1965), concessions to conservative contentions are few, and adherence to the popular critical opinions is strong.

E. The Minor Prophets

Before dealing with the individual minor prophets let us note several works which deal with them as a whole. The prolific Artur Weiser wrote the first volume of *Das Buch der zwölf Kleinen Propheten* (Göttingen: Vandenhoeck und Ruprecht) in 1949 for the series *Das Alte Testament Deutsch,* and Karl Elliger completed the second volume in 1950. The former was responsible for Hosea through Micah while the latter covers Nahum through Malachi. George L. Robinson wrote *The Twelve Minor Prophets* (Grand Rapids: Baker) which appeared in 1952. Another conservative commentary or introduction is Jack Lewis' *The Minor Prophets* (Austin, Texas: Sweet), which appeared in 1966.

The crucial element for interpreting the prophecy of Hosea is one's understanding of the autobiographical sections. Evangelicals are still divided on the questions of Gomer's original morality and over her literal existence.

Heading this select list of post-war contributions is H. Wheeler Robinson's *Two Hebrew Prophets: Studies in Hosea and Ezekiel* (London: Lutterworth; Naperville, Ill.: Allenson, Inc.; 1948). He regards the first chapter as biography and the third as autobiography. The commentary on Hosea which Van Gelderen left unfinished at his death in 1945 was completed by W. H. Gispen and published in 1953 (Kampen: Kok). These two professors of the Free University of Amsterdam stoutly oppose tampering with the text while at the same time present sound linguistic scholarship. That same year Norman Snaith wrote *Mercy and Sacrifice: A Study of the Book of Hosea* (London: S.C.M.), a theological word study.

The year 1966 witnessed two significant projects on Hosea. J. M. Ward produced the first full-length commentary on the prophecy in half a century, *Hosea: A Theological Commentary* (New York: Harper & Row). Although Ward is more interested in the theology of the book than in exegesis, his commentary is a substantial work. That same year appeared *Studies on the Books of Hosea and Amos* which consisted of papers of the seventh and eighth meetings of Die O. T. Werkgemeenskap in Suid Afrika. These are all from a conservative point of view. The latest conservative work is David Hubbard's *With Bands of Love* (Grand Rapids: Eerdmans, 1967).

The only noteworthy study devoted solely to Joel is Arvid S. Kapelrud's *Joel Studies* (Uppsala: Lundequistska) which appeared in 1948. Reflecting the Scandinavian school, Kapelrud sees Joel as a temple-prophet who lived around 600 B.C. The strength of the *Studies* is in the large use of the Ras Shamra materials. An example is the extensive study on the word *haṣ-ṣᵉpônî* which occurs in Joel 2:20 and means "northern (er) " or something similar.

Amos is perhaps the most popular of the so-called minor prophets, at least more seem to choose to write about him than any other. From a rather conservative point of view is Andre Neher's *Amos: contribution à l'étude du prophétisme* (Paris: J. Vrin, 1950). Five years later appeared R. S. Cripps' second edition of *A Critical and Exegetical Commentary on the Book of Amos* (London: S.P.C.K.; Naperville, Ill.: Allenson, Inc.; 1955). It does not differ essentially from his 1929 edition.

J. D. W. Watts has produced two books on Amos in our period. In 1955 appeared his *Vision and Prophecy in Amos* (Grand Rapids: Eerdmans), which contains the novel thesis that the book is a composite of two documents, both going back to Amos. The fact that one source is Judaic and the other Israelitish explains such passages as the restoration of the House of David. In 1966 appeared his *Studying in the Book of Amos* (Nashville: Broadman). One of the most valuable books on Amos appeared in 1961: Kapelrud's *Central Ideas in Amos* (Oslo: Aschehoug). Like his *Joel Studies,* mentioned above, much is made of Ugaritic literature, which sheds light on, for example, a rare word like *nōqᵉḏîm* (herdsmen) of 1:1. In addition there have been published other less scholarly but nevertheless noteworthy works from conservative pens. We mention Ralph L. Murray's *Plumblines and Fruit Baskets* (Nashville: Broadman, 1966); P. Kelley's *The Book of Amos* (Grand Rapids: Baker, 1966); D. Garland's *Amos* (Grand Rapids: Zondervan, 1966); and Roy L. Honeycutt's *Amos and His Message* (Nashville: Broadman, 1963).

Regarding Obadiah, the smallest of Old Testament books, only two works are to be mentioned, both from a conservative point of view. In 1947 Frank Gaebelein wrote *The Servant and the Dove: Obadiah and Jonah* (New York: Our Hope) and twenty years later John D. Watts wrote *Obadiah: A Critical and Exegetical Commentary* (Grand Rapids: Eerdmans, 1967).

Jonah has attracted a little more study than Obadiah but not much. Besides Gaebelein's treatment mentioned above, there is the conservative view maintained by Aalders in his pamphlet which appeared in 1948, *The Problem of the Book of Jonah* (London: Tyndale) and by Theodore Epp in *Jonah the Prophet* (Lincoln: Back to the Bible, 1960). Two works from the negative critical school appeared in 1950: von Rad's sixteen-page pamphlet, *Der Prophet Jona* (Nuremberg: Laetare), and G. A. F. Knight's *Ruth and Jonah* (London: S.C.M. Press; Naperville, Ill.: Allenson, Inc.). In 1956 James H. Kennedy published *Studies in the Book of Jonah* (Nashville: Broadman).

On Micah mention will be made only of *A Study of the Prophet Micah* by B. A. Copass and E. L. Carlson, which Baker published in 1950. Micah is credited with the entire book, except for the "mountain of the Lord" passage in Chapter 4. Besides the commentary, which is substantially done, there is a fine section on the history of prophecy in Israel, an appendix on the Moabite stone, and another on servant worship.

In 1947 one of the more noteworthy of the Swedish school, Alfred Haldar, wrote *Studies in the Book of Nahum* (Uppsala: Lundequistska). Like Kapelrud, he makes full use of Ugaritic and other extra-biblical materials. A more traditional approach is found in Walter Maier's commentary *Nahum* which appeared in 1959 (St. Louis: Concordia).

For Haggai one must note two studies. From the conservative point of view is Richard Wolff's *The Book of Haggai* (Grand Rapids: Zondervan); and from the critical school, H. W. Wolff's *Haggai* (Kreis Moers: Erziehungsvereins Neukirchen, 1951) —a thorough study of all aspects of the prophet.

Zechariah, the longest minor prophet, has not often been treated in a separate volume. Charles Feinberg wrote *God Remembers: A Study of the Book of Zechariah* (Wheaton: Van Kampen, 1951). In our decade Merrill Unger produced his *Commentary on Zechariah* (Grand Rapids: Zondervan, 1963).

Significant post-war publication on Malachi has yet to appear.

III. The Prophetic Movement

In addition to the commentaries and special studies in the individual prophets there have been many other books on the practice of prophecy and the preachments of the prophets. Much stress is put on the ecstatic element both in the preliterary and in the literary prophets. Most of this stress comes from the liberal camp. Such titles as the following point in that direction: *The Cultic Prophets in Ancient Israel* by Aubrey Johnson (Cardiff: University of Wales; Mystic, Conn.: Verry; 1944) ; *Associations of Cult Prophets Among the Ancient Semites* by Alfred Haldar (Uppsala: Almquist and Wiksells, 1945) ; *Die Offenbarungserlebnisse der Propheten Amos, Jesaja, und Jeremia* by Ivar P. Seierstad (Oslo: Dybwad, 1946) ; *Inspiration and Revelation in the Old Testament* by H. Wheeler Robinson (Oxford: Clarendon; New York: Oxford University Press; 1946) ; *The Hebrew Prophetic Consciousness* by H. Knight (London: Lutterworth, 1947) ; *Literary and Psychological Aspects of the Hebrew Prophets* by George Widengren (Uppsala: Lundequistska, 1948) ; *L'Essence de Prophétisme* by Andre Néher (Paris: Universitaires de France, 1955) ; and W. C. Klein's *The Psychological Pattern of Old Testament Prophecy* (Evanston: Seabury-Western Theological Seminary, 1956) . On the matter of prophetic transmission one must note Mowinckel's *Prophecy and Tradition* (Oslo: Dybwad, 1946) , and Claus Westermann's *Basic Forms of Prophetic Speech* (Philadelphia: Westminster, 1967) . To complete the listings in this section are Harold H. Rowley's essays on the prophets in his *Men of God* (New York: Nelson, 1963) and one of the most commendable books of all, Johannes Lindblom's *Prophecy in Ancient Israel* (Philadelphia: Fortress, 1962) .

General works on the prophets and their message are legion. We will list but a few of them. J. Phillip Hyatt wrote *Prophetic Religion* in 1947 (New York: Abingdon) and in the same year appeared C. C. Torrey's *Lives of the Prophets* (Philadelphia: Society of Biblical Literature). With the same title appeared Stephen Caiger's popular study in 1949 (New York: Macmillan). Of the same popular sort is John Peterson's *The Goodly Fellowship of the Prophets* (New York: Scribner's, 1948) . Norman Gottwald wrote *All the Kingdoms of the Earth* (New York: Harper & Row, 1964) and *A Light to the Nations* (New York: Harper's, 1959) . The next year saw Curt Kuhl's *The Prophets of Israel* (Richmond, Virginia: John Knox). Two Jewish works deserve mention in this general category: the prophetic sections in Yehizkiel Kaufmann's *The Religion of Israel* (Chicago: Univ. of Chicago, 1960) and Abraham Heschel's *The Prophets* (New York: Jewish Publication Society, 1962) . That same year Bernhard Anderson and Walter Harrelson edited *Israel's Prophetic Heritage* (New York: Harper & Row). In 1963 B. D. Napier expanded his *Interpreter's Bible Dictionary* article (Vol. III, pp. 896–919, Nashville: Abingdon, 1962) into the book, *Prophets in Perspective* (New York: Abingdon). In this section belongs the conservative work of Edward J. Young, *My Servants the Prophets* (Grand Rapids: Eerdmans, 1955) . One of the most outstanding collections was *Studies in Old Testament Prophecy* given to T. H. Robinson, edited by Harold H. Rowley in 1950 (Edinburgh: T. & T. Clark; Naperville, Ill.: Allenson, Inc.) .

In a category by itself is Oswald T. Allis' *Prophecy and the Church* (Philadelphia: Presbyterian and Reformed, 1945) which is a critique of dispensationalism's approach to prophecy. The year 1956 saw the English reprint of a monumental four-volume work on messianic prophecy, Hengstenberg's *Christology of the Old Testament* (Grand Rapids: Kregel). That same year another conservative, Aaron Kligerman, published *Messianic Prophecy in the Old Testament* (Grand Rapids: Zondervan, 1957). Samuel J. Schultz in 1968 wrote *The Prophets Speak* (New York: Harper & Row). Also in 1968 appeared *An Introduction to the Old Testament Prophets* by Hobart E. Freeman (Chicago: Moody).

To conclude this survey of study on the Old Testament prophets since World War II, let us note the appearance of five liberally oriented Old Testament introductions and four conservatively oriented ones, all of which treat the prophetic movement and its products. In 1948 appeared Robert Pfeiffer's classic, *Introduction to the Old Testament* (New York: Harper & Row); in 1951 the English translation of Aage Bentzen's two-volume *Introduction to the Old Testament* (Copenhagen: G. E. C. Gad, 1948–49); and in 1963 Samuel Sandmel's *The Hebrew Scriptures* (New York: Knopf). Otto Eissfeldt's massive contribution appeared in 1965, *The Old Testament: An Introduction* (tr. P. R. Ackroyd, New York: Harper & Row). The latest is Georg Fohrer's *Introduction to the Old Testament* (tr. D. Green, New York: Abingdon, 1967).

Introduction to the Old Testament (Grand Rapids: Eerdmans) by Edward J. Young appeared in 1949 and was enlarged and revised in 1964. It is still a standard work. We have also Merrill F. Unger's *Introductory Guide to the Old Testament* (Grand Rapids: Zondervan, 1951), Samuel Schultz's *The Old Testament Speaks* (New York: Harper's, 1960), and Gleason Archer's *A Survey of Old Testament Introduction* (Chicago: Moody, 1964). The most recent is Roland K. Harrison's massive *Introduction to the Old Testament* (Grand Rapids: Eerdmans, 1969).

In conclusion, let us summarize the major issues as they are found in some of these cited books. The most significant matters to affect or augment our study of the prophets in the area of lower criticism are perhaps to be distilled from the study of the Dead Sea Scrolls and the literature from Ras Shamra. Both of these areas are treated elsewhere in this volume. Briefly put, light now shines on occasional obscure words and phrases. Ugaritic is a sister language to Hebrew. Most of what has been uncovered tells and often clarifies difficult Biblical expressions. One example is the weeping for Hadadrimmon (Zech. 12:11) and the weeping for Tammuz (Ezk. 8:14). They are like the mourning of El and Anat for Baal.[1] One of the several *hapax legomenoi* in Isaiah 3, *bāttê-han-nepeš* (v. 20) finds some analogy in two Ugaritic offering lists[2] where *nephesh* clearly means perfume. Some scholars try to draw from such bases conclusions which are quite strained. Amos' original vocation among the *nōqᵉd̲im,* for instance, led Kapelrud to consider him as a sort of temple functionary, since the same word appears in Ugaritic as the title of *Atn prln,* a high priest.[3]

In regard to the Dead Sea Scrolls, our appreciation of the Septuagint has gone up, while our long-standing trust in the Masoretes is shaken. The Dead Sea Scrolls have shown that the LXX translators were not as poor Hebrew students as had been thought. They apparently did translate accurately from the Hebrew text which they had before them, for such a text tradition has appeared in the desert of Judea. The same applies to some of the New Testament quotations of the Old. For example, the indicative of John 12:40 has support in the Dead Sea Scroll of Isaiah from Cave 1 (IQIsᵃ), chapter 6, verse 10, whereas the MT reads *hshmn,* taken as an imperative. Romans 11:26 reads "out of Zion" whereas Isaiah 59:20 has "to Zion" in the standard text. Paul quotes the LXX, which we now realize has support from the Hebrew tradition, represented by IQIsᵃ at this point.

We are, of course, still plagued by the question of what happened between the time when a given prophet spoke or wrote an individual sermon or "burden" and the time of our oldest manuscripts. Yet within the prophetic writings themselves are hints of secretaries (Jer. 36:4), collections (Isa. 38:9), and of subsequent editing (Amos 1:1). Evangelicals have been accused of dodging questions by appealing to unavailable *autographa.* We must answer the challenges regarding oral transmission, possible pious or impious additions or alterations, and the whole matter of canon. With the discoveries of the Dead Sea Scrolls, Old Testament textual criticism is approaching the complexity which has long characterized that discipline in New Testament study. Some of the questions may be even harder, such as that of the long and short versions of Jeremiah.

Sober evangelical interpretation of the prophets is plagued on both sides. Bible believers once saw Allenby's aircraft over Jerusalem in 1918 as predicted in Isaiah 31:5 (*Amplified Bible*) or the boasts of Zionism as justified by the prophets. On the other hand the flood of neo-orthodox Biblical theologies reaches conclusions that are neither Biblical nor theological. The history-of-religions school characterizes most of liberalism's interpretation of the Old Testament. The prophets are reduced to whirling dervishes and the ark of the covenant to a Bedouin *kubbe.* The age of the writing prophets is but the time when Israelite religion advanced from a purely vertical relation between man and the gods to a horizontal one between man and man, so it is said.

In short, universalism, social duty, and a more subjective response to the *Monotheos* came about with the literary prophets. If anything prior to this time should teach such advanced principles, then that passage is to be labeled as a later gloss.

Evangelicals, being a minority, have a twofold task. We must teach true interpretation with conviction, scholarship, and devotion; and with no less apology, documentation, and Christian grace, we must reveal and renounce the false. Let us be sure of our position. Let us love God, our friends, and our enemies. Let us be first class in our academic integrity.

Notes

1. Cyrus H. Gordon, *Ugaritic Handbook* (Rome: Pontificium Institutum Biblicum, 1947), 67:vi.

2. *Ibid.*, 5:15; 9:1.

3. *Ibid.*, 69:19.

SOME PRINCIPLES IN THE INTERPRETATION OF ISAIAH AS ILLUSTRATED BY CHAPTER 24

Allan A. MacRae

To many Christians the greater part of the prophetical books consists of material that is rarely studied. Although occasionally read through as part of a complete reading of the whole Bible, most of the prophets leave little impression. A few outstanding sections and an occasional verse are memorized and frequently quoted. The rest remains a dark and seldom noticed area. The verses that are singled out for special attention consist of descriptions beforehand of the coming of Christ or of His return in glory. It is easy to receive the impression that much of the material in the prophetical books consists of isolated pictures of events that would occur long after the time when the prophets lived, with little if any relation to the period of their activity.

In contrast to this rather common attitude among Bible believers, critical scholars of the past century often described the prophets as social reformers interested merely in the developments of their own day. It was assumed that everything in the prophetic writings must be interpreted as a message for contemporaries or as part of a controversy with priestly or other forces representing elements of Israelite society holding views and objectives differing widely from their own. More recently some of the critical writers have interpreted the prophets as conservative forces rather than radical reformers, but they have also generally considered references to the distant future as something to be explained away if possible. Thus we have two groups of interpreters putting their emphasis on different sections of the prophetical books and presenting entirely different impressions of the books as a whole.

Actually there is a measure of truth in both approaches, although the liberal approach involves certain rather fundamental errors. It is a misinterpretation to think of the prophets as social reformers in the modern use of the term. They do indeed inveigh heavily against injustice, meanness, personal selfishness, and hypocrisy. Rebukes to individual sin, regardless of the class of society in which it is involved, are common in their writings, but the prophetical books contain no presentation of a new social system and no suggestion that the ills of life would be eradicated if only the system of government or of society were changed.

There is also a fundamental difference of attitude toward the prophets. Were they mere human thinkers, applying their own ideas to the situation as they saw it, or were they spokesmen for God, declaring His revelation, and presenting the message that He had ordered them to declare? We, as Bible believers, are committed to the second position. We do not simply adopt this as a presupposition. We find it clearly expressed in the claims of the prophets and in the New Testament attitude toward them. The mistake that we often make, however, is in thinking of them as merely being God's mouthpiece for giving forth predictions of a far distant future, and as writing only for us, with little thought of the needs of their own time.

I. Purposes of the Prophets

A. Judgment

Indeed, if the prophets were spokesmen for God, and if it was God's will that some of their material be written down, we are justified in expecting that that portion of their messages that God desired should be preserved would have a purpose not only for their own day, but also for believers in distant ages. Yet we often make the mistake of tending to overlook the relation to the contemporary situation. Here the liberal approach contains an emphasis which, while it needs correction, is nevertheless a worthy corrective to an error that we can easily make. The prophets, I think we can say without exception, were intensely interested in the situation of their own day. God sent them directly to their own people. Almost without exception their messages begin with material that is closely related to the affairs of their own time. God had a message for the people then living, and there was doubtless much of prophetic speaking that was not preserved, because it did not have a great deal to say to future ages. But if the prophets are not simply human observers, but carriers of a divine message, and if God is omnipotent and not only knows the future but controls it, it would be strange indeed if they did not drive home the importance of their messages by declaring God's intentions for the future and by presenting future events as a consideration that should influence immediate actions. Much of this, of course, consists of declarations of the judgment that God will bring upon the people for their sin. Much of it consists of description of the terrors of the exile and of various features of the chastisement that God intends to bring to His erring people. But there is another aspect that is widely found among the prophets, one that the liberal interpreters tend almost universally to overlook. This aspect relates to the attitude of the prophets to those people who were firmly convinced that the prophets spoke from God and who therefore would tend to accept all their declarations as true.

As the prophets in verse after verse, sometimes in chapter after chapter, declare the misery of the exile and destruction that God will bring upon the people for their sin and for their forgetfulness of God's righteous law, that portion of the people that we can rightly call "the godly" must have been stricken to the heart by the prophets' words. There were doubtless many who were doing their utmost to follow the teachings that God had given in the past. Yet they saw the nation as a whole going further into sin, rejecting God's law, and even sometimes persecuting the prophets whom God had sent. They heard the prophetic declarations against the widespread sin of their nation and must have been greatly disturbed as they observed how little the bulk of the people were heeding the prophet's words.

B. Restoration

It is a common practice among the great writing prophets, after rebuking the sin of the people, declaring the punishment that is bound to come, and exhorting the people to turn away from their sin, then to turn their attention to the little group of the godly. These people believed that the prophets spoke from God. They accepted the prophetic message as true. They knew that the nation, if it did not repent, must inevitably be punished for its sin. They felt themselves to be implicated in the sin of the nation; as they saw their associates rushing headlong toward disaster they might easily give way to despair and think that God in His wrath would cast away the people whom He had so blessed in the past. Time after time, after declaring a great message of rebuke, a prophet would turn to this godly element and would look far beyond the coming judgment to give them assurance that God was not through with His people, that God would indeed fulfill His purposes, that after the fulfillment of the judgment there was blessing ahead for those who put their trust in Him. Most of the passages that are memorized and beloved by Bible-believing Christians fall into this category. They are messages addressed to the godly, and in the great majority of cases they come after a message of rebuke to the nation as a whole.

The original headings in the King James Version sometimes receive a measure of criticism because they seem constantly to attribute all the judgments to Israel and all the blessings to the Church. Such an attitude would be quite wrong. God had both rebuke and blessing for Israel. He has both rebuke and blessing for His followers in the present age. Yet the headings of the King James Version are not as far from the truth as some might think. God's righteous people all through the ages make up a church; they are a group gathered out from the mass of people, including all who put their trust in God and His righteous promises, whether looking forward to the One who is to come, or looking back to the One who has been so marvelously revealed and who is yet to return to complete His work. His great work of redemption is finished, but the working out of the redemption in purifying the earth and its people is still future. Even though originally addressed to the prophet's contemporaries, the rebukes have significance for the professing church, and we lose something we need when we fail to study them carefully and see to how great an extent they may be applied to ourselves. The blessings, similarly, are for Israel. Some of them, indeed, are intended for the physical descendants of the ancient Israelites. All of them have some reference, and some have a very specific reference, to the remnant of grace, which may be exemplified in our own day by the church invisible, contained in the professing church but to some extent to be contrasted with it.

Examination of the prophetical books as a whole shows many occasions when the prophet begins with pointing out the sin of his contemporaries, sharply rebukes them for it, urges them to turn away from it, points to the calamities that God has determined to bring upon the nation as a result of its sin, and then looks far beyond the predicted misery to reassure the righteous that God is still interested in them and will eventually bring to pass great undeserved blessings that are part of His marvelous plan. The immediate purpose of most of the very distant predictions, whether of Christ's first coming, or of His second, is to bring encouragement and comfort to the godly.

II. Illustration via Isaiah 24

Let us now turn our attention to Isaiah 24. Since it has rightly been declared that a text without a context is only a pretext, it is proper that we should note that this particular chapter is sharply separated from what precedes and from what follows. Often a chapter of the Bible is not correctly interpreted unless taken in close relation to the preceding or following chapters. In fact there are many instances where a vital division of a book comes in the middle of a chapter, so that each section of the chapter has a far greater relation to the preceding or following material than to the rest of the chapter. In chapter 24 this is not the case. The chapter is easily seen to be a definite unit by itself, separated from the discussion of Tyre in chapter 23 and from the prayer in chapter 25.

Looking at chapter 24 another fact soon becomes apparent. There is a sharp difference of thought at about the middle of the chapter. In the first twelve verses all is gloom and misery. It is a picture of judgment and desolation. The second half of the chapter, while containing a number of verses that picture desolation or calamity, contains a still larger number that describe future blessing to the godly. Under these circumstances our first duty is to determine the exact relevance of the first half of the chapter. Is it a prediction looking far into the future, or is it a passage dealing directly with the prophet's own time? The analogy of the greater part of the prophetic writings would suggest the latter interpretation. Although occasionally a prophetic message may begin in the distant future, it is far more common for the prophet to start with a picture of what is near. In view of this usual analogy the most natural suggestion would be that the first half of the chapter is describing the punishment that God will bring upon the sin of the prophet's contemporaries, and that the latter half looks beyond this judgment to some aspect of God's future plan as a means of encouragement to the godly.

A. Isaiah 24:1–12: Immediate and Local Judgment

One consideration seems at first sight to militate strongly against this interpretation. Some of these verses create an impression of worldwide calamity—an impression that is derived mainly from the frequent use of the word "earth," which suggests a prediction about the whole world. Yet this interpretation may perhaps be a false one. The word "earth" is a translation of the Hebrew 'ereṣ. While this word is often used to describe the entire globe it is still more frequently used to denote a particular area, such as the land of Egypt, the land of Israel, or the land of Assyria. If the word were to be translated "land" in this passage—an equally possible interpretation of the word—the cosmic impression would largely disappear.

As we look more closely at these twelve verses we find a great many statements that seem far more appropriate to a prediction of God's wrath upon the land of Israel for its sin than to a picture dealing with the world as a whole. Thus we see at the end of verse 1 the statement that He "scattereth abroad the inhabitants thereof." Does this mean that the people of the whole world are scattered from one nation to another? It fits somewhat better the idea of exiling the inhabitants of Israel from their land. Verse 2 refers specifically to certain classes of people: the priest, the servant, the master, the buyer, the lender. While this verse could picture the world as a whole, it surely fits appropriately with Israel itself. In verse 3 'ereṣ is rendered "land" in the KJV. Verse 5 speaks of the defilement caused by the inhabitants, of their transgressing the laws, changing the ordinances, and breaking "the everlasting covenant." This would fit appropriately with a picture of the people of Israel to whom God had originally given His laws, and whom He had charged to obey His everlasting covenant.

Verse 10 says that "the city of confusion is broken down." Verse 12 says that "in the city is left desolation, and the gate is smitten with destruction." We immediately ask, "What city?" If we should speak about the world as a whole, there are so many cities that the phrase "the city" would be rather out of place in these two verses. The Hebrew text does not say "every city." It does not use the plural, "cities." It would seem to be speaking specifically of one city. If one speaks of England and refers to "the city" he naturally means London. In France it would be Paris. Similarly, speaking of Israel "the city" would be Jerusalem. It is the outstanding individual city in the land.

Verse 13 begins with the words: "When thus it shall be in the midst of the land." The word that was rendered as "earth" six times in earlier verses is here translated "land," (as was already the case in verses 3 and 11). "Earth" would seem quite out of place in this verse, which is most naturally interpreted as referring to the midst of a particular country rather than to the midst of the whole world.

Thus many specific statements in these twelve and one-half verses fit best with the interpretation that is suggested by the parallel with the general practice of the prophets, who so often begin a passage with rebuke for the sin of the people of their own day, and then go on to provide specific encouragement to the godly. This leads naturally to the conclusion that Isaiah 24:1–12 is a prediction of exile, rather than a description of eventual judgment upon the earth as a whole. Such judgment may well be contained in statements later on in the chapter. Here it seems most unlikely. The only thing that makes the other impression seem so probable is the frequent use of the English word "earth."

In verses 1 to 13 the word 'ereṣ occurs nine times. The King James Version translates it "earth" six times and "land" three times. To the English reader, unfamiliar with the Hebrew, these appear to be two different words. Yet it would seem most likely that the word in this unified passage is either "earth," referring to the whole globe, or "land" referring to Israel. Surely it would be better to translate it one way or the other. Here at first sight the Revised Standard Version seems to be superior, in this passage, to the King James Version. In every one of these instances it translates 'ereṣ by the same English word. Unfortunately, however, it selects the wrong one of the two. To my mind it is not nearly as important which word is selected as that one be used consistently throughout this unified passage and that a footnote be inserted in case of doubt to give the student the authority to make his own determination as to which is meant. If 'ereṣ were always translated "land" in verses 1 to 12, it would bring out the true meaning of the passage, fit better with its contents, and also with the analogy of prophetic usage elsewhere.

At this point someone may well raise the question, how can Hebrew be so absurd as to use one word to express two such different ideas as to mean either the whole globe, or just a small section of the globe such as the land of Egypt or the land of Israel? In answer we must say, "Yes, indeed; like all languages, Hebrew has its absurdities. It is surely absurd that one word should have two such different meanings. Yet it is not nearly as absurd as the corresponding situation in the English language. In English the word 'earth' is frequently used to indicate the entire globe. Yet it is equally common in a very different sense. A man could fill a pail with earth, carry it into a house, and then pour out the earth upon the floor. Surely English is a step more absurd than the two meanings of Hebrew when it uses the same word either to represent the entire globe or to indicate a mere pailful of soil."

B. Isaiah 24:13–23: Future Restoration

Interpreted in this way, with *'ereș* translated as "land," verses 1 to 12 present a clear picture of the sad effects of exile and depopulation so often predicted by Isaiah and Jeremiah. All is gloom, despair and misery until we reach verse 13. By the time we reach verses 14 and 15 we know that we are in a different atmosphere. They are verses of joy and happiness. Verse 13 is a transition verse. It reads: "When thus it shall be in the midst of the land among the people, there shall be as the shaking of an olive tree, and as the gleaning grapes when the vintage is done."

This verse might be approached in either of two ways. It might be taken as showing the greatness of the calamity. Nothing remains but the little that will fall when an olive tree is shaken, or that is overlooked in the harvest. There is left only "the gleaning grapes when the vintage is done." Yet it may be suggested that the emphasis is not on the thorough-going nature of the destruction, but on the fact that something will still remain to receive God's blessing. The destruction is not complete. There is yet to be a remnant of grace.

Verse 13 does not make this idea clear. It is only a suggestion. But the suggestion is shown to be a correct one by what is said in verse 14: "They shall lift up their voice, they shall sing for the majesty of the Lord, they shall cry aloud from the sea." It is difficult to imagine verse 14 as occurring earlier in the chapter. Then there was nothing for which to lift up one's voice in song. All was gloom and despair. Now we see that after God has punished the nation there will still remain a remnant of grace, able to lift up its voice and sing for the majesty of the Lord.

1. *Universal praise.* Thus we find a suggestion of a new idea in verse 13, and verse 14 makes it clear that this suggestion is not imaginary but is really there. Similarly we have a new suggestion at the end of verse 14: "they shall cry aloud from the sea." The words "to cry aloud" could suggest agony and misery in English, though they are sometimes used for a cry of joy. In Hebrew *șāhal* usually means a shout of happiness. They

are crying aloud with joy, but we note they are crying aloud from the sea.

When one realizes the location of the land of Israel, much of it elevated ground only a short distance from the Mediterranean sea, he is apt to be amazed to realize how comparatively seldom the sea is mentioned in the Old Testament. Most of the action of the Old Testament takes place on land. A partial reason for this is the fact that the seacoast of the land of Israel is straight, with few good natural harbors. Jaffa and Haifa have been improved in modern times, but they are quite in contrast with the coast of Phoenicia to the north where there is an abundance of good harbors and small islands to tempt the inhabitants out to maritime travel and adventure. The Israelites were a land people; Jonah went down to Joppa to get a ship to go to Tarshish. This is almost the only instance in the Old Testament where we read of a man taking a boat from Israel.

God called Abraham and followed up the call with His promises to Isaac and Jacob and His continuing blessing upon Israel, in order that through Israel He might keep alive the knowledge of the one true God and might prepare the way for the coming into the world of the Savior who would bring light to all nations. The revelation of God in the Old Testament is mostly confined to the people of Israel; and, except for a few incidents in Egypt or in Mesopotamia, almost all of the events depicted occur in the land of Israel. Yet here we have a note rarely struck in the Old Testament: "They shall cry aloud from the sea." The suggestion is clear that at some time beyond the coming exile there will be an occasion when those who are true to God will praise Him not only in the land of Israel, but in regions from which at Isaiah's time His praise had rarely ascended.

This suggestion is barely touched upon in verse 14; but when we look at 15, and at the beginning of 16, we find it clearly repeated and emphasized. Verse 15 reads, "Wherefore glorify ye the Lord in the fires, even the name of the Lord God of Israel in the isles of the sea." Verse 16 begins with the words, "From the uttermost part of the earth have we heard songs, even glory to the righteous." Here the word "righteous" is in the singular and refers, of course, to the righteous God. Thus the succeeding verses bring out the fact that we are not reading something into verse 14 when we suggest that it is promising that the knowledge of God will not die with the exile and that a remnant of grace will continue in the land of Israel. Going far beyond this, the praise of God is to be extended into other parts of the world so that even in the islands of the sea there will be those who will be giving praise to the Lord God of Israel.

Can we doubt that as Isaiah penned these words the Lord gave him a glimpse of the extension of the knowledge of the true God in future times? Did he perhaps foresee the apostle Paul sailing westward to bring the message of salvation through God's Son to Greece and Rome, and perhaps even to Spain? Did he see missionaries bringing the message of salvation to Britain? Did he see the Word of God crossing the ocean, and great centers for its belief and promulgation being established in America? Did he see missionaries going still farther westward, carrying the message across the sea from America to the eastern shores of Asia? "They shall cry aloud from the sea."

As we have already noted, the next verse and a half develop the hint contained in verse 14. What was previously a vision confined to the land of Israel now spreads out into large portions of the globe. The Word of God is to be widely extended. God's plan is not to be nullified by the fact that so much of Israel has fallen into sin. It is His purpose that there shall go forth from Israel a light to the nations, and this promise is indeed to be fulfilled.

2. *Universal frustration.* As we look at the fuller development in verses 15–16a of the hint contained in verse 14, we again find a suggestion of something new. Verse 15 begins with the words: "Wherefore glorify ye the Lord in the fires." An edition of the Bible that I used as a boy has a marginal note opposite the word "fires" which reads: "Or valleys." So far as I know the reading "valleys" is not contained in the text of any English version, though it is found in Portuguese and Spanish translations. I have no idea where it originated. The Hebrew word used generally refers to a fire, or its flame, and is similar to a word meaning "light." Not all English versions follow the kjv in rendering the word as "in the fires." The rsv says, "Therefore in the east give glory to the Lord." One Hebrew dictionary calls the plural of *'ûr* a separate word, translating it "region of light—east" and giving Isaiah 24:15 as its only occurrence. This is obviously a mere guess, based on the verse that we are now considering. Certain commentaries state that since the latter part of the verse, which speaks of glorifying God in the isles of the sea, would refer to the west, we must conclude that "in the fires" should logically refer to the east. In order to provide a basis for this interpretation it is alleged that the "fires" in this verse must refer to the reddish sky at sunrise in the east.

This is surely a forced interpretation. As a rule sunsets are more colorful than sunrises. There would certainly be no more reason to use the word "fires" to describe the east than to use it to describe the west. Surely this is reading something into the Scripture, in order to produce a desired symmetry. What the Bible says is "fires" and it does not seem to fit with the preceding thoughts. A new idea is rather being added.

The most natural way to interpret the idea of glorifying God in the fires is to take it as referring to the fires of persecution and adversity. Did Isaiah, as he wrote these words, have a glimpse of Israel in Maccabean days, facing the effort to destroy the true religion? Did he see men tortured and murdered for their faith, and therefore cry out, "Glorify

God in the fires"? Did he look forward and see the early Christian martyrs tied to posts in Nero's garden, covered with pitch and then ignited to give light to Nero's festivals? Did he see the martyrs of Reformation days, many of whom were burned at the stake for their faith? Surely this is the most logical way to interpret the expression, "Glorify the Lord in the fires." But we must be careful not to read something into the passage. This is a remarkable idea, but we must not extract it merely from one word.

It is primary rule of Biblical exegesis that we must never build a teaching upon one word alone, or even on one verse alone. Often we find an idea suggested by a word, but if we are to accept the idea as definitely God's teaching we must not build merely upon a suggestion. We must look elsewhere in the Scripture for evidence that our interpretation is really what is intended. Here we do not need to look far for such evidence.

At first sight verse 16 is a very strange verse. We recognize, of course, that the verse divisions were not made by the original writers of the Bible. They are quite old and probably were determined long before the chapter divisions. We do not know who inserted them. They are convenient for finding references, but one often wonders on what basis they were made. Frequently a sentence is divided into two verses. Occasionally, as in Psalm 19:4 we find a verse composed of the concluding sentence of one stanza, combined with the first phrase of a long sentence that begins a new stanza.

Some of these verse divisions are strange, but one wonders whether there is a verse anywhere in the Scripture that is quite as strange as verse 16 of chapter 24. Here we have two separate complete sentences that appear to have little in common. The first expresses great joy, while the second grieves over a sad disappointment. Yet it is not as strange as it appears, for the two sentences really present one complete thought. In the providence of God there are combined in verse 16 two different ideas, one of which carries on the principal idea of verse 15, while the other develops the new idea that was suggested by one word of that verse.

The first part of verse 16, as we have already noticed, repeats the principal thought of verse 15, that the praise of God is to be extended to the uttermost part of the earth. The last two-thirds of the verse, however, which forms a complete sentence, expresses a very different idea: "But I said, My leanness, my leanness, woe unto me! the treacherous dealers have dealt treacherously; yea, the treacherous dealers have dealt very treacherously."

Here is a presentation that seems quite different from anything earlier in the chapter. One wonders who is speaking. Could it be one of those who were heard singing the songs of glory to the righteous God? Do they come to realize that some treachery has occurred? Has an enemy crept in and planted tares? Does the phrase, "My leanness, my leanness" express disappointment that the great amount of fruit that might have been expected has failed to materialize?

Here we naturally think of events of the past century. Only a little more than a generation ago the cry was widely heard, "The evangelization of the world in this generation." Yet today there are more heathen in the world than there were a century ago. Only a short time ago many American denominations were sending missionaries to the far corners of the earth, leading countless souls to salvation through faith in the atoning death of Jesus Christ the Savior and in the teaching of the Scriptures. Today many old-line denominational missions are largely controlled by individuals who are convinced that the Bible is to a great extent a combination of myths and legends, and that no statement in it is dependable except as it may happen to coincide with their own philosophical or speculative ideas. A century ago, in the United States there were churches on almost every corner proclaiming the gospel of Christ. Today many of them are merely discussing sociology. How does this fit with Isaiah's prophecy? As God gave him this wonderful vision of the future, Isaiah saw that God was not ending His witness to lost humanity. God was not through with Israel. Israel would return from exile and would again become an instrument for the preservation of the name of God and for the bringing of His Son into the world. It would be a center from which the Word of God would be made known throughout the world. But the spread of the gospel throughout the world would not be simply a joyous progress of victory. It is God's will that the progress be mixed with persecution, disappointment and frustration. It would be a progress in which eventually unbelief and false doctrine would gain such power that they could transform many institutions that at one time were devoted to Biblical teaching into centers for denial of the primary truths of Scripture.

It is reasonable to consider the verses following verse 16 as showing the later results of this development. Time does not permit that they be examined in detail. Like the earlier picture in verses 1–12 they are quite lacking in joy. They portray upheaval, turmoil, fear, and destruction. The conclusion is plain. God is here revealing to Isaiah that even while the message of God's mercy is being taken to the very ends of the world, men will turn to unbelief and treachery. There will be a leanness, a failure to produce the expected fruit. The age will end, not in a great paean of joy, but in a time of disappointment and destruction even worse than the one described in the first twelve verses of the chapter.

In these four verses the word "earth" occurs several times. When the question is raised whether it should be interpreted as "earth" or "land" it is found that not even one of the many evidences that pointed to the land of Israel in verses 1–12 is present here. By this time, as we have seen, the perspective has been extended to the very islands of the sea. Now a time of tribulation for the whole world is in view. The four verses, with their terrible picture of confusion, upheaval and misery, show what can reasonably be expected after great nations that have had the opportunity to know the Word of God have deliberately turned away from it.

The passage ends differently from the first part of the chapter. Verse 20 concludes with the words "it shall fall, and not rise again." The great worldly civilization that would become possible when the Word of God was widely proclaimed, but that would turn away from this gospel and forget it, is eventually to fall and not rise again.

Thus the Lord revealed to Isaiah that human efforts would never establish lasting happiness. Not even the widespread preaching of God's Word by consecrated men would produce lasting joy on earth. Only through the direct interposition of divine power could such a result be accomplished.

3. *Universal triumph.* This interposition is described in verse 21: "And it shall come to pass in that day, that the Lord shall punish the host of the high ones that are on high, and the kings of the earth upon the earth."

The word translated "punish" in verse 21 and "visit" in verse 22 would be better rendered "intervene regarding." *Pāqad* is translated in a number of different ways in the King James Version. Thus it is rendered "appoint" 6 times, "call to remembrance" once, "enjoy" once, "look" once, "remember" once, "count" twice, "number" 110 times, "punish" 7 times, and "visit" 57 times.

Such a variety of translations might almost suggest that the word had little definite meaning but could be fit into the context in various ways that seemed reasonable to the translator. But examination of all the occurrences reveals the basic meaning of the word. It is used to indicate the intervention of a higher power in the affairs of a lower one. Thus many times it is used of a king numbering his soldiers for battle, or numbering the people from whom he can draw individuals for military or other service. Aside from a king dealing with his troops, use of *pāqad* is nearly always limited to divine activity. It represents the intervention of a higher authority to make a change in one's situation. This change need not mean punishment or injury; it may equally well denote a blessing. Thus we read in Ruth 1:6 that "the Lord had visited his people" in giving them relief from the famine. While Exodus 34:7 says that God visits the iniquities of the fathers upon the children to the third and fourth generation, and Psalm 89:32 says that God will "visit their transgression with the rod," Psalm 106:4 says, "O Lord, . . . visit me with thy salvation."

Though verse 21 is speaking of God's intervention to destroy the power of the forces of evil, it is premature to translate the word as "punish" here; "intervene" would come nearer, even if not exactly giving the full meaning. There is usually the meaning not only of taking an action, but of taking with power an action that will make a difference to the fate of those with whom it deals. In this case, the result is shown at the beginning of the next verse, which says that those whom God thus "visits" will be gathered together and shut up in prison.

Verse 21 speaks of "the host of the high ones on high and the kings of the earth upon the earth." Here God has given Isaiah a glimpse of the truth revealed in Ephesians 6:12 that we wrestle not merely against earthly opponents, but also "against principalities, against powers, against the rulers of the darkness of this world." God will intervene not only against the human forces of wickedness but also against the supernatural forces that are directing and inciting them.

Verse 22 is a very interesting verse. These evil forces are to be gathered together and shut up in a prison. Then we read, "after many days shall they be visited." The word is again pāqaḏ. "Visit" here has nothing of the common present meaning of paying someone a visit, or making a call. It does not mean that someone will visit these people in prison. The Hebrew word is never used in that sense. It means that after many days a change will be made in their condition. The nature of the change is not stated. If one were speaking of an earthly court, one might well say that criminals will be put into jail, and then, after a long time, when finally the slow processes of justice reach the point of taking care of their case, they will receive their punishment. To make such a criticism of divine justice would hardly be in keeping with the attitude of Isaiah. Yet this interpretation would be easily derived from the translation of the rsv, which seems to declare that punishment will be given after a long period of awaiting judgment. The rendering of verse 22 in the kjv is much better than that in the rsv, in that it leaves the matter open. It does not tell us whether the visitation is for punishment or for release.

The latter idea, while thus more logical in the context, seems indeed a strange one. Why would God intervene against the forces of evil, shut them up in prison for many days, and then release them for a time? Professor Franz Delitzsch deals with the problem as follows: "So far as the thing itself is concerned, we have a parallel in Rev. xx. 1–3 and 7–9: they are visited by being set free again, and commencing their old practice once more; but only (as ver. 23 affirms) to lose again directly, before the glorious and triumphant might of Jehovah, the power they have temporarily reacquired."[1]

The chapter ends with a marvelous picture. Verse 23 describes the glory of the Lord of hosts when He reigns in Mt. Zion and in Jerusalem, a glory so great that before it the glory of the moon and the sun pale into insignificance.

Isaiah contains many wonderful truths at which Christians seldom glance. We gain much value from studying the precious Messianic passages, but we lose a great deal when we neglect the rest of the book and consequently miss the many other important teachings that God desires His people to receive.

Notes

1. Franz Delitzsch, *Biblical Commentary on the Prophecies of Isaiah*, 1859 edition, I:435.

—11—

THE ARAMAIC OF THE "GENESIS APOCRYPHON" COMPARED WITH THE ARAMAIC OF DANIEL

Gleason L. Archer, Jr.

One of the most remarkable discoveries from the First Cave of Qumran was the Genesis Apocryphon, a midrash of Genesis composed in Aramaic. Because of its caked and brittle condition, it required a special technique, carried out with infinite patience, to unroll this document strip by strip and to decipher five columns of text out of at least twenty-three (and probably much more) of which the manuscript was originally composed. It finally saw publication in Naḥman Avigad and Yigael Yadin's 1956 edition of *The Genesis Apocryphon*.[1]

The scholarly world had been waiting expectantly for this production ever since the first announcement of the discovery of what was at first mistakenly identified as the "Lamech Scroll" (so called because the name "Lamech" appeared in the outermost column in the scroll). It was recognized that the language was Aramaic rather than Hebrew, and because of its inclusion in the same collection as the great Isaiah Scroll and the Habakkuk Commentary, it promised to be the earliest extra-Biblical manuscript in Aramaic apart from the Elephantine Papyri of the 5th and 4th Centuries B.C.

Subsequent to the publication of the *Apocryphon*, various brief discussions of its linguistic importance and informational content appeared in the scholarly journals, such as Paul Winter's *Das Aramäische Genesis-Apokryphon*,[2] and E. Y. Kutscher's "The Language of the Genesis Apocryphon: a Preliminary Study."[3] But none of these have ventured into a really detailed comparison with the Aramaic chapters of Daniel; so far as this writer is aware, this has not yet been done in any subsequent article. It would be interesting to speculate on what a spate of discussions would have appeared had the language of the Apocryphon shown noteworthy resemblances to that of Daniel. This would have demonstrated once and for all the soundness of the theory that Daniel was written in the second century B.C. and have refuted the contention of evangelical scholars that it was actually composed in the late sixth century, as it purports to have been. As it turned out, however, the linguistic data proved to point in quite the opposite direction; and therefore the subject of language comparison was quietly dropped. But it seems altogether incumbent upon conservative scholars to exploit this new body of evidence to its fullest extent and demonstrate the comparative lateness of the *Apocryphon* in relationship to Daniel. Here at last we have an authentic Aramaic manuscript, copied out within a century of the supposed publication date of the Book of Daniel, according to the Maccabean Date Theory. Surely it should manifest many and striking points of resemblance in grammar, style, and vocabulary. But in actuality the differences are so striking and essential in all three of these categories as to make it impossible to remain intellectually respectable and still hold to the theory of the Book of Daniel as a Maccabean pseudepigraph. Although the Qumran copy of the Apocryphon may have been written down in the late first century, or even a few decades later, say the editors, nevertheless the original was composed earlier than *Jubilees* or *Enoch,* and very likely in the third century B.C.—which would be a century earlier than the Maccabean revolt!

In his brief discussion Winter pointed out that the *Apocryphon* was written in a later kind of Aramaic than the Imperial Aramaic of Daniel and Ezra.[4] This dictum was confirmed by Kutscher, who stated that the language of the *Apocryphon* was neither Reichsaramäisch in general nor Biblical Aramaic in particular.[5] Furthermore, he added, Biblical Aramaic shows distinct indications of eastern origin, in contrast to the western traits of the *Apocryphon*. The implications of this judgment are quite devastating for the theory of Maccabean origin for Daniel, which assumes and insists that this alleged pseudepigraph was composed by an anonymous Jewish patriot in Palestine around 168 B.C. But if the Aramaic of Daniel was of an eastern cast, this would seem to rule out composition in Palestine altogether, and to point towards an origin in Babylonia where the historic sixth-century Daniel carried on his ministry. Western traits singled out by Kutscher in the *Apocryphon* (but lacking in Daniel) include the form *kamān* for *kᵉmā* ("how much?" "how great?") in 21:14, and *tammān* for *tammā* ("there"), which otherwise occur only in Galilean Aramaic. The same is true of the *pᵉal* infinitive *mišbôq* ("to leave") which appears instead of *mišbaq,* the standard form, in 19:15. W. B. Stevenson[6] confirms this *miph'ōl* form as Palestinian Talmudic or Midrashic only, since it does not appear in the targums of Onkelos or Jonathan.

I. Contrasts in Morphology and Spelling

In regard to the personal pronouns, it is noteworthy that the 3rd fem. sing. suffix "her" is usually spelled *-hā,* in the *Apocryphon* rather than the earlier *ah*. Stevenson labels this as Targumic, for it does not occur before Onkelos or Jonathan.[7] Similarly the 3rd plural masc. suffix *-ôn* occurs in *mᵉdittôn* ("their city") for the usual *mᵉdinaṯôn* of Daniel and the Elephantine Papyri. Stevenson lists this as a variant form of *-hôn* not employed until the Palestinian Talmud and Midrashim.[8] As for demonstrative pronouns, the form *dēn* is almost always used for the *dᵉnā* of Biblical Aramaic and the Elephantine Papyri; this again is a Talmudic-Midrashic variant unknown in the Targums.[9] Similarly 2:17 shows *kᵉdēn* for the earlier *kiḏᵉnā* for "thus, such."

In the area of verb morphology the uniform practice of the *Apocryphon* is to use the non-aspirated form of the *haphel* causative and of the reflexive-passive *hithpᵉel* or *hithpa'al*. Only occasionally does unaspirated *aphel* or *ithpa'al* occur in Daniel, but these are invariably used in the Apocryphon and in later Aramaic and Syriac; e.g. *'iṯbaḥᵃlēṯ* ("I was frightened") in 2:3, and *'itbᵉniyat* ("she was built") in 19:9 instead of the Biblical *hiṯbᵉnāṯ*. Note also that this latter example uses an ending for the 3rd sing. perf. which does not occur until Onkelos and Jonathan.[10] Another late verb form is *yiḥē* (*h*) ("he will live") in 20:23 rather than the Biblical *yiḥyē* (*h*). Stevenson notes this as a good Onkelos-Jonathan form,[11] but it never occurs in Biblical Aramaic or the Elephantine Papyri.

In the area of noun-spelling, it is quite startling to find such a late form as *bê* in 21:6 instead of *bêṯ* for "house"; Jastrow includes it as a Talmudic or Rabbinic form. The spelling of Sodom is peculiar: it shows a *waw* after the *samekh* but not after the *daleth* (*swdm* instead of *sdwm*), although even in Syriac the *waw* occurs after the *daleth*. But this tendency to retain a full u-vowel or o-vowel in the first syllable shows up in the spelling of two prepositions which do have counterparts in Syriac: *qwdm* pointing to *qōḏem* rather than *qᵉdām* (the Biblical form) for "before, in front of" (cf. Syriac *qūḏᵉmō*, "forepart, front"), and (*qūḇᵉlê* or *qōḇᵉlê*) for the biblical *qᵉbēl*.

Lastly it should be observed that in the matter of spelling the *Apocryphon* almost always uses *aleph* as the vowel lengthener at the end of words, hardly ever the *he* of Biblical Aramaic (which, to be sure, uses *aleph* occasionally as well) and of the Elephantine Papyri. Kutscher notes just one instance of determinate-*ā* spelled with *hē*: *ḥelmā* (*h*) in 19:18 (with the same word occurring earlier in the same line as *ḥelmā* (')) with final *aleph*. Two or three feminine nouns end in *hē* (*'intā* (*h*) in 20:27, 34, *minḥā* (*h*) in 21:2, and *mūmā* (*h*) "oath" in 20:30), but all the rest in *aleph*. Three third-weak-radical verbs exhibit a final *hē* (*'aṯā* (*h*) "come," *rᵉmā* (*h*) "fall upon," and *qᵉnā* (*h*) "acquire"); all the rest end in *aleph*. In Biblical Aramaic and in the Egyptian papyri there is a great preponderance of feminines in *hē*, and a fair number of definite masculines in *hē* (although the *aleph* is the usual spelling). Syriac and the Aramaic of the Babylonian Talmud dropped the *hē*-ending altogether in favor of the *aleph,* and so in this respect also the *Apocryphon* exhibits a distinctly later usage than the Aramaic of Daniel and Ezra.

II. Targumic Words Not Found in Biblical Aramaic or the Papyri

At the outset it needs to be emphasized that there are barely ten chapters in the Aramaic sections of Daniel and Ezra, and the entire bulk of the Elephantine Papyri (many of which are fragmentary) is hardly sufficient to form a firm basis for vocabulary statistics. It may well be that more extensive documentation from the sixth and fifth centuries B.C. would reveal that some of the words not appearing in the extant literature of that period were already in use, even before their occurrence in the *Apocryphon* and in Targumic times. Nevertheless, it is hardly feasible to explain away the entire list of post-Biblical terms in this scroll after such a fashion. In many cases these same objects or ideas do appear in Daniel, Ezra or the Papyri, but in entirely different words or divergent forms. It is of course possible that a certain number of synonyms co-existed, some of which may not have turned up until the *Genesis Apocryphon* but were actually in use back in the fifth century. But if a very large number of Targumic words characterize the vocabulary of the *Apocryphon* (and they do), the only reasonable deduction to draw is that this scroll comes from a substantially later period than do the Biblical books or the Egyptian papyri. Had there proven to be a great similarity between the *Apocryphon* and Daniel, it would surely have been triumphantly adduced by liberal scholarship as proof positive of the lateness of the composition of Daniel. Since the cumulative evidence points altogether in the opposite direction, it is only fair to say that the linguistic data indicate a considerable time-interval between the two documents.

The following list contains these Targumic or Talmudic words occurring in the *Apocryphon,* in the order of their appearance in the five legible columns of its text. In every case the word listed has been checked in Gesenius-Buhl's *Aramäisches Lexikon* (referred to as BA for Biblical Aramaic), in the word-index of Cowley's *Aramaic Papyri* (CAP), and (usually) in Lidzbarski's *Handbuch der Nordsemitischen Epigraphik* (Lidz.), and has been found to be missing, although listed in the two volumes of Jastrow's Lexicon of post-Biblical Hebrew and Chaldee. In some cases the Aramaic word in question does appear in Biblical Hebrew, and was therefore known in its Hebrew form, at least in the Palestinian area. It may have been known to speakers of Aramaic and adopted into their language even in early post-exilic times. But on the other hand this borrowing may not have taken place until later centuries, and such words cannot safely be left out of the present reckoning, particularly since this tendency to adopt Hebraisms may have been fostered in later times by continuous study of the Hebrew Scriptures on the part of Aramaic-speaking Jews.

Column Two is rather fragmentary and contains but two such "late" words:

1. *'antā'*, meaning "time" (the Hebrew *'ēt*) ;
2. the adverb *hākā*, meaning "here."

Column Nineteen

3. Line 16 has *'akl°yât*, an aphel of *k°lā* (') , meaning "call, cry out." Note the late form of the 3rd fem. sing.: *-yât* instead of *-āt*.

4. Line 18 has *'ištā'ê*, an ithpa'al imperative masc. sing., meaning "tell" (a dream to someone) , from *š°'ā* (') , which is earlier found only in the meaning "to smooth, to paste over."

5. Line 19 uses *yôm* "day" in the feminine, modifying it with the feminine demonstrative *dâ*. In BA, CAP, and Lidz., this word is always masculine.

6. Line 21 uses *b°dîl* in *b°dîlîkî* "for thy sake," a common Syriac locution not found in BA, CAP or Lidz.

Column Twenty

7. Line 3 has *yā'în*, a plur. of *yā'e (h)*, meaning "fitting, right, nice" (cf. the Targumic *yā'ayûtā* (') "beauty, grace") , and applied to Sarah's fair breast, hair, and hands. The fem. sing. *yā'ā* (') occurs in line 4.

8. Also in line 3 is *nēṣ*, translated by Avigad and Yadin as "radiance," but defined in Jastrow as "blossom."

9. Line 5 offers *maḥzê*, meaning "appearance," coming from a common enough root (*ḥ°zā* (') "to see") , but not extant in any of the three (BA, CAP, or Lidz.) .

10. Line 5 also has the adjective *'°rîk* in the sense of "long"; Biblical Aramaic uses it only to mean "right" or "befitting" (Ezr. 4:14) ; CAP and Lidz. do not use it at all.

11. Thirdly, line 5 uses *qaṭṭîn* to mean "slender, thin, fine"; only Lidz. shows this word in the sense of "meager, slight." Of course it is related to the common Hebrew adjective *qāṭôn*, which means "small."

12. Line 6 uses *ginnûn* meaning "bridal chamber" or "wedding canopy," also "cover, shade."

13. In line 10 occurs a locution built on *dî* similar to the *b°dîl* just mentioned, namely *'al dîl*, "because of." The sequence *zî lî* is found in CAP, and Lidz. cites *zî lāk, zî lēh*, etc.; but none of them contains this combination with the preposition *'al*.

14. Line 10 also has an ithp°el participle of *t°gar*, "travel about, trade": *mitt°gēr*, "making profit, being benefited." Lidz. lists the noun *tagrā* (') , "merchant" (cf. Arabic *tājirun*) but not the verb itself.

15. Line 16 uses *ḥ°ša* (') , "be quiet" or "be grieved" in the latter sense: *ḥ°šêt*, "I was grieved" (according to Avigad and Yadin) . This is cognate

with the Biblical Hebrew *ḥāšā,* "be silent," but it has not hitherto been found in pre-Targumic times.

16. In line 18 we meet with *nigdā* ('), meaning "a lash, punishment, affliction."

17. In line 20, and again in 21:14, we find the conjunctive particle *'ᵃrê,* used as "because, that." This may be ultimately related to *'ᵃrû,* "behold," which occurs in BA and Lidz., although not in CAP.

18. Line 20 also has the verb *'ᵃraq* "to flee," which also occurs in 21:32. The root of this word may be the same as an *'rq* in the Elephantine Papyri, which serves apparently as a preposition meaning "toward," but there is no observable semantic connection between the two.

19. Line 33 has the phrase *laḥᵃda* ('), which properly means "singularly," but here has developed into "very much" or "too much"—a usage unknown in BA, CAP or Lidz.

Column Twenty-One.

20. In line 1 we meet with *maršᵉyâṭî,* from the Targumic *mašrîṭā* ('), "camp, resting-place," from the root *šᵉrā* (') "to loosen, to encamp."

21. In line 9 we see *šᵉqal,* as a verb meaning "lift up" (one's eyes), rather than in the more familiar meaning of "to weigh, be heavy"—if this be a Hebrew borrowing equivalent to the Aramaic *tᵉqēl* (which is more than doubtful).

22. Line 15 has the verb *sᵉḥar,* meaning "to go, to journey about," which does not appear in BA or Lidz., and probably not in CAP either (although Aḥiqar 175 shows a *samekh-ḥeth* that may have had *rōsh* as its third letter). Yet the Hebrew cognate *sāḥar* is quite common in the O.T.

23. Line 33 contains the noun *'ugᵉyi'în,* which is apparently a masculine-type plural of the feminine *'ûgᵉyā* ('), defined by Jastrow as "a cavity dug around a tree; a rut." Avigad and Yadin render it as "pits."

Column Twenty-Two

24. On line 2 occurs the noun *'ān* for "cattle," which is cognate with the Hebrew *ṣô* (') *n,* "small cattle: sheep or goats." But it does not occur in BA, CAP or Lidz., perhaps by mere chance.

25. In line 5 we meet with *ḥᵃlam* in the ithpa'al, which the translators render as "grow strong." Jastrow lists the pa'el as meaning "join closely," but cites no ithpa'al.

26. Line 21 has the noun *'arqā* (') meaning "strap, band," or in this context: "shoelatchet."

27. In the same line is *mᵉsân,* meaning "shoe," apparently cognate with the verb participle *sō'ēn* in Isaiah 9:4 meaning "booted warrior," and the noun in construct with it: *šᵉ'ôn,* "shoe."

28. Lastly, in line 23 we meet with an adverb very common in Syriac: *kᵉḇar,* meaning "already, long ago." It is not cited, however, either in BA, the Elephantine Papyri, or in Lidz.

The cumulative evidence of this long list of words in the *Genesis Apocryphon* which do not occur in any pre-Christian Aramaic literature known to us prior to its discovery but which are in current use in Targumic times can lead only to the deduction that by the first century B.C. (or possibly the second or third century B.C., if Avigad and Yadin are correct in conjecturing an earlier origin), the vocabulary and spelling had substantially altered from that which prevailed in Daniel and Ezra. If linguistic testimony has any weight whatever, it is difficult to resist the conclusion that the Maccabean Date Theory for the composition of Daniel must be altogether surrendered—at least so far as the Aramaic chapters are concerned. But since these chapters (2–7) already contain much predictive material that did not find fulfillment until the second or even the first century B.C. (understanding the Fourth Kingdom of chapter 2 as foretelling the Roman conquest of the Near East), there is little point in maintaining that the Hebrew chapters of Daniel might still have been composed around 168 B.C. The stumbling block of fulfilled prophecy remains for the rationalist to cope with, and he cannot any longer explain it away as a mere pseudepigraph. The linguistic evidence of this scroll points to a far earlier date than 168 B.C. for the Aramaic of Daniel. Not only the divergent vocabulary but also the basic sentence structure of the two documents demonstrates a different period and provenance, irreconcilable with the second century theory. The characteristic pattern in Daniel is to defer the verb until later in the clause, often after the object itself (doubtless a reflection of the characteristic word-order of the Akkadian earlier spoken in Babylon). The *Apocryphon,* on the other hand, tends to conform more faithfully to normal Semitic order: first the verb, then the subject, and then the object (unless of course the verb consists of a participle in a periphrastic construction). It is therefore out of the question to regard the author of Daniel as living in the same geographical and cultural orbit as the author of the *Apocryphon,* and at approximately the same period of time, as is necessarily demanded by the Maccabean Date Theory. To disregard this linguistic testimony amounts to the grossest obscurantism unworthy of responsible scholarship.

III. Earlier Words with Later Meanings

The later origin of the *Genesis Apocryphon* is discernible not only by its use of new words, but also by the employment of older words with a new and different meaning.

1. A good instance in point is the verb $d^e \underline{b}aq$, which is very often used to mean "reach" or "arrive at" (19:8, 21:1, and frequently throughout Col. 21 and Col. 22). In Daniel 2:43 (the only occurrence in BA) it means "connect together"; in the Elephantine Papyri it often appears

with the meaning "adjoin" (of contiguous parcels of real estate) , cf. CAP 5:5; 8:6; 25:5, 8; 66:7. Only in the Apocryphon does it acquire the meaning of motion to, or arrival at a destination.

2. Another example of changed meaning is the verb *n^egaḏ* in 19:8, 22:3, etc., which seems to mean "go forth on one's way" or "follow after." In BA it occurs only in the pa'el, with the meaning "to stream, to flow." In CAP it appears as a passive participle (or p^e'īl?) *n^eḡîḏā,* meaning " (it is) described," or again as a hithp^e'el meaning "it is described, or drawn up." Possibly this is to be regarded as a different root altogether, although a homonym.

3. In *Apocryphon* 20:5 *k^elîl* is used to mean "perfect," as in Biblical Hebrew, *kālîl,* rather than "entire" or "whole burnt offering," "wreath" or "circle," as in the rest of extant Aramaic literature.

4. Two nouns are used as prepositions in a way hitherto unexampled in the pre-Christian period. In 19:16 *ṭ^elal,* which means "shade, shadow, screen" appears in the combination *biṭ^elal* to mean "for the sake of." So also in 19:20 with the following 2nd fem. sing. pronominal suffix: *b^eṭallêḵî,* "on thine account."

5. The second example of this type is *bārā (')* , which commonly appears in Biblical Aramaic as "forest" or "prairie," and in CAP as "desert"; but here in the *Apocryphon* it is used with a following *min* to mean "outside of" or "except" (22:23 and 22:31) —a common usage in Syriac.

IV. Formal Hebraisms in the Apocryphon

By "formal" Hebraisms we mean those words which show a specifically Hebrew form, as opposed to what they would normally be in Aramaic (rather than words adopted from Hebrew and then Aramaicized) . There are perhaps five of these in this scroll.

1. *'^enôš,* "man" instead of the normal Aramaic *'^enāš*—in 19:15 and 20:32.

2. The masc. plur. *'ōlāmîm* (or perhaps here *'āl^emîm*), instead of the usual Aramaic *'āl^emîn* (20:13) .

3. The precative or hortatory particle *nâ* is used in 20:25 in the common Hebrew way, but not hitherto known in Aramaic.

4. An amazing example of a converted imperfect is found in 21:6: *wayyiḇen,* "and he built"—the exact word used in the Hebrew original of Genesis 12:7 and related passages speaking of Abraham's altar-building. Since in this case the word is directly followed by the Aramaic "dative,"— *lēh*—rather than the Hebrew form *lô,* it can hardly be regarded as a quotation from the Hebrew, but must have been intended as an Aramaic word (for which the normal Aramaic would have been *ûḇ^enā (')* .

5. The Hebrew pronominal suffix is used in 21:10 *l^emoh^erātô,* "on its morrow."

V. Words or Expressions Not Previously Found in Aramaic Literature

It usually happens that each new document unearthed by modern archaeologists brings to light new words never before noted in the history of that language. To this the *Genesis Apocryphon* is no exception; this writer has found at least fourteen or fifteen terms and usages hitherto unknown in Aramaic literature. It may be of some use to list these words in the order of their appearance, appending the conjectural renderings offered by the ever-resourceful editors, Avigad and Yadin.

Column Two

1. Line 1, *hry't*, "conception" (compare the more conventional form *hrwn'* in 2:15).

2. Line 6, *hls*, "loin, waist" (BA shows only *hᵃras*—Dan. 5:6; CAP lacks the word in either spelling).

3. Line 9, *y'* as the interjection "Oh!" (but CAP does have *yh* in Ahiqar 127, 129).

4. Line 9 also has *'dynty* "pleasure" (cf. Jastrow's *'addîtā* (') "booty, lion's share").

Column Twenty

5. Line 3, *rgg* as an adjective: "pleasing" (cf. Jastrow's *rᵉgag* "to desire, long for, covet," and *rᵉgāgā* (') "desirable").

6. In Line 7, *dl* is the "tip" of Sarah's hands (cf. the adjective *dal* "thin, sparse").

7. Line 9 has *'wb'* rendered "at once."

8. Line 10 employs the combination *kdy* to mean "in order that"; BA uses it only as "when," while Jastrow's definitions include "when, now that, incidentally, as such, alone, merely, for no cause."

9. In Line 16 we meet with *mkdš*, which is translated "pestilential," but without any ascertainable basis in etymology.

10. Line 26 has the verb *ytwk* rendered "will depart"; possibly this is an ithpe'el of *hāk*, an abbreviation of *hᵃlak*, "to go"; but if so it is impossible to account for the *waw*.

11. In Line 26 is the mysterious term *šhlnp'* rendered "the evil," but possibly an idolatrous name of some sort.

Column Twenty-one

12. Line 31 contains a possible preposition, *'wr'* which is interpreted to mean "against." It is barely conceivable that this is cognate with the verb *'ᵃraq*, "to meet some one in battle."

Column Twenty-two

13. In Line 4 we find *hlt'*, translated as "valley," but with no ascertainable etymology or cognate. It goes without saying that words of this sort, which cannot be identified with any previously known period of

Aramaic literature, are of no help in establishing the point under discussion in this paper. They are simply listed to complete the vocabulary profile for this document.

Summary and Conclusion

By way of summary it may be said that the *Genesis Apocryphon* furnishes very powerful evidence that the Aramaic of Daniel comes from a considerably earlier period than the second century B.C. The fact that Targumic and Talmudic words abound in this first-century document indicates a considerable interval in time between its composition and that of Ezra and Daniel. Its use of normal Semitic word order in the clause as over against Daniel's tendency to follow a policy of placing the verb late in the clause points to a definite difference either in geographic origin (which would eliminate the possibility of Daniel's Maccabean composition in Palestine) or in epoch. Either inference is fatal to the pseudepigraph theory. It is fair to say, therefore, that the overall testimony of this scroll leads to abandonment of a long-cherished position of higher criticism, and makes the genuineness of Danielic authorship of Daniel an even more attractive option than it was before.

Notes

1. Nahman Avigad and Yigael Yadin, *The Genesis Apocryphon* (Jerusalem: Magnes Press, 1956).

2. Paul Winter, "Das Aramäische Genesis-Apokryphon," *Theologische Literatur Zeitung*, 4 (1957).

3. E. Y. Kutscher, "The Language of the Genesis Apocryphon: a Preliminary Study," *Scripta Hierosolymitana* (Jerusalem: 1958).

4. Winter, *op. cit.*, p. 260.

5. Kutscher, *op. cit.*, p. 30.

6. William B. Stevenson, *A Grammar of Palestinian Jewish Aramaic*, 2nd ed. (New York: Oxford University Press, 1962), no. 20.

7. *Ibid.*, no. 13.

8. *Ibid.*, no. 4.

9. *Ibid.*, no. 5.

10. *Ibid.*, no. 27.

11. *Ibid.*, no. 319.

—12—

THE GREEK WORDS IN DANIEL IN THE LIGHT OF GREEK INFLUENCE IN THE NEAR EAST

Edwin M. Yamauchi

I. The Problem

One of the strongest of the stock arguments for a late Hellenistic date for the composition of the book of Daniel has been the presence of three Greek words in the text. It is an argument which has been used without change in most critical commentaries from the end of the nineteenth century to the present.[1] S. R. Driver phrased it succinctly in a famous dictum: "The *Persian* words presuppose a period after the Persian empire had been well established: the Greek words *demand,* the Hebrew *supports,* and the Aramaic *permits,* a date *after the conquest of Palestine by Alexander the Great* (B.C. 332)"[2] (the italics are Driver's).

At the time when Driver's statement was made in 1897 there was widespread an understandable conviction that Greek contacts with Palestine and with Mesopotamia were very limited before the conquests of Alexander. Although this concept may still prevail in some quarters, there is little excuse for it today in the light of the accumulated evidence of early contacts between the Aegean and the Near East. James Montgomery, writing in 1927, was aware of the implications of the increasing knowledge of such an interchange: "The rebuttal of this evidence for a low date lies in the stressing of the potentialities of Gr. [sic] influence in the Orient from the 6th cent. and on. . . ."[3]

II. The Fragmentary Nature of the Evidence

The argument for a late date from the Greek words in Daniel is basically an argument from silence. It is reasoned that since we do not have certain corroborative evidence for something mentioned in the textual tradition, the reference must be anachronistic. Two examples, however, of such an argument from the classical world show how precarious such arguments can be.

Homer constantly refers to the bronze corselets of his heroes. As recently as 1950 in a comprehensive work on the archaeological data then available, Lorimer wished to regard these references as late interpolations, since there were no known bronze corselets of a Mycenaean date.[4] But in 1960 the first example of such a Late Bronze corselet was found at Dendra in the Argolid.[5] Then in 1963 a second Mycenaean example was found at Thebes in Boeotia.[6]

In 1948 Hanfmann denied that there was evidence for a major Greek migration to Ionia in western Asia Minor before the eighth century.[7] Writing in 1965, he now acknowledges that we have substantial evidence confirming the Greek tradition of an eleventh-century migration.[8]

Why are arguments from the silence of inscriptional and of material evidence so precarious? For the sake of those who are tempted to use such arguments and also for those who are not impressed by the evidence of a potsherd here and a potsherd there, one must grant the fragmentary nature of the non-traditional evidence. We have at our disposal but a fraction of a second fraction of a third fraction of a fourth fraction of the possible evidence.

First only a fraction of what is made or what is written ever survives. Speaking of Greek literature, Baldry notes: "Of scores of epic poems, we have a mere half dozen; of thousands of plays, forty-five; of countless speeches, enough to fill a few volumes."[9] This is true of even the works of the three greatest Greek dramatists—Aeschylus, Euripides, and Sophocles. Only about ten percent of their works have been transmitted to us. Of all the Greek lyric poets who wrote in the seventh and sixth centuries we have manuscripts only for Theognis and Pindar. Even for Pindar all but the victory odes are fragmentary. From Sappho, apart from fragments, we have only one complete poem.

If so little of highly prized literature survived, it is no surprise that even a smaller portion of mundane writing survived. To take an extreme example from the Roman world:

> In the first three hundred years of the empire there were never less than twenty-five Roman legions, and each legion had five thousand men. The legions were paid three times a year, so that there were 375,000 pay vouchers a year. Multiply that by three hundred, and the result is 112.5 million.[10]

Of this grand total of pay vouchers we have recovered only six and a fragment of a seventh.

In the second place only a fraction of the possible sites have been surveyed, and only a fraction of the surveyed sites have been excavated. In Greece over 300 Mycenaean sites are known.[11] But this number could be readily multiplied by more intensive and more extensive surveys. In 1944 the Palestine Gazette listed a total of about 3,000 sites in Cis-Jordan and several hundred in Trans-Jordan. In 1963 the total of known sites increased to about 5,000.[12] Paul Lapp estimated that of this total there had been scientific excavations at about 150 sites, including 26 major excavations. "To be sure, many of the sites on record would not merit extensive excavation, but if only one in four were promising, major excavations have till now been carried out at only two per cent of the potential sites."[13] Seton Lloyd notes that by 1949 more than 5,000 mounds had been located in Iraq.[14] As of 1962 Beek's atlas records twenty-eight major excavations in Iraq.[15]

Even those sites which have been chosen for excavation have rarely included sites which would yield evidence for the problem at hand. For example, Yeivin in his survey of excavations carried out by the Department of Antiquities in Israel from 1948–1958 counts a total of 320 operations—many of them salvage excavations which are excluded from Lapp's count. Of these only five operations touched the Late Israelite period (ca. 580–330 B.C.). Saul Weinberg, a classical archaeologist, speaking before the Israel Academy of Sciences and Humanities in March, 1968, stressed the lack of excavations in Israel designed to focus on the problem of Greek contacts.[16]

In the third place, with the exception of small and shallow sites such as Qumran and Masada, it is almost always the case that only a small fraction of any given site is actually excavated. The wealthy Oriental Institute excavations at Megiddo from 1925 to 1934 succeeded in completely removing the top four strata. But this grandiose scheme was abandoned in later seasons and has not been attempted at any site of comparable size. Yadin with a large staff of over thirty archaeologists and a crew of over a hundred laborers worked but a fraction of the site of Hazor in four seasons (1955–58). "He has suggested that it would take eight hundred years of about four of five months work per year to clear the entire site."[17] Now Garstang, who had made soundings at Hazor in 1928, concluded that Hazor was not an important city in the 14th and 13th centuries because of "the complete absence of Mykenaean specimens."[18] Yadin's excavations found houses littered with Mycenaean pottery.[19] From 1902–04 Sellin excavated nearly a fifth of Tell Taanach and concluded that there were no more important structures to be found and that the city had never been surrounded by a fortification wall. Both a fortification wall and important structures were found by Lapp in 1963.[20] The British excavated at Zakro in eastern Crete in 1901. They found houses but missed a palace, which was not found until the excavations under Platon begun in 1962.

In areas where a modern city rests upon an ancient site, excavations are costly and difficult, if not impossible. Chance discoveries in the course of building operations sometimes yield materials missed by the excavator. Part of the acropolis of Thebes in Greece was excavated in 1906 and 1921. In 1937 another part of the palace of Cadmus was discovered and again in 1963 an even more spectacular discovery was made during the course of building operations. Most of ancient Thebes, one of the most promising sites in Greece, remains unexcavated. Just the cost of appropriating the land and displacing the present town would cost one million dollars.[21] The Austrian mission of 1894 at Ephesus found magnificent late remains but nothing of the Bronze Age. In 1963 Turks building a parking lot found a Mycenaean burial there.[22] For decades no Mycenaean remains were found at Halicarnassus. In 1962 George Bass saw a man walking down the street, carrying a Mycenaean jar—obtained from a burial from a nearby village.[23]

In the fourth place, only a fraction of the materials and of the inscriptions produced by the excavations have ever been published. About 500,000 cuneiform documents have been excavated—"even this total seems to represent but a small fraction of those that still remain underground."[24] Kramer has estimated that only ten percent of this total have been published. Because of the scarcity of scholars who can publish ancient inscriptions and other factors, there is often a serious time lag between the acquisition and the publication of texts. Quite often texts acquired in the nineteenth century have been published only in the 1950's and 1960's. A Babylonian king list acquired in the 1880's by the British Museum was published in 1954.[25] The Aramaic papyri from Elephantine acquired by Charles Wilbour in 1893 were published in 1953.[26] A Demotic papyrus acquired in 1880 was published in 1959.[27] The Berlin Coptic Codex acquired in 1896 was not fully published until 1955.[28]

There are at times delays in the publication of material remains from excavations. The results of the 1900–1909 excavations at Phaistos on Crete were not fully published until 1951. Apart from the publication of the Lachish letters and of the fosse temple, the first major publication on the Lachish excavations—cut short by Starkey's murder in 1938—appeared in 1953. The reports on the Beth Shean dig completed in 1933 have not been fully published, though a work on the Iron Age levels was published in 1966.

The publication of Greek pottery found in the Near East has been incomplete and unsatisfactory, especially with regard to some of the earlier excavations. Clairmont, one of the few specialists concerned with Greek pottery in the Near East, comments:

> Scholars excavating Near Eastern sites in the late 19th and the first two decades of our century, have treated Greek pottery as a stepchild whenever it occurred among their finds. They undertook the excavations not in order to find Greek pots but to discover remains of the ancient civilizations of Egypt and the Near East for which sherds of the Bronze Age and the Early Iron Age are representative. In order to reach these lower levels, they had to dig through the upper levels of settlements which in many cases had been inhabited during

Iron Age II (9th to 6th cent. b.c.) and Iron Age III (Persian domination). As long as the technique of excavation had not been methodized in the modern sense, the excavators generally paid little or no attention to smaller finds from levels with which they were not immediately concerned, and ignored the stratification. . . . Sherds of pots, however, even Greek pottery with painted decoration, may have been light-heartedly thrown away if they happened to be covered with incrustations and the dirt of the centuries during which they had been hidden in the earth.[29]

Iliffe, writing in the 1930's, refers to a situation in which "few students of Palestinian archaeology have thought Greek pottery worthy of their serious attention."[30] Auscher regrets the fact that some of the earlier excavation reports from Palestine simply mention the existence of Greek sherds on a site without mentioning the number or the type.[31]

Clairmont's own survey of Greek pottery in the Near East, although it is one of the most complete in recent times, is far from comprehensive. It is based on materials from museums in Alexandria, Antioch, Beirut, Cairo, Damascus, Jerusalem, and some American and European collections. It refers to but does not incorporate finds from excavation reports. It does not include some major collections, e.g. Berlin, the British Museum, Baghdad, etc. Clairmont refers to numerous black-glazed Attic pottery in the Iraq Museum, noting, "As a whole they have never been published."[32]

If by a generous estimate one can guess that one-tenth of the artifacts and texts has survived, that one-tenth of the sites has been identified and excavated, that one-tenth of any given site has been touched, that one-tenth of what has been unearthed has been published—we would have in hand but one ten-thousandth of the potential evidence. Yet even that fraction of the evidence is impressive, and incorporates the evidence for early contacts between the Aegean and the Near East.

III. The Greek Words

There are three indisputable Greek words in Daniel—all of them musical terms. A fourth word kārôzâ (Dan. 3:4) has been derived by some scholars from the Greek word kērussein "to preach, to be a herald." But recent studies have not maintained a Greek etymology for this word.[33] The three musical terms that occur, for example in Daniel 3:5, are: 1) qaytᵉrōs, i.e. the Greek kitharis; 2) pᵉsantᵉrîn, i.e. the Greek psaltērion; and 3) sûmpōnᵉyā, i.e. the Greek sumphōnia. The concern of this chapter is not with the precise meanings of these terms, as this has been discussed elsewhere.[34]

There is no question as to the antiquity of the first word kitharis, which refers to a type of lyre. It is found in Homer (8th cen. b.c.) and in Herodotus (5th cen. B.C.) . There is, however, a question as to the early attestation of the two other terms. Driver asserted:

> But no such exception can be made in the case of *psaltērion* and *sumphōnia*, both *derived* forms, the former used first by Aristotle, the latter first by Plato, and in the sense of concerted music (or, possibly, of a specific musical instrument) first by Polybius. These words, it may be confidently affirmed, could not have been used in the Book of Daniel unless it had been written *after the dissemination of Greek influences in Asia through the conquests of Alexander the Great*[35] (italics are Driver's) .

The same position has been repeated without variation in most commentaries. For example, A. Jefferey holds that these two words "have a history within Greek which show that they could hardly have come into Oriental languages until that spread of Greek culture which followed the campaigns of Alexander the Great."[36]

The fragmentary nature of the extant remains of Greek literature, particularly of the lyric poets who might be expected to refer to musical instruments, should make one chary of dogmatic statements made from negative evidence. Driver holds that the word *psaltērion* was not used until the time of Aristotle (384–22 B.C.) . Yet the verbal root from which the noun is derived is found in Herodotus I, 155: *kitharizein te kai psallein . . . paideuein tous paidas* "to teach their sons lyre-playing and harp-playing." It is assumed that the *psaltērion* was a triangular-shaped instrument because of its epithet *trigōnon* in Aristotle; a triangular-shaped instrument is pictured as early as the ninth century on a Greek geometric vase.[37]

Driver also maintained that *sumphōnia* was first used by Plato (427–347 B.C.) , who uses it in the sense of "harmony of notes" and "agreement," and by Polybius (204–122 B.C.) in the sense of "concerted music." The idea that *sumphōnia* is a "bagpipe" is based largely on a late rabbinic interpretation, and has been abandoned by recent commentators. Yet in the general sense of "harmony" a close variant of the word is used by Pindar (6th cen. B.C.) in the Pythian Ode I, 70: *damon gerairōn trapoi sumphōnon es asuchian* "honor the people and prompt them to harmony and peace." Surely the secondary use of the word to mean harmony in human relations presupposes the earlier use of the word in its etymological sense of the harmony of sounds.

IV. Channels of Transmission

It appears to be no accident that the three Greek words are musical terms. Musical instruments and types of music, because of their exotic appeal, lend themselves to distribution and to acceptance in foreign lands—in many cases together with their original foreign names. To cite two recent American examples: in the early twentieth century there was a rage for the Hawaiian *ukulele,* as today there is a craze for the Indian *sitar.*

The lyre was introduced into Egypt from the east during the Hyksos period. "For many years after its introduction into Egypt it continued to be regarded as a 'foreign' instrument, and is often represented in tomb paintings of the Eighteenth Dynasty as being played by a Syrian."[38] Asiatic orchestras are portrayed in the palace of Akhnaton; in the Wenamon story an Egyptian singing woman appears at the court at Byblos.[39] In the third millennium B.C. an Elamite musical instrument from the mountainous region of Sabun became popular in Babylonia, where it was known as *sabitum.*[40] In China a kind of lute or mandolin from Bactria was called *p'i-pa;* a similar instrument in Persia was called *barbat,* and in Greece *barbiton.*[41]

Recent studies have shown that the ancient Mesopotamian musical notation was probably transmitted to the Greeks. F. Galpin had doubted that there was evidence for Mesopotamian notation.[42] But Anne Kilmer, a cuneiformist, and M. Duchesne-Guillemin, a musicologist, have collaborated to decipher a tablet from 1500 B.C. as the earliest evidence for notation.[43] The *kitharis* itself was probably borrowed originally from the Near East. Ellenbogen considers the name to be a foreign loan in Greek.[44]

The transmission of the musical terms may have taken place through the exchange of goods, the travels of musical guilds, or the capture of prisoners. The exchange of goods requires no further comment. Ancient societies were characterized by guild organizations, among whom musicians were prominent (Odyssey XVII, 381–86). Ugaritic guilds had the *shrm* "singers," and *mṣlm* "cymbalists." Cyrus Gordon has suggested that the travels of these minstrels, singing their epic tales to the accompaniment of lyres, may have been the means of transmitting some of the tales from the Near East to Greece.[45]

It is known that the Babylonians and Assyrians required their captives to perform on their own musical instruments for the victors (Ps. 137:1–3). In striking confirmation of this practice are two Assyrian reliefs.[46] The first celebrates Ashurbanipal's defeat of the Elamites and portrays six Elamite musicians. The second relief comes from Sennacherib's palace. It portrays three captive lyrists, perhaps from Lachish in Judah. In the Taylor Prism Sennacherib says, "As for Hezekiah, the awful splendour of my lordship overwhelmed him . . . male and female musicians he sent me later to Nineveh, my lordly city."[47] The Persians considered musicians to be prize captives. After a battle, the Medes selected for Cyrus the Great "the lady of Susa, who was said to be the most beautiful woman in Asia, and two of the most accomplished music girls (Xenophon, *Cyropaedia* IV, 6.11; cf. also V, 1.1; V, 5.2; and V, 5.38).

One further means of transmission may have been the presence of mercenary soldiers in the Near East, as music was long used for martial purposes. Another relief from Ashurbanipal's palace at Nineveh pictures a four-member military band, consisting of a hand drum, cymbals, an eight-stringed lyre, and a five-stringed lyre.[48] David used his musical talents to inspire his men to fight as a unit (II Sam. 1:18; Ps. 60:1). Achilles was an accomplished lyrist as well as a warrior. Tyrtaeus inspired Sparta to victory in the Second Messenian War (7th cen. B.C.) with his martial elegies. The Proto-Corinthian Chigi vase from the mid-seventh century B.C. portrays a piper playing to keep the hoplite warriors in step.[49] Archilochus of Paros (7th cen. B.C.), one of the earliest lyric poets, was also a mercenary soldier. He expressed his twofold interest as follows: "I am two things: a fighter who follows the Master of Battles, and one who understands the gift of the Muses' love."[50]

V. Contacts before 1000 B.C.

In his presidential address given in December, 1964, to the Society of Biblical Literature, Professor Frederick V. Winnett remarked:

> The list of Japhethite peoples in the table of nations in [Genesis] 10:2–5 points to an even later date, for judging from the other references to Japhethite peoples in the Old Testament, the Hebrews did not become acquainted with most of them until the time of Ezekiel and Deutero-Isaiah.[51]

Yet trade and interchange between the Aegean and the Near East is documented long before the sixth century B.C.

A mold from Mesopotamia has been found in Smyrna, on the west coast of Anatolia, carried there by an itinerant smith. Products from this and similar molds (ca. 2500–2200 B.C.) have been found in Mesopotamia, Cilicia, Troy, and Lemnos—an island in the Aegean west of Troy. Canby comments, "Whatever his purpose, the evidence of a merchant's travelling from Mesopotamia across Anatolia to the Aegean coast at the end of the Third Millennium B.C. lends credence to what had once seemed an unlikely tradition of the Akkadian kings' far flung adventures in this area."[52]

There are evidences of mutual relations between Mesopotamia and Crete early in the second millennium. From Platanus on Crete comes a Babylonian cylinder seal of hematite, dated to the time of Hammurabi (18th cen. B.C.).[53] Conversely there is documentary evidence from Mari on the middle Euphrates that there was trade with *Kaptara* (Biblical Caphtor), i.e., Crete at this time. Zimrilim, the king of Mari, sent Hammurabi an object from Crete.[54] An inscription of Naram-Sin of Eshnunna was found on Cythera off the south coast of Greece; this is also from the Old Babylonian period.[55]

Daggers from Byblos in the Levant have been found in Cyprus and in Crete from the early second millennium.[56] There is evidence of a Lycian from southwest Anatolia at Byblos ca. 2000 B.C.[57]

About 1850 B.C. a syllabic script called Linear A was developed on Crete. This continued in use until about 1450 B.C. This has been found mainly at Hagia Triada, but also at a number of other sites on Crete. Isolated texts have also been found at Melos, Thera, and Ceos in the Aegean, at Argolis and Messenia in Greece, and at Ugarit.[58] In 1962 Cyrus Gordon announced that he had succeeded in analyzing Linear A and related Eteocretan ("original" Cretan written in Greek letters from 600–300 B.C.) as Semitic.[59] The decipherment has been questioned by classicists not at home in Semitic, disputed by some Semitists,[60] and defended by others.[61] One of the problems is the relative paucity of the Linear A texts as compared with the later Linear B texts. Whereas there are nearly 4,000 of the latter, there are little over 200 of the former. Rival suggestions have been made that Linear A is Luwian, an Anatolian dialect,[62] and that it is Hittite.[63] If Gordon is correct—as I believe he is—then we have further evidence of contacts between the Aegean and the Near East. According to his analysis Hurrian and Ugaritic names occur in the Semitic Linear A texts. An analysis by Astour of an Egyptian text from 1500 B.C. of fourteen names of Keftiu, i.e. Crete, lends support to Gordon's analysis. Astour found that the list contained two Akkadian names, four West Semitic names, six Hurrian names, one mixed Hurro-West Semitic name, and one North Syrian name.[64]

About 1450 B.C. the Mycenaean Greeks seem to have taken over Knossos. From Knossos Evans found almost 3,000 tablets written in Linear B. Since 1939 about 1,000 Linear B tablets have been found at Pylos and about 40 at Mycenae since 1950. In 1963 seven Linear B tablets were found at Thebes in Boeotia. These texts used from 1450 to 1150 B.C. were deciphered as Greek by a young British architect, Michael Ventris, in 1952.[65]

Among the names in Linear B are: *Arasiyo* "the Cypriote," *Aradayo* "the man from Arad" in Lebanon, *Perita* "the man from Beirut," and *Turiyo* "the man from Tyre." Among the most interesting words in Linear B are *ponike* and *ponikiya*, the former referring perhaps to a griffin and the latter to crimson dye—both associated with Phoenicia.[66] Contrary to the opinion of many critics, Homer was not speaking amiss when he described in the Odyssey the early contacts of the Greeks with the Phoenicians.

Already at this early date there are in addition to the ethnic names a number of Semitic loanwords in Greek. Most of these are the names of imported products: *kuruso* "gold" (cf. Semitic *kharuṣ*); *kumino* "cummin" a spice (cf. Ugaritic *kmn*, Hebrew *kammōn*, Akkadian *kamūnu*); *kuparo* "cyperus" a spice (cf. Hebrew *kōper*); *sasama* "sesame" (cf.

Akkadian *shammashammu,* Ugaritic *shshmn*) ; *kito* "tunic" (cf. Akkadian *kitintu,* Ugaritic *ktnt*) . The various spices were probably transported in the "Canaanite" jars which have been found at Mycenae.[67]

One of the interesting Linear B words is *erepateyo,* i.e. *elephanteia* "of ivory." There are numerous examples of carved ivory in the Aegean, probably from Syria where elephants were still to be found. These ivories incorporate numerous eastern motifs such as griffins and sphinxes, and are to be compared with the Megiddo ivories of the thirteenth century. The Mycenaeans made their own adaptations and subsequently influenced ivory carving on Cyprus, and in Syria and Palestine.[68]

Bronze figurines of a smiting god from Syria were imported into Greece in the fifteenth and fourteenth centuries, and became the models of Greek images of the smiting Zeus.[69]

A spectacular confirmation of relations between Greece and the Near East came in the course of building operations in 1963 at Thebes in Boeotia. A cache of 36 cylinder seals of lapis lazuli, 14 with cuneiform inscriptions, was uncovered. One of these bears the name of an official of Burraburriash II (1367–46 B.C.) , a Kassite king of Mesopotamia.[70] Thebes is appropriately the legendary home of Cadmus, the Phoenician prince and brother of Europa.[71]

The movement of the Mycenaeans and their wares eastward can be best traced through the distribution of their pottery. Excavations in the last twenty years have turned up Mycenaean pottery at an increasing number of sites in western Asia Minor and even as far inland as Sardis. Farther east great quantities of Mycenaean pottery have been found on Cyprus especially from 1400 B.C. on. Although some of the pottery must have been locally made, recent laboratory tests indicate that the mass of fourteenth and thirteenth century Mycenaean pottery on Cyprus was still imported from the Aegean.[72] The strategic position of Cyprus as a crossroads is indicated by the fact that in one excavation six seal impressions were found to have the following origins: one Babylonian, one Minoan, three Minoan-Mycenaean, and one Mycenaean-Cypriote.[73]

Northeast of Cyprus, Greek influence is attested by Mycenaean pottery in Cilicia. A Greek tradition related that some of the Greeks under Mopsus migrated to Cilicia after the Trojan War in the thirteenth century. This has been strikingly confirmed by the famous bilingual inscription from Karatepe. In it a ruler of the eighth century, Azitawadda, claims descent from the house of Mopsus, rendered *Mukshush* in Hittite and *Mupsh* in Phoenician.[74]

East of Cyprus at Minet el-Beida, the port of Ugarit, there seems to have been a Mycenaean trading settlement as evidenced by the Aegean type corbel-vaulted tombs there. The famous ivory pyxis lid from Minet el-Beida, portraying a bare-breasted goddess flanked by two goats, is an interesting example of an Oriental motif in Mycenaean dress.[75]

The distribution of Mycenaean pottery in Phoenicia and Palestine is well attested.[76] Mycenaean pottery is divided into several chronological phases: Myc. I, 1550–1500; Myc. II, 1500–1425; Myc. III A, 1425–1300; Myc. III B, 1300–1230; and Myc. III C, 1230–1025. Myc. II pottery is rare in the Levant: sherds have been found at Alalakh, Ugarit, Byblos, Gezer, Lachish, Tell el-Ajjul, and recently at Ashdod.

In north Syria Myc. III A sherds have been found at Alalakh, at Ugarit, and at the inland Orontes sites of Hama, Katna, and Kadesh. Myc. III A pottery has been found at Hazor, Tell Abu Hawam, Beth Shean, Jerusalem, Gezer, Beth Shemesh, Jericho, Gaza, Askalon, Lachish, Tell el-Ajjul, Gerar, and Tell Beit Mirsim. Tell el-Ajjul and Askalon in the south and Tell Abu Hawam, near Mount Carmel, served as ports of entry.

Myc. III B sherds have been found in the northern Levant at Alalakh, Ugarit, Byblos, and Sarepta. In Palestine they have been found at Hazor, Tell Abu Hawam, Megiddo, Taanach, Shechem, Gezer, Beth Shemesh, Ashdod, Lachish, Askalon, Tell el-Ajjul, Tell Fara, Tell el-Hesi, Tell Jemmeh, and Tell Beit Mirsim.

Mycenaean pottery has also been found in Trans-Jordan. Sherds have come from Madaba on the Moabite plateau, and from Tell es-Sa'idiyeh, "deep in the Jordan Valley, separated from the obvious trade routes by the barriers of a high mountain and a river."[77] It has been found as far inland as Tell Achari on the banks of a tributary of the River Yarmuk, twenty-five miles east of the Sea of Galilee. Stubbings asks, "One may well speculate why such imported pottery should penetrate so far inland. Is there some hint of a link with caravan routes to Mesopotamia?"[78] As a matter of fact, although it is scant evidence, one Mycenaean sherd from Babylon has been published.[79]

The widespread interchange in the Late Bronze Age between the Aegean and the Near East left not only the evidence of abandoned potsherds, but a more permanent legacy of ideas and motifs. As Martin Nilsson shrewdly reasoned twenty years before the decipherment of Linear B, the roots of Greek mythology go back to the Mycenaean period.[80] The recent finds at Thebes lend credence to the Greek traditions of a near Eastern origin of Cadmus, the eponymous founder of the city. Gordon's decipherment of Linear A as Northwest Semitic fits perfectly the tradition that Cadmus's sister, the Phoenician princess Europa, was the mother of Minos, the legendary king of Knossos.[81] It is widely recognized that the original inspiration for the Greek theogony recorded by Hesiod is the Hurrian-Hittite myth of Kumarbi.[82]

The close analogies between the Greek and Mesopotamian concepts of the afterlife are probably not fortuitous.[83] The Greeks, as is well known, had their famous ferryman Charon who transported the dead across the river Styx. Not so well known is the fact that the Mesopotamians also had a similar concept. In the Sumerian myth of "Enlil and Ninlil: Birth of the Moon God," a boatman ferries the dead across a "man-devouring" river.[84] In the Babylonian Theodicy, we read " (Men must) go the way of death; 'You shall cross the river Hubur,' they are ordered from eternity."[85] The ferryman was called *Humuṭ-taba* "Bear Swiftly."

At the end of the Late Bronze Age the lands bordering the eastern Mediterranean were in ferment. Primitive Dorian Greeks succeeded in destroying most of the Mycenaean centers except Athens. The Hittite Empire also came to a demise at this time, overrun by northern barbarians. Uprooted peoples from the Aegean and Anatolia, known in Egyptian records as the "Sea Peoples," attacked the Levant and Egypt during the reigns of Merneptah (ca. 1220) and of Ramesses III (ca. 1170). Among the groups were the Akaywash, who have been identified with the Achaean Greeks.[86] Waldbaum suggests that these may have been responsible for the "900" tombs at Tell Fara. These were based on Mycenaean prototypes and contained Myc. III B pottery.[87]

The most famous of the Sea Peoples were the Philistines. Their exact origin has been the subject of debate. Amos 9:7 reads: "Have not I brought up Israel out of the lands of Egypt and the Philistines from Caphtor (i.e. Crete) . . . ?"[88] The Phaistos disk found in southern Crete (dated ca. 1700 B.C.) portrays a man with a feathered headdress similar to those worn by the Philistines. Eight lentoid Minoan seals from the end of the second millennium were found at Gaza, a Philistine center.[89]

In 1964 at Deir 'Alla in the Jordan Valley in a stratum dated to the thirteenth century three inscribed tablets were found.[90] The script resembles the Minoan Linear A syllabary from Crete. Albright has suggested that these might be Philistine texts.[91] The excavator, however, notes that the texts were found in the stratum previous to that which contained Philistine pottery.[92] Perhaps these should be associated with a pre-Philistine Sea People from the Aegean.

Albright has added his voice to those who favor an origin of the Philistines from southwestern Anatolia.[93] In any case what has become crystal clear is that the Philistines came from the area of the Aegean and that they were in close contact with the Mycenaean Greeks. Their organization resembles that of the Greek amphictyony.[94] There are a number of striking parallels with the Aegean world in the Biblical account of the Philistine champion Goliath (I Sam. 17).[95] Philistine pottery is derived from Myc. III C pottery. The recent study by Trude Dothan has shown close affinities between Philistine *kernoi* (ring-shaped vessels with small figures attached at intervals) and Greek examples.[96]

The later "500" tombs like the earlier "900" tombs at Tell Fara are derived from Aegean prototypes; the "500" tombs contain the anthropoid clay coffins which have been attributed to the Philistines.[97]

The name of the Philistine lords in the Old Testament, *serānīm*, is thought to be related to the Greek word *turannos* "tyrant"—which is itself evidently a loan from Anatolia. But there are other words in early Hebrew that may be Greek. Cyrus Gordon has argued that "since the language of Minoan Linear B is Greek, it is not surprising that *early* Hebrew vocabulary has loanwords familiar to us from Greek. Hebrew *mᵉkērā (h)* has long been identified (already in rabbinic literature) as Greek *machaira* 'sword,' . . ."[98] Speiser rejected this suggestion of a Greek etymology for *mkrtyhm* in Genesis 49:5 as an anachronism, not taking into account the considerable contact between Palestine and the Aegean in the second millennium.[99] Other suggestive parallels listed by Gordon are: Hebrew *liškā (h)* "chamber" with Greek *leschē;* Hebrew *lappîd* "torch" with Greek *lampas,* genitive *lampados;* and Hebrew *mûm* "blemish" with Greek *mōmos* "blame."[100] Another Hebrew word which can best be explained as an early Greek loanword is the word for ship which occurs as *'anâji* in the Amarna letters.

> This word *'anâji* has long been recognized as the primitive, uncontracted form, represented in later Hebrew by the word *'ôniyâh* (for **'anajiâ*). What is the etymology of *'anâji?* It has no Semitic root and can only be from the Indo-European root of *naus-navis* (ship), perhaps preceded by the article. This means that a certain type of ship was already brought to the Levant by the Mycenaean Greeks by the 14th century B.C., and had been a familiar sight, and a study of the use in the Hebrew Bible of the word *'ôniyâh* shows that it described a heavy, sea-going ship, usually in the phrase *'ôniyat Taršiš,* a ship of Tarshish, which I think we can show was a Phoenician development of the Mycenaean ship.[101]

VI. Contacts between 1000 and 700 B.C.

In the Aegean, the period after the Dorian invasions of the twelfth century was a Dark Age. But recent studies have shown that this Dark Age was not as dark or dark for as long as had been supposed. Excavations in the Ceramicus in Athens show that after the degenerate Sub-Mycenaean style of 1125–1075 a vigorous, well-proportioned ware known as Proto-Geometric developed from 1075–900. This is characterized by the use of compass-drawn concentric circles and semi-circles. Its wide distribution attests to the vigor of Athenian culture at this time.[102]

Proto-Geometric ware has been found in western Asia Minor at Miletus, Smyrna, Phocaea, and Clazomenae—confirming the Greek traditions of the Aeolic and Ionian migrations, which had been doubted by critics.[103] Recently Sub-Mycenaean and Proto-Geometric sherds were found inland at Sardis.[104] In the Near East there is evidence of Proto-Geometric ware at Cyprus, at Tarsus and Mersin in Cilicia, and at Judaideh, Tell Tayinat, Hama, and Hammam in Syria. At Nineveh one Sub-Mycenaean and one Proto-Geometric sherd have been discovered.[105] In Palestine the ware has been found at Askalon and at Tell Abu Hawam.[106] It is worth noting that the latter served as a port of entry for both the earlier Mycenaean pottery and for the later Geometric pottery. This implies that contact with the Aegean although diminished was not altogether broken during the Greek Dark Age.

Another evidence for continued contact with the Greek world during this period is the distribution of the fibula, a type of safety pin. In the early eleventh century semi-circular fibulae associated with Aegean immigrants appeared on Cyprus. In addition to the Greek colonies on Cyprus this type of fibula has been found in the Amuq in Syria, and at Tell en-Nasbeh and Tell Abu Hawam in Palestine.[107] It should be noted that fibulae in general are worn and not traded.

In the ninth and eighth centuries the Geometric style of pottery flourished in Greece. As the name implies this style used a number of geometric designs, such as the meander, the swastika, and the herringbone. Geometric ware has been found at various sites on Cyprus, and at Mersin and Tarsus in Cilicia. At the latter site numerous fragments of Ionian ware were found in the levels below that marked by the destruction of the city by Sennacherib in 696 B.C.[108]

In Syria Geometric ware has been found at Amuq, Hama, Hammam, and Al Mina. Al Mina, established in 800 at the mouth of the Orontes River, was the most important Greek trading station in the Levant. The memory of the site may have been transmitted through the Dark Age; Mycenaean sherds have been found three miles upstream. The site is especially significant since there is evidence of the continual importation of Greek and Cypriote ware from this period, with but a small break in the sixth century, until 312 B.C.[109] In Mesopotamia Geometric ware has been found at Tell Halaf in the northwest. An unpublished example from Nineveh has been reported.[110] From Babylon come two Geometric sherds from the eighth century.[111] In Palestine two ninth-century sherds have been found at Megiddo, and an eighth-century crater from Argos at Samaria. Other sherds have been found at Achzib and at Tell Abu Hawam.[112]

In the ninth and eighth centuries carved ivories known collectively as "Nimrud ivories" were distributed widely over the Near East and the Aegean probably from Phoenicia.[113] In the west these ivories or their imitations have been found at Samos, Ephesus, Rhodes, Crete, Delphi, Athens, Corinth, and Sparta.[114] In Palestine they have been found appropriately at Samaria (cf. II Kgs. 22:39; cf. Amos 6:4). In the east these have been found at Zinçirli, Carchemish, Arslan Tash, Khorsabad, Ashur, and above all at Nimrud.

Mallowan's excavations at Nimrud have produced many ivory master-works, including some of native Assyrian workmanship. Ivory and lime-stone lions have been found that may be paralleled by examples in Iran, Samos, and Greece.[115] Ivory plaques portraying a man thrusting a sword in the mouth of a winged griffin dated 730–720 are paralleled in metal work at Cyprus and in the Aegean not more than 50 years later.[116] A lovely ivory chair of the eighth century is now paralleled by a contempo-rary chryselephantine chair found on Cyprus; both recall the descrip-tion in Homer's *Odyssey* of Penelope's chair.[117] A wax writing tablet dated 715 B.C. recalls the tablets in the story of Bellerophon in the Iliad. A nearly contemporary tablet in an Etruscan tomb is but one of many articles which indicate oriental influence, or even the presence of oriental craftsmen in the far west.[118] The image of a cherubic female was proba-bly transmitted from the east through Cyprus to Etruria.[119]

Many finds from Sparta, Perachora, and Corinth are similar to finds from Nimrud. The Orientalizing lead plaques from eighth-century Sparta can be compared with bronze plaques from Nimrud. Mallowan suggests that at the outset Oriental workmen may have introduced the fashion, which over the years became wholly modified to suit Greek tastes.[120] Bone and ivory figurines from Perachora and Sparta though of Greek workmanship are related to nearly contemporary works in As-syria.[121] The ivory heads of females may have served as the inspiration for the later Greek *korai*.[122]

In the eighth and seventh centuries Phoenician metal bowls decorated with a mixture of Egyptian, Syrian, and Mesopotamian motifs were widely distributed. They have been found in Assyria, Cyprus, Greece, and Etruria.[123] In a siege scene on a bowl from Cyprus we see Assyrian archers and horsemen attacking a fort defended by soldiers with Greek shields.[124] The fact that men with Aegean shields are also to be found among the Assyrians is not just a stock device. Nothing is clearer from the history of mercenary warfare than the fact that mercenaries from the same group will be found fighting on both sides of a battle—e.g. Philis-tines fighting both for and against Egyptians, Greeks fighting both for and against Persians at Cunaxa.

In the seventh century tridacna shells from the Red Sea incised with elaborate designs have been found in many areas. "The distribution of these in the Near East points to Assyria as the source, although the style is perhaps more Phoenician."[125] A survey of these shells has been made by Amandry: one was found at Etruria; in the Aegean, nine at Lindos, one at Camiros, one at Cos, two at Aegina; in Egypt, five at Naucratis, one at Daphnae, one at Memphis; in Palestine, one at Bethlehem; and in Mesopotamia, five at Ashur, two at Babylon, one at Warka, one at Obeid, two at Nineveh, and one at Sippar.[126] Also in the seventh century various Assyrian motifs are adopted in Corinthian art.[127] An Assyrian cylinder seal has been found at Olympia.[128]

A possible contribution of Phoenicia to the Greeks may have been the Proto-Aeolic (or Proto-Ionic) columns. Harden, who regards these columns as Phoenician, points out the fact that thus far no examples have been found in Phoenicia itself.[129] The earliest prototype seems to be from Ashur in the eleventh century.[130] Examples have been found in Cyprus[131] and in Palestine from the tenth century on at Megiddo, Samaria, Hazor, and recently at Jerusalem,[132] and at Ramat Rahel.[133] It has also been found at Medeibi' in Transjordan. Albright feels that the Greeks of Cyprus and of Ionia borrowed them from the Phoenicians about the eighth century, as they become more frequent among the Greeks in the seventh century.[134]

In the eighth century products from distant Urartu, north of Assyria, were exported to the west. The Urartians were especially known for their skill in metallurgy. One of their products was a cauldron decorated with bull, lion, or griffin protomes. Such objects and their imitations have been found on Cyprus, at Gordion in Anatolia, on Rhodes, on Crete, at Olympia, Delphi, Athens, and Argos in Greece, and in Etruria.[135] Amandry has suggested that the cauldrons were first imported at the end of the eighth century, copied in an oriental style at the beginning of the seventh century, and made in an independent style by the middle of the seventh century.[136]

From even farther east came objects from Luristan in western Persia. A Luristan pendant was discovered at Knossos and a Luristan ewer at Samos[137] Exotic tapestries from Persia were probably imported. All of these fluid and sometimes florid designs helped to liberate Greek art from "the tyranny of the ruler and compass" which prevailed in Geometric art, producing the Proto-Corinthian and Proto-Attic wares of the seventh century known as "Orientalizing" styles. Ghirshman has assembled a striking collection of examples illustrating the influence of Urartian and of Persian motifs on various arts and crafts in Greece during the eighth and seventh centuries.[138]

Without question the most important contribution of the east to the west in this period was the transmission of the Phoenician alphabet to the Greeks at the latest by the eighth century.[139] It is interesting to note also that there are loanwords coming into Greek from the Semitic languages as well as Greek words coming into Semitic at this time. A spindle whorl with a short Phoenician inscription of the eighth century from Çatal Hüyük in north Syria (not the site by the same name in Asia Minor) contains a Greek loanword for thread.[140] In Homer (8th cen.) appear the Akkadian loanwords *krokos* "crocus" from *kurkanu,* and *pelekus* "axe" from *pilakku*.[141] The word (*F*) *rodon* for "rose" from *amaridu* (*amurdinnu*), another Akkadian word, was absorbed into Greek by the seventh century. Many other Mesopotamian words—including *mna* from mina in Herodotus, and *siglos* from shekel in Sophocles— were absorbed into Greek before the end of the fifth century.[142]

VII. Contacts between 700 and 400 B.C.

The eighth century witnessed the expansion of the militant empire of the Assyrians westward. The Assyrians came into direct contact with the Greeks in Cilicia and in Cyprus. In 713 seven Greek kings of Cyprus came to do homage to Sargon II at Babylon.[143] Greek fibulae were found in Sargon's palace in Assyria.[144] In 712 Sargon was forced to take action against Yamani—the Ionian Greek[145]—who had rebelled after having been enthroned by the people of the Philistine city of Ashdod.[146]

Sennacherib (705–682). Sargon's successor, had to contend in 696 B.C. with a revolt in Cilicia, led by Kirua, the Assyrian governor of Illubri. Kirua was supported by Greeks from Ingira (Greek Anchiale) and Tarsus. Sennacherib ruthlessly suppressed the revolt, and transported the captives to Mesopotamia. The account of the revolt is also recounted in the writings of Berossus, a Babylonian priest of the third century B.C. who wrote in Greek.[147] In 694 Sennacherib assembled a navy built by Phoenicians at Nineveh and Til Barsip to hunt down the ambitious Babylonian king Merodach-Baladan. The ships, staffed by Tyrians, Sidonians, and Ionian Greeks, were floated downstream to Chaldea in an unsuccessful attempt to capture the rebellious Babylonian.[148]

Esarhaddon (681–70) took up his residence at Nineveh and at the beginning of his reign undertook the construction of a number of buildings in a new suburb. For the materials he turned to the west. The list of contributors included ten rulers from Cyprus, whose names are Greek.[149] In 671 Esarhaddon succeeded in conquering Egypt. The Egyptians, however, rebelled and Esarhaddon died in 670 on his way to suppress the revolt.

Ashurbanipal (669–33) proceeded to Egypt in 667 and took not only Memphis in Lower Egypt, but also sacked Thebes in Upper Egypt. Over the years 658–51, Psammetichus I, founder of the Saite Dynasty, succeeded in ousting the Assyrians with the aid of Ionian and Carian mercenaries sent to him by Gyges (687–52), king of Lydia in western Anatolia. Earlier Gyges had sought Assyrian help against invading Cimmerians. For this subsequent act of treachery by Gyges, Ashurbanipal prayed for the Lydian king's death and was able duly to record the fulfillment of this prayer. Herodotus (II, 152–54) describes how the Egyptians set up these Ionians and Carians (Caria is in southwest Anatolia) in camps by the Nile, and how the Egyptians had their boys learn Greek to serve as interpreters. Excavations at Daphnae on the Pelusiac arm of the Nile uncovered a camp that would have held 20,000 men.

The next pharaoh, Necho (610–595), employed Greek mercenaries in his conflict with Nebuchadnezzar at Carchemish in northwest Mesopotamia in 605. At Carchemish Leonard Woolley and T. E. Lawrence (of Arabia) found arrowheads and a Greek shield in a house that contained Egyptian objects and sealings of Necho.[150]

There is now evidence that some Greek mercenaries, probably from Egypt, found employment in the seventh and sixth centuries in Palestine. In 1960 between Ashdod and Jaffa at Meṣad Ḥashavyahu a fortress covering one and one-half acres was excavated. East Greek ware in large quantity dating to the end of the seventh century was found here.[151] The site was established by Greeks about 630–25. Although there is no actual evidence of Egyptian control, the settlers were probably Greek mercenaries employed by Psammetichus I. The fortress was conquered by Josiah a few years before 609 and never resettled.[152]

Farther inland just west of the Dead Sea at Arad inscribed ostraca were discovered from the fortress which was destroyed in Nebuchadnezzar's first campaign (c. 600–598). These ostraca come from the archive of Eliashib, who was in charge of distributing supplies to the *Kittim*. Since the term in the Old Testament refers to Greeks of the Aegean and of Cyprus, Aharoni, the excavator of Arad, has concluded that these Kittim in the ostraca were Greek mercenaries serving in the remote forts of Judah.[153] Some of the personal names in the ostraca are apparently Greek.[154] Although no Greek pottery has been found at Arad as yet, East Greek ware has been found at nearby Tel Malḥata.[155]

In the areas north of Palestine seventh- and sixth-century archaeological evidence of continuing Greek penetration has been found. Pottery, mainly Corinthian and Rhodian, is found in Anatolia as far inland as Midas City, Gordion, Boghaz-koy, and Alishar. It is found on Cyprus, in Cilicia at Mersin and Tarsus, in Syria at Sakçe Gozu, Çatal Hüyük, Zinçirli, and Al Mina. There is an interesting gap at Al Mina that corresponds with the rise of the Neo-Babylonian Empire. The Babylonians may have suppressed Al Mina in favor of Tell Sukas, fifty miles to the south, to compete with Tyre. At Tell Sukas there is a great amount of Greek pottery, especially from 600–550. At this site was recently found a spindle whorl, dated to 600, with a woman's name of Ionian type in Greek script.[156]

In the east at the end of the seventh century a coalition of Medes, Scythians, and Babylonians overturned the once formidable Assyrian Empire, capturing Nineveh in 612. The greatest ruler of the Neo-Babylonians was Nebuchadnezzar (605–561). The last king of the rather short-lived empire was Nabonidus (555–39), whose son Belshazzar was in charge of Babylon during Nabonidus' self-imposed, ten-year exile in Arabia.

As already noted above, Necho employed Greek mercenaries in his battle with Nebuchadnezzar at Carchemish in 605. It is more than possible that Greek mercenaries fought for the Babylonians there also. We know that Antimenidas, the brother of the famous poet Alcaeus, fought for Nebuchadnezzar as a mercenary against Askalon in 604.[157]

Nebuchadnezzar also employed Greek craftsmen, as twice a group of eight and twice a group of seven Ionian craftsmen are named.[158] Included in the groups are some with Luwian names from southwestern Anatolia. The walls of the king's throne room at Babylon were decorated with a row of yellow columns superimposed with Ionic capitals. Clairmont suggests that these are the work of Ionian artisans.[159]

In 585 during Nebuchadnezzar's reign, Nabonidus (who is called Labynetus in Herodotus I, 74) was sent to Anatolia to arrange peace between the Medes and the Lydians. It is of interest to note that a late seventh or early sixth-century Babylonian seal has been found at Sardis, capital of Lydia.[160] According to tradition one of the factors that worked for peace was the occurrence of an eclipse in 585, just as Thales—the father of Greek science—had predicted.[161] Greeks, probably Cypriotes, were well known to Nabonidus. His annals record that iron was imported to Babylonia from Iamana, i.e. an area associated with Ionians (cf. Ezk. 27:19).[162] Oppenheim notes, "Even before Cyrus occupied Babylon in 539 B.C., the economic texts from the great sanctuaries in Sippar, Babylon, and Uruk offer evidence of trade relations that reached to the Mediterranean (Cilician iron) and even as far as Greece."[163]

Greek pottery of the seventh and sixth century has been found in Mesopotamia. One Rhodian sherd of the late seventh century has been found at Nineveh.[164] At Babylon one Greek sherd of Ionian fabric of the seventh century and sherds of nine Greek vessels of the sixth century have been found.[165]

Cyrus, who was half-Median and half-Persian, seized the leadership of the Medes and the Persians by 550. He first expanded his domain by marching westward to engage the wealthy Croesus, king of Lydia. Cyrus took the city of Sardis in 546. His general Harpagos captured the Ionian cities. Greek cities were now an integral part of the Persian Empire.

Elements of Greek style may be seen in the architecture of Pasargadai, the palace which Cyrus built c. 550. The use of folds in the sculptured garments as Pasargadai came from the Ionian Greeks.[166] The tomb of Cyrus was decorated with a Greek molding.

Cyrus was succeeded by his son Cambyses II (529–22), whose most noteworthy accomplishment was the conquest of Egypt in 525. In this campaign he was aided by a Greek mercenary, Phanes of Halicarnassus, who had defected from the army of Psammetichus III (Herodotus III,

4 and 11). After Cambyses' death a Magian seized the throne for seven months. Darius succeeded in gaining control in 522 and ruled until 486.

In 513 with the aid of Ionian Greeks Darius embarked on an ambitious but futile campaign against the Scythians west of the Black Sea. In 499 the Ionians revolted and were not suppressed until 494. Miletus was besieged and sacked. Most of the survivors of this city were transplanted to Mesopotamia by the mouth of the Tigris River (Herodotus VI, 18 ff.). During the Ionian Revolt Athens and the city of Eretria, on the island of Euboea, had sent aid to the Ionians. Darius sent a fleet in 492 to punish these two cities. In spite of a storm which wrecked the fleet Darius was able to establish control in Thrace, a part of Europe. In 490 another punitive force of the Persians was defeated at the famous battle of Marathon. The Persians were successful, however, in taking the city of Eretria. The prisoners were transported to "Kissian" country along the borders between Babylonia and Persia. Some fifty years later Herodotus saw them "still preserving their ancient language" (Herodotus VI, 119). Their fate was bemoaned by Plato, a generation later:

> Leaving the rough Aegean's surge and swell,
> Afar in inland Median plains lie.
> Farewell, Eretria famed, our home; farewell
> Athens, our neighbour there; farewell, dear sea.[167]

The Ionian Greeks that Darius had with him proved useful in many ways. Early in his reign, Democedes of Croton, a famous physician cured the king's foot and healed a swelling on the breast of Atossa the queen (Herodotus III, 129 ff.). Darius used Scylax, a navigator from Caria, and other trusted persons, probably Ionian Greeks, to explore the Indus River Valley in 510 (Herodotus IV, 44).[168] Pliny states how the eminent sculptor Telephanes of Phocaea executed many important works for Darius and Xerxes.[169]

Other anonymous Greeks were employed as craftsmen for building enterprises. In his famous building inscription from Susa, Darius enumerated the various contributions from his empire, including the following references to Ionians:

> This palace which I built at Susa, from afar its ornamentation was brought. . . . The cedar timber, this—a mountain by name Lebanon—from there was brought. The Assyrian people, it brought it to Babylon; from Babylon the Carians and the Ionians brought it to Susa. . . . The ornamentation with which the wall was adorned, that from Ionia was brought. . . . The stone-cutters who wrought the stone, those were Ionians and Sardians. . . . The men who wrought the baked brick, those were Babylonians.[170]

The last word of the citation is simply rendered "Babylonians" in the Old Persian and Elamite versions, but the Akkadian version seems to indicate that this means "Ionians resident in Babylonia."[171] The line which speaks of cedar being transported from Babylon to Susa implies that Ionians were resident in Babylon.

There is evidence from the still unpublished Fortification Tablets (508–493) that Greeks also worked in Persepolis. "Fortification Tablet 1711 has even a short text in Greek and another, Fort. 3821, bears the impression of an Athenian coin with an owl."[172] The Treasury Tablets from 490–60, published by Cameron in 1948, also mention Ionians at Persepolis.

The statements that Darius used Ionian craftsmen are confirmed by several lines of material evidence. Achaemenian sculpture shows clear indications of the Archaic Greek style.[173] A graffito on the foot of a statue of Darius portrays a bearded face that is an exact replica of some of the faces in the Greek vase paintings of 510–500.[174] A recent study shows that certain marks on the Persian sculptures and buildings can be attributed to the toothed chisel. This instrument was first used in Greece from 550 and in Persia from 520. Nylander suggests that its use may be associated with the importation of Greek craftsmen.[175]

During the early Persian period (late 6th and 5th cen.) evidence of increased Greek influence comes from pottery remains. About 530, black-figure pottery was largely replaced by the more brilliant red-figure style, although mass-produced black-figure ware was still exported until about 475. Plain vases with a black gloss were developed at the beginning of the fifth century and became popular in the fourth and third centuries.

About ninety pieces of red-figured ware have been found at Susa. Clairmont suggests that this was brought to Susa by the Greeks who worked for the Persian kings.[176] Already mentioned are the nine sherds of black-figure ware from the sixth century at Babylon. Black-figure ware is also found at Carchemish.[177] Deubner reports nine fifth-century red-figure sherds at Babylon;[178] Clairmont adds a tenth red-figure example.[179] In Syria sixth-century black-figure ware has been found at Al Mina, Tell Sukas, Deve Hüyük, Çatal Hüyük, Aleppo, Tell Tayinat, and Neirab.

The many sites in Palestine with Greek pottery of the sixth and fifth centuries, may be listed in rough geographical order from north to south. Unless otherwise indicated the information is derived from Auscher's chart.[180] At Tell Abu Hawam were found two black-figure (BF), two red-figure (RF), and one early (ca. 500) black-glaze (BG) sherd.[181] In the fall of 1967 at Tell Megaddim on the coast, numerous Attic, Rhodian, and Cypriot wares from the Persian period were found.[182] At Atlit two kilometers to the south a sixth-century RF has been found, as have a number of fifth-century BG. Four Greek scarabs found there indicate a small settlement of Greeks.[183] At Dor (Tantura) a RF ware was found. Inland at Megiddo three BF sherds were found. BF sherds of the early fifth century have been found at Shechem.[184] Large quantities of Greek pottery of various types were found at Samaria. Uncovered were four BF, other sherds of the sixth century, over thirty RF of the fifth century, and numerous BG sherds of about 500 B.C. Together with twenty-seven Greek lamps, the sherds indicate that there was a Greek enclave at Samaria.[185] BF has been found at Tell Qasile. An unusual amount of BF and RF from Bat Yam on the coast south of Jaffa may indicate that this served as the port of entry.

In the interior at Tell en-Nasbeh north of Jerusalem were found: two BF (500), one RF (525–500), one BG (520–490), and one Clazomenian ware (540–30).[186] Three BF and two RF ware have been found at Gezer. On the coast many sherds of "Greek red-and-black painted ware" from the Persian period have been reported by the current excavation at Ashdod.[187] Three BF, a number of RF, and one early BG ware have been reported from Askalon. About a dozen BF and a dozen RF sherds have been reported from Tell Jemmeh. Finally inland on the shore of the Dead Sea at Ein Gedi, Mazar recently found one East Greek sherd of about 500, together with another sherd imitating this ware.[188] He found numerous Attic sherds dating from 475–350, with the majority coming from 450–400.[189]

Another material evidence for the spread of Greek influence in the sixth and fifth centuries is the distribution and also the imitation of Greek coins. Coinage had been introduced to the Greeks by the Lydians in the seventh century. In the middle of the sixth century Peisistratus, the dictator of Athens, began the practice of stamping the head of Athena on one side and an owl on the other—emblems that were to become widespread with the imitation of Attic coinage in the fifth century.

An important hoard of sixth-century Thracian coins was found at Ugarit.[190] "At Persepolis a number of coins were found in association with the foundation deposits for the Hall, or 'Apadana,' of Darius (511 B.C.); there are eight Lydian staters, and in silver one Aeginetan, one Thracian, and three Cypriot pieces."[191] Darius minted his own coins—the famous gold darics. Greek workmanship can be detected in the engraving of these coins.[192] Woolley, in excavating Ur, came across a coin collector's hoard, which included impressions of Greek coins from 450–350.[193]

In Palestine two coins of the sixth century have been published. A coin from Thasos was found at Shechem.[194] In 1960 an Attic coin from the time of Peisistratus was found in a suburb of Jerusalem.[195] Three "atticizing" tetradrachms from the fifth century have come from Samaria, and a fourth example from Beth Zur.[196] It seems that from 450 Attic coins were imitated in Palestine and became the medium of exchange there.[197]

It is of interest that in Ezra 2:69, 8:27, and Nehemiah 7:70–72 coins called *dark^emônîm* and *'ǎdarkōnîm* are mentioned. C. C. Torrey's belief that this and other words were Greek led him to date the work of the

Chronicler—i.e. Ezra, Nehemiah, and Chronicles—to about 250 B.C.[198] Weingreen holds that both terms refer to the Persian daric and that this reference is "proof that the accounts given in these memoirs were written at a time close to the events which they describe."[199] Even if the first word *dark⁽e⁾môn* were to be interpreted as the Greek drachma, and the second word *'ădarkōn* as the Persian daric, this would not make these references anachronistic, as the Greek coins appear in Palestine already in the Persian period.[200]

It should not be surprising that the word for the Greek coin "stater" should be found in the fifth-century Aramaic papyri from Egypt, especially since Greek influence in Egypt was very strong from the seventh century on.[201] When Emil Kraeling published *The Brooklyn Museum Aramaic Papyri* (New Haven: Yale University Press, 1953), he asserted that the Aramaic of Ezra reflected the use of the language in the fifth and fourth centuries because of its resemblance to the Egyptian Aramaic papyri. C. C. Torrey in a review of Kraeling's work in JNES (1954) criticized Kraeling's remark, and asserted that the Aramaic of Ezra must belong to the third century because of the occurrence of a Greek word. Recent studies have indicated that there are indeed a number of Greek words in the fifth-century Aramaic documents. For example, Yaron interprets *drmy* in Brooklyn Papyrus 9 (404 B.C.) as the Greek *dōrēma* "gift" in a passage in which a father gives his daughter the gift of half a house.[202] Rabinowitz interprets the Aramaic *prtrk* as the Greek *prō-tarchēs* "first-beginning."[203]

In conclusion, we may safely say that the presence of Greek words in an Old Testament book is not a proof of Hellenistic date, in view of the abundant opportunities for contacts between the Aegean and the Near East before Alexander. The evidence which I have presented is but a small fraction, which no doubt will be amplified many times by future discoveries.

Notes

In addition to the abbreviations listed elsewhere, the following are also used in this study:

AJA   *American Journal of Archaeology*

ANE   *The Aegean and the Near East,* ed. Saul Weinberg (Locust Valley, N.Y.: J. J. Augustin, 1956).

AOT   *Archaeology and Old Testament Study,* ed. D. Winton Thomas (Oxford: Clarendon Press, 1967).

Arch   *Archaeology*

CAH f.   The revised edition of volumes I and II of the *Cambridge Ancient History* (Cambridge: Cambridge University Press), issued as fascicles (f.).

GO   John Boardman, *The Greeks Overseas* (Baltimore: Penguin Books, 1964).

IEJ   *Israel Exploration Journal*
ILN   *Illustrated London News*
JHS   *Journal of Hellenic Studies*
QDAP   *Quarterly of the Department of Antiquities in Palestine*

1. Cf. Norman W. Porteous, *Daniel* (Philadelphia: Westminster, 1965).

2. Samuel R. Driver, *An Introduction to the Literature of the Old Testament* (New York: Meridian Library, 1960, reprint of the 1897 edition).

3. James A. Montgomery, *Daniel* (Edinburgh: T. and T. Clark, 1927; Naperville, Ill.: Allenson, Inc., 1959), p. 22; and Charles Boutflower, *In and Around the Book of Daniel*, published in 1923, presented the evidence for contacts available at that time. This has been reprinted (Grand Rapids: Zondervan, 1963).

4. Hilda Lockart Lorimer, *Homer and the Monuments* (London: Macmillan & Co., 1950).

5. Anthony Snodgrass, *Early Greek Armour and Weapons* (Edinburgh: University Press; Chicago: Aldine; 1964), p. 71.

6. N. Platon and E. Stassinopoulou-Touloupa, "Ivories and Linear-B from Thebes," ILN, (Dec. 5, 1964): 896–7.

7. George M. A. Hanfmann, "Archaeology in Homeric Asia Minor," AJA, 52 (1948): 135–55.

8. George M. A. Hanfmann, "Archaeology and the Origins of Greek Culture: Notes on Recent Work in Asia Minor," *The Antioch Review*, (Spring, 1965): 41–59.

9. H. C. Baldry, *Ancient Greek Literature in Its Living Context* (New York: McGraw-Hill, 1968), p. 9.

10. Alan E. Samuel, *The Mycenaeans in History* (Englewood Cliffs, N.J.: Prentice-Hall, 1966), p. 82.

11. *Ibid.*, p. 101.

12. The Israeli surveys of 1968, covering the Golan Heights, Samaria, and Judah, have increased this total. Moshe Kochavi, the director of the Judean survey writes (in a letter of Nov. 14, 1968): "Our Survey surveyed about 1200 sites of which some 20–30 per cent are new sites previously unrecorded. A second phase of the Survey, which is being carried out now, may lead to the same results. . . . I estimate that not more than one-third of the amount of possible sites were recorded, and a thorough survey is a question of many years (including the yet unsurveyed parts of pre-war [that is, the 1967 war] Israel)." One result is that Albright's identification of Tell Beit Mirsim with Debir may have to be abandoned in favor of the new site of Rabud, excavated by Kochavi in the summer of 1968.

13. Paul Lapp, "Palestine: Known but Mostly Unknown," BA, 26 (1963): 122–3; and Yohanan Aharoni, *The Land of the Bible* (Philadelphia: Westminster, 1967), map 5, p. 90, lists 18 major and 23 large excavations in Israel and Trans-Jordan.

14. Seton Lloyd, *Mounds of the Near East* (Edinburgh: Edinburgh University Press; Chicago: Aldine; 1963), p. 99.

15. M. A. Beek, *Atlas of Mesopotamia* (London and Camden, N.J.: Nelson, 1962), map 2.

16. Professor Weinberg's excavation at the non-Biblical site of Tell Anafa, in which the writer participated, is intended to focus on this problem. The first season in 1968 reached mainly Hellenistic levels, with but a few sherds of the Persian period. See Saul S. Weinberg, "Tel Anafa—A Problem-Oriented Excavation," *Muse*, 3 (1969): 16–23.

17. William F. Albright, *New Horizons in Biblical Research* (London and New York: Oxford University Press, 1966), p. 3.

18. Garstang's statement, cited by Yigael Yadin, "Hazor," AOT, p. 247.

19. *Ibid.*, pp. 248 ff.

20. Lapp, *op. cit.*, p. 130.

21. S. Marinatos, "Archaiologika Chronika," *Athens Annals of Archaeology*, 1 (1968): 17.

22. George M. A. Hanfmann, *The Antioch Review, op. cit.*, p. 43.

23. *Ibid.*, p. 42.

24. Samuel N. Kramer, *Cradle of Civilization* (New York: Time Inc., 1967), p. 123.

25. A. Sachs and D. Wiseman, "A Babylonian King List of the Hellenistic Period," *Iraq*, 16 (1954): 202–12.

26. Emil G. Kraeling, *The Brooklyn Museum Aramaic Papyri* (New Haven: Yale University Press, 1953), p. 9.

27. Richard A. Parker, *A Vienna Demotic Papyrus on Eclipse- and Lunar-Omina* (Providence: Brown University Press, 1959).

28. W. Till, *Die gnostischen Schriften des koptischen Papyrus Berolinensis 8502* (Berlin: Akademie-Verlag, 1955).

29. C. Clairmont, "Greek Pottery from the Near East," *Berytus*, 11 (1955): 85.

30. J. Iliffe, "Pre-Hellenistic Greek Pottery in Palestine," QDAP, 2 (1932–33): 15.

31. D. Auscher, "Les relations entre la Grèce et la Palestine avant la conquête d'Alexandre," VT, 17 (1967): 9.

32. C. Clairmont, "Greek Pottery from the Near East, II," *Berytus*, 12 (1956–57): 3, note.

33. F. Rosenthal, *A Grammar of Biblical Aramaic* (Wiesbaden: Otto Harrassowitz, 1961); M. Ellenbogen, *Foreign Words in the Old Testament* (London: Luzac & Co.; Mystic, Conn.: Verry; 1962). A. Shaffer, "Hurrian *kirezzi, West-Semitic *krz," *Orientalia*, 34 (1965): 34, concludes, "In view of the priority of the present text dating from *ca.* 1500 B.C., this identification rules out the traditional theory of a Greek loan-word origin for *krz. . . ."

34. See Ovid R. Sellers, "Musical Instruments of Israel," BA, 4 (1941): 33–47; E. Werner, "Musical Instruments," in *The Interpreter's Dictionary of the Bible*, ed. George Buttrick (New York: Abingdon Press, 1962), III, 469–76; and especially T. Mitchell and R. Joyce, "The Musical Instruments in Nebuchadrezzar's Orchestra," in *Notes on Some Problems in the Book of Daniel* by Donald Wiseman *et al.* (London: The Tyndale Press, 1965), pp. 19–27.

35. Driver, *op. cit.*, p. 502.

36. A. Jefferey, IB, VI: 349.

37. M. Guillemin and J. Duchesne, "Sur l'origine asiatique de la cithare grecque," *L'Antiquité Classique*, 4 (1935): 118, and fig. 35; cf. B. Aign, *Die Geschichte der Musikinstrumente des Ägäischen Raumes bis um 700 vor Christus* (Frankfurt am Main, 1963).

38. W. C. Hayes, *The Scepter of Egypt* (Cambridge, Mass.: Harvard University Press, 1959), II, 23–25. Cf. Pierre Montet, *Everyday Life in Egypt* (London: Edward Arnold; New York: St. Martins; 1958), p. 95.

39. W. Ward, "Egypt and the East Mediterranean in the Early Second Millennium B.C.," *Orientalia*, 30 (1961): 36, n. 3.

40. W. Hinz, *Persia, ca. 2400–1800* B.C. (CAH f. 19, 1963), p. 30. The Kassite court of the 12th cen. B.C. used Subarian and Elamite singers. The later Assyrian court at Nimrud used Kassite and north Syrian singers.

41. L. Carrington Goodrich, *A Short History of the Chinese People* (New York: Harper's, 1959), p. 55.

42. Francis W. Galpin, *The Music of the Sumerians and Their Immediate Successors . . .* (Cambridge: University Press, 1937).

43. M. Duchesne-Guillemin, "Survivance orientale dans la désignation des cordes de la lyre en Grèce?" *Syria*, 44 (1967): 233–46; cf. Anne Kilmer, "The Strings of Musical Instruments: Their Names, Numbers, and Significance," in *Studies in Honor of Benno Landsberger . . .* (Chicago: University of Chicago Press, 1965), pp. 261–72.

44. Ellenbogen, *op. cit.*, p. 148.

45. Cyrus Gordon, "Ugaritic Guilds and Homeric dēmioergoi," ANE, pp. 136–43; cf. Thomas B. L. Webster, *From Mycenae to Homer* (London: Methuen & Co.; New York: Barnes and Noble; 1958). Cf. also Jack M. Sasson, "Instances of Mobility among Mari Artisans," BASOR, no. 190 (1968): 46–54.

46. James B. Pritchard, ed. *The Ancient Near East in Pictures* (Princeton: Princeton University Press, 1954), pictures 204 and 205.

47. DOTT, p. 67.

48. Pritchard, *op. cit.*, picture 202.

49. John Boardman, *Greek Art* (New York: Frederick A. Praeger, 1964), fig. 38.

50. Richmond Lattimore, trans., *Greek Lyrics*, rev. ed., (Chicago: University of Chicago Press, 1960), p. 1.

51. Frederick V. Winnett, "Re-examining the Foundations," JBL, 84 (1965): 4.

52. J. Canby, "Early Bronze 'Trinket' Moulds," *Iraq*, 17 (1965): 54.

53. F. Matz, *Minoan Civilization: Maturity and Zenith* (CAH f. 12, 1962): p. 24.

54. G. Dossin, "Les archives économiques du Palais de Mari," *Syria*, 20 (1939): 111–12. Cf. further R. Dussaud, "Rapports entre la Crète ancienne et la Babylonie," *Iraq*, 6 (1939): 53–65; S. Smith, "Middle Minoan I–II and Babylonian Chronology," AJA, 49 (1945): 1–24.

55. E. Weidner, "The Inscription from Kythera," JHS, 59 (1939): 137–38; Henri Frankfort, *et al.*, *The Gimilsin Temple* . . . (Chicago: University of Chicago Press, 1940), p. 139.

56. Keith Branigan, "Byblite Daggers in Cyprus and Crete," AJA, 70 (1966): 123–6.

57. William F. Albright, ". . . a Lycian at the Byblian Court," BASOR, 155 (1959): 31–4.

58. W. Brice, *Inscriptions in the Minoan Linear Script of Class A* (Oxford: University Press, 1961); J. L. Caskey, *Greece and the Aegean Islands in the Middle Bronze Age* (CAH f. 45, 1966): p. 24.

59. Cyrus H. Gordon, "Minoica," and "Eteocretan," JNES, 21 (1962): 207–14; "The Decipherment of Minoan," *Natural History*, 72 (Nov., 1963): 22–31; *Evidence for the Minoan Languages* (Ventnor, N.J.: Ventnor Publishers, 1966); *Forgotten Scripts* (New York: Basic Books, Inc., 1968), chap. 7.

60. Jonas C. Greenfield, "Review of Evidence for the Minoan Language," by Cyrus H. Gordon, JBL, 86 (1967): 241–4.

61. Michael C. Astour, "The Problem of Semitic in Ancient Crete," JAOS, 87 (1967): 290–5.

62. Leonard R. Palmer, *Mycenaeans and Minoans* (New York: Alfred A. Knopf, 1962), pp. 232–50.

63. S. Davis, *The Decipherment of the Minoan Linear A. and Pictographic Scripts* (Johannesburg: Witwatersrand University Press, 1967).

64. Michael C. Astour, "Second Millennium B.C. Cypriot and Cretan Onomastica Reconsidered," JAOS, 84 (1964): 240–54.

65. Michael Ventris and John Chadwick, eds., *Documents in Mycenaean Greek* (Cambridge: Cambridge University Press, 1956); and John Chadwick, *The Decipherment of Linear B* (New York: Vintage Books, Random House, 1958).

66. Michael C. Astour, "The Origin of the Terms 'Canaan,' 'Phoenician,' and 'Purple,'" JNES, 24 (1965): 346–50.

67. V. Grace, "The Canaanite Jar," ANE, pp. 80–109.

68. Helene J. Kantor, "Ivory Carving in the Mycenaean Period," *Arch*, 13 (1960): 14–25; "Syro-Palestinian Ivories," JNES, 15 (1956): 153–74, especially 169 ff.

69. Robert Houston Smith, "Near Eastern Forerunners of the Striding Zeus," *Arch*, 15 (1962): 176–83.

70. N. Platon and E. Stassinopoulou-Touloupa, "Oriental Seals from the Palace of Cadmus . . . ," ILN (Nov. 28, 1964): 860.

71. Michael C. Astour, "Greek Names in the Semitic World and Semitic Names in the Greek World," JNES, 23 (1964): 193–201.

72. H. W. Catling, *Cyprus in the Neolithic and Bronze Age Periods* (CAH f. 43, 1966): 55–57.

73. J. Benson, "Aegean and Near Eastern Seal Impressions from Cyprus," ANE, pp. 59–79.

74. H. Bossert, "Die Phönizisch-Hethitischen Bilinguen vom Karatepe," *Oriens*, 2 (1949): 72–128; Richard D. Barnett, "Mopsus," JHS, 73 (1953): 140–3.

75. Kantor, "Ivory Carving," *op. cit.*, 23–4.

76. F. H. Stubbings, *Mycenaean Pottery from the Levant* (Cambridge: Cambridge University Press, 1951).

77. James B. Pritchard, "A Cosmopolitan Culture of the Late Bronze Age," *Expedition*, 7 (1965): 26–33.

78. Stubbings, *op. cit.*, p. 107.

79. O. Deubner, "Die griechischen Scherben von Babylon," in F. Wetzel *et al.*, *Das Babylon der Spätzeit* (Berlin: Gebr. Mann, 1957), p. 52.

80. Martin P. Nilsson, *The Mycenaean Origin of Greek Mythology* (New York: W. W. Norton & Co., 1963, reprint of the 1932 edition).

81. A. Horon, "Canaan and the Aegean Sea: Greco-Phoenician Origins Reviewed," *Diogenes*, 58 (1967): 59 ff.

82. Richard D. Barnett, "The Epic of Kumarbi and the Theogony of Hesiod," JHS, 65 (1945): 100–1; Hans G. Güterbock, "The Hittite Version of the Hurrian Kumarbi Myths: Forerunners of Hesiod," AJA, 52 (1948): 123–34; cf. Michael C. Astour, "Semitic Elements in the Kumarbi Myth: An Onomastic Inquiry," JNES, 27 (1968): 172–6. Cf. also P. Walcot, *Hesiod and the Near East* (Cardiff: University of Wales Press, 1966).

83. Cyrus H. Gordon, *The Common Background of Greek and Hebrew Civilizations* (New York: W. W. Norton, 1965), pp. 85–6.

84. Samuel N. Kramer, "Death and Nether World according to the Sumerian Literary Texts," *Iraq*, 22 (1960): 64.

85. H. W. F. Saggs, "Some Ancient Semitic Conceptions of the Afterlife," *Faith and Thought*, 90 (1958): 165.

86. William F. Albright, "Some Oriental Glosses on the Homeric Problem," AJA, 54 (1950): 166.

87. Jane C. Waldbaum, "Philistine Tombs at Tell Fara and Their Aegean Prototypes," AJA, 70 (1966): 339–40.

88. Cf. J. Prignaud, "Caftorim et Kerétim," RB, (April, 1964): 215–29.

89. V. E. G. Kenna, *Cretan Seals* (Oxford: Clarendon Press; New York: Oxford University Press; 1960), pp. 65, 78, 151 ff.

90. Hendricus J. Franken, "Clay Tablets from Deir 'Alla, Jordan," VT, 14 (1964): 377–9.

91. William F. Albright, *The Amarna Letters from Palestine; Syria, the Philistines and Phoenicia* (CAH f. 51, 1966): 27.

92. Hendricus J. Franken, *Palestine in the Time of the Nineteenth Dynasty* (CAH f. 67, 1968): 8.

93. Albright, *The Amarna Letters*, p. 30.

94. Bruce Donald Rahtjen, "Philistine and Hebrew Amphictyonies," JNES, 24 (1965): 100–4.

95. See the writer's *Greece and Babylon* (Grand Rapids: Baker Book House, 1967), pp. 45–6.

96. Trude Dothan, *The Philistines and Their Material Culture* [in Hebrew with an English summary] (Jerusalem: Bialik Institute, 1967).

97. Waldbaum, *op. cit.*, pp. 332 ff. Cf. G. Ernest Wright, "Philistine Coffins and Mercenaries," BA, 22 (1959): 54–66.

98. Cyrus Gordon, "The Role of the Philistines," *Antiquity*, 30 (1956) : 23.

99. E. A. Speiser, *Genesis* (Garden City, N.Y.: Doubleday & Co., 1964), p. 365.

100. Gordon, *Antiquity, op. cit.*

101. Richard D. Barnett, "Early Shipping in the Near East," *Antiquity*, 32 (1958) : 225.

102. Vincent R. d'A. Desborough, *Protogeometric Pottery* (Oxford: Clarendon Press, 1952).

103. J. M. Cook, *Greek Settlement in the Eastern Aegean and Asia Minor* (CAH f. 7, 1961), p. 13.

104. George M. A. Hanfmann, "The Ninth Campaign at Sardis (1966)," BASOR, 186 (1967) : 17, 27–37.

105. Robert M. Cook, "Ionia and Greece in the Eighth and Seventh Centuries B.C.," JHS, 66 (1946) : 83, n. 143.

106. W. Heurtley, "Note on Fragments of Two Thessalian Proto-Geometric Vases Found at Tell Abu Hawam," QDAP, 4 (1935) : 181.

107. J. Birmingham, "The Development of the Fibula in Cyprus and the Levant," *Palestine Exploration Quarterly*, 95 (1963) : 109.

108. George M. A. Hanfmann, "On Some Eastern Greek Wares Found at Tarsus," ANE, pp. 165–84.

109. Carl Roebuck, *Ionian Trade and Colonization* (New York: Archaeological Institute of America, 1959), pp. 62 ff.; S. Smith, "The Greek Trade at Al Mina," *Antiquaries Journal*, 22 (1942) : 87–112.

110. GO, pp. 68–9.

111. Deubner, *op. cit.*, p. 52.

112. Auscher, *op. cit.*, p. 12.

113. A. Millard, "Alphabetic Inscriptions on Ivories from Nimrud," *Iraq*, 24 (1962) : 41–51, notes that some inscribed ivories are labeled as coming from Hama and Lu'ash, sites in Syria.

114. Richard D. Barnett, "The Nimrud Ivories and the Art of the Phoenicians," *Iraq*, 2 (1935) : 179–210; "Early Greek and Oriental Ivories," JHS, 68 (1948) : 1–25.

115. Max E. L. Mallowan, *Nimrud and Its Remains*, Two Vols. (New York: Dodd, Mead & Co., 1966), pp. 135–6, 182.

116. *Ibid.*, p. 586.

117. *Ibid.*, pp. 510–12; cf. V. Karageorghis, "Unique Ivories from Cyprus," ILN, (Dec. 16, 1967) : 27–9.

118. Mallowan, *op. cit.*, pp. 152–60, cf. 136–7. W. Llewellyn Brown, *The Etruscan Lion* (Oxford: Clarendon Press, 1960).

119. Mallowan, *op. cit.*, p. 496.

120. *Ibid.*, p. 642, n. 52. The discovery in 1967 of a 9th-cen. grave in Athens yielded gold earrings which "presuppose a far more intimate association of Greek and oriental than isolated imports have hitherto suggested." Evelyn L. Smithson, "The Grave of an Early Athenian Aristocrat," *Arch*, 22 (1969) : 24; cf. William Culican, *The First Merchant Venturers* (New York: McGraw-Hill, 1966), pp. 62–63.

121. Mallowan, *op. cit.*, pp. 212–15, cf. p. 330, n. 18.

122. *Ibid.*, p. 212.

123. Donald Harden, *The Phoenicians* (N.Y.: Frederick A. Praeger, 1963), 188–90; Henri Frankfort, *The Art and Architecture of the Ancient Orient* (Baltimore: Penguin, 1963), pp. 195 ff.

124. John Myres, "The Amathus Bowl," JHS, 53 (1933) : 36; William S. Smith, *Interconnections in the Ancient Near East* (New Haven: Yale University Press, 1965), p. 53, and fig. 81.

125. GO, p. 91.

126. P. Amandry, "Objets orientaux en Grèce et en Italie aux VIIIe et VIIe siècles avant J.-C.," *Syria*, 35 (1958) : 82.

127. Andrew R. Burn, *The Lyric Age of Greece* (New York: St. Martin's Press, 1960),
p. 86.

128. GO, p. 91.

129. Harden, *op. cit.*, pp. 194, 196.

130. Auscher, *op. cit.*, pp. 28–9.

131. Harden, *op. cit.*, p. 194.

132. Kathleen M. Kenyon, *Jerusalem* (London: Thames and Hudson, 1967), p. 59.

133. Yohanan Aharoni, "Ramat Rahel," AOT, p. 179.

134. William F. Albright, *The Archaeology of Palestine* (Baltimore: Penguin, 1960),
pp. 126–7.

135. P. Amandry, "Chaudrons à protomes de taureau en Orient et en Grèce," ANE,
pp. 238–61; R. Barnett, "The Archaeology of Urartu," *Compte Rendu de la troisième
Rencontre Assyriologique Internationale* (Leiden: E. J. Brill, 1954), pp. 10–18; R. Barnett and W. Watson, "Russian Excavations in Armenia," *Iraq*, 14 (1952): 132–47;
K. Maxwell-Hyslop, "Urartian Bronzes in Etruscan Tombs," *Iraq*, 18 (1956): 150–67.

136. Amandry, *Syria*, *op. cit.*, 108–9, cf. 73–80.

137. Frankfort, *op. cit.*, p. 189.

138. Roman Ghirshman, *Perse: Proto-Iraniens, Mèdes, Achéménides* (Paris: Galli-
mard, 1963), pp. 330–43.

139. Lilian H. Jeffery, *The Local Scripts of Archaic Greece* (Oxford: Clarendon
Press; New York: Oxford University Press; 1961).

140. S. Gevirtz, "A Spindle Whorl with Phoenician Inscription," JNES, 26 (1967):
13–16.

141. R. Crossland, "Indo-European Origins: The Linguistic Evidence," *Past and
Present*, 12 (1957): 36.

142. For other examples of Mesopotamian words absorbed into Greek by the end of
the 5th cen., see R. Thompson, "The Debt of Europe to Babylon," *Cambridge Ancient
History* (Cambridge: Cambridge University Press, 1925), III: 248–50.

143. Frankfort, *op. cit.*, pp. 195–6.

144. Gordon Loud, *The Palace of Sargon II* (Chicago: University of Chicago Press,
1938), pl. 59.

145. H. Tadmor, "The Campaigns of Sargon II of Assur," *Journal of Cuneiform
Studies*, 12 (1958): 80, disputes the usual rendering of Yamani as the "Ionian." See,
however, H. W. F. Saggs, "The Nimrud Letters," *Iraq*, 25 (1963): 77–8.

146. DOTT, pp. 62–3.

147. A. T. Olmstead, *A History of Assyria* (Chicago: University of Chicago, 1923),
pp. 310–11; cf. J. Boardman, "Tarsus, Al Mina, and Greek Chronology," JHS, 85
(1965): 5–15.

148. Olmstead, *op. cit.*, p. 290.

149. *Ibid.*, pp. 368–9.

150. C. Leonard Woolley, *Carchemish* (London: British Museum, 1921), II, 128,
and plate 24.

151. Greek pottery of the 7th cen. has also been found at Tell Abu Hawam, Ascalon,
and Tell Jemmeh. Auscher, *op. cit.*, p. 12.

152. J. Naveh, "The Excavations at Meṣad Ḥashavyahu—Preliminary Report," IEJ,
12 (1962): 89–113.

153. Yohanan Aharoni, "Hebrew Ostraca from Tel Arad," IEJ, 16 (1966): 4; "The
Negeb," AOT, pp. 398–9; "Forerunners of the Limes: Iron Age Fortresses in the
Negev," IEJ, 17 (1967): 14.

154. Yohanan Aharoni, "Arad: Its Inscriptions and Temple," BA, 31 (1968): 11.

155. M. Kochavi, "Notes and News," IEJ, 17 (1967): 273. In a personal conversation
with Professor Kochavi in May, 1968, he reported that a Greek oinochoe of the second
half of the 6th cen. had been found.

156. *Arch* 17, (1964) : 206–7.

157. J. Quinn, "Alcaeus 48 (B16) and the Fall of Ascalon (604 B.C.) ," BASOR, no. 164 (1961) : 19–20; cf. Dennis L. Page, *Sappho and Alcaeus* (Oxford: Clarendon Press, 1955) , pp. 223 ff.

158. E. Weidner, "Jojachin, König von Juda, in Babylonischen Keilschrifttexten," *Mélanges Syriens offerts à M. René Dussaud* (Paris: Paul Geuthner, 1939) , II, 923–35; William F. Albright, "Cilicia and Babylonia under the Chaldaean Kings," BASOR, no. 120 (1950) : 25.

159. In a letter of October, 1966.

160. Hanfmann, "Archaeology in Asia Minor," *op. cit.*, p. 154.

161. Otto Neugebauer, "The Survival of Babylonian Methods in the Exact Sciences of Antiquity and Middle Ages," *Proceedings of the American Philosophical Society,* 107 (1963) : 533, on the basis of the Babylonian evidence available denies that the Babylonians could have predicted a solar eclipse.

162. Roebuck, *op. cit.,* p. 102.

163. A. Leo Oppenheim, *Ancient Mesopotamia* (Chicago: University of Chicago Press, 1964) , p. 65.

164. R. Cook, *op. cit.,* p. 83, n. 143.

165. Deubner, *op. cit.,* pp. 52–3.

166. Richard N. Frye, *The Heritage of Persia* (Cleveland: World Pub. Co., 1963) , pp. 80–1. For other Greek elements at Pasargadai see GO, p. 120; D. Stronach, "Excavations at Pasargadae: Second Preliminary Report," *Iran,* 2 (1964) : 26 f.

167. Anthologia Palatina VII, 259, cited by Andrew R. Burn, *Persia and the Greeks* (New York: St. Martin's Press, 1962) , p. 253.

168. Max Cary and E. H. Warmington, *The Ancient Explorers* (Baltimore: Penguin, 1963) , pp. 78–9; William Culican, *The Medes and Persians* (New York: Frederick A. Praeger, 1965) , p. 74.

169. G. Perrot and C. Chipiez, *History of Art in Persia* (London: Chapman and Hall, 1892) , p. 27: "Out of Greece also had come bronze and marble statues, distributed about the capitals of the (Persian) empire, where the Macedonians found them, as lasting trophies of western campaigns . . . . Some of these were from the best sculptors of the sixth century . . . ."

170. R. Kent, *Old Persian* (New Haven: American Oriental Society, 1953) , p. 144.

171. *Ibid.,* p. 143, n. on line 53.

172. Carl Nylander, "Old Persian and Greek Stonecutting and the Chronology of Achaemenian Monuments," AJA, 69 (1965) : 55, n. 39.

173. Henri Frankfort, "Achaemenian Sculpture," AJA, 50 (1946) : 6–14; K. Erdmann, "Griechische und achaemenidische Plastik," *Forschungen und Fortschritte,* 26 (1950) : 150–3.

174. Gisela M. A. Richter, "Greeks in Persia," AJA, 50 (1946) : figs. 26–28.

175. Nylander, *op. cit.* Cf. C. Nylander, "A Note on the Stonecutting and Masonry of Tel Arad," IEJ, 17 (1967) : 56–9. Yohanan Aharoni, the excavator of Arad, has new evidence that such tools were used in Assyrian palaces before the 6th cen. That a tool originally from the Near East should have been adopted by Greeks, and then used by them in the Near East is not surprising. It is one example of many (cf. the alphabet, coinage) of an original inspiration from the Near East that has been adapted by the Greeks and brought back to the Near East.

176. Clairmont, "Greek Pottery," *op. cit.*, p. 90.

177. GO, p. 79.

178. Deubner, *op. cit.*, pp. 53–4.

179. Clairmont, "Greek Pottery," p. 93.

180. Auscher, *op. cit.*, pp. 12–13.

181. A. Hamilton, "Excavations at Tell Abu Hawām," QDAP, 4 (1935) : 5.

182. M. Broshi, "Notes and News," IEJ, 17 (1967): 278.

183. Auscher, op. cit., p. 17.

184. G. Ernest Wright, "The Fourth Campaign at Balâṭah (Shechem)," BASOR, no. 169 (1963): 1–60.

185. Auscher, op. cit., p. 16.

186. D. von Bothmer, "Greek Pottery from Tell en-Naṣbeh," BASOR, no. 83 (1941): 25–30.

187. Jerusalem Post Weekly, (Aug. 19, 1968): 1.

188. B. Mazar and I. Dunayevsky, "En-Gedi, Fourth and Fifth Seasons of Excavations-Preliminary Report," IEJ, 17 (1967): 137.

189. Ibid., p. 138.

190. C. Schaeffer, "Une trouvaille de monnaies archaiques Grecques à Ras Shamra," Mélanges Syriens, I, 461–87.

191. GO, p. 79.

192. Richter, op. cit., p. 27; cf. E. Robinson, "The Beginnings of Achaemenid Coinage," The Numismatic Chronicle, 18 (1958): 187–93. Greek influence may also be traced in the engraving of Persian gems and seals of the late 6th and early 5th cen. B.C. See Gisela M. A. Richter, "Greek Subjects on 'Graeco-Persian' Seal Stones," Archaeologica Orientalia in Memoriam Ernst Herzfeld (Locust Valley, N.Y.: J. J. Augustin, 1952), pp. 189–94; also in the same volume, H. Seyrig, "Cachets Achéménides," pp. 195–202.

193. Edith Porada, "Greek Coin Impressions from Ur," Iraq, 22 (1960): 228–34.

194. G. Ernest Wright, "Shechem, 'The Navel of the Land,'" BA, 20 (1957): 29, fig. 10.

195. Y. Meshorer, "An Attic Archaic Coin from Jerusalem," 'Atiqot, 3 (1961): 185.

196. Auscher, op. cit., p. 24.

197. Albright, The Archaeology of Palestine, p. 143.

198. William F. Albright, "The Date and Personality of the Chronicler," JBL, 40 (1921): 113.

199. DOTT, p. 232.

200. Jacob M. Myers, ed., I Chronicles (Garden City, N.Y.: Doubleday, 1965), p. lxxxviii.

201. A. Cowley, Aramaic Papyri of the Fifth Century B.C. (Oxford: Clarendon Press, 1923), p. 131; cf. Kraeling, op. cit., p. 40.

202. Reuven Yaron, "Two Greek Words in the Brooklyn Museum Aramaic Papyri," Hebrew Union College Annual, 28 (1957): 49.

203. J. Rabinowitz, "Grecisms and Greek Terms in the Aramaic Papyri," Biblica, 39 (1958): 76–82. For an appraisal of these suggestions see Kenneth Kitchen, "The Aramaic of Daniel," in Notes on . . . Daniel, pp. 46–7.

V. TEXTUAL CRITICISM

—13—

THE DEAD SEA SCROLLS AND THE OLD TESTAMENT TEXT

R. Laird Harris

The discovery of the Dead Sea Scrolls in 1947 was an event of major importance in Bible study. It has been called the greatest archaeological find of this century—a century replete with major archaeological discoveries. More Dead Sea Scrolls are still coming to light and some important ones remain to be published. Interest in them therefore remains high, and even yet much study is needed on these remarkable documents of ancient time.

The Scrolls have had a definite bearing on the study of the backgrounds in thought and organization of the Christian church. They have been useful in sharpening our knowledge of gnosticism and of contemporary Jewish history. But above all they are important in the study of the text of the Old Testament and its transmission. In the present study we shall endeavor to bring together the general conclusions on text transmission that may be drawn from the Scrolls and also give some detailed examples of textual study taken from the better preserved scrolls of Isaiah and Psalms.

I. Early Types of Text

As is well known, our earliest manuscripts of the Hebrew Old Testament heretofore came from about A.D. 900. The first impression gained from the new scrolls is that here we have manuscripts earlier by a thousand years, yet differing in no major way from the material we already had. There is an obvious general confirmation of our text of the Old Testament.

More detailed study of the Scrolls has led to further significant observations. Not only do some scrolls resemble the Hebrew text tradition called Masoretic; some of the scrolls are significantly closer to the Septuagint text. To make the picture complete, we add that some other scrolls of the Pentateuch follow the text style of the Samaritan Pentateuch.[1]

It is now apparent, as pointed out by Albright[2] and Cross,[3] that these text types are found in manuscripts going back to about 200 B.C. The text types themselves are probably considerably older.

Consequences for study of the various types of text are interesting. It is fair to say that Septuagint study has been repristinated. Cross remarks that "the polemic against the trustworthiness of the Septuagint translators and the usefulness of their version as a witness to the pre-Masoretic text had come close to winning the day,"[4] but this is now no longer the case.

The School of Kahle indeed had argued that there never was a unified Septuagint but only an amorphous group of translations of individual books. This view also is answered by the newer evidence. There are now available Hebrew manuscripts going back to 200 B.C. showing the type of text found in the LXX, and comparison of the LXX with these manuscripts shows that the Greek translators were careful workmen. The LXX can therefore be used with new confidence as a witness to a Hebrew text current in Palestine in 200 B.C. Cross, following Albright, suggests that this LXX text type separated out as early as the fifth century and was preserved in both Palestine and Egypt. The proto-Samaritan type text, he thinks, "cannot have diverged much later."[5]

As to the Masoretic type of text, there are representatives of this also in Qumran going back to the early second century B.C. We shall speak more in detail about this text later, but in any event its history doubtless reaches back long before Qumran. Albright argues that this type of text was current in Babylon and was brought back "by the returning exiles during the late sixth and the fifth centuries B.C."[6] He studies several Assyro-Babylonian names occurring in the Dead Sea Scroll of Isaiah and shows that the peculiar spellings of the Scroll are correct and suggests that eastern scribes had been at work.

There are several consequences of these remarkable discoveries and studies. In the first place, the practice of ancient scribes is illustrated. The marvelous fidelity of the scribes who copied the Masoretic text through the middle ages is seen to extend back at least to the first half of the first Christian century. Examples of such constancy will be given. And it should be added that even in the great Isaiah scroll from the mid-second century B.C., the scribal work, though somewhat careless, is still as good as is found in many New Testament manuscripts. It is easy to compare the few and unimportant Dead Sea variations listed in the bottom of Kittel's pages on Isaiah with the relatively numerous variations on every page of Nestlé's edition of the Greek New Testament. It is clear that the scribes were careful workmen, even when they were not working under the most meticulous principles which some scribes followed. We have been told much about sleepy scribes and redactors and glossators who were thought to have played fast and loose with their texts. Our evidence rather is that the typical scribe copied industriously and faithfully what was before him. Sleepy scribes at Qumran probably were given some of the penalties which were meted out rather freely in that strict "monastery." The scribes made mistakes indeed. Several good examples of homoioteleuton, dittography, false word division, etc. can be pointed out in all of these manuscripts. There is even a striking example of homoioteleuton in Kittel's Hebrew Bible (Neh. 7:67)! But Albright is correct in saying "most of the Scrolls and fragments present a consonantal text which is virtually indistinguishable from the text of corresponding passages in our Masoretic Bible."[7]

It is of interest to note that this careful scribal activity antedated the upheavals in Palestine when Jerusalem fell and when the Christian church was formed. It even antedated the Syrian persecutions and the Maccabean revolt. We may suggest that the men of the honored scribal profession customarily copied carefully, also in antiquity.

An interesting sidelight comes from study of the Samaritan type of text. Our previous copies of this type of text were medieval. But when these copies are compared with Qumran manuscripts of the first half century of the Christian era and others, we learn that the Samaritan scribes also were careful. Skehan says, "The Samaritan recension . . . is shown by this scroll to have been preserved with a measure of fidelity, from a time somewhere near the origin of the recension that compares not unfavorably with the fidelity of transmission of MT itself."[8]

Likewise the new estimates of the value of the LXX involve the view that it was not only a careful translation but also that its copies which have come down to us are relatively faithful to the originals. We have no right to assume that the early Jewish scribes of the monarchy and post-exilic times were less careful.

II. Dating

A second consequence of textual study of the Qumran scrolls involves the dating of the books of Chronicles. The argument is circuitous, but convincing. Of Chronicles itself, a mere scrap has been found at Qumran. Cross remarks that in this case "worms have gorged themselves on Holy Writ. The result is leather lace with only four complete words legible."[9] Nevertheless the Scrolls have led Cross and others to a date for Chronicles of about 400 B.C. instead of about 250 B.C. as held by R. H. Pfeiffer.[10]

The argument is that the scrolls of Samuel found at Qumran (4QSam) show the Septuagint type of text. This type of text in Hebrew circles is early and was less highly regarded later on. But the books of Chronicles in their quotations from Samuel-Kings follow this type of text more closely than they follow the Masoretic type. Therefore the work of the Chronicler must be earlier than had been supposed. Other considerations doubtless enter into the argument, such as the view that Chronicles and Ezra are from the same workshop and the Aramaic of Ezra can now be dated early. But the textual relations are thought to favor the early date.

A further consequence of the new textual studies of the Old Testament is to throw light on several problems of Old Testament quotation in the New Testament. For instance, the number of individuals in the family of Jacob, seventy-five, as given by Acts 7:14 contrasts with the number seventy in the MT of Exodus 1:5. The LXX of Exodus 1:5, however, gives the number seventy-five and doubtless this is the source of the Acts quotation. A new fragment of Exodus now supports the LXX, and a good case can be made out that this is the correct reading. Since most other problems of quotation between the New Testament and the Old arise from the usual New Testament use of the LXX, and since the LXX can now be defended as old and often preserving the correct reading, these problems are more amenable to solution. Other examples are the quotation of Deuteronomy 32:43 (LXX) in Hebrews 1:6 and the use of the LXX and Samaritan reading of Exodus 12:40 in Galatians 3:17.

III. Detailed Consideration of Typical Old Testament Texts

Much has been said above of a general nature. It may be of value to check the statements that have been made by reference to three extensive and published Dead Sea Scrolls, the two major scrolls of Isaiah and the Psalm Scroll of Cave 11.

In such studies it may be helpful to keep in mind the purposes of textual criticism. It is to be feared that in evangelical circles textual criticism of the Old Testament has lagged behind other studies. This has been unfortunate. There have perhaps been reasons. Liberal scholars have so mingled their textual critical studies with extensive conjectural emendation and a generally critical approach that evangelicals have had a tendency to react to the other extreme and declare the MT inviolable. It may also be feared that Old Testament textual criticism languishes sometimes because it requires a fair knowledge of both Greek and Hebrew (at least!), and it is easier for a student to refuse these burdens.

Nevertheless evangelical scholars have taken a large part in textual critical studies of the New Testament, and such studies are widely considered and appreciated. Both B. B. Warfield and A. T. Robertson, of undoubted orthodoxy, have extensive handbooks on this area of New Testament introduction.[11]

The science of textual criticism deals with factual material, and the principles of such study are similar for the Old Testament, the New Testament, or for any other document. It would be well, therefore, for more evangelical Old Testament scholars to enter this field.

Furthermore, textual criticism is important in connection with the doctrine of Scripture. Warfield remarks that the purpose of textual criticism is twofold. Everyone knows that one purpose of such work is to reach, insofar as possible, the original text of the document in question. But Warfield adds "It is as important to certify ourselves of the correctness of our text as it is to correct it if erroneous; and the former is as much the function of criticism as the latter."[12] These words should be applied also to the Old Testament. There are several places in the Book of Isaiah where we can compare various witnesses and still be at a loss to know whether the word for deity was originally the Tetragram or Adonay. But when we stop to think, what difference does it make? The words are synonymous and overlap so greatly that we can say the decision makes little difference whichever was original. Indeed, it is because the difference is slight that the scribes were led into this variation! If this sort of thing is the only problem with the text we shall say that we are fully as close to the ancient text as it is needful to be. This conclusion thus supports the idea of the providential preservation of Scripture free from material error.

A. The Isaiah Scrolls

Others have made extensive comparisons of the readings of the Dead Sea Scrolls. For our purposes we shall try to summarize the results of such study. The important variants of the major Scrolls of Isaiah (DSIs a) are found as footnotes in the third paragraph at the bottom of the pages of Kittel's Hebrew Bible, 8th ed. and following. They are also given in convenient listing by Burrows.[13] A similar listing is given by Loewinger for the other extensive manuscript of Isaiah (DSIs b).[14]

One point must always be kept in mind. In comparing a variant manuscript or text with MT, it must always be remembered that neither manuscript is to be considered a perfect standard. Formerly when the LXX was found to vary from MT, the LXX was practically always adjudged guilty. This viewpoint is fallacious. The MT must be tested like any other manuscript text. It so happens, however, that in these comparisons the MT has usually carried off the palm.

To begin with, it must be noted that we are basically testing the consonantal text. The vowel points of course are much later. In DSIs a there is a puzzling use of excessive vowel letters which do not occur in all the Dead Sea Scrolls. Whether these vowel letters were inserted in this type of text or whether this type of text had them from antiquity and other text types have exscinded them is not certain. They may merely reflect a current pronunciation which is not made specific in more formal texts.

In any event, these vowel letters do not usually affect the sense at all and are omitted in the present study.

In the first page of Kittel's Isaiah there are five variant Dead Sea spellings, one added article, two added conjunctions, and one added word. In the last case MT says (1:7) "and it is a desolation." The Scroll turns the noun into a verb adding a preposition, "they are appalled at it." Surely the differences are slight.

On the second page three prepositions are added which express what the context already makes clear. Two conjunctions are added and one taken away. A series of three words is used in the plural where MT has a collective usage. One feminine verb is used instead of a masculine form to express an abstract, and the singular of "scarlet" is used in 1:18. Surely these differences are quite inconsequential and could be called differences of style. There is one larger variant. In 1:15 MT reads "your hands are full of blood." DSIs *a* adds "your fingers with iniquity." This probably is an unconscious harmonizing with 59:3. Many such harmonistic readings occur in the Gospels. Whether this reading was original we do not know—though it is not supported by other evidence—but in any case how slight are the divergencies between the witnesses!

The sixth chapter may be taken as another sample. There are several differences marked by Kittel consisting of vowel letters where the consonants agree with MT. Beyond these a conjunction is lost. One article is lost and another article added, an equivalent preposition and an alternative tense is used. Besides these the Tetragram is substituted for Adonay, and the verb "and he said" is dropped. In this scroll the Seraph says "Holy" only twice, and the phrase "six wings" is used only once. Perhaps here MT has a dittography. In any case the whole chapter is very close to MT—except for inconsequential details.

These sections are typical of the whole book, although occasionally an outright error occurs and there are a few larger variations. But even then the larger errors can usually be easily corrected and the variations, though interesting, are not disturbing.

Burrows lists three cases of clear homoioteleuton (4:5; 16:8, 9; and 23:15). The 16:8 passage is preserved in DSIs *b*, where this omission does not occur. Other omissions concern only two or three words which are often mere emphasizing words which do not vary the sense. Indeed, this is the impression one gets from the manuscript. It is not a carefully made manuscript, as all agree, and very seldom do its readings seem better than those of MT. But neither is the manuscript excessively defective so that the meanings are significantly altered. The scribal tradition is careless but not bad! Burrows' introductory comment is valid, "Differing notably in orthography and somewhat in morphology, it agrees with the Masoretic text to a remarkable degree in wording. Herein lies its chief importance, supporting the fidelity of the Masoretic tradition."[15]

When we come to DSIs *b,* we are in an altogether different position. Major parts of this scroll are preserved from chapters 38 to 66 with a few earlier fragments. Here the orthography is like MT. No longer is the conjunction "that, because," spelled *kî'* but *kî* as in MT. The negative does not have the medial *waw.* The 2nd masc. sing. perfect and the 2nd masc. sing. pronoun suffix do not have the overhanging *he.* The writing looks comfortably like the MT.

And the text is remarkably close to MT. Chapter 39 is identical with MT except for a few vowels. Chapter 41 has a few (very few) vowel differences, one less conjunction, and one mistake. In verse 11 the phrase "they shall perish" is replaced by "they shall be ashamed," which is repeated erroneously from earlier in the verse.

In chapter 45 there is an extra conjunction and in verse 2 an "r" replaces a "d" of MT. Actually in this case DSIs *a* also has the "r"; and, since the word in question is uncertain, MT may be in error (so RSV). This is the only problem for the half of chapter 45 that is preserved—one letter!

In chapter 53 there are two places where the conjunction is added and one where it is dropped (In DSIs *a* the conjunction varies ten times). The only other consonantal change is the addition of the word "light" after "see" in verse 11. This addition agrees with the Septuagint and DSIs *a,* but it is puzzling as to its meaning. Again the difference is one word in the whole chapter. Accuracy like this would be the envy of New Testament textual critics!

There are of course other variations in DSIs *b,* but really nothing of consequence. There is a beautiful example of homoioteleuton in 60:19, 20 where fifteen words are omitted between "light" and "light." An occasional word is skipped or a letter interchanged. The reading sometimes agrees with the MT Kethib reading when it is clearly in error (e.g. 49:6), but this only emphasizes the constancy of the MT tradition! All in all the manuscript reads like a very good copy of MT.

This conclusion is of considerable importance. Here is a scroll dated to the first half of the first Christian century. It already shows the standard MT text formerly associated with the rabbis of about A.D. 100. Likewise a manuscript with five Psalms was discovered by Yadin at Masada exhibiting the same MT text (see below). The work of the rabbis of about A.D. 100 has thus perhaps been overemphasized.

We do not know how far back the strict MT tradition goes. The fact that DSIs *a* shows a poor copy of the MT type in about 150 B.C. need not prove that good copies were not available at that time. Cross calls 4QJer[a] of 200 B.C. a "proto-Masoretic" manuscript.[16] The evidence is in favor of an early date for MT and a remarkably early date for the Old Testament text from which the later families of text divided. This parent text can be reconstructed in all essentials back some considerable time before

200 B.C. Albright speaks from evidence when he argues for an MT tradition reaching back to the exile in Babylon, and an Egyptian, Septuagint type of text going back to the fourth or fifth centuries B.C. It is extreme criticism today to think that we have a text form notably differing from that read by Ezra and Nehemiah in their great celebration of the feast of tabernacles (Neh. 8). Cross makes the remark that this text history only applies to the early books. It may be true that our evidence is not full, or in most cases is lacking, for some of the later books. But it should be said that there is no evidence against including such books in these conclusions. It is only that evidence is lacking. Naturally if one holds that certain books were written only in the Grecian period he would deny them an early text history. But if these books are held to be pre-exilic they could indeed exhibit the early text history. Further study of books like Ecclesiastes with these points in view might be of interest.

In fairness it must be added that Cross differs from Albright's reconstruction of the text history.[17] Cross argues for an early type of text separating out in Palestine about the fifth century B.C. Shortly afterward an Egyptian type of text broke off from this—enshrined in the LXX and the 4Q books of Samuel. In Babylon, meanwhile, a type of text was developing which was introduced into Palestine in late Maccabean times and became the Masoretic text.[18] Cross says that these types of text are not found in all books, especially the books of the Hagiographa. Of these, however, we cannot be so sure either way, for the evidence on some of them from the Dead Sea Scrolls is meager. The Cave IV manuscripts and the large Samuel Scroll remain to be published. There is still something to say for Albright's position that the text type of DSIs *a* is that of the Masoretic family although its orthography is peculiar. In any case varying text types represented in the Masoretic, Septuagint, and Samaritan texts and possibly others are traceable in the Dead Sea Scrolls to around 200 B.C.

As mentioned above, Cross calls 4QJer[a] of 200 B.C. "proto-Masoretic" and says that 4QJer[b], of slightly later date, is a type "identical with that which underlies the Old Greek (Septuagint) translation." There are, of course, problems between the MT and LXX texts of Jeremiah, and Cross discusses them. He holds that MT is the later expansionist type of text. Yet the 200 B.C. copies witness to this text type. It still is true that some of the omissions in the LXX of Jeremiah can be ascribed to errors due to homoioteleuton. Other parts thought to be additions in MT may be due to insertion of parallel material from Jeremiah (most often) or from Kings or the Pentateuch. There is little extra material in MT which cannot be thus explained or defended as original.

B. The Psalm Scroll

In 1965 there was published a scroll from Cave 11 at Qumran which contained parts of 37 canonical Psalms and, mixed among them, 9 other poems some of which had been previously known and others not.[19] This manuscript, like DSIs *b,* comes from the first half of the first Christian century, and is of interest from several angles. If it be considered a Bible scroll, the question arises about the varying order of the canonical Psalms and the presence of the non-canonical material. Skehan has argued that it is not a Bible scroll, but a hymn book with a variety of contents based upon the canonical Psalter.[20] In the present discussion the state of the text is the significant matter. And it may be said that the text is close to the Masoretic tradition. In the tattered parts of the manuscript, Sanders notes at the bottom of almost every column, "Aside from orthographical considerations, MT is indicated for the lacunae."

This manuscript differs from DSIs *b* by showing a wider use of the vowel letter *waw,* e.g. in the word *kôl* "all" and *lô'* "not," and in the Qal active participle, etc. Otherwise the orthography is more like DSIs *b* than DSIs *a.* Some examples of the readings should be given.

Psalm 148 has ten verses preserved with the left extremity of each line gone. In one place it reads "above with reference to the heavens" instead of MT "above the heavens." The difference is an "l" instead of "h." Also at the beginning of verse 5 the jussive "let them praise" is changed to an imperative "praise"—the dropping of a Hebrew *yodh.* Otherwise it follows MT except for ten instances of the vowel letter *waw.*

The next Psalm, number 121, also interchanges an "h" for "l," drops one conjunction, omits "Lord" twice, and adds "by night" once. Other variations concern vowel letters. Psalm 122 has about the same number of variations. These two Psalms have more variations than most, but even these are not excessive.

Psalm 124 omits one word of MT apparently by mistake. It adds a relative pronoun and the adverb "all." Otherwise it alters the readings slightly by way of pronoun endings and of course has a few extra vowel letters.

Psalm 126, however, has no word differing from MT but disagrees in a few vowel letters.

Of Psalm 119 there are 109 verses preserved in whole or in part in eight columns of text. Again the text is on the whole close to MT but there are a number of minor differences. An attempted tabulation can hardly give the whole picture, but it may be of some help. There are about twelve cases of substitution of synonymous words. For instance, the Scroll has "words" for "mercies"; "judgments" for "word"; "do" for "keep"; "statutes" for "mercies"; "word" (*dbr*) for "word" (*'mr*); and a couple of changes of words probably due to outright mistakes in copying letters. The name of God "Adonay" is added once. Several times pronouns or prepositions are interchanged with no change of meaning. In the phrase "for ever and ever," the first "ever" is omitted. The conjunction is omitted four times and added once. This is about all, beside variations in the use of vowel letters. The manuscript thus gives the impression of being a copy of MT like DSIs *b,* but a somewhat careless copy. It does not use vowel letters as frequently as DSIs *a,* however, and shows fewer outright mistakes.

The evaluation of the Psalm scroll is difficult and much more study will be done of course. The present writer believes that Skehan's judgment, that it is a hymn book based on the canonical Psalter but including other pieces, is sound. It would fit the idea that the text of the canonical Psalms here preserved from the first half of the first Christian century is not strictly the MT, yet is a representative of that type of text in relatively good condition. It seems to lie between DSIs *a* and DSIs *b* in quality. One might suppose that if this were a purely canonical Psalter from this later date that its text would be more like that of DSIs *b.* It is instructive to compare the five Psalms found by Yadin in the excavations at Masada, which clearly date to before A.D. 70. This scroll contained Psalms 81 to 85 in fragmentary form but in the canonical order. As to their text he says, "The text corresponds to the Masoretic text, in both contents and the spelling except for an interesting variant in 83:7" where two letters are reversed.[21] It would seem therefore that the MT was standardized at least by the early first century of the Christian era and was copied with increasing accuracy from then on. This type of text can be traced back to 200 B.C. in copies from Qumran and can be inferred as early as the exile.

Before leaving this subject we return again to Warfield's note as to the second purpose of textual criticism—to validate the existing text. For this purpose the recent discoveries are most welcome. The Masoretic and Septuagint types of text can be traced back to 200 B.C.; the Samaritan type almost as far. By comparing these text families it is possible for the student to solve some ancient problems between variant readings. But with the new repristination of the Septuagint and Samaritan texts he can go further. It is clear now that whichever text is chosen—even the worst of all the various readings—the result will not be unsatisfactory. The worst text is not far off from the best text.

It might not be amiss to remember that for over three hundred years the Christian church used the Septuagint almost exclusively for its Old Testament text. When Jerome reverted to the Hebrew as a basis for his Latin Bible, the shock was not in the variant text so much as in the new translation! And even today it may be said that new translations differ among themselves more in the choice of words and idioms than in the basic text reflected. Any of the texts we use are of satisfactory accuracy except for the details which concern the scholar. The Masoretic text when improved upon by reference to the ancient copies and versions now available can be considered a most faithful reproduction of those copies used by Ezra the scribe and his immediate successors traditionally called the men of the Great Synagogue. In the time preceding Ezra the evidence for types of text becomes more slender, but there are other evidences, such as archaeological confirmation of little details and the confirmation of the preservation of names, which would support the general picture of antiquity that ancient scribes worked faithfully and reproduced their texts with care.

Notes

1. Patrick W. Skehan, "Exodus in the Samaritan Recension from Qumran," JBL, LXXIV (1955) : 182–7.

2. William F. Albright, "New Light on Early Recensions of the Hebrew Bible," BASOR, 140 (Dec. 1955) : 27–33.

3. Frank M. Cross, Jr., *The Ancient Library of Qumran* (Garden City: Doubleday-Anchor, 1961), pp. 188–94.

4. *Ibid.*, p. 176.

5. *Ibid.*, p. 193, though he dates the actual Samaritan text to Hasmonean times, p. 172.

6. Albright, *op. cit.*, p. 29.

7. *Ibid.*, p. 28.

8. Skehan, *op. cit.*, p. 183.

9. Cross, *op. cit.*, p. 41.

10. Robert H. Pfeiffer, *The Books of the Old Testament* (New York: Harper's, 1957), p. 165; Cross, *op. cit.*, p. 189.

11. Benjamin B. Warfield, *Textual Criticism of the New Testament* (New York: T. Whittaker, 1889); Archibald T. Robertson, *An Introduction to the Textual Criticism of the New Testament* (New York: Doran, 1925).

12. Warfield, *op. cit.*, p. 10.

13. Millar Burrows, "Variant Readings in the Isaiah Manuscript," BASOR, 111 and 113 (Oct. 1948 and Feb. 1949) : 16–23 and 24–32.

14. Samuel Loewinger, "The Variants of DSIs II," VT, IV (1954) : 155–63. He has marked with an asterisk those places where DSIs *b* differs from MT and agrees more or less closely with DSIs *a*. It is illuminating, however, for the student to go through at least some of the material for himself to get the feel of the subject and to see the proportion of the variations to the totality of the text and to judge the consequences and perhaps the causes of the errors.

15. BASOR, 111:16 f.

16. Frank M. Cross, Jr., "The Contribution of Qumran Discoveries to the Study of the Biblical Text," *Israel Exploration Journal* XVI (1966) : 82.

17. *Ibid.*, p. 89 n.

18. *Ibid.*, p. 93 f.

19. J. A. Sanders, *The Psalms Scroll of Qumran Cave 11*, Discoveries in the Judaean Desert of Jordan, IV (Oxford: Clarendon Press; New York: Oxford University Press; 1965).

20. Patrick W. Skehan, "The Biblical Scrolls from Qumran and the Text of the Old Testament," BA, 28 (1965) : 100.

21. Yigael Yadin, "The Excavation of Masada—1963/64," *Israel Exploration Journal* XV (1965) : 104.

—14—

THE SAMARITAN PENTATEUCH
AND THE TEXT OF THE OLD TESTAMENT

Bruce K. Waltke

In this chapter the writer hopes to show the contribution of the Samaritan Pentateuch to the textual critic and the higher critic of the Old Testament. The Samaritan Pentateuch (sp) has two primary values for the literary critic of the Old Testament: (1) it points up the relative purity of the Massoretic Text (mt) ; and (2) when used in conjunction with the Septuagint (lxx) it can be a useful, though limited, tool in the hand of the critic as he seeks to restore the original text. In the field of higher criticism, the sp helps to establish the antiquity of the Pentateuch.

In order to show its value in pointing up the relative purity of the Massoretic Text in a paper of this limited scope, the writer will define its text type by selecting representative variants from mt and classifying them according to their nature. In order to show why it must be used in conjunction with the lxx to restore an original reading, the writer will demonstrate the historical connection in the fifth century b.c. between the lxx and the sp. If he can establish that the text of sp has been revised and modernized as early as about 450 b.c., then obviously the archaic text of mt antedates this text by many years. First of all then, the writer will seek to define the character of sp's text, and secondly he will endeavor to trace the history of this text in the pre-Christian era with emphasis upon its historical contact with lxx.

I. The Character of the Text

Gesenius,[1] the first to classify the variants between the sp and mt in a thorough and convincing way, concluded that all the variants of sp can be classified "comfortably" into these categories: (1) readings in which emendations of a grammatical nature have been attempted, (2) glosses or interpretations received into the text, (3) conjectural emendations of real or imaginary difficulties in the mt, (4) readings corrected or supplemented with the help of parallel texts, (5) large additions interpolated from parallel passage, (6) emendations of passages and words of the mt which were objectionable to the Samaritans because of historical difficulties or a seeming lack of dignity in terms applied to the Creator, (7) morphological alterations in favor of the Samaritan dialect, (8) alterations made in favor of Samaritan theology and hermeneutics. Although this classification of variants implies the secondary character of the SP's readings, Gesenius cautions "there are left some readings of the SP [Gen. 4:8; 22:13; 49:14; and 14:14] which are recommended by internal arguments and which are therefore not to be rashly confounded."[2]

Undoubtedly Gesenius accurately appraised the text,[3] and to ignore his work, as some recent writers have done, is to court failure. But the work is often a *tour de force* and too radical. Gesenius carefully selected his material to prove his conclusions and never tried to control his research by selecting a single passage and considering all variants within that passage. Often he assumed the superiority of the MT and rejected arbitrarily a reading of the SP without philological reason. In addition, some of the variants he considered are in reality inner Samaritan variants, for with other scholars of his century he was limited by a lack of a critical edition of the SP.

Later scholarship has corrected and modified Gesenius's conclusions, and has supplemented his material. This writer is heavily indebted to that heritage. He has classified (see below, note 95) the secondary variant readings of SP from MT into these eight classes: (1) the Samaritan text has been corrupted by scribal error; (2) the Samaritan text preserves a linguistic tradition which differs from the linguistic tradition preserved by the Tiberian grammarians; (3) the Samaritan text has been modernized by replacing archaic Hebrew forms and constructions with forms and constructions of a later Hebrew linguistic tradition; (4) the Samaritan text has been smoothed exegetically and linguistically by removing grammatical difficulties, and by replacing rare constructions with constructions that occur more frequently; (5) the Samaritan text has been supplemented, clarified and corrected by small additions, and interpolations both large and small from parallel passages; (6) the Samaritan text has been clarified and interpreted by small changes; (7) the Samaritan text has been corrected to remove historical difficulties and objectionable passages; (8) the Samaritan text has been adapted to conform to the theology of the Samaritan sect.

In this limited discussion the writer will consider only classes three, four, five, and seven, and he will treat these only to the extent necessary to indicate to the reader the true nature of this text.

A. Class I

The Samaritan text has been modernized by replacing archaic Hebrew forms and constructions with forms and constructions of a later Hebrew linguistic tradition.

Many readings clearly betray the fact that they originated from the scribal practice of adapting the text to the linguistic tradition of the post-exilic period by replacing archaic forms with late Hebrew and Aramaic forms. Ben-Ḥayyim observed and demonstrated:

> On the whole the Samaritan tradition, known to us mainly from the readings of the Pentateuch, is closer to Mishnaic Hebrew than is the Tiberian tradition. This is at first glance strange, for the Samaritans rejected even the non-Pentateuchal parts of the Old Testament, and would have no truck with the oral law of the Jews. We have here another proof that at any definite point of time and in any definite area the language is common to the population as a whole, not the special possession of sects and groups separated from the main body on religious grounds.[4]

The following variants of the SP serve to illustrate that the scribes of this tradition have substituted archaic forms with later forms.

1. *In orthography.*

a. *The 3rd masc. sing. pronominal suffix.*[5] The use of *he* for final *ō* was a feature of early Hebrew orthography.[6] The MT occasionally preserves a remnant of this early, orthographic practice; but to the writer's knowledge the SP systematically alters the *he* to the later *waw;* cf. Gen. 9:21, the MT reads *'hlh,* but the SP reads *'hlw;*[7] Gen. 49:11, the MT reads *'yrh,* but the SP reads *'yrw;* Ex. 22:26, the MT reads *kswth,* but the SP reads *kswtw.*

b. *Defectiva versus plene writing.* The SP replaces *scriptio defectiva* writing with *scriptio plene* writing. Both texts had a tendency in this direction, but the SP went further than the MT. In the Rabbinic period the Jewish scribes chose a text with conservative orthography. There were some secondary attempts to establish its principles and to level the text according to them.[7a]

2. *In morphology.*

a. *The SP replaces the short form of the imperfect with waw-consecutive with the long form of the imperfect.* It is now fairly certain that in fourteenth-century (B.C.) Hebrew, the Hebrew verbal scheme was: "punctual *qatala,* durative *yaqtulu,* jussive *yaqtul,* 'emphatic' jussive *yaqtula.*"[8] Moran noted that in the Canaanite dialect of Byblos at this time the jussive form may refer to the past, and that with the exception of two forms ". . . not one of the 69 examples of *yaqtul* with past meaning refers to continued action."[9] Undoubtedly, the "short" form of the prefixed conjugation with *waw-consecutive* in Biblical Hebrew derives from this preterite use of the *yaqtul* form.[10] With the later loss of final short vowels the two forms, *yaqtulu* and *yaqtul,* fell together, though they remain distinct in the *hiphil* stem and in certain forms of the so-called weak verbs. To the writer's knowledge, wherever the distinction is observed the *waw-consecutive* construction occurs with the short form in the Pentateuch of MT. But in the SP the distinction is no longer perfectly observed. Perhaps the later Aramaic influence caused this blurring of the forms, for in Aramaic this distinction is lacking. Sperber cites many examples of this well-known phenomenon:[11]

   i. *Hiphil* with preservation of the *yodh:*

      Num. 16:10, MT reads *wyqrb* but SP reads *wyqryb.*

      Gen. 31:42, MT reads *wywkḥ* but SP reads *wywqyḥ.*

      Num. 31:50, MT reads *wnqrb* but SP reads *wnqryb.*

   ii. *Tertiae infirmae* verbs with preservation of the *he.*

      Deut. 10:3, MT reads *w"ś . . . w"l* but SP reads *w"śh . . . w"lh.*

      Gen. 41:22, MT reads *w'r'* SP reads *w'r'h.*

      Deut. 3:1, MT reads *wnpn wn'l* but SP reads *wnpnh wn'lh.*

   b. SP *frequently introduces "pseudo-cohortative" forms, an archaizing practice in late Hebrew writing.* This feature is rare in the Pentateuch and the Prophets, but very common in the Hagiographa.[12] The MT rarely has the "pseudo-cohortative" form. A few examples will suffice to illustrate the construction in the SP.[13]

      Ex. 6:5, MT reads *w'zkr* but SP reads *w'zkrh.*

      Deut. 10:2, MT reads *w'ktb* but SP reads *w'ktbh.*

      Deut. 10:3, MT reads *w'psl* but SP reads *w'pslh.*

      Deut. 3:4, MT reads *wnlkd* but SP reads *wnlkdh.*

      Deut. 2:13, MT reads *wn'br* but SP reads *wn'brh.*

   c. SP *sometimes replaces waw-consecutive ("conversive") and the perfect with the waw conjunctive and the normal tense.* Moran has demonstrated conclusively the use of *waw* conversive with the perfect in proto-Hebrew of the Amarna period, a usage well attested in the MT.[14] But in the SP the construction is dropped occasionally in favor of *waw* conjunctive and the simple imperfect; e.g.:[15]

      Ex. 8:12, MT reads *whyh* but SP reads *wyhy.*

      Ex. 8:23, MT reads *wzbḥnw* but SP reads *wnzbḥh.*

Sometimes a *waw-consecutive* with the imperfect is substituted by a *waw* with the perfect; e.g. Gen. 27:22, MT reads *wymšhw* but SP reads *whmšhw.*

   d. SP *replaces the infinitive absolute with an imperative or a finitive verb forms.* Concerning the use of the infinitive absolute in early Hebrew, Moran comments:

> The use of the infinitive absolute instead of a finite verb was not unknown to Hebrew grammar, but it was not given due consideration nor, as a result, brought to bear on the solution of certain problems of the Hebrew text. It was Karatepe and, in its light, Ugaritic and Amarna, which demanded a serious investigation of the infinitive absolute and the extent of its use. This Huesman has given us in two articles,[16] demonstrating that the substitution of the infinitive absolute for the finite verb was a fairly common construction. Amarna and Ugaritic have shown the antiquity of the construction . . .[17]

Whereas Moran points out the early use of the infinitive absolute, Kropat points out that this use of the infinitive as an imperative or a command is entirely lacking in Chronicles.[18] "When such a construction occurs in Samuel–Kings, it is represented in the parallel text of the Chronicler by a finite verbal form."[19] Undoubtedly, then the SP reflects a later modernization of the text in those passages where it replaces the infinitive absolute with an imperative or a finite verb form.

In pre-exilic Hebrew this use of the infinitive absolute was more extensive than in the MT.[20] It appears, therefore, that the scribes of the Massoretic tradition have also eliminated many of these forms but not nearly as systematically as the scribes of the Palestinian-Samaritan tradition.

The following examples illustrate the replacement of the infinitive absolute with an imperative:[21]

Num. 15:35, MT reads *rgwm* but SP reads *rgmw*.

Num. 25:17, MT reads *srwr* but SP reads *srrw*.

Deut. 31:26, MT reads *lqh* but SP reads *lqhw*.

The following illustrate the substitution of another finite verb continuing a finite verb for the infinitive absolute:[22]

Gen. 8:3, MT reads *wyšbw . . . hlwk wšwb*
        SP reads *wyšbw . . . hlkw wšbw*

Gen. 8:5, MT reads *hyw hlwk whswr*
        SP reads *hyw hlkw whsrw*

Gen. 8:7, MT reads *wyṣ' yṣw' wšwb*
        SP reads *wyṣ' yṣ' wšb*

Probably those instances should be included here where the SP replaces an infinitive construct after a particle with a finite tense construction:[23]

Gen. 46:30, MT reads *'ḥry r'wty*
        SP reads . . . *r'yty*

Deut. 12:30, MT reads *'ḥry hšmdm*
        SP reads . . . *hšmydm*

Num. 3:13, MT reads *bywm hkty* but SP reads *bywm hkyty*

Num. 9:15, MT reads *wbywm hqym* but SP reads *wbywm hwqm*

e. *SP has a distinct predilection for the hiphil stem.* Because the same tendency is distinctive in Chronicles in contrast to the parallel text in Samuel–Kings, this predilection is best considered as a feature of late Hebrew.[24] The Canaanite material and the early Hebrew inscriptions do not have this predilection while occasionally the MT has the *hiphil* form in opposition to the SP. The following examples are but a few of the many times the SP replaces the stem of the MT with the *hiphil* stem:[25]

    I. *Hiphil for qal:*
       Gen. 22:23, MT has *yld* but SP has *hwlyd*.
       Deut. 20:8, MT has *wyspw* but SP has *wywsypw*.

    II. *Hiphil for piel:*
       Num. 33:52, MT has *te'abbēḏū* but SP has *t'bydw*

f. SP *replaces enclitic mem construction with the normal construct state ending.* H. D. Hummel has demonstrated that enclitic *mem* was a feature of early Hebrew as well as of Ugaritic, Akkadian, and certain South Semitic dialects.[26] Moran has demonstrated its presence in the Byblos letters of the Amarna period.[27] Though the MT rarely preserves this ancient construction, it was consistently replaced by the normal construct forms in the SP; e.g.[28] in Deut. 33:11, MT reads *mtnym qmyw* but SP reads *mtny qmyw*.

g. SP *"treats the he locale rather roughly."*[29] Both the textual evidence and the Jewish ridicule of the Samaritan exegetes indicate Samaritan ignorance of the *he locale* suffix.[30] The presence of the *he locale* afformative in Ugaritic indicates that its absence in the SP is best understood as a later modernization of the text of the SP. The following examples suffice to show its omission:[31]

Ex. 10:19, MT has *ymh swp* but SP has *ym swp*.

Ex. 33:9, MT has *h'hlh* but SP has *h'hl*.

Gen. 37:24, MT has *hbrh* but SP has *hbwr*.

On the other hand, sometimes the SP preserves the form where it is omitted in the MT.

h. SP *replaces rare and early indefinite pronouns with later and more customary forms.* To the Hebrew pronouns Ugaritic has added the indefinite interrogative *mn,* discovered by Albright in Deut. 33:11.[32] But the SP reads *my* here instead of *mn*.

The archaic *zû* of the MT in Ex. 15:16 finds parallels in the dialect of Byblos, Ugaritic and in Mari names,[33] but in the SP it is changed to the more customary *zh*.

Likewise *nḥnw* is revised to the later form *'nḥnw* in Gen. 42:11; Ex. 16:7, 8; Num. 32:32. These are the only places where the MT reads *nhnw*.

i. *The SP drops the paragogic yodh and waw occasionally found in the MT.* Gesenius writes: "In the formation of nouns the paragogical letters *yoḏ* and *waw* added to the *nomen regens* are omitted almost constantly [in SP]; e.g. *škn* for *škny* Deut. 33:16, . . . *ḥyt* for *ḥytw* Gen. 1:24. . . ."[34]

B. Class II

SP *presents an exegetically and linguistically more straightforward text than MT by removing grammatical difficulties, and replacing rare constructions with more frequently occurring constructions.*[35]

1. SP *has a more consistent orthography than MT.* Talmon observed: "But whilst the MT might use the same word in the same sentence once in *plene* and once in defective spelling, S is more consistent and harmonises such instances as, for example, in Gen. 1:14, 15, 16; 7:2; 8:20."[36]

2. SP *replaces the asyndetic constructions of MT with the smoother syndetic constructions.*[37] By changing the asyndetic *'ṣ* (Gen. 1:11), *'l* (Gen. 3:16), *hnplym* (Gen. 6:4), *tmym* (Gen. 6:9) into *w'ṣ,* etc., the SP

obtained greater clearness. On the other hand, it will be observed that
less frequently the sp has the asyndetic construction where the mt employs the conjunction.

3. sp *corrects discrepancies in syntax.* Scholars have tried to explain in
various ways the discrepancies in gender and number between subject,
predicate, and attributes, which form such a disconcerting peculiarity
of the mt. This lack of agreement is an early feature of Hebrew syntax
for as Moran demonstrated: ". . . the syntax of agreement in the Byblian letters is paralled in most in detail in Biblical Hebrew."[38] He there-
upon cited examples of syntactical disagreement in the Byblian letters
similar to that encountered in the mt. The scribes of the Samaritan
tradition smoothed the text by removing these discrepancies.

a. *The verb or attribute corrected to agree with the customary gender
of the noun:*[39]

	MT	SP
Gen. 13:6[40]	*nš̆' . . . h'rṣ*	*nš̆'h . . . h'rṣ*
Gen. 49:20	*š̆mnh lḥmw*	*š̆mn lḥmw*
Gen. 49:15	*mnwḥh . . . ṭwb*	*mnwḥh . . . ṭwbh*

b. *The verb corrected to agree with the number of the subject:*[41]

Num. 9:6[42]	*wyhy 'nš̆ym*	*wyhw 'nš̆ym*
Gen. 30:42	*whyh h'ṭpym*	*whyw h'ṭpym*
Ex. 4:29	*wylk mš̆h w'hrn*	*wylkw mš̆h w'hrn*
Gen. 10:25	*yld š̆ny bnym*	*yldw š̆ny bnym*
Gen. 46:27	*wbny ywsp 'š̆r yld*	*wbny ywsp 'š̆r yldw*

c. *The verb corrected to agree in number with other verbs:*[43]

Ex. 39:3	*wyrq'w . . . wqṣṣ*	*wyrq'w . . . wqṣṣw*
Lev. 14:42	*wlqḥw . . . whb'yw . . .*	*wlqḥw . . . whb'yw . . .*
	yqḥ wṭḥ	*yqḥw wṭḥw*
Lev. 19:27	*l' tqpw wl' tš̆ḥyt*	*l' tqpw wl' tš̆ḥytw*
Num. 13:2	*š̆lḥ . . . tš̆lḥw*	*š̆lḥ . . . tš̆lḥ*
Num. 21:32	*wylkdw . . . wywrš̆*	*wylkdw . . . wywryš̆w*

4. sp *tends to discard the collective form in favor of plurals.*[44]
Another feature common to the Samaritan text and Chronicles, in distinction from the Massoretic Pentateuch and Samuel–Kings, is the tendency to discard the collective forms in favor of plurals.[45] In this respect
too the Samaritan text and Chronicles represent a younger linguistic
stage than the Massoretic Pentateuch and Samuel–Kings. As in many
other cases, the development seems to have proceeded in an Aramaizing
direction, for in Aramaic most of the old collectives are converted into
plural forms.[46] The following examples are but a few cited by Sperber:

	MT	SP
Lev. 20:27	*b'bn*	*b'bnym*
Lev. 8:13	*'bnṭ*	*'bnyṭym*
Ex. 35:28	*hbśm*	*hbśmym*
Num. 4:15	*mś'*	*mś'y*
Lev. 23:40	*w'np*	*w'npy*

5. SP *combines collective nouns with singular or plural verbs more consistently than* MT. Gerleman misrepresented the SP when he said, "In these Books [Samaritanus and Chronicles] collectives are combined much oftener than in the Massoretic Pentateuch, or Samuel–Kings, with plural verbs." To prove his point he cited examples of the different construction of the verb with *'m* "people," in Ex. 1:20; 4:31; 16:4; 17:3; 33:10. But when the examples of this feature cited by Sperber[47] are examined, it is discovered that in these instances the collective is used with the plural verb in the MT in contrast to the use of the singular verb in the SP. Talmon stated the case more precisely: "Collective nouns are treated somewhat haphazardly by the Massoretes. The number of verbs and adjectives connected with them is flexible and apparently influenced by the context. S, on the other hand, strives to establish a more consistent treatment and, in most cases, deliberately chooses between given possibilities. Once accepted, a definite number will be used predominantly in connection with the collective noun concerned."[48]

6. SP *replaces passive constructions with active constructions.* By replacing passive constructions with active constructions the scribes of the Palestinian tradition achieved a more readable text. The following passages illustrate this feature:[49]

	MT	SP
Num. 28:17	*yē'āḵēl*	*tô'ḵēlû*
Lev. 11:13	*yē'āḵ'lû*	*t'klw*
Lev. 25:34	*yimmāḵēr*	*ymkrw*
Num. 28:15	*yē'aśe(h)*	*y'św*
Gen. 10:1	*wayyiwwāl'dû*	*wywlydw*
Ex. 34:34	*y'ṣuwwe(h)*	*yṣwhw*
Num. 3:16	*ṣuwwā*	*ṣwhw*
Lev. 6:23	*yûḇá*	*ybw'*
Lev 4:35	*yûsar*	*ysyr*
Ex. 27:7	*w'hûḇā'*	*whb't*

7. SP *replaces rare forms with more customary forms; e.g.*
   a. *Forms of infinitive construct of tertiae infirmae verbs:*[50]

MT	SP
Ex. 2:4[51] *l°ḏē'ā*	*ld't*
Gen. 50:20 *'°šō (h)*	*'šwt*
Ex. 18:18 *'°šōhû*	*'šwtw*

b. *Form of "pe-waw" verb:*[52]

| Gen. 11:30 *wld* | *yld* |

c. *Assimilation of taw in hithpa'el stem:*[53]

| Num. 21:27 *w°tikkōnēn* | *wttkwnn* |
| Num. 24:7 *w°tinnaśśê (')* | *wttnś'* |

8. SP *replaces rare and lively expressions with customary and prosaic expressions.* Geiger observes: "For him [the scribe of SP] the lively expressions are no longer fitting, and so he chooses the more sober, and seemingly more regular expressions."[54]

Gen. 7:2. In the MT of Gen. 7:2 the formula of words *'îš w°'ištô* appears alongside the synonymous pair of words *zāḵār ûn°qēḇa.* This variety of expression disappears in the SP and LXX, which use the latter formula in both verses probably because the latter formula seemed more appropriate with animals.

Gen. 17:17. The MT reads *hlbn m'h šnh yiwwālēḏ:* "Shall a child be born to one who is an hundred years old?" The LXX is in perfect agreement with this linguistic usage found also in Gen. 4:18 etc. But the Samaritan clarifies the construction by the easier *'wlyd.* The text now reads: "Shall I beget a child at the age of an hundred years."

Ex. 21:28. The verb *ngḥ* used in Ex. 21:28, 29, 31, 32, 36 with respect to the "pushing" of an ox is replaced by an easy change to the more familiar verb *nkh* "to strike."

Ex. 25:20. In describing the position of the two cherubim, the MT reads *'yš 'l 'ḥyw.* For this the SP substitutes the more banal expression *'ḥd 'l 'ḥd.*[55]

C. Class III

The text of the Samaritan tradition has been supplemented and clarified by the insertion of additions and the interpolation of glosses from parallel passages.

1. *Small additions have been added to the text of the SP to achieve greater clarity.*

a. SP *inserts a subject to achieve greater clarity:*[56]

MT	SP
Gen. 2:24 *whyw lbśr*	*whyw šnyhm lbśr*
Gen. 21:33 *wy't*	*wy't 'brhm*
Gen. 29:23 *wyb' 'lyh*	*wyb' 'lyh y'qb*
Ex. 15:25 *wyṣ'q 'l yhwh*	*wyṣ'q mšh 'l yhwh*
Ex. 2:6 *wtḥml 'lyw*	*wtḥml 'lyw bt pr'h*

b. SP *inserts an appositive to achieve greater clarity:*[57]

Gen. 26:5 *'qb 'šr šm'*   . . . *'šr šm' 'brhm 'byk* . . .
     'brhm bqly
Gen. 48:7 *mth 'ly rḥl*   *mth 'ly rḥl 'mk*
Gen. 38:13 *wygd ltmr*   *wygd ltmr kltw*
Gen. 48:7 *bb'y mpdn*   *bb'y mpdn 'rm*

c. SP *inserts various nouns to achieve greater clarity:*[58]

Lev. 5:24 *mkl 'šr yšb'*   *mkl dbr 'šr yšb'*
Num. 23:26 *kl 'šr ydbr*   *kl hdbr 'šr ydbr*
Ex. 15:22[59] *wylkw šlšt*
    ymym   *wylkw drk šlšt ymym*
Gen. 48:14 *wyšlḥ* . . . *'t*
    ymynw   *wyšlḥ* . . . *'t yd ymynw*

d. SP *inserts various prepositions to achieve greater clarity:*[60]

Ex. 12:43 *'l mšh w'hrn*   *'l mšh w'l 'hrn*
Ex. 12:28[59] *'t mšh w'hrn*   *'t mšh w't 'hrn*
Gen. 48:5 *kr'wbn wšm'wn*   *k'r'wbn wkšm'wn*
Ex. 2:14 *l'yš šr wšpṭ*   *l'yš šr wlšpṭ*

e. SP *inserts the particle 't to achieve greater clarity.*[61]

Gen. 44:26 *lr'wt pny h'yš*   *lr'wt 't pny h'yš*
Ex. 2:9 *wtqḥ h'šh hyld*   *wtqḥ h'šh 't hyld*
Lev. 4:17 *wṭbl hkhn*
    'ṣb'w   *wṭbl hkhn 't 'ṣb'w*
Num. 22:41[62] *wyr' mšm*
    qṣh h'm   *wyr' mšm 't qṣh h'm*
Deut. 26:2 *lškn šmw šm*   *lškn 't šmw šm*

f. SP *inserts various particles to achieve greater clarity.*[63]

Ex. 29:33 *lml' 't ydm*   *lml' bm 't ydm*
Ex 18:21 *tḥzh*   *tḥzh lk*
Gen. 2:12 *ṭb*   *ṭb m'd*
Gen. 2:19 *wyṣr yhwh*
    'lhym   *wyṣr yhwh 'lhym 'wd*
Ex. 21:8 *'m r'h b'yny*
    'dnyh   *'m r'h hy' b'yny 'dnyh*

2. *The Samaritan text has been harmonized and supplemented by parallel passages.* One of the outstanding characteristic features of the Samaritan text is its predilection for duplicates and supplementations of the text with the aid of parallel passages. Concerning this characteristic Gesenius stated: "The Samaritan critics seem to have put forth a special

effort to achieve complete consistency in the sacred text and to make sure that nothing would be omitted which seemed to be required for a complete statement."[64] This feature is also a characteristic of the Chronicles in contrast to Samuel–Kings, for Gerleman noted: "Here too [in the Chronicles] we find numerous interpolations and a distinct tendency to eke out the text with the aid of parallel passages."[65]

a. *SP has harmonized and supplemented one passage by another with little alteration of the text.* Concerning this class of variant readings Gesenius wrote:

> Most of the emendations of this kind are made in such a manner that the meaning is little changed; only the words and forms of the words are harmonized with some parallel passage. Here are a few examples! Gen. 18:29, 30 for *l' "šh* Samaritan has *l' 'šhyt* harmonized from vv. 28, 31, 32. Gen. 37:4 *bnyw* for *'hyw*, corrected by v. 3. Ex. 21:25 *mkwh* for *kwyh*, harmonized from Lev. 13:24, 25, 28. ". . . Into this same class belong many proper names which appear in the Hebrew text in more than one form, but in the Samaritan text they consistently have the same form. Thus Moses's father-in-law is always called *ytrw, Jetro*, and the successor of Moses is everywhere called *yhwš'*, while in the Hebrew text the former is sometimes called *yeter* and other times *yit'rō*, and the latter is sometimes called *y'hōšu"'*, and other times *hōšê"'*. In some passages the reading is harmonized in a manner which conflicts with his ultimate purpose as in Lev. 14:44, 48; here *prh* (to harmonize with v. 43) is read for the vulgar *pšh*, [a change] which is very inept in this passage.
>
> Only rarely is the meaning of the passage changed by such corrections. Obviously, however, this happened in Gen. 36:2 and 14 where the Samaritan critics proposed a son in place of a daughter for *Zibeonis*. Unquestionably he was fooled by the parallel passage in vs. 14. Without much more reflection and preceded by the Alexandrine translation the same error was committed by Hubigantius, Kennicottus, J. D. Michaelius. But confer also the second thoughts of Michaelius, De Rossius, Ilgenius and Vaterus on this passage who all demonstrate conclusively that the Hebrew text is right.[67]

Even more convincing are the examples cited by Geiger:

> In order to give Israel's borders round about, the SP also changes the borders of Canaan so that in Gen. 10:19 he describes the borders of Canaan as *mnhr mṣrym 'd hnhr gdwl nhr prt w'd hym h'hrwn* exactly as he also alters the text of Dt. 34:1–3 from Gen. 15:18 (cf. Ex. 23:31). In like manner he adds to the text of Gen. 30:36 from 31:11–13 (that an angel appeared to Jacob in a dream revealing his portion in Laban's herds). To Gen. 42:16 he adds the text of 44:22 (that Benjamin could not leave his father) . . . .[68]

b. *SP has expanded the text by larger interpolations from parallel passages.* This feature is so unique that Gesenius classified these variants as a class by themselves. His treatment, though now antiquated in some details, has stood the test of time. He wrote:

> This matter leads us to those larger additions, which are completely peculiar to the Samaritan text, interpolated from parallel passages in such a way

that wherever something is commemorated as having been said or done by Moses previously this same thing is found expressed with as many words in the preceding passage, and also that whatever is commanded by God this very same thing is repeated with as many words where it is narrated as being carried out by Moses. A large harvest of these examples is offered in Exodus where you have interpolations either from the same book or from Deuteronomy; v. c. 6:9 (cf. 14:12) ; 7:18 (cf. vv. 16–18) ; 7:29 (cf. vv. 26–28) ; 8:19 (cf. vv. 16–19) ; 9:19 (cf. vv. 13–19) ; 10:3 [10:2] (cf. vv. 3–6) ; 11:3 (cf. 4:22, 23) ; 18:25 (cf. Dt. 1:9–18) ; 20:17 (cf. Dt. 27:2, 5–7) ; 20:21 (cf. Dt. 5:26, 28; 18:18–22; 5:27, 28) . In addition Num. 4:14; 10:10; 12:16 [13:1]; 13:33 [13:34]; 20:13; 21:11, 12, 20; 27:23; 31:24; Dt. 2:7; 4:21; 10:6 [10:7].

Already Morinus, who is otherwise a strenuous defender of the Samaritan readings, made a proper judgment about the authenticity and origin of these insertions. He excused these interpolations of the Samaritans by the example of the Greek fathers, especially Origen, who supplemented one translation of the Old Testament by another one. Grotius is also right when he calls stupid these unnecessary efforts of the transcribers though he is not quite consistent with himself for he admits some of them into his text. Of the more recent critics after Whiston these Samaritan readings found patrons in Hubigantius and Kennicottus who were seconded by Geddesius. Kennicottus follows the explanations of the Samaritans themselves. He writes in his preface to the Sam. Aramaic translation of the Pent. in the Bodleian library: 'Some of the Jews omitted some repetitions for the sake of simplification, but the Samaritans, careful not to leave out anything, retained them.' Following the Samaritans he did not doubt that genuine pericopes of the more ancient text were omitted by the Jews at the time of King Ptolemy. This was done out of an effort to abbreviate the text so that they would be freed from the burden of copying both in the original text and in the Greek translation. In order to defend his cause Hubigantius refers to the ancient custom of writing. Characteristic of Homer's style is the feature that the commands of the gods and the heroes when addressed to men are given twice with just about the same words. Once they are found when the command is given, and again where they are narrated as being carried out by those who received them. We answer him that though it is right to refer to the analogue of ancient ways of writing, it is not right to appeal to the Greek poets whose way of speaking differs considerably from the Hebrew. We should rather study the Oriental writers and especially the Hebrews. Now the study of this literature proves the very opposite of what Hubigantius desired to prove for wherever in the Hebrew commentaries things are repeated of which they spoke previously, such repetition is never done with the same words; the thought is repeated, but not with the same words. Unfortunately Kennicottus draws arguments partly from the brevity and necessity of some repetitions and partly from the testimony of the Jews themselves. This second argument was already answered by Sabastian Ravius who easily demonstrated that in the analysis of the testimony of the Jews this celebrated critic of his age was very wrong. Concerning his first argument it is so far from the truth that no weight can be given to it. Rather, many of these interpolations intrude themselves into the text in such inept passages that they betray themselves like shrews. As examples of these one should mention the interpolations after Ex. 6:9; 20:21; Num. 27:14, of which Vaterus already judged well.

In addition, the slight knowledge of ancient Hebraisms found in the passages reveal the freedom which the interpolators took. So for example in the passage inserted after Gen. 28:5 where for *nšym* we read *'yšwt women* which form of the word is completely alien from the old and pure Hebraism. By the way, in thinking up his unfortunate conjecture Kennicottus overlooked completely the religion of the Jews who were already very solicitous from these times on not to lose by carelessness even an *iota* from these most sacred documents. These men would have never permitted themselves to drop entire sections in order to serve the laziness of the copyist. Furthermore, even if we assume that some codices were mutilated in such a way that even those from which the Alexandrine translation came were effected, how can we explain that such mutilation having invaded all codices, only the Samaritan ones were left intact?

Concerning the origin of these interpolations I can hardly agree with Sabastian Ravius who attributed them exclusively to the envy and resentment of the Samaritans. [He wrote:] 'Since the Greek translation does not recognize these interpolations and the Jews cannot be considered as having suppressed certain pericopes for the reasons given by Kennicottus . . . nothing seems more probable to me than that the Samaritans because of their hatred towards the Jews, and to give more occasion to it, decided, to interpolate their Pentateuch and in this way made it fuller and larger thus implying that the Jews mutilated their codices.' This opinion cannot be brought in harmony with those rules which we see the Samaritans followed in their making of their Pentateuch. We prefer, therefore, to see these interpolations as the endeavor of the Samaritans to render their text more plain and more complete. This opinion has the support of the obvious analogue of the smaller additions of which we spoke above. So it cannot be accepted with some other critics that these pericopes were derived from the authority of some ancient codices or glosses on their margins.

If you ask about the time when these interpolations were inserted into the text, it appears that they were introduced between the time of the Alexandrine translation and Origen because Origen mentions such a passage which he certainly found in the Samaritano-Greek translation.[69]

The arguments advanced by Gesenius which are still valid today are: (1) these interpolations are not found in the lxx, which historically arose from the same recension of the sp and not the mt; (2) deliberate omissions of this sort would hardly be expected in the conservatively transmitted Massoretic tradition; (3) interpolations of this kind can be expected in a text which is generally characterized by "scholarly" reworkings.

D. Class IV

The Samaritan text has been corrected to remove historical difficulties and objectionable passages.

Gen. 50:23. The mt reads *bny mkyr bn mnšh yldw 'l brky ywsp* but the sp changes the phrase *'l brky ywsp* to *bymy ywsp* evidently because it seemed improper that the great grandchildren of Joseph should be born upon his knees.

Deut. 25:11. In this passage it was found unacceptable to say in naked obscenity that in a fight a woman would grab a man at his private parts. Therefore the text of the SP has been changed to read *bśrw* "his flesh" in place of *mbšyw* "his private parts."

Deut. 28:30. In the curse formula it is predicted: *'šh t'rś w'yš 'ḥr yšglnh*. Apparently the verb *šgl* was deemed too vulgar for public use and the oral tradition read *yškbnh* in its place. This Q'*re* reading is taken up into the text of the SP.

Conclusion

One may conclude that the text of the Samaritan Pentateuch displays a text which has been modernized with scholarly revisions. The large number of clearly demonstrable secondary readings in the SP, and the even larger number of such readings in the LXX, stand in sharp contrast to the strikingly few number of such readings in the MT. F. F. Bruce stated the point concisely: "While in certain details the Samaritans have preserved a true reading lost by the Jewish text (in which case the true reading has usually been preserved by the Septuagint as well), the chief value of the Samaritan Pentateuch is the witness which it bears to the essential purity of the Masoretic text of the first five books of the Bible."[70] Cross also praised the Massoretic text of the Pentateuch: ". . . the Rabbinic text is normally short, not conflate or expansionist in the Pentateuch and Samuel. To be sure, there are secondary expansions in the Pentateuch, but by and large it is a superb, disciplined text."[71]

II. The History of the Text

Here the writer is not concerned with the history of the text of SP after its origination as a sectarian text, but prior to its origination as a sectarian text. To put this study into focus, however, one must first establish the date of the origin of the sectarian text.

A. The Date of the Origin of the Sectarian Text

With the discovery of new sources, scholars were able to date the origin of the SP with a fair degree of accuracy, by comparing the phenomena of the Samaritan Pentateuch with other dated Biblical and non-Biblical MSS. As the proper turning of the dial of a combination lock releases the lock, so the proper matching of the phenomena of the SP with the phenomena of these sources resolved the problem: the SP as a sectarian recension originated in the Hasmonean era.

William F. Albright first reached this conclusion through a comparison of the oldest lapidary examples of Samaritan writing with the coins of the Hasmoneans dated ca. 137 B.C. This external evidence of the script harmonized with the historical record; since the Jewish conquest of Samaria and Shechem occurred between 128 and 110 B.C., it was only natural to date the final schism between the sects somewhere in this period.[72]

Frank M. Cross, Jr. continued the work of matching the evidence. As Albright had compared the script of the SP with the coins of the Hasmonean period, Cross compared the script with the Dead Sea Scrolls [DSS] written in Palaeo-Hebrew forms. The new material yielded the same answer: the Samaritan script separated in the Hasmonean period.[73] In addition to the palaeographic evidence, he considered the orthographic evidence. From this study he concluded:

> Samaritan orthography reflects neither the restricted use of *matres lectionis* characteristic of the third century and earlier, nor the revised spelling principles of the rabbinic text. Rather it exhibits the characteristic full orthography of the Maccabean and especially Hasmonean eras.[74]

James D. Purvis most recently concluded a thoroughgoing study of the problem of the origin of the sect and its Pentateuch.[75] In his study of the scripts, Purvis was careful to establish the separation of the Palaeo-Hebrew script into branches after the Hasmonean period: the one represented in the Palaeo-Hebrew writing of the coins and manuscripts of the Roman period, the other represented in the archetype of the Samaritan script.[76] Such a distinction can be seen, for example, in the *daleth.* There is a tendency toward a rounded head in the Hasmonean coins; this characteristic is developed in the Samaritan script, but not in the coins of the Roman period. Other consonants where the two traditions most clearly diverge after the Hasmonean era are *he, yodh,* and *resh.* He concluded: "Thus, some tendencies which are initiated in the script of the Hasmonean period are taken up in the Samaritan script, but are not developed in the Palaeo-Hebrew script of the Roman period."[77]

Purvis found the orthography of the SP conformed to the orthography of the Qumran Scrolls dated in the Hasmonean era in the following ways: in the full use of *matres lectionis,* the use of *waw* and *yodh* in medial and final positions for o/u and i/e respectively, the use of *'aleph* as a *mater lectionis* for ā, the appearance of the "pseudo-cohortative," the behavior of the laryngals, the shorter orthography in 2, 3 masc. pl. of the suffixes and pronouns, and the evidence of the predominant penultimate stress.[78]

He found further confirmation for this date in the agreement of the textual tradition of the SP with Hebrew texts of the Hasmonean period.[79]

These three independent witnesses argue that the Samaritan Pentateuch originated in the Hasmonean period.

B. The History of the Text Before Its Origination as a Sectarian Recension

Unlike Aaron's golden calf, the Samaritan Pentateuch did not suddenly come forth in the Hasmonean era as a creation *ex nihilo*. Unquestionably the Samaritans adopted a text already in existence. In this section an attempt will be made to uncover and expose the age, provenance, and vicissitudes of the recension which gave birth to the Samaritan Pentateuch.

Fortunately the text of the sp exhibits strong correspondences to other texts belonging to Jewish circles; by comparing the correspondences and differences of the text of the sp with these other texts, to a large extent the prehistory of the sectarian text can be inferred. More particularly, the sp shares unique readings with the New Testament, a coterie of Qumran MSS, the lxx, the mt, the Book of Jubilees, and the Chronicler.

In a paper of this limited scope, the writer will confine his study of the relationship of sp to the Qumran scrolls, the lxx, and the Chronicler in an attempt to reconstruct the prehistory of sp.

1. *The Samaritan Pentateuch and the Qumran scrolls.* One hundred years ago Geiger recognized that the variant readings of the sp—aside from Aramaism and purely sectarian readings—are not the product of specifically Samaritan recensional activity; rather they derive from an old recension.[80] The later empirical evidence of the dss has completely substantiated this judgment. In fact, even the Aramaisms cannot be attributed to the Samaritans. By identifying and localizing this "old recension" in the dss, Cross and Skehan contributed the first major advance beyond this thesis.

Three MSS have been published or announced which ally themselves with the "Samaritan" recension either wholly or partially: 4QNum[b],[81] 4QEx[a],[82] 4QTestimonies.[83] The most significant of these is 4QEx[a]. The affinities of this scroll with sp are striking not only with respect to script but also with respect to textual characteristics. Skehan in his first study concluded:

> The recension in question is the 'Samaritan' recension, with all the essential characteristics of that fuller text, including its repetitious manner of recounting the plague episodes, its borrowings from Deuteronomy and its transpositions; *this is true at almost every point where the extant fragment makes verification possible.*[84]

At the end of this article Skehan presents much additional evidence to support this conclusion. Both texts are collateral witnesses to one recension. Its one truly unique reading *wbzrw' ḥzqh* is the product of textual corruption because in no other passage is *ḥzqh* used with *zrw'* but rather with *yd*.

Later examination of 4QEx[a] led to the certain conclusion that it belongs to a local recension and not the Samaritan sectarian recension; *i.e.* the SP emerged from a Proto-Samaritan recension. In his first article Skehan refused to answer the question ". . . by whom, and for what purpose, such texts were prepared. . . ."[85] Cross believed it had no relationship with the sectarian text: "There is not the slightest reason to suppose that the 'Proto-Samaritan' is in any sense a sectarian recension."[86] In a later article Skehan presented conclusive evidence vindicating this judgment:

> The paleohebrew Exodus described in JBL, LXXIV (1955), 182–87 has proved on further study to contain all the expansions of the Samaritan form of Exodus, with one notable exception: it did not contain the addition to the Ten Commandments after Ex. 20:17, referring to the unhewn altar on Mt. Gerizim. . . . The conclusion is that the paleohebrew Exodus is not a Samaritan sectarian document, though it does offer the type of text the Samaritans have preserved as their own.[87]

Emphatically, the variants of the SP—aside from the purely sectarian readings—are not the product of specifically Samaritan recensional activity. Therefore, the Samaritans must have adopted and adapted a recension shared by the Jewish community in the Hasmonean era. One can now confidently speak of a Proto-Samaritan recension.

This recension is but one of at least three recensions attested at Qumran. According to Cross:

> In the Pentateuch three types of text are present. Some texts, especially that of Genesis, are closely allied with the *textus receptus;* others reflect close relations with the Samaritan, or properly, with the Palestinian text; a third group is closely affiliated with a text of the type which underlies the Septuagint.[88]

Cross solved the problem of the origins of such recensionally different texts by his theory of local texts.[89]

Furthermore, one may conclude safely that *the provenance of 4QEx[a] and consequently the Proto-Samaritan recension is Palestine.* Cross argued for the provenance of the "Samaritan" recension on the basis of its script. 4QEx[a] is written in the Palaeo-Hebrew script: "The script [of 4QEx[a]] cannot by any stretch of the imagination be called Samaritan. It is now by far the fullest example we have, and a very fine one, of a quite regular Palaeo-Hebrew bookhand."[90] As indicated the Samaritan script is a later branch of the Palaeo-Hebrew script. Thus Cross writes: "There can be no doubt that the proto-Samaritan text is Palestinian. If for no other reason, this can be argued from the fact that the Palaeo-Hebrew script survives thanks to its transmission in texts of this type."[91]

But SP also shows a strong affinity with the LXX.

2. *The SP and LXX and Massoretic traditions.* The obvious relationship of the SP and the LXX intrigued scholars from the time of Morinus[92]

until the present. To explain this relationship is to explain the early history of the Proto-Samaritan tradition. A survey of the literature reveals, however, that it has seldom been noted that the SP has a much closer relationship with the MT than with the LXX. The reason for this oversight was that no one bothered to make a thorough collation of the three texts. E. Castellus[93] made no more than a feeble attempt to collate them for he omitted the greatest number, "cum nullam sensus varietatem constituant." More satisfactory was the collation of the SP and the MT by Petermann,[94] but a precise and analytical collation of all three texts together was still lacking. The writer, therefore, undertook such a collation for the first ten chapters of Exodus. Originally he purposed to collate the entire book of Exodus, but after collating ten chapters he realized that the percentage of agreement or disagreement among the texts remained constant. Therefore, for the purpose of this study ten chapters constituted a sufficient sample of material from which to draw firm conclusions.[95]

From this study the writer can now draw the following conclusions: a. *The "Samaritan" [Palestinian] textual tradition and the "Septuagintal" [Egyptian] tradition stem from an earlier, common [Old Palestinian] textual tradition which differed from the Massoretic [Babylonian] tradition.*

In the first ten chapters of Exodus SP and LXX share 75 readings against MT. According to Gesenius,[96] in the entire Pentateuch there are more than a thousand instances where LXX and SP agree against MT. But the number alone is not significant; it is the nature of the agreement: for the most part *they do not share original readings, but secondary readings.* If they merely shared original readings this would not prove any significant or unique historical contact of the two recensions; but because they share scores of secondary readings one must propose some unique historical contact between the two traditions. Most of the longer readings of the SP and the LXX against the shorter readings of the MT are transparently secondary; in passages where the SP and the LXX have a different grammatical number from the MT they present a much smoother text. Gesenius summarized the nature of their agreement thus:

> 1. There is a large measure of agreement between the two codices in variant readings which seem to be glosses inserted into the text, and conjectural emendations of more difficult passages. Now this occurs in such a manner that one cannot suppose that it is a coincidence[32][32 Vaterus in his commentary on Ex. 12:40 and Michaelius in *Bibl. Orient.,* XXII, 196, observes this very smartly]. The following examples exhibit this genre of variant agreement: Gen. 2:2, 24; 14:19; 15:21; 17:14; 18:19; 24:62; 25:8; 27:27; 29:1, 26:6, 41:15; 47:21; 49:3, 4, 12, 22, 26; Lev. 18:21; Numb. 16:15; 21:28; 34:6; Dt. 32:5 *et. cet.*
>
> 2. Furthermore, they agree with each other in such small and minute detail in many passages that they do not change the meaning at all. Their agreement

in transposition and confusion of letters even less can be attributed to mere accidental coincidence. For example, the prefix *waw* is added two hundred times and deleted one hundred times; the LXX, with very few exceptions, follows the SP exactly[34][34 Hassencampius in his book says, p. 225: "If you think that the LXX made these changes when they translated the text into Greek and they agree with the Samaritan by mere accident—if you imagine this— why then do you agree with Cicero when he pokes fun at Epicurus for his position about his atoms?].[97]

Though Gesenius typically overstated the case, the point that they are related by secondary readings must stand. In both recensions identical secondary expansions are added; e.g. explicative nouns (1:22; 2:3, 6, 21), conjunctions (2:24; 3:6, 8), the article (5:18; 9:24), *lk* (7:5), etc. are inserted into the texts. In contrast, the MT tends to be a short, clean text, though occasional expansions occur. To this writer's knowledge Thomson alone rejected an historical relationship of the two traditions, but he failed to observe the cogency of Gesenius' argument concerning the nature of agreement.[98]

Having established that they are historically related, it is proper to ask the reason behind this relationship. Gesenius' answer to the question remains a classic. He wrote:

> As far as we are concerned if we try to inquire about this matter, what was the cause of this agreement or disagreement, there can be found three reasons: it is possible that the LXX came from the Samaritan, or that one codex was interpolated from the other, or finally that the Greek Pentateuch had a common source with the Hebrew Samaritan—namely, a recension of the books of Moses which was somewhat different from the one which obtained public authority with the Palestinians. We will say something about each one of these possibilities respectively.[99]

Gesenius ruled out the possibility that the LXX came from the Samaritan primarily for these three reasons: (1) There is no evidence that the LXX was translated from the Palaeo-Hebrew script; (2) fragments of the Samareitikon, a Samaritan Greek translation which is completely different from the Alexandrian translation, argues conclusively that the Alexandrian Greeks used a different recension for their translation from the Samaritan recension; (3) the thesis runs contrary to history. As Gesenius wrote:

> Flavius Josephus' history teaches us that during the time of the Ptolemies there was fresh and very savage hatred between the Jews and the Samaritans living in Egypt. There was also a public discussion staged by the two sects in the presence of the king. When it was finished the Samaritans coming out as the losers were beheaded. Now how is it possible that the Jews of Alexandria would have accepted and adopted the Greek translation of their law from this sect which they hated more than Vatinianus, and that this translation could have obtained so quickly such great authority in spite of its origin?[100]

He argued against the hypothesis of an interpolation on the basis of the nature of the agreement:

Hassencampius has observed very much to the point,[49][49 Hassencampius, p. 226] the nature of the agreement as explained above is contrary to this hypothesis. All those who see some truth in this reasoning agree that the agreement is even in minutiae and matters which normally escape the attention of an interpolator, and which are numerous. It is of such a nature that it reveals the work is not that of an interpolator but that of a translator.[101]

He concluded, therefore, that they spring from a common source:

We have left the third explanation which we accept without any uncertainty even though we admit it does not solve all the problems mentioned above, and does not lack completely some of the difficulties of the other hypotheses. We stated earlier that *the Alexandrian translation like the Samaritan text came from Judaean codices which were similar to each other. But they followed a different recension [ekdosis] of the Pentateuch from the one which obtained public authority with the Palestinians. The Samaritan exemplar, on the other hand, was later corrected and interpolated in many passages by half-learned scribes.*

That body of sacred books of the Old Testament, which we use now, had many exemplars which teach us that the same piece (such as a song, or a narration, or a genealogy) sometimes have different recensions which sometimes disagree in their readings (e.g. Ps. 18 and 2 Sam. 22; Ps. 14 and Ps. 53; or Ps. 105 and 1 Chron. 16) ; sometimes they differ in the order of their chapters and verses, (as we can observe in the prophecy of Jeremiah whose Hebrew text differs a great deal from the one found in the Alexandrian translation) . Now the form of this second edition very clearly shows the tampering of a second editor in some passages. This editor wanted to earn honor by removing difficulties of words, and thoughts, and other things either true or as in most of the cases imaginary. Of this sort of thing we have abundant examples in the pericopes of the books of Samuel and Kings found also in the Chronicles[55][55 I gathered quite a number of examples in *historia linguae et scripturae hʹbraicae*, p. 12, which I do not repeat here]. Similarly we believe that the Jews in addition to the Hebrew text of the Pentateuch, which we use presently, had another one in which the authors endeavored to render their content more simply and shorter, and who tried to correct the difficulties and imaginary problems of the text in such a way that they received into the text glosses and conjectural emendations. The exemplars of this other edition which you could call *Alexandrino-Samaritanus* . . . were received by the Alexandrians as well as by the Samaritans. But others, first of all the Jews of Jerusalem, tried to conserve piously the ancient reading unchanged even though it was harder to understand and more obscure, and not completely free of defects.[102]

Geiger modified Gesenius' view by allowing merely the Aramaism and sectarian readings as purely Samaritan contributions to the text.[103] The DSS allow only the sectarian readings to the Samaritans. All serious scholars accept Gesenius' hypothesis that the LXX and the SP diverged from a common earlier source: Swete says: "A careful analysis of the Samaritan text led Gesenius to the conclusion, which is now generally accepted, that the fact of two Pentateuchs often making common cause against the printed Hebrew Bibles indicated a common origin earlier than the fixing of the Massoretic text. . . ."[104]

This conclusion for the Pentateuch is in complete harmony with Cross's conclusion concerning the recensional history of the text of Samuel. He argued that a common text of Samuel lies behind the LXX and the Chronicler. This hypothesis rests on the foundation "that Chronicles often utilize an edition of Samuel closer to the tradition of the Cave IV Scroll [4QSam[a]] than to that which survived in the Masoretic recension." Moreover, "the text type of Samuel underlying the LXX is closely allied to that used by the Chronicler not long after 400 B.C. in Palestine."[105] This would argue that the LXX derives from an Old Palestinian recension. He concludes from the evidence of 4QSam[b]:

> Again, the archaic Samuel manuscript (4QSam[b]) obviously reflects at many points a text which antedates both the proto-Masoretic recension and that underlying the Septuagint, though its affinities are clearly with the latter. Since the manuscript itself dates from the end of the third century, and there is no strong reason to suppose that several texts imported from Egypt came to Qumran, we must conclude that it is a witness to a collateral line of tradition that persists in Palestine from a time antedating the divergence of the Chronicler's Palestinian text of Samuel and the Hebrew textual tradition surviving in Egypt. Perhaps it is easiest to suppose that this Old Palestinian text type derives from the fifth-century Jewish community in Palestine, and that the ancestral Egyptian textual tradition diverged from this Old Palestinian text no earlier than the fourth century, no later than the early third century B.C.[106]

This suggestion of a Palestinian provenance and date of the fifth century B.C. nicely fits the Pentateuchal evidence for this early recension. One must propose that this common ancestry occurred at an early period, to allow time for the differences between the two traditions to develop. The collation also showed that the LXX recension privately developed many secondary readings which are product of traditional growth. Albright has brought forth convincing evidence that in the fifth century B.C. there was Egyptian influence on the Hebrew recension underlying the Greek translation.[107] Although not as numerous, secondary readings were gradually introduced into the Proto-Samaritan tradition. Cross's proposed date for the Old Palestinian recension precisely fits the Pentateuchal evidence.

3. *The SP and Chronicles.* Cross argued that underlying those passages in Chronicles which are synoptic with Samuel and the allied Hebrew text-type behind the LXX translation, lies an Old Palestinian recension that was in the possession of the fifth-century Jewish community. Empirical evidence of this old recension is found in the three scrolls of Samuel

from Cave IV. These scrolls are widely at variance with the text of the traditional Massoretic text of Samuel but follow systematically the rendering of Septuagintal Samuel, and in the case of 4QSam[a] bear close resemblance to Chronicles. The writer has posited that collateral lines of the old recension also underlie the allied Samaritan and Septuagint recensions of the Pentateuch. Now if the LXX and Samaritan texts emerge from collateral lines of this Palestinian recension of the fifth-century Jewish community, then they should show affinity with the synoptic portions of the Pentateuch found in the first nine chapters of Chronicles composed in Palestine not long after 400 B.C. In this source the theory can be tested.

But first it is necessary to determine whether the Chronicler himself modernized his Pentateuchal source and corrected it according to the linguistic and stylistic ideals of time, or whether the recensional source he had in hand already possessed these revisions. Martin Noth[108] and A. Kropat[109] proposed that the Chronicler himself modernized and corrected his sources in the historical books, but Gerleman[110] reasoned otherwise because of the similarities of Chronicles with the text of Samuel used by the LXX translation. He concluded: "The Septuagint thus strongly conflicts with the current view that the sources of the Chronicler must have been more or less identical with our Books of Samuel–Kings, and that the Chronicles in their present form are the result of a deliberate attempt at modernization on the part of the Chronicler." The scrolls of Samuel from Cave IV put the issue beyond doubt. Cross stated: "In sections where Chronicles overlaps with Samuel in this section I Sam. 1–2 Sam. 11:1, the text of Chronicles normally agrees with 4Q and LXX[BL] against MT."[111] Undoubtedly, then, the Chronicler relied upon a Pentateuchal recension current in Palestine in his time. Its correspondences with the LXX, 4QSam and the Samaritan text settle the issue.

Since Gerleman was completely under the influence of Kahle, however, he came to the erroneous conclusions that the Books of Samuel-Kings were carefully revised and archaized after the production of Chronicles and the LXX, whereas the Hagiographic Books of the Chronicles remained in a precritical, vulgar textual stage. As indicated, Cross refuted this theory.[112]

Gerleman pointed out the strong correspondences between the Samaritan Pentateuch and the synoptic passages of the Pentateuch in 1 Chron. 1–9. "It is a fact which has not received due attention," he wrote, "that the latter [*the genealogies and the lists of names in 1 Chron. 1–9*] *show greater resemblance to the Samaritan Pentateuch than to the Massoretic.*"[113] This statement is backed up by many convincing examples of correspondences or partial correspondences between the Chronicler and the SP. The texts show an affinity in the following textual and linguistic features: in their forms of the names; in their use of *waw* in the genealogical tables—both of them preferring the later syndetic construction against the more archaic asyndetic construction; in their preference for *plene* spellings; in their use of "pseudo-cohortative" forms with *waw consecutive* and the imperfect; in their preference for *'l* against *'l;* in their Aramaizing tendencies; in their tendency to replace collectives by plural forms; and their preference for infinitive absolute with finite verb forms. Gerleman wrote: "It is evident that the Pentateuch text from which the Chronicler has taken his genealogies was precisely a vulgar text of the same kind as Samaritanus."[114] Furthermore, "it is, however, not only in morphological and syntactical details that the textual tradition of the Chronicler shows affinity with the Samaritan Pentateuch. The resemblance extends also to the actual composition, the arrangement of the material, the form of the narrative."[115]

The correspondences pertain to the LXX as well. Concerning this relationship he concluded: "We have seen that the texts from which the lists of names in 1 Chronicles 1–9 have been taken show remarkable correspondences not only with Samaritanus, but also with the Septuagint."[116]

The differences between Chronicles and the SP are easily explained as the product of secondary, later growth within the Palestinian recension, the later influence of the reintroduced Proto-Massoretic text on this recension, and the later Jewish textual criticism on Chronicles. These strong correspondences between the Chronicler's Pentateuch and the Samaritan Pentateuch place beyond doubt the existence of a "Samaritan" text-type in Palestine about 400 B.C. Here is the oldest witness to the existence of a Palestinian text.

Conclusion

From this history of the text one can conclude: (1) When the SP and the LXX agree against MT, they bear witness to an Old Palestinian recension as old at least as the fifth century B.C. Normally, therefore, SP shares an original reading with LXX. Though this reading is older than either recension per se, it is not necessarily superior to the reading of MT, for already in this early period the Palestinian recension was being revised by scholarly reworkings. One should realize that this conclusion is opposed to presentations in recent, popular introductions to textual criticism. Indeed these writers appear to ignore the essentially sound conclusions of Gesenius. For example, R. H. Pfeiffer concluded that "the SP is a valuable aid in emending erroneous readings, particularly when it is supported by the LXX or other ancient versions."[117] B. Roberts also ignored Gesenius. He concluded: "Where the LXX and the SP coincide, it may be conceded that the text offered is generally preferable to the Masoretic, and the readings are frequently suggested as emendations for it."[118] Likewise A. W. Adams asserted: "But more recent views, which see the MT as only one line in the transmission of the text, and notably the striking agreement of some of the DS fragments with Samaritan readings, have disposed some scholars to find in the SP one of the best preserved traditions of the Hebrew text."[119] Indeed, according to A. W. Adams, the reviser of Kenyon's handbook, in cases of variants the SP is probably nearer to the original text than the MT! Likewise F. F. Bruce is not sufficiently cautious when he writes: "Where the Samaritan and Septuagint texts agree against the Masoretic text, there is a *prima facie* case in form of the former."[120]

(2) Time and space did not permit the writer to present evidence that the proto-MT text probably contaminated the text of SP at about the time it branched off from the Palestinian recension. Accordingly, when SP and MT agree against the LXX, the relationship is less meaningful for this contamination would account for some of this agreement.

(3) In addition to that canon of textual criticism which asserts that the reading with widest geographical support is to be preferred, one can now add the canon that the reading found in two historically unrelated traditions is to be preferred. According to the former canon one would suppose that "the likelihood is great that a variant attested by such diverse traditions as the Samaritan and the LXX is closer to the original than the MT reading,"[121] but the second proposed canon would correct this misinterpretation of the evidence. More precisely, one can say only that the likelihood is great that a variant attested by such historically unrelated traditions as the LXX and MT is closer to the original than the SP reading.

(4) Finally, the Pentateuch itself must be older than the fifth century. If the scribal scholars of the second Jewish commonwealth found it necessary to modernize the Pentateuch to make it intelligible to the people (cf. Neh. 8) in the fifth century, then obviously the original Pentateuch antedates this period by many years.

Notes

1. Guilielmus Gesenius, *De Pentateuchi Samaritani origine, indole et auctoritate: commentatio philologico-critica* (Halle, 1815).

2. *Ibid.,* p. 61.

3. Patrick W. Skehan, "Exodus in Samaritan Recension from Qumran," JBL, 74 (1955) : 187.

4. Z. Ben Hayyim, "Traditions in the Hebrew Language with Special Reference to the Dead Sea Scrolls," *Scripta Hierosolymitana*, Vol. IV: *Aspects of the Dead Sea Scrolls,* ed. C. Rabin and Yigael Yadin (Jerusalem: 1965) : 208.

5. Gesenius, *op. cit.,* p. 26.

6. Frank M. Cross, Jr., and David N. Freedman, *Early Hebrew Orthography* (New Haven: Yale Univ. Press, 1952) , p. 69.

7. Cf. Gen. 12:8; 13:3.

7a. Cross and Freedman, *op. cit.,* pp. 69 f.

8. William L. Moran, "The Hebrew Language in Its Northwest Semitic Background," *The Bible and the Ancient Near East,* ed. G. Ernest Wright (Garden City, N.Y.: Doubleday, 1961) , p. 64.

9. William L. Moran, "A Syntactical Study of the Dialect of Byblos as Reflected in the Amarna Tablets" (Ph.D. diss., Johns Hopkins University, 1950), p. 51.

10. G. Bergsträsser, *Hebraische Grammatik*, 28th edition of *Wilhelm Gesenius' hebräische Grammatik* (Hildesheim: 1962), Part II, p. 10.

11. A. Sperber, "Hebrew Based Upon Biblical Passages in Parallel Transmission," HUCA, XIV (1939), ¶ 49: 187 ff, and ¶ 53B: 193. Obviously Sperber has made a substantial contribution by his comprehensive grouping and classification of grammatical variants of the SP from the MT. The work is limited, however, by his failure to distinguish inner Samaritan variants from original variants in the SP. Examples taken from his work have been screened to eliminate inner Samaritan variants.

12. Gillis Gerleman, "Synoptic Studies in the Old Testament," *Lunds Universitets Arsskrift* (N. F. Avd. 1), 44 (1948): 15.

13. Sperber, *op. cit.*, ¶ 103–07: 228–32.

14. Moran, "Hebrew Language," *op. cit.*, pp. 64 f.

15. Sperber, *op. cit.*, ¶ 97: 225 f.

16. John Huesman, S.J., "Finite Uses of the Infinitive Absolute," *Biblica*, 37 (1956): 271–95, 410–34.

17. Moran, "Hebrew Language," pp. 61 f.

18. A. Kropat, "Die Syntax des Autors der Chronik verglichen mit der seiner Quellen," Beihefte ZAW, 16 (1909): 23.

19. Gerleman, *op. cit.*, p. 18.

20. Moran calls attention to the use of the infinitive with the additional *i* vowel in Amarna and Ugaritic and suggests that this construction underlies the text of Gen. 30:8, 49:11, Ex. 15:6. Cf. Moran, "Hebrew Language," *op. cit.*, p. 62.

21. Sperber, *op. cit.*, ¶ 98: 226. He does not cite any examples where the SP retains the inf. abs. form.

22. *Ibid.*, ¶ 101: 227 f.

23. *Ibid.*, ¶ 99: 226 f.

24. Kropat, *op. cit.*, pp. 14 f.

25. Sperber, *op. cit.*, ¶ 62: 201 f., Sperber cites many examples of what he considers to be "the i-imperfect *qal*." Cf. ¶ 50: 90. Apart from the interchange of *'ayin-waw*, *'ayin-yodh roots* (e.g. Ex. 13:22; 33:11), Sperber does not cite any reference where the MT has the *yodh* form.

26. Horace D. Hummel, "Enclitic *Mem* in Early Northwest Semitic, especially Hebrew," JBL, 76 (1957): 87–107.

27. Moran, "Hebrew Language," *op. cit.*, p. 60.

28. Sperber, *op. cit.*, ¶ 77: 209; cf. Hummel, *op. cit.*, *passim*.

29. Abraham Geiger, "Einleitung in die biblischen Schriften. 11. Der Samaritanische Pentateuch. 20. Uebersetzungen unter den Samaritanern," *Nachgelassene Schriften* (1876) IV: 54–67, 121–32.

30. Cf. *Jer. Jeb.* 1, 6; *Kiddushin*, 75 a.

31. Sperber, *op. cit.*, ¶ 108: 232 f.

32. William Foxwell Albright, "The Old Testament and Canaanite Language and Literature," CBQ, 7 (1945): 23, n. 64.

33. Moran, "Hebrew Language," *op. cit.*, p. 61.

34. Gesenius, *op. cit.*, p. 27. Cf. Moran, "Hebrew Language," *op. cit.*, p. 60.

35. Many variants of this type can be found in Gesenius's third class; cf. Gesenius, *op. cit.*, pp. 36–45.

36. Shemaryahu Talmon, "The Samaritan Pentateuch," JJS, 2 (1951): 147.

37. Cf. Gerleman, *op. cit.*, pp. 10–12.

38. Moran, "Syntactical Study," *op. cit.*, p. 60.

39. Sperber, *op. cit.*, ¶ 88: 217 f.

40. In the dialect of Byblos, Moran cites an example where a masc. sing. verb precedes a fem. sing. subj.; cf. Moran, "Syntactical Study," *op. cit.*, p. 60.

41. Sperber, *op. cit.*, ¶ 89: 218 f.

42. In Byblos a masc. pl. subject may be used with a third sing. masc. of the verb. Moran, "Syntactical Study," *loc. cit.*

43. Sperber, *op. cit.*, ¶ 90: 219–20.

44. *Ibid.*, ¶ 91: 220 f. In all but one example cited by Sperber, the MT has the singular form, and the SP has the plural form. The one exception is Num. 11:31 where the MT has *šlwym* and the SP has *šlwy*.

45. Gesenius, *op. cit.*, p. 28; Kropat, *op. cit.*, pp. 9 f.

46. C. Brockelmann, *Grundriss der vergleichenden Grammatik der semitischen Sprachen* (Berlin: 1908), I: 428.

47. Sperber, *op. cit.*, ¶ 92: 221.

48. Talmon, *op. cit.*, 147 f.

49. Sperber, *op. cit.*, ¶ 61: 199, 200. He does not cite any passages where the SP retains a passive construction.

50. *Ibid.*, ¶ 56: 195. He does not cite any reference where the SP retains a rare form.

51. Cited in Blayney's edition of the SP.

52. Gesenius, *op. cit.*, p. 28.

53. Sperber, *op. cit.*, ¶ 58: 196; Gesenius, *op. cit.*, p. 28.

54. Geiger, *op. cit.*, p. 58.

55. Cf. Ex. 26:3.

56. Sperber, *op. cit.*, ¶ 122 a: 242 f.

57. *Ibid.*, ¶ 122 b: 243.

58. *Ibid.*, ¶ 124 a: 243 f.

59. Cited in Blayney.

60. Sperber, *op. cit.*, ¶ 118: 238 f.

61. *Ibid.*, ¶ 119: 239 f.

62. Cited in Blayney.

63. Sperber, *op. cit.*, ¶ 124 b: 244 f.

64. Gesenius, *op. cit.*, p. 45.

65. Gerleman, *op. cit.*, p. 21.

66. Argument is dubious.

67. Gesenius, *op. cit.*, p. 45.

68. Geiger, *op. cit.*, pp. 60–61.

69. Gesenius, *op. cit.*, pp. 46 ff.

70. Frederick F. Bruce, *The Books and the Parchments* (Old Tappan, N.J.: Fleming H. Revell, 1950), p. 126.

71. Frank M. Cross, Jr., "The History of the Biblical Text in the Light of Discoveries in the Judean Desert," HTR, 57 (1964): 289.

72. William Foxwell Albright, *From the Stone Age to Christianity* (Baltimore: Johns Hopkins, 1940), pp. 345 f., n. 12.

73. Frank Moore Cross, Jr., "The Development of Jewish Scripts," *The Bible and the Ancient Near East. Essays in Honor of William Foxwell Albright*, ed. George E. Wright (New York: Doubleday, 1961), p. 189, n. 4.

74. Frank M. Cross, Jr., *The Ancient Library of Qumran and Modern Biblical Studies*, rev. ed. (Garden City: Doubleday Anchor Books, 1961), pp. 172 f.

75. James D. Purvis, "The Origin of the Samaritan Sect" (Ph.D. diss., Dept. of Old Testament, Harvard Divinity School, 1962).

76. Milik contended that the Samaritan script separated from the main stream of Jewish tradition in the Roman period (J. T. Milik, *Dix ans des découvertes dans le Desert de Juda* [Paris, 1957]).

77. Purvis, *op. cit.*, p. 104.

78. *Ibid.*, pp. 125–9.

79. *Ibid.*, pp. 130–45.

80. Geiger, *op. cit.*, p. 67.

81. News Letter from Frank Moore Cross, Jr., Archaeological Director, Hebrew Union College–Jewish Institute of Religion, and Biblical and Archaeological School, Jerusalem, December 1, 1963; and *idem, Ancient Library of Qumran.*

82. Skehan, *op. cit.*, pp. 182–7; and *idem,* "Qumran and the Present State of Old Testament Text Studies: The Massoretic Text," JBL, 78 (1959) : 22, 23. In addition to the material published by Skehan, a photograph of a fragment from 4QEx^a appears in Solomon Birnbaum, *The Hebrew Scripts,* Part Two (London: 1954–57) , No. 32; and in Harold H. Rowley, *The Dead Sea Scrolls and the New Testament,* photograph on cover.

83. John M. Allegro, "Further Messianic References in Qumran Literature," JBL, 75 (1956) : 174–87; for this "Document IV," see pp. 182–7 and the corresponding plate. Patrick W. Skehan, "The Period of the Biblical Texts from Khirbet Qumran," CBQ, 19 (1957) : 435–40.

84. Skehan, "Exodus," *op. cit.*, p. 182.

85. *Ibid.*

86. Cross, *Ancient Library of Qumran, op. cit.*, p. 192.

87. Skehan, "Qumran and O.T. Studies," *op. cit.*, p. 22.

88. Cross, "History of the Biblical Text," *op. cit.*, pp. 286, 287.

89. Cross, *Ancient Library of Qumran, op. cit.*, pp. 163–94.

90. Skehan, "Exodus," *op. cit.*, p. 182.

91. Cross, *Ancient Library of Qumran, op. cit.*, p. 193.

92. Joannis Morinus, *Exercitationes ecclesiasticae in utrumque Samaritanorum Pentateuchum. De illorum religione et moribus* (Paris: 1631) .

93. B. Walton, *Biblia Sacra Polyglotta,* VI, 19.

94. J. H. Petermann, "Versuch einer hebräischen Formenlehre nach der Aussprache der heutigen Samaritaner, nebst einer darnach gebildeten Transscription der Genesis" (Leipzig: 1868) , *Abhandlungen für die Kunde des Morgenlandes,* 5: No. 1.

95. For collation see writer's dissertation: Bruce K. Waltke, "Prolegomena to the Samaritan Pentateuch" (Ph.D. diss., Dept. of Old Testament, Harvard University, 1965) , pp. 226–46.

96. Gesenius, *op. cit.*, p. 10.

97. *Ibid.*

98. John Ebenezer Honeyman Thomson, *The Samaritans: Their Testimony to the Religion of Israel* (Edinburgh: 1919) , p. 332.

99. Gesenius, *op. cit.*, p. 11.

100. *Ibid.*, p. 12.

101. *Ibid.*, p. 13.

102. *Ibid.*, p. 15.

103. A. Geiger, *Urschrift and Uebersetzungen der Bibel in ihrer Abhängigkeit von der innern Entwickelung des Judenthums* (Breslau: 1857) .

104. H. B. Swete, *An Introduction to the Old Testament,* rev. by Richard Rusden Ottley (New York: KTAV Publishing House, Inc., 1968) , p. 438.

105. Cross, *Ancient Library of Qumran, op. cit.*, p. 188.

106. *Ibid.*, p. 189. Gerleman also says: "The Hebrew text which served as the basis for the Greek books of Sam.–Kings . . . was identical or closely related with Chronicles," *op. cit.*, p. 34.

107. William F. Albright, "New Light on Early Recensions of the Hebrew Bible," BASOR, 140 (1955) : 27–33.

108. Martin Noth, *Ueberlieferungsgeschichte Studien* (Tübingen: 1957) .

109. Kropat, *op. cit.*

110. Gerleman, *op. cit.*, p. 34.

111. Cross, "History of the Biblical Text," p. 293.

112. *Ibid.*

113. Gerleman, *op. cit.*, p. 9.

114. *Ibid.*, p. 12.

115. *Ibid.*, p. 21.

116. *Ibid.*, p. 28.

117. Robert H. Pfeiffer, *Introduction to the Old Testament* (New York: Harper's, 1941) , p. 102.

118. Bleddyn J. Roberts, *The Old Testament Texts and Versions* (Cardiff: 1951) , p. 193. After the discovery of the Qumran Scrolls, Roberts modified his views; cf. "Text Old Testament," IDB, 4: 580–94.

119. Frederick Kenyon, *Our Bible and the Ancient Manuscripts*, rev. by A. W. Adams (New York: Harper's, 1958) , p. 91; cf. p. 145 also.

120. Bruce, *op. cit.*, p. 125.

121. Gleason Archer, Jr., *A Survey of Old Testament Introduction* (Chicago: Moody Press, 1964) , p. 52.

VI. THEOLOGY

—15—

THE B'RITH OF YAHWEH

J. Barton Payne

The literary division of holy Scripture into the books of the Old and New Testaments corresponds to the theological division of holy history into the two divine administrations of the older and newer testaments. Old Testament prophets (Jer. 31:31–33, Ezk. 16:60) and New Testament apostles (II Cor. 3:6, 14; Heb. 9:15–18) unite in affirming progressive redemption via the former and the latter covenant—b'rith (Heb) or *diathēkē* (Gr); and the question of their actual meaning has taken on an increasing significance in recent theological discussion. It bids fair to assume even greater importance in the future, particularly among evangelicals.

I. Modern Scholarly Concern

A. *Reappraisals of the B'rith*

At the outset of the present century, the Wellhausen school of negative criticism had succeeded in reducing the concept of the b'rith, in the minds of most Old Testament scholars, to the status of a magical rite of blood relationship with one's deity, which the Hebrew prophets of the eighth century B.C. struggled to convert to one of moral relationship, and which yet failed to become central in Israelitish thinking until an additional 100 years had passed.[1] Unreconstructed liberalism reached its extreme in Robert H. Pfeiffer's presidential address before the Society of Biblical Literature in 1950. Pfeiffer asserted that no reference to a divine b'rith with Israel could be found in passages earlier than Josiah's reformation late in the seventh century.[2]

But while some may yet speak of the origin of the b'rith as "unclear in the Old Testament tradition,"[3] archaeology has produced striking parallels to it in the form of mid-second millennium Hittite suzerainty treaties. In these, a vassal would enter into an oath of loyalty and trust toward the king and his dynastic successors, out of gratitude for royal favors already received.[4] Though published as early as 1931,[5] such treaties were first seriously related to the b'riths of the Old Testament by G. E. Mendenhall in 1954 and Klaus Baltzer in 1960.[6] Their thesis was this: that while the Hittite Empire came to an end by 1200 B.C., its treaty-form still matches that of the Decalogue[7] and, to some extent, that of Joshua's final charge to Israel (Josh. 24) ;[8] hence, they concluded, these Biblical documents must possess a correspondingly early origin.[9] Thorough treatment of the subject appeared in D. J. McCarthy's *Treaty and Covenant,* 1963,[10] with detailed studies by F. C. Fensham and others.[11]

Conservative writers such as Meredith Kline (1960) ,[12] Walter Moran (1962) ,[13] J. A. Thompson (1963) ,[14] and Kenneth Kitchen (1967) ,[15] have proceeded to stress the apologetic value of these new correlations, especially for the Book of Deuteronomy. Yet their implications reach even farther, going back to Genesis itself. Earlier critical evaluations of the patriarchal b'riths, as if they were mere reflections projected backward from the time of David,[16] are now openly rejected.[17] Mendenhall, for one, insists relative to their pre-Sinaitic character, that the Abrahamic b'rith must now be understood as the model for the Davidic and that it would be "difficult, if not impossible, to account for the invention of this narrative in post-Mosaic times."[18]

Paralleling and even preceding this renewed appreciation for its antiquity, has occurred a reawakened awareness of the centrality of the b'rith concept for Biblical revelation. Walther Eichrodt's epoch making *Theologie des alten Testaments,* 1933, proclaimed "covenant" as the theme of the Old Testament, with covenantal history as basic to Israel's election and its content as basic to Hebrew law. In certain areas, e.g., Old Testament wisdom literature, this centrality may appear as less than obvious;[19] but thirty-five years of discussion have served to underline, even among those who would charge Eichrodt with "artificiality,"[20] how successful was this choice of his for a unifying principle.[21] Thus, the leaders of early Israel, such as Moses, Joshua, Samuel, or Eli, have taken on fresh color when viewed in their role of "covenant mediators";[22] and the prophets and apocalyptists of later Israel, in their invocations both of natural phenomena and of political disaster, have had their preaching illuminated by the maledictions of the ancient Near Eastern suzerainty treaties.[23] Confessedly, among the seven eighth-century prophets[24] only Isaiah makes consistent reference to the b'rith concept—the prophets knew of it (Hos. 6:7, 8:1), but they may have feared a perversion of its judicial character into an externalized or legalistic religion (Mic. 3:11) —yet the goal of all the great prophets, from this time onward, seems to have been that of reactivating national commitment to the "covenant stipulations" (cf. Amos 3:2) .[25] Scholarly debate appears now to have shifted over into questioning whether this dominant b'rith of Yahweh was real or simply a matter of Israel's thinking, but the fact of its centrality is increasingly presupposed.[26] Here then is exhibited a prime example of scholarly reappraisal toward true Biblical teaching, based upon the history of a literary form.

B. Formgeschichte

While critically minded writers prefer to speak of the Old Testament as containing narratives and speeches *about* treaties[27] rather than, as conservatives state (especially for Deut.), "the text of a treaty,"[28] this very preference renders their recognition of such ancient covenant forms within Scripture all the more significant. Three sub-"forms" are generally discerned: parity covenants, suzerainty treaties, and promissory testaments.[29] Certain features are held in common by all three forms: e.g., the very name *b⁰rît;* or the accompanying ceremony of dismembering animals (Jer. 34:18–20), hence the verb *kārat,* to *cut* a b'rith, signifying a threat of similar dismemberment against the one who should violate the arrangement (cf. Ruth 1:17, I Sam. 3:17, Ezk. 17:13, and the parallels from Mesopotamia[30]). But it is the non-parity forms, initiated by Yahweh, whether of the treaty or of the promissory variety, that are seen as determinative for Old Testament religion. In particular, Exodus 19:5–6, on Yahweh's Sinaitic choosing of Israel as His "peculiar" people, affects all subsequent formulations of the b'rith.[31] The Decalog (Ex. 20) then offers a more detailed expression of the suzerainty features at Sinai. Its historical prologue (v. 2b), which is part of the b'rith form, makes reference moreover to Israel's exodus from Egypt; and this seriously undercuts von Rad's radical view of the originally independent existence of the Sinaitic and of the exodus traditions.[32]

It is in Moses' renewal of the b'rith on the Plains of Moab (cf. Deut. 29:1)[33] that the six elements of Mendenhall's non-parity Hittite treaty form appear most clearly:[34]

1. A preamble, introducing the sovereign (Deut. 1:1–5), often in an "I-thou" form (cf. Ex. 20:2a);[35]

2. Historical prologue, outlining the previous relations of the parties concerned and emphasizing the vassal's debt of gratitude toward his suzerain (Deut. 1:6–ch. 3);

3. Stipulations, deliniating their respective obligations, both basic (4, 5–11) and detailed (12–26);

4. Preservation, including arrangements for periodic public rereading of the treaty (27:1–8; 31:24–27), the disposition of the text (31:9–13), and the dynastic successors of the parties (31:1–8, 14–16a, 23; 32:46–ch. 34);[36]

5. Witnesses enlisted, among the Hittites a list of heavenly and earthly gods (but 31:19–22, 31:28–32:45 in Deut.);

6. Curses and blessings, depending upon the non-fulfillment or the fulfillment of the stipulations (27:9–ch. 30; 31:16b–18).[37]

Subsequent Old Testament materials, even in the different literary Gatung of narrative or exhortation (e.g., Josh. 24, I Sam. 12), demonstrate this same dependence upon the form of the written Hittite treaty;[38] McCarthy has in fact asserted, "There is not another literary form among those of the ancient Near East which is more certainly evident in the Old Testament."[39]

C. Confrontation with Accepted Criticism

As a result of such comparative Formgeschichte, modern scholarly consensus is having to rethink its position in respect to at least four major issues.

1. Mutuality. Critics of the Biblical doctrine of divine sovereignty have been slow to recognize the monergism of God's older b'rith:[40] the more brash may speak of "man's making an agreement with his God";[41] while even the more careful insist that "the parties to the agreement . . . regard one another as being free and with equal rights. . . . It is never a one-sided decision."[42] But while mutuality may have been true of certain parity covenants, the suzerainty treaties simply did not consist of matters reached by agreement.[43] W. G. Most is now thus demanding clarification over the meaning of "bilateral" b'riths and concludes that within suzerainty forms mutuality is restricted to resultant obligations;[44] it does not concern initiation, determination of content, inauguration, or effectuation. Biblical terminology bears this witness saying, on the one hand, "to establish" or "to command" a b'rith or, on the other, "to obey" or "to transgress" it (Josh. 23:16, Jer. 34:10). The initiator, moreover, normally makes a b'rith *l*ᵉ (prep.), *to* or *for* the recipient rather than *'im* or *'ēṯ, with* him;[45] and the b'rith so constituted becomes equivalent to a *ḥōq, statute* (Josh. 24:25).[46] In respect to the etymology of the noun *b*ᵉ*rîṯ,* much dispute exists; yet among those who reject Gesenius-Buh's *baraya, decide* or *allot to* (per I Sam. 17:8) and who still prefer roots that favor mutuality, whether with a meaning of "to bind" or "to eat bread with,"[47] even Köhler, representing the last-cited, now proposes a "table-fellowship, which a healthy person offers to a sick person."[48] John Murray has thus been vindicated in his definition of b'rith as "a sovereign administration of grace and promise. It is not a 'compact' or 'contract' or 'agreement' that provides the constitutive or governing idea but that of 'dispensation' in the sense of disposition";[49] and as Jocz goes on to conclude, "The one-sided nature of the covenant relationship is decisive for a theological understanding of the Bible."[50]

2. Sanction. Critical interpreters tend to restrict the Old Testament b'rith to cultic situations.[51] G. M. Tucker insists on the ceremonial sanction of an oath or a self-curse by the petitioner, "pledging something valuable, usually one's own life,"[52] and calling on God or the king to hold him responsible for his assertion or promise; so even God Himself is said to swear by His holiness (Ps. 89:35). That a close relationship does exist between the b'rith and the oath has been indicated long since by J. Pedersen's subsuming "covenants" under the oath concept;[53] and Tucker would then designate both the Near Eastern and the Old Testament b'riths as simply an "elaborated oath form."[54] But while the Old Testament may indeed speak of Yahweh's swearing a b'rith,[55] and while it may at points use terms such as $\check{s}^e\underline{b}\hat{u}^{'a}$ "oath,"[56] or '$\bar{a}l\bar{a}$ "curse"[57] along with b'rith, the Bible may make at other points a distinction. For instance, just as among the Hittites the curses and the blessings formed but a concluding section within the treaty form, so in the Old Testament, Ezekiel 17:18 seems to speak of interrelationship rather than identity, "He hath despised the '$\bar{a}l\bar{a}$, (curse) by breaking the b'rith."[58] In respect to the $\check{s}^e\underline{b}\hat{u}^{'a}$ "oath," the very evidences that are adduced by Tucker appear likewise to favor the distinction.—Jeremiah 11:5 inculcates obedience to the b'rith made at Sinai, "that I may establish the $\check{s}^e\underline{b}\hat{u}^{'a}$ which I sware unto your fathers [the patriarch Abraham, etc.], to give them a land flowing with milk and honey."[59] Biblical oaths frequently involve no b'rith; and as McCarthy says of the b'rith: "It may involve an oath or it may not."[60] Moshe Weinfeld stresses the variability of the sanctions of Old Testament b'riths, how ritual meals or sacrifices[61] came to be replaced in later contexts by verbal oaths.[62] Even Mendenhall, who states that covenants *"usually* [italics mine] had sanctions of a religious nature," grants that the oath is lacking in both the Israelite and Hittite covenant forms.[63] The b'rith of the Old Testament must therefore not be restricted in its meaning by equation with other terms or particular forms of ratification; it is simply an obligation, a relationship under sanctions,[64] the particular nature of which is to be determined on no other basis "but simply on the parties concerned."[65]

3. *Deuteronomy*. While most negatively critical scholars still follow DeWette and Wellhausen in assigning the present book of Deuteronomy to the Josianic age, it has become a truism in critical circles to state that the Deuteronomic problem, particularly in reference to the origin of its source materials, is now almost as controversial as it was once "assured."[66] Some interpreters, such as H. J. Kraus and J. J. Stamm, would still hold to von Rad's view that Deuteronomy, along with Joshua 24 and probably Exodus 20 and the Book of the Covenant that follows it, must have arisen out of a cultic ritual, rather than directly from the treaty Gattung.[67] Others, such as E. Gerstenberger, would trace these codes, and particularly the apodictic law, to wisdom literature and its maxims.[68] Yet the point-by-point correspondence of Deuteronomy with the treaty form of the Hittites is increasingly compelling today's critics to concede, with Weinfeld, that "the structure of Deuteronomy follows

a literary tradition of covenant writing."[69] The real question now seems to be, "Which tradition?"

Extant treaties from the ancient Near East fall predominantly into two groups: one of the second millennium, consisting primarily of Hittite documents of the fourteenth and thirteenth centuries B.C.; and another of the first millennium, primarily Assyrian and Aramean, of the ninth to the seventh centuries. McCarthy, with others, holds that there is no basic change in pattern that can be established,[70] which would mean that Deuteronomy could be safely left sleeping in its Josianic bed! Its above cited agreement, however, with the six major elements of the earlier Hittite treaties entails its equally consistent divergence from later Assyrian forms, both in content and in arrangement.[71] The first-millennium covenants uniformly omit parts 2 (historical prologue),[72] 4 (preservation arrangements), and 6-b (blessings); and in their sequences they allow parts 5 and 6-a (witnesses and curses) to come before part 3 (stipulations). Indeed, the regularity of arrangement that is so characteristic of the second-millennium form seems to be lacking altogether. Yet these matters form an integral part of Israel's b'riths, both in Exodus and in Deuteronomy;[73] little wonder that Mendenhall's position, that the Sinaitic b'rith corresponds to the second-millennium treaties rather than to the first, is sweeping the field.[74] Furthermore, as both Clements and Kline have clearly perceived, "The institution of a covenant required a permanent witness setting out its origin, purpose, and stipulations, so that future generations might know them." As a result, "covenant and canon are two inseparably related entities in the Old Testament;"[75] nothing less than the entire literary history of the Old Testament lies at stake!

Yet sceptical criticism has so far failed to take seriously the implications of this confrontation. Kitchen, and others, have spelled it out, saying, "The literary characteristics of the ancient Near Eastern treaties make nonsense of the usual criteria of conventional literary criticism." He then grows specific and adds:

> McCarthy blithely makes the astonishing assumption that the casual combination of J, E sources and rearrangement of text (by redactors *centuries* later than second millennium covenants, of course) should just happen to produce a direct correspondence with a covenant-form half a millennium obsolete! A miracle indeed.[76]

Yet, willy-nilly, P. Buis still pleads JEDP "sources" behind what he calls the "reconstitutions purement artificielles" of the Old Testament![77]

4. Jeremiah's New Testament. Relative to the prophets, the attacks of negative criticism concern not so much the dates and sources but the validity of the contents. By limiting the sphere of predictive prophecy to such situations as could have been contemporaneous with, or immediately future to, the prophets themselves.[78] Scepticism has thus reduced Jeremiah's anticipation of the New Testament in 31:31–34 to the category of a pious but essentially false pronouncement. As Noth has concluded,

> Shortly before the collapse of the Judean kingdom . . . the saying about the future new covenant explicitly assumed that the covenant made at the exodus from Egypt was now at an end. . . . However, the heralding by Jeremiah and Ezekiel of a new covenant seems to have played no special role in later times; it fades before the hope of a speedy restitution of the old order.[79]

Such devaluations, however, must now face not only the apostolic teaching that Jeremiah *was* predicting, at a supernaturally long range, a fulfillment over six centuries ahead of himself (Heb. 8:6–13; see below, II:C, 7) until which time the Sinaitic b'rith stood in no danger of abrogation; they must also contend with the earlier, authentically pre-Sinaitic fact of analogously promissory testaments which validate the conceivability then, during the continuation of the Old Testament dispensation, of a graciously internal relationship with God. McCarthy points out that it was the restoration community which most desperately needed just such testamentary promises and that as a result, in light of their known appeals to the patriarchal b'riths, the graciousness of Jeremiah's New Testament assumes a "special role"; indeed, this "kind of covenant . . . was not only acceptable, it became the backbone of [their] theological structure."[80]

D. A Question for Conservatives

Yet as has been true of archaeological contributions in general, so too the effect of these new b'rith evidences has not been limited to a confronting of scepticism with confirmations of Scripture to the detriment of "the assured results of higher criticism"; previously unanticipated problems may also result for evangelicalism. Witness such dilemmas as the case of Ai or of the date of the exodus.[81] Relative to the treaty-forms, discussion of this sort centers about the curses. For while first-millenium Assyria completely dropped part 5-b (the blessings) of the Hittite treaties, it greatly augmented their part 5-a (the curses).[82] It is not just that the extensive maledictions of Deuteronomy 27 and 28:15–68 are disproportionate to the blessings of 28:1–14; Weinfeld and others have gone on to claim them as taken "directly" from Assyrian treaties that are contemporary with Josiah.[83] The parallels that are cited include the general content of the curses—for instance, water being made poisonous or flooding the land; devouring animals invading inhabited areas; people being caught like birds in a trap; the breasts of nursing mothers drying up; captives going stripped like prostitutes; bodies being left unburied—and even verbalisms: for example, "to love (= be loyal) with all your heart," or "to hearken to his voice."[84] R. Frankena has even hypothesized deliberate reproduction of form, so as to underscore Josiah's 626 B.C. transfer of allegiance away from Ashurbanipal to Yahweh.[85]

The question, however, is not about the existence of the parallels but about the sources for these parallels. In another article, Weinfeld freely recognized that they included similarities with the fourteenth-century Amarna letters, as well as with the ubiquitous second-millennium Hittites.[86] Kitchen refers to his further citation of Old Babylonian data and describes his theory of Assyrian dependence as "naïvety." So while the problem of first-millennium curse-parallels remains a matter for evangelical scholarly concern, Kitchen's apologetic seems to summarize the modern mood, with its appreciation for the b'rith form as "a long-standing tradition going well back into the second millennium at least, which could have become known in the Westlands even before Moses."[87]

II. Evangelical Perspective

A. Method

But what utilization of this b'rith data may now be anticipated, particularly among conservative theologians? An immediately recognizable area is that of methodology. Despite the recent upsurge of a form-analysis epitomized by the hyper-source-criticism of Allenson's Studies in Biblical Theology, Second Series, whose primary goal seems to be one of discovering new alternatives to the Bible's own teachings about its composition and authenticity,[88] Formgeschichte may yet be found to possess a greater potentiality for construction than for destruction. Even as Oswald T. Allis was able, over fifty years ago, to utilize a formal poetic analysis to substantiate the long-range predictive character of Isaiah's Cyrus prophecies,[89] so conservatives may be expected, now, to develop the implications of the treaty form so as to validate far more comprehensive aspects of Old Testament truth. At least three avenues appear, not simply for challenging the liberal "establishment," but more positively for opening up new areas of evangelical creativity.

1. *The B'rith of Yahweh as an organizing principle for Old Testament study.* It is true that as far back as patristic times the early church organized its sacred documents into an "Old Testament" and "New Testament." Even the notes of the Scofield Bible speak of "the great covenants of Scripture which condition life and salvation, and about which all Scripture crystallizes."[90] But today more than ever, because of insights brought about by the Near Eastern treaty-form, students are discovering Pentateuchal b'rith concepts—whether or not the actual term appears—from the Garden of Eden to the Plains of Moab.[91] In the historical books "covenant renewal" has become the lodestar of Joshua 24, of the amphyc-

tionic judges, and of Israel's royal revivals.[92] The Psalms are being increasingly explained by evangelicals in terms of b'rith rituals.[93] The covenant lawsuit, or *rib* pattern, is seen as pervading much prophetic discourse.[94]

A certain tardiness on the part of Bible believers to take up the challenge of synthesis via the b'rith may be explained, partly because of the stigma of negative Biblical criticism and of Religionsgeschichte that has pervaded the attempts of the Eichrodtian school to construct Old Testament theology around the b'rith concept, and partly because of increasing antipathy demonstrated by modern dispensationalists against traditional "covenant theology."[95] The revised edition of the Scofield Bible, for a significant example, has deleted the above-quoted statement which appeared in the first edition.[96] Yet the author trusts that his own recent volume[97] holds portent for an ever broader evangelical adoption of the testament as an organizing principle.

2. Historical study. Meredith Kline's *Treaty of the Great King* (1963) on Deuteronomy, has established an obvious precedent for a wider evangelical employment of the Near Eastern treaty-form for detailed historical analysis. The entire history of Israel and, indeed, universal providence rests, as Jocz adduces, upon "the covenant-keeping God."[98] Two later examples may illustrate this process, both of which hold promise of fruitful study. On the one hand, the Qumran community witnesses to an intertestamental belief that the *bᵉrît ʾēl*, "God's covenant," with the Hebrew patriarchs had been violated by sinful Israel (CD, i*) but that Yahweh would continue to "make good His everlasting covenant" with the faithful remnant (iii, 12) in accordance with Deuteronomy 7:9 (viii, 5). They referred specifically to God's "new covenant in the land of Damascus" (vii, 9–viii, 21), under which they chose to identify their own sect[99] and, on the basis of Jeremiah 31, claimed to be God's true Israel. Yet on the other hand, shortly after these "covenanters," and with far better right,[100] Jesus Christ stated about the communion cup at the Last Supper, "This is my blood of the testament ['new testament" in I Cor. 11:25] which is shed for many for the remission of sins" (Matt. 26:28). His words are best understood historically, as the conscious fulfillment of Jeremiah 31[101] and probably of Isaiah 42:6 and 49:8.[102] As Alan Richardson has pointed out, Christ's death as a deliberate ransom (Mark 10:45) accomplishes that new redemption which fulfills Isaiah's prophecies, both of the b'rith and of the Suffering Servant (Isa 53:10–11).[103] It also serves as a passover sacrifice, "by which a new and better covenant was ratified between God and a new Israel,"[104] and all history, but particularly that of the Old Testament, takes on meaning.

3. Apologetics. While it remains a fact that the evangelical believes

* CD = Cairo Damascus Document.

the Bible because of the authority of Christ and not because of rational arguments,[105] he still utilizes for confirmation such of these latter as may appear; and in this regard the potentialities of the b'rith form for counteracting the assaults of a negative higher criticism have by no means been exhausted by the already discussed defense of Deuteronomy. Weinfeld, for example, in the midst of an otherwise destructive argument,[106] notes almost incidentally how rituals from the documents of Mari and Alalakh validate Exodus 24, as authentically second millennium. A. R. Millard has observed how parallels to the ancient treaty forms appear in the Psalter, in Israel's summons to worship,[107] thus providing further prospective validation for its already increasingly appreciated antiquity. The late E. J. Young's prophetic studies,[108] as well as Hobart Freeman's introduction to the prophets,[109] have emphasized the overt function of this institution as a guardian to the Mosaic theocracy (Deut. 18:9–22); and now, in light of the pre-prophetic origin of the b'rith form, the authenticity of such appeals may no longer be rejected as mere "Deuteronomic redaction."[110] The treaty-form is thus opening up unlimited vistas for Biblical apologetics.

B. Crucial Passages

Without attempting exhaustive exegesis, the writer would propose the following six passages as representative portions which the b'rith of Yahweh seems to place in a new light, latent for significant development by evangelical commentators in time to come.

Genesis 15:17–18 describes how "a smoking furnace . . . passed between the pieces [of dismembered animals]. In that day Yahweh made a b'rith with Abram." As is now universally recognized, this is the same b'rith-making ritual that appears both in Jeremiah 34:18–20 and in the Mesopotamian culture, particularly that of the second millennium.[111] What is not so consistently recognized is that it is Yahweh (represented by the furnace-oven) who assumes to himself the threat of dismemberment. As Derek Kidner has stated, "The accent is on His initiative and His giving. . . . This emphasis persists throughout Scripture"; and he goes on specifically to cite Hebrews 9:15 ff. in its sense of "[last] will."[112] So early does the theme of One who would lay down His life for His friends, to effectuate the testament in His blood, enter Scripture.

Leviticus 24:8 says, "Every sabbath day he shall set it [the show-bread] in order before Yahweh continually; it is on behalf of the children of Israel, an everlasting b'rith." This verse then serves to illustrate the exegetical process of having to select the proper connotation for the noun b'rith, whether parity covenant, suzerainty treaty, or promissory testament (see above, I:B). The first meaning, a mutual contract, is foreign to this context. But does the noun signify more than the second option, the imposed will of Israel's sovereign, so that b'rith becomes equivalent to an everlasting *ḥōq,* or *statute?* The showbread in this case stood as a symbol of God's graciously redeeming presence, so that to make provision for it was to carry out an ordinance that contributed to man's participation in divine salvation. Minor as it may have seemed, it expressed Israel's faith in the gracious Testator. It was, as Keil states, "a pledge or sign of the everlasting b'rith"; and he goes on to adduce the promissory parallel of circumcision (cf. Gen 17:13).[113]

Hosea 2:18–20, "In that day will I make a b'rith for them with the beasts of the field . . . and I will break the bow and the sword and the battle out of the land and will make them to lie down safely . . . I will even betroth thee unto me in faithfulness; and thou shalt know Yahweh." This mid-eighth-century revelation was God's first disclosure of a yet future b'rith. Hosea, seemingly in despair because of his Baal-worshiping surroundings (2:17), here looks forward to a better time ahead which would possess two aspects: an internal, of one's personal knowledge of God; and an external, of universal peace upon God's earth. These aspects then came to a more complete expression during the next two centuries, in Jeremiah's new testament (31:31–34) and in Ezekiel's testament of peace (34:25–31).

Meanwhile, Hosea's younger eighth-century contemporary in Jerusalem was carrying forward the internal portion of his prophecy of a future b'rith. In his messages of comfort to Judah subsequent to the devastating attack of Sennacherib in 701 B.C.,[114] Isaiah spoke of the deliverance that would be accomplished through God's Suffering Servant (Jesus Christ, Lk. 22:37) and, specifically, how Hosea's future b'rith would be embodied in Him: "I, Yahweh, have called thee in righteousness . . . and will give thee for a b'rith of the people, for a light of the Gentiles," Isaiah 42:6 (cf. 49:8). That is, what had so far been considered as a legal disposition is now summed up in a Person.[115] Through crucial passages such as this, one may be led to appreciate Jesus, not only as the everlasting God who establishes the testament,[116] but also as the priest who officiates at the death (52:15), as the Testator, the sacrificial offering who dies (53:8), and as the inheritance, being Himself the living blessing of reconciliation that is bestowed; as the Father said to the Son, "that thou mayest be my salvation" (49:6). Christ, in other words, is the b'rith.

Zechariah 11:10, "And I cut my staff assunder, that I might break my b'rith which I had made with all the peoples." The prophet's context is this: that while God has heretofore been ordering world history in favor of Israel (cf. Deut. 32:8), He now frees all peoples from this "b'rith" obligation. It is an almost unique statement, in which Yahweh is described as involved in a suzerainty covenant, but without a pervasively redemptive, testamentary character. It does, however, provide understanding for Jeremiah 33:20, 25.

Hosea 6:7, "But they like Adam have transgressed the b'rith." The kjv translates it, "But they like men . . ." which is possible but seems somewhat pointless. When one adopts the proper-noun rendering of asv and the modern versions, however,[117] he is projected back to Eden itself. He sees in this reference the implication that the human race is not only living under God's gracious promissory b'rith subsequent to Adam's fall but is also living subject to a prior suzerainty covenant of works—man's original and most fundamental relationship with his God (see part C, 2, below).

C. Theological Concerns

The doctrinal potential of the b'rith concept has already been suggested by the above selection of verses. It remains, however, briefly to identify seven areas of theological tension now appearing in evangelical attitudes toward the b'rith of Yahweh and yet auguring fruitful resolution in days ahead.

1. *The unity of God's b'rith.* While Scripture assigns unquestioned prominence to a number of redemptive b'riths,[118] a question that is still at issue concerns their uniting to form a single coherent testament of grace. Dispensational theology in particular hesitates "to project the general idea of covenant in the Bible."[119] Yet all evangelicals agree that redemption occurs only through a sinner's identification by faith with the atoning sacrifice of Christ (Mt. 3:15, I Pet. 2:24) [120] and that this truth applies equally to the saved of all ages, to those of the Old Testament as well as of the New Testament (Heb. 10:40).[121] Israel at Sinai stood quite literally under the blood (Ex. 24:8, Heb. 9:19), and the effectiveness of that blood lay not in the bulls and goats (Heb. 10:4) but in its anticipation of the offering of the body of Jesus Christ once for all (v. 12). Hebrews 9:15 speaks of Christ as the mediator both of "the new testament" and of "the first testament"; but, with only one class of transgression, one atoning death, and the same divine mediator, there appears to exist but one basic testament. Thus Matthew 26:28 records the words of our Lord, "This is my blood of *the* testament [the adjective 'new' is not present at this point in the better MSS], which is shed for many for the remission of sins."

A similar unity appears even prior to the fulfillment of Yahweh's b'rith in Christ; for Moses could anticipate deliverance for Israel on the basis, either of his own Sinaitic b'rith (Lev. 26:45) or of God's remembering His b'rith with Abraham, Isaac, and Jacob (v. 42), with no seemingly essential distinction being felt. The rediscovered law book of 622 b.c., which probably included the whole Pentateuch, is called simply, "the book of the b'rith" (II Kgs. 23:2). Scripture later refers also to "the reading of the old *diathēkē* (II Cor. 6:14) as equivalent to "whenever Moses is read" (v. 15); and this latter must include the b'riths of Genesis as well as those of Exodus 19, Numbers 25, and Deuteronomy 29. David called upon his contemporaries to remember, not his own Davidic b'rith, or even Moses' Sinaitic, but rather that which Yahweh made with Abraham, Isaac, and Jacob: "His b'rith . . . which he commanded to a thousand generations" (I Chr. 16:15–16). Two centuries thereafter, in the bleak days of Jehoahaz, God was still preserving Israel "because of His b'rith with . . ." the three patriarchs (II Kgs. 13:23). Finally, the Asaphite singers of the exile prayed God to "have respect unto the b'rith" (Ps. 74:20); it is impossible to tell which of its various Old Testament revelations may have been intended—more likely, it is the entire testament of Yahweh, viewed in its unity.

2. *Testamentalism.* In previous publications and papers of the Evangelical Theological Society, the writer has supported the more precise rendering of b'rith as "testament," or, last will, rather than the more general "covenant."[122] That is, if Hebrews 9:18 calls God's "first" (Sinaitic) disposition a testament, and if its author is correct, then testament is what it must be! Suffice it here merely to adduce two additional considerations that have arisen out of the recent Near Eastern correlations. On the one hand has come the testamentary factor that is evident in the Hittite treaties. As Kline has summarized it,

> From the viewpoint of the subject people a treaty guaranteeing the suzerain's dynastic succession is an expression of their covenantal relation to their overlord; but from the viewpoint of the royal son(s) of the suzerain the arrangement is testamentary . . . it is not in force while the testator lives.[123]

On the other hand has come the death element, so prominent in the Mesopotamian enactments of the second millennium with their ceremonial slayings of asses or sheep; compare with these the b'rith rituals of Exodus 24:4–8 or of Deuteronomy 27:5–7. Even the Noachian testament, which has been disparaged as not directly redemptive due to its purported lack of "bloody, sacramentally dividing signs"[124] was in fact introduced by the sacrificial death of clean animals, so that "Yahweh smelled the *rê*ᵃ*ḥ han-nîḥō*ᵃ*ḥ,* or placating odor" (Gen. 8:21). By means of this proposed emphasis upon testamentalism, it is hoped that future evangelical studies of the b'rith may transcend the present-day connotations of "covenant theology," which is now so often limited to theories of infant baptism, and to concentrate upon the more primary considerations of Calvary love as underlying all Scripture from Genesis 3:15 onwards.

3. *Monergism.* The subject of monergism derives from the preceding subject, for a testament is, by definition, a gracious bestowal by "one worker." It rules out not simply the concept of mutuality in the establishment of the b'rith, but also any claim to the necessity for cooperative works in its effectuation, which may be designated as "synergism." A promising field of inquiry in this regard lies in comprehensive compari-

son of the non-testamentary (yet covenantal) [125] relationship of God toward man that is described in Genesis 2 with what may be called the promissory testament that is introduced after Adam's fall in the next chapter. The legitimacy of such a procedure, however, or the supposition that Genesis 3:15 (as noted in the paragraph above) actually marks such a fundamental shift to monergistic b'rith administration, has become a subject of evangelical dispute, and from two viewpoints.

On the one hand, certain covenant theologians, such as Kline, out of a zeal to guard against anthropocentric religion and to safeguard the ultimate sovereignty of God against unwarranted claims upon His grace, are tending currently to minimize the promissory elements of the b'rith. All parties agree on its outcome of reconciliation with God, as stated from the first book of the Bible to the last: "Its constant refrain is the assurance, 'I will be your God, and you shall be my people' [cf. Gen. 17:7, Rev. 21:3]."[126] But while John Murray then says, "This is the promise of grace upon which rests the communion of the people of God in all ages," Kline prefers to define the b'rith as "a sovereign administration of the Kingdom of God . . . an administration of God's lordship, consecrating a people to Himself under the sanction of divine law."[127] Kline rightly stresses the priority of law and obedience in God's original covenant of works with Adam (II:B, 6, above), but his definition seems to neglect the fact that in every subsequent b'rith it is the redemption by divine grace that becomes central.

On the other hand, certain dispensational theologians, such as C. C. Ryrie, are criticizing the "covenant of grace" concept, both as a general category for Biblical redemption beyond Genesis 2 (see II:C, 1, above) and as a specific designation for Genesis 3:15, where the noun b'rith does not itself occur.[128] Reference at this point may, however, be made to the writer's comparison of the features of Genesis 2 and 3, and of Genesis 3 with the major features of the subsequent b'riths of Yahweh, as charted in his *Theology of the Older Testament*.[129] It seemingly confirms the recent study of L. Alonso Schökel on the status of Genesis 3 as an actual b'rith of monergistic grace.[130]

4. Conditionality. Eichrodt insists that b'rith involves both grace and precept;[131] for redemption under the b'rith, though monergistic, yet requires a response, man's meeting of the conditions of faith and obedience that God the suzerain has laid down. This subject too is related to the concept of b'rith as testament; for a last will does carry requirements: an heir may break his testamental obligation, but by so doing he forfeits his standing. The writer would thus define the b'rith of Yahweh as "a legal disposition by which *qualified* heirs are bequeathed an inheritance through the death of the testator."[132] As a result, to quote from Eichrodt, "The Hebrew *bᵉrit̲* has to cover two lines of thought: . . . 'legal system' . . . and 'decree of salvation' . . . which can yet only in conjunction render the whole content of that divine activity covered by the term $b^e r \hat{\imath} \underline{t}$."[133]

Such conjunction, however, requires the maintenance of a proper balance, in the violation of which theologians seem constantly to stand in danger! Antinomianism may be represented by the much used, and abused, term, "conditionless covenant."[134] Yet even when the conditions remain unrepresented in quoted formulations of the Biblical b'riths, one need never proceed far in the surrounding contexts to discover characteristics of contingency. Even the Abrahamic b'rith was specifically conditional, for only as the patriarch's children did justice would God bring upon them what He had spoken (Gen. 18:19). Theoretical legalism, on the other hand, did not die with the New Testament Pharisees. Modern critics are adept at discovering in Sinai a mutual quid-pro-quo "which is almost directly opposite, and which is in origin almost completely unrelated," to the other Biblical b'riths.[135]

Among modern dispensational interpreters the sentiment expressed so bluntly in the first edition of the Scofield Reference Bible, when it described how "Israel rashly accepted the law . . . [and] at Sinai they exchanged grace for law," is by no means defunct either.[136] Recourse is even had to such doctrines as the glory or sovereignty of God, which, despite their greatness, may hardly be invoked as a rationale by which to account for differing dispensations, to the disparagement of a consistently unfolding plan of redemption.[137] As Galatians 3:17 makes clear, the law did not disannul God's previous b'rith and its promises; and, within the Pentateuch itself, Deuteronomy 7:7–8 and 9:4–6 clearly base the contemporary Sinaitic b'rith on the reality of God's continuing love. Indeed, as G. E. Wright has remarked, it is the graciousness of her testament that uniquely distinguishes the faith of Israel, preserving humility on the part of the inheritors and checking any tendencies toward legalistic distortions or toward any necessary equating of God with the national interests.[138]

5. *Dispensations.* Within the basic unity of God's b'rith there exists, however, an equally discernible historical development—those "distinguishable economies in the outworkings of God's purpose."[139] A prime theological issue that is awaiting resolution in modern evangelicalism is that of the nature and extent of these differences within the b'rith concept. Signs of progress appear on the horizon: many dispensationalists are making it explicit that salvation is always to be based on the work of Christ and to be appropriated through a response of faith; and covenant theologians are increasingly recognizing that the conscious *content* of men's faith does exhibit change in the various dispensations—Israel's knowledge of the personal Messiah may have been minimal or even (especially at the first) non-existent.[140] But, as men manifest their sincere faith in God through a response of obedience, wherein do the "dis-

tinguishable" areas of this obedience actually lie? Dispensationalist writers manifest ambiguity as they speak on the one hand of "law under grace" but on the other hand of complete freedom from law as a medium for sanctification.[141] It would appear preferable to distinguish between the particularistic Mosaic codes, whose underlying principles remain valid but whose specific applications should be limited to the ancient Hebrews—for example, the principle of "safety devices" which applied to Israel in the form of required "battlements" placed around the flat roofs of their houses—and the general moral laws of Sinai—for example, the ten commandments—whose origin in God's own moral perfection renders them inherently changeless and authoritative in application, though progressively revealed because of man's limited capacity to receive and obey. Law then culminates in the teachings and personal example of Christ, yet with the moral legislation of Moses as still quotable by the New Testament and normative for God's people today.[142] Ceremonial obedience, however, is marked by augmentation from stage to stage in the revelations of the older testament; and, with its realization in the newer dispensation of the church, many of its typical rites have been fulfilled and are thus no longer observed (Col. 2:16–17, Heb. 9:8–9).[143] A proposed definition for dispensation would therefore be as follows: a testamentary period within which faith in God is manifested by a distinctive form of ceremonial obedience.

6. *Ceremonial initiation.* Within the above subject, an aspect of the b'rith of Yahweh that has produced recent doctrinal discussion is that of the relationship of man's initial ceremonial response, whether by circumcision or by baptism, to the sanctions of the ancient Near Eastern treaty-form. Specifically, Meredith Kline has called into question the traditional consensus that circumcision and baptism exist as signs of divine grace and blessing; and he has preferred to identify them as symbols of malediction, to enforce men's pledges of consecration.[144] But while an actual self-maledictory oath is reflected in Genesis 15 (see above, II:B, 1, and Jer. 34, in I:B) it is God the testator who is symbolized by the torch and invokes the destruction upon Himself (Isa. 53:8, Col. 1:22; cf. Heb. 9:16), not the man Abraham. Furthermore, while threats of a man or of his descendants being "cut off" do find representation within the ceremonies of the b'rith, it was always the uncircumcised male, not the one who had participated in the ceremony, against whom the threat was directed (Gen. 14:14; e.g., Moses's son in Ex. 4:21–23).[145] For, instead of "confessing themselves under the judicial authority and more precisely under the sword of the Almighty,"[146] those who took part in the rite of circumcision were precisely the ones who became released from the wrath of God (Jer. 4:4). Likewise in the New Testament, when John the Baptist uttered threats of chaff that should be burned in fire (Mt. 3:12), it was those who would *not* be baptized in the Holy Spirit

and in "fire" (v. 11, a different fire!) against whom he spoke.[147] Kline has made a significant point on Christ's use of the term "baptism" to describe His own passion (Lk. 12:50, Mk. 10:38); but this negative usage seems to be based upon the Greek verb *baptizo*'s meaning of *immersion,* and hence of drowning and of destruction (cf. Col. 1:11), rather than upon the initiatory ceremonies of the testament, with their consistent connotations of cleansing and regeneration.[148]

7. *Eschatological fulfillment.* Since the inheritance granted under Yahweh's b'rith constitutes "both the basis and the theme of Old Testament eschatology,"[149] its interpretation assumes a corresponding importance in this final doctrinal area. Specifically, today's three major evangelical alternatives seem to hinge basically upon the relationship that one discovers between Jeremiah's new testament and Ezekiel's testament of peace (see above, II:B).

(a) Amillennialists hesitate to affirm a literal (millennial) fulfillment for Ezekiel's prophecies of a future earthly kingdom, with its international security and agricultural prosperity (34:27–29). Thus they tend to equate such external events with the spiritual achievements of the Christian church, militant or triumphant, as anticipated in Jeremiah's internal new testament. As a neo-orthodox, but amillennial, author has put it, "God would make with Israel, forgiven and restored, a new and everlasting marriage covenant (Ezk. 16:60–63). The New Testament writers think of this prophecy as having been fulfilled in the marriage covenant between Christ and His church."[150] Jeremiah's new b'rith is thus identified with Ezekiel's prophecies and becomes the final word in testamentary revelation, "not to be displaced by any other more complete realization of what covenant grace embodies."[151] The difficulty with this approach seems to lie, not simply in the Old Testament's unequivocal assertions of literal, national fulfillment (e.g., Jer. 31:36, 32:42), but also in the New Testament's corresponding references to Mt. Zion and to the post-millennial city of the saints, on earth (Rom. 11:26, Rev. 20:8–9).

(b) Yet traditional millennialists, who favor a more literal realization for the earthly-kingdom prophecies, must likewise face a difficulty, in that the newer b'rith in Christ's blood is an everlasting, an "eternal testament" (Heb. 13:20). In reply they would contend that an eternal program may yet exhibit a series of progressive developments. Thus, a chronological distinction is maintained between the b'riths of Jeremiah and of Ezekiel, though not a complete separation. For at the second coming of Christ the four features of Jeremiah's presently existing, church-centered new testament are said to be, not transcended or displaced, but rather expanded, brought to fulfillment, and rendered determinative for life throughout the entire world, under Ezekiel's testament of peace. Specifically, men's internal religion will become productive of a totally consistent external pattern of conduct (Ezk. 37:24). Their reconciliation with God, expressed at all points in history by the Biblical promise, "I will be their God, and they shall be My people" (v. 27), will then eventuate into the fullness of divine fellowship. The Christian's present blessing of direct faith will become that of direct sight (v. 26), and the explicit forgiveness that is now granted to the saints (Jer. 31:34) will be honored by the whole creation together (Ezk. 37:28). The testament of peace will then, after the final judgment, be resolved into the new heavens and the new earth of Revelation 21–22.

(c) A final segment of evangelicalism, that of dispensational premillennialism, seeks to locate *both* Jeremiah's new testament and Ezekiel's testament of peace in the future kingdom of the millennium. A chief difficulty for dispensationalists, however, springs from the quotation of Jeremiah 31:31–34 in Hebrews 8–10. They would grant that today's church receives *similar* blessings and that the "better testament" mentioned in Hebrews 8:6, of which Christ is the mediator and which supersedes the older testament of Moses, does indeed refer to the church. But this better testament must then be distinguished from the "second testament" in the verse that follows, which is equated with Jeremiah's new testament, which in turn is cited at length (in vv. 8–12). The prophet's words are said to have been quoted in the New Testament to show that, since in the millennium there will be a superseding of the older testament by the new testament made with the nation of Israel, it is not impossible now to think of a superseding of the old by that better *diathēkē* of the church.[152] Such unelaborated subtlety of thought, however, might not have answered the temptation to lapse into Judaism which faced the first-century readers, as well as the fact that Jeremiah had simply predicted the church.

Dispensationalism is also faced with three contextual problems. (i) Hebrews 8:13 notes that Jeremiah's new testament is what makes the first old. Yet the period of the first *diathēkē* was limited to the pre-Christian era (9:8). As Ryrie has said, "In Hebrews 9 the Christian order supersedes the sacraments of the Mosaic covenant."[153] It would seem to follow that the Christian order should itself be Jeremiah's new testament.[154]

(ii) In 9:14, forgiveness is said to exist for Christians (cf. 8:12 = Jer. 31:34) because of Christ's mediating the new testament (Heb. 9:15); so Ryrie concludes that there must be two "new testaments" in Hebrews, the future one in chapter 8 and the present one in chapter 9.[155]

(iii) Since Hebrews 10:16–17 again quotes Jeremiah's new testament, this passage should also be understood as future; but because of the remission of sins that result from it the writer adds, "Having therefore, brethren, boldness . . ." (v. 19). It would appear that while the concluding portion of Jeremiah 31 may well present a parallel to Ezekiel's millennial b'rith of peace (e.g., vv. 38–40), its central message on the new testament (vv. 31–34) accords best with the chronologically prior, internal b'rith of Christ with His church. Under any of the three above-listed interpretations, however, the b'rith of Yahweh assumes primary significance for the direction of future evangelical thought.

Notes

1. Julius Wellhausen, *Prolegomena to the History of Israel* (Edinburgh: A. & C. Black; Magnolia, Mass.: Peter Smith; 1885), pp. 418–19.

2. Robert H. Pfeiffer, JBL, 70 (1951): 2; cf. Pfeiffer's *Religion in the Old Testament* (New York: Harper's, 1961), p. 163, and as followed, e.g. by C. F. Whitley, JNES, 22 (1963), 37–48, or, *The Prophetic Achievement* (Leiden: Brill, 1963), p. 30.

3. TWNT, II:121.

4. Cf. ANET, pp. 203–5, with the discussion and bibliography of Gerhard von Rad, *Old Testament Theology* (New York: Harper & Row, 1962), 1:132.

5. F. Korošeç, *Hethitische Staatsvertrage* (Leipzig: 1931).

6. G. E. Mendenhall, BA, 17 (1954): 26–46, 49–76: reprinted as *Law and Covenant in Israel and the Ancient Near East* (Pittsburgh: Biblical Colloquium, 1955), Klaus Baltzer, *Das Bundesformular*, 2nd ed. (Neukirchen: 1964).

7. BA, pp. 35–41.

8. *Ibid.*, pp. 42–3.

9. So even von Rad grants "some connection," *loc. cit.*

10. D. J. McCarthy, *Treaty and Covenant*, Analecta Biblica, 21 (Rome: Pontifical Biblical Institute); cf. his summary of recent debate in *Der Gottesbund im Alten Testament* (Stuttgart: 1966).

11. E.g., ZAW, 74 (1962): 1–9; 75 (1963): 155–75; BA, 25 (1962): 1–9; VT, 13 (1963): 133–43; *Theologische Zeitschrift*, 23 (1967): 305–22.

12. Meredith Kline, WTJ, 22 (1960): 123–46, and 23 (1960): 1–15, reprinted in Kline's *Treaty of the Great King* (Grand Rapids: Eerdmans, 1963); *idem*, WTJ, 27 (1964–65): 1–20, 115–39, and 28 (1965): 1–37, reprinted as *By Oath Consigned* (Grand Rapids: Eerdmans, 1968).

13. Walter Moran, *Biblica*, 43 (1962): 103–4; *Verbum Domini*, 40 (1962): 3–17; CBQ, 25 (1963): 417.

14. John Arthur Thompson, TB, 13 (1963): 1–6; *The Ancient Near Eastern Treaties and the Old Testament* (1964).

15. Kenneth A. Kitchen, *Ancient Orient and Old Testament* (Chicago: Inter-Varsity Press; London: Tyndale Press, 1967), esp. pp. 90–102.

16. As in W. Zimmerli's, "Promise and Fulfillment," *Essays on Old Testament Hermeneutics,* ed. C. Westermann and J. L. Mays (Richmond: John Knox, 1963), p. 91.

17. Frank M. Cross, Jr., "Yahweh and the God of the Patriarchs," HTR, 55 (1962): 225–59; or Gerhard von Rad, *Genesis* (Philadelphia: Westminster, 1961), pp. 154–6.

18. IDB, I:717–18.

19. Cf. Robert C. Dentan, *The Knowledge of God in Ancient Israel* (New York: Seabury, 1968), p. viii.

20. Norman W. Porteous, "Old Testament Theology," *The Old Testament and Modern Study,* ed. Harold H. Rowley (London: Oxford, 1951), pp. 326–7.

21. *Ibid.*, p. 326; cf. J. Jocz's "presupposition" of the covenant as a unifying principle, *The Covenant* (Grand Rapids: Eerdmans, 1968), p. 9.

22. Murray Newman, "The Prophetic Call of Samuel," *Israel's Prophetic Heritage,* ed. B. W. Anderson (New York: Harper's, 1962), p. 95.

23. G. Ernest Wright, "The Lawsuit of God: a Form-Critical Study of Deuteronomy

32," *Israel's Prophetic Heritage,* ed. B. W. Anderson (New York: Harper's, 1962), p. 53.

24. Hosea, Joel, Amos, Obadiah, Jonah, Micah, plus Isaiah.

25. Ronald E. Clements, *Prophecy and Covenant,* Studies in Biblical Theology, Ist Ser., #43 (Naperville, Ill.: Allenson, Inc., 1965), pp. 69–71; cf. J. Muilenberg's analysis of Jer. 7:2–7 as a development of Ex. 19:5–6, VT, 9 (1959): 354–5; B. R. Hillers, *Treaty Curses and the Old Testament Prophets,* Biblical & Orientalia, #16 (Rome: Pontifical Biblical Institute, 1964); or W. Bruggemann, "Amos 4:4–13 and Israel's Covenant Worship," VT, 15 (1965): 1–15.

26. G. Ernest Wright, *God Who Acts,* Studies in Biblical Theology, 1st Ser., #8 (Chicago: Regnery, 1952), p. 54; cf. Jocz, *op. cit.,* p. 31, that the theological aspect is "not vitally affected" by the historicity of the Sinaitic b'rith; contrast J. Barton Payne, BETS, 11 (1968): 116–17.

27. Cf. D. J. McCarthy, "Covenant in the Old Testament: the Present State of Inquiry," CBQ, 27 (1965): 229.

28. Meredith G. Kline, "Oath and Ordeal Signs," WTJ, 27 (1965): 113.

29. Cf. Mendenhall, IDB, I:716–17; his "patron"-form appears to be simply one type (the most significant) of the promissory, namely that of a superior party binding himself to grant benefits to an inferior.

30. As granted in TWNT, II:118, cf. ANET, pp. 353–4, despite previous argumentation for the idea of an "extension of blood brotherhood," TWNT, II:115–17.

31. Muilenberg, *op. cit.,* p. 352.

32. Cf. Ernest W. Nicholson, *Deuteronomy and Tradition* (Philadelphia: Fortress, 1967), p. 43, or H. B. Huffmon, "The Exodus, Sinai, and the Credo," CBQ, 27 (1965): 101–13, and P. B. Harner, "Exodus, Sinai, and Hittite Prologues," JBL, 85 (1966): 233–6.

33. This in itself is a cause of no minor perplexity to the negative critics: why it should be in the relatively late Deuteronomic texts, even if assigned to a previous North Israelite source, that this form is reflected most clearly (McCarthy, "Covenant in the Old Testament," p. 224). C. F. Whitley connects the texts with the Canaanitish Baal B'rith of Shechem (JNES, 22 [1963]: 38).

34. Kitchen develops in detail both the Hittite and the Deuteronomic forms, adding to the former three other, non-written elements and including the possibility of a separate and yet complete recapitulation in Deut. 29–30. (Kitchen, *op. cit.,* pp. 92–4, 96–8).

35. D. J. McCarthy has argued with H. B. Huffmon over the indispensability of a historical prologue to Hittite treaties ("Covenant in the O.T.," *op. cit.,* pp. 227–8, note 23). But prologues appear even earlier (18th cen.) and, whether indispensable or not, the fact that they *are* included in the Pentateuch testifies to the latter's 2nd-millennium origin.

36. Sec. 4, on the guarding of the treaties, is not as regular as the others among the Hittites.

37. The Decalog proper lacks sec. 6, the curses, except that Ex. 23:20–33 seems applicable; J. l'Hour would insert curses from Deut., transposing the whole to Josh. 24 ("L'Alliance de Sichem," RB, 69 [1962]: 5–36, 161–84, 350–68.

38. McCarthy, "Covenant in the O.T.," p. 229, note 25.

39. *Ibid.,* p. 221. Belief, however, in his counter-claim that "literary forms . . . may well be the product of similar circumstances in different times and different places without there necessarily being an historical connection among the different appearances," requires abnormal credulity (*ibid.,* p. 229).

40. Walther Eichrodt, *Theology of the Old Testament* (Philadelphia: Westminster, 1961), I:37.

41. J. Stanley Chesnut, *The Old Testament Understanding of God* (Philadelphia: Westminster, 1968) , p. 166.

42. Ludwig Köhler, *Old Testament Theology* (Philadelphia: Westminster, 1958) , p. 62.

43. Cf. the discussion of G. M. Tucker, "Covenant Forms and Contract Forms," VT, 15 (1965) : 487–503.

44. W. G. Most, "A Biblical Theology of Redemption in a Covenant Framework," CBQ, 29 (1967) : 3.

45. TWNT, II:109.

46. Von Rad, *op. cit.*, I:54, 63.

47. Cf. J. Barton Payne, *Theology of the Older Testament* (Grand Rapids: Zondervan, 1962) , pp. 78–9.

48. Köhler, *loc. cit.*

49. John Murray, *The Covenant of Grace* (London: Tyndale Press, 1953) , p. 31; cf. pp. 10–12, 14–16.

50. Jocz, *op. cit.*, p. 31; cf. p. 42. Cf. also Payne, *Theology*, pp. 80–81, 87, on the problem of Ps. 50:5 and on the three exegetical situations in which a dipleuric covenant may indeed concern Yahweh.

51. Cf. even Geerhardus Vos's insistence upon religious sanctions in *Biblical Theology* (Grand Rapids: Eerdmans, 1948) , pp. 32–3, 277; contrast their apparent lack in I Sam. 11:1 or 18:3 (though this does appear later in 20:8, 42) .

52. Tucker, *op. cit.*, p. 491; cf. pp. 488–94 in this VT article.

53. Johannes Pedersen, *Der Eid bei dem Semiten* (Strasbourg: 1914) .

54. Tucker, *op. cit.*, p. 495; cf. P. Buis, "Les Formulaires d'Alliance," VT, 16 (1966) : 396–411, and "La Nouvelle Alliance," VT, 18 (1968) : 1–15.

55. Deut. 4:31, 8:18; Ps. 89:3, 34–35; cf. Ezr. 10:3, 5, "Let us make a covenant to put away the foreign wives . . . Then Ezra made them swear that they would do according to this word."

56. Josh. 9:20; cf. v. 16; or II Chr. 15:15, cf. v. 12.

57. Gen. 26:28; Deut. 29:13.

58. *Bāzā 'ālā lᵉ hāpēr bᵉrîṭ;* cf. v. 13, Nebuchadrezzar "made a covenant with him; he also brought him under an *'ālā*," curse; or vv. 16 and 19.

59. KD, Jeremiah, I:212. See also II Kgs. 11:4, Jehoiada "made a covenant with them, and took an oath of them"—*way-yašbaʻ 'ōṯām*, etc., in Tucker, *op. cit.*, pp. 488–9; cf. Ezk. 16:8, "I sware unto thee, and entered into a b'rith with thee."

60. McCarthy, *Treaty and Covenant*, p. 169.

61. Gen. 15:9, 26:30, 31:54, Ex. 24:8–11.

62. Moshe Weinfeld, "Deuteronomy: The Present State of Inquiry," JBL, 86 (1967) : 255.

63. Mendenhall, IDB, I:714, 720. He would then also propose an interchangeable usage of b'rith with *'ēḏuṭ*, "testimony" (p. 716, cf. Ex. 31:18, "the two tables of the testimony") . But *'ēḏūṭ* connotes "reminder" (KB, p. 683) , is more specific than b'rith, and seems here to refer rather to "the basic stipulations of the Sinai covenant, particularly the 'ten commandments' " (Kitchen, *op. cit.*, p. 108) .

64. Kline, WTJ, 27 (1964) : 3.

65. Louis Berkhof, *Systematic Theology* (Grand Rapids: Eerdmans, 1941) , p. 262.

66. Cf. Weinfeld, *op. cit.*, pp. 250–1.

67. The argument is traced by McCarthy, "Covenant in the O.T.," *op. cit.*, p. 225.

68. E. Gerstenberger, "Covenant and Commandment," JBL, 84 (1965) : 38–51.

69. Weinfeld, *op. cit.*, p. 253.

70. McCarthy, *Treaty and Covenant*, pp. 80–2; so also F. C. Fensham, ZAW, 74 (1962) : 1, and Thompson, *Ancient Treaties*, pp. 14–15. Cf. its utilization for "critical apologetics," by G. Fohrer, (Sellin's) *Introduction to the Old Testament* (Nashville:

Abingdon, 1968), p. 73, or by Ronald Clements, *God's Chosen People* (London: SCM, 1968), who dismisses Kline's 2nd millennium date as an "unsupportable conclusion" (p. 27), and yet confesses that his concept of the O.T. canon depends on parallels with the 2nd-millennium Hittite documents (p. 99).

71. Cf. Kitchen's analysis, *op. cit.*, pp. 95–6.

72. A. Goetze has sought to justify the omission on the grounds that a rehearsal of previous acts of grace would have been antithetical to the Assyrian mentality, per Weinfeld, *op. cit.*, p. 253.

73. Even in chs. 5–11; cf. Nicholson, *Deuteronomy and Tradition*, p. 44.

74. BA, 17 (1954): 56–76; so Moran, *op. cit.*, p. 103; J. Harvey, *Biblica*, 43 (1962): 185; Huffmon, *op. cit.*, pp. 109–10.

75. Clements, *op. cit.*, p. 98; cf. also Kline's chapter that follows in this present symposium.

76. Kitchen, *op. cit.*, p. 101.

77. P. Buis, VT, 16 (1966): 411.

78. E.g., Jeremiah's anticipation in 31:27–30 of his own generation's exile and the Persian restoration that followed it.

79. Martin Noth, *The Laws of the Pentateuch* (Philadelphia: Fortress, 1967), pp. 63–7.

80. McCarthy, "Covenant in the O.T.," pp. 235–6.

81. As discussed above in this symposium, in Leon Wood's chapter on the date of the exodus.

82. Cf. Donald J. Wiseman's publication, "The Vassal Treaties of Esarhaddon," *Iraq*, 20 (1958): 1–99.

83. Weinfeld, "Traces of Assyrian Treaty Formulae in Deuteronomy," *Biblica* 46 (1965): 414–27; cf. Hiller's study, *Treaty Curses and the Old Testament Prophets* (Rome: Pontifical Biblical Institute, 1964).

84. Cf. William L. Moran, "The Ancient Near Eastern Background of Love of God in Deuteronomy," CBQ, 25 (1963): 77.

85. R. Frankena, *Oudtestamentische Studien*, 14 (1965): 152–4.

86. Weinfeld, in JBL, 86 (1967): 254–5.

87. Kitchen, *op. cit.*, p. 100, n. 49.

88. A veritable crusade against the "unreconstructed" text of the Bible; cf. Samuel J. Schultz, *The Prophets Speak* (New York: Harper & Row, 1968), p. 12.

89. Oswald T. Allis, "The Transcendence of Jehovah God of Israel," *Biblical and Theological Studies* (Princeton Theological Seminary, 1912); cf. his later, *The Unity of Isaiah* (Philadelphia: Presbyterian & Reformed, 1950), ch. 5.

90. C. I. Scofield, ed., *Scofield Reference Bible* (New York: Oxford, 1917), pp. 5–6.

91. E.g., John M. L. Young's use of the Hittite pattern to illumine God's covenant of works in Gen. 2, *Christianity Today*, 13 (1968): 163.

92. Cf. J. Jocz, *The Covenant*, pp. 31–2; e.g., "The Bible is best viewed as the history of the covenant."

93. E.g., D. J. A. Clines, "Psalms Research Since 1955: The Psalms and the Cult," TB, 18 (1967): 103–26; cf. Huffmon, JBL, 79 (1958): 286–95.

94. Huffmon, *loc. cit.*

95. E.g., Charles C. Ryrie, *Dispensationalism Today* (Chicago: Moody, 1965), ch. 9.

96. *Scofield Reference Bible*, rev. ed. (New York: Oxford, 1967), p. 5; though cf. a modified recognition, p. vii.

97. Payne, *Theology*, *loc. cit.*

98. Jocz, *op. cit.*, p. 33.

99. Perhaps figuratively identified as "Damascus" (cf. Amos 5:27), though a literal Syrian exile has also been proposed.

100. The "covenanters" of Qumran exhibit an unresolved tension. On the one

hand they rightly appreciated the new b'rith as a divine enactment, on the basis of which God would forgive the iniquities (Cairo Damascus Document [CD] iv, 10) of those whom He had "chosen to be partners of His eternal covenant" (*Manual of Discipline* [IQS], iv, 22). Yet on the other hand, Qumran's stress upon rigid observance of the Sinaitic Law (CD, iv, 8) accords more closely with Pharisaic legalism than with the internal religion anticipated by Jeremiah and they could speak of their own "entering into a covenant, in the presence of God, to do according to all that He has commanded" (IQS, 1, 16), namely to observe the Qumranic discipline. To "be admitted to the covenant of the community" (iii, 16) thus came to mean simply to join the sect (cf. Helmer Ringgren, *The Faith of Qumran* [Philadelphia: Fortress, 1963], p. 128). In their rituals they might indeed confess their sins and invoke upon themselves the blessings, or curses of God (i, 16–ii, 18). But the covenant became a mere human oath, representing either initiation or subsequent annual resubscription (per Bk. Jub. 6:17) to the life of the community. While the concept of "the new covenant" may thus be said to sum up the beliefs of Qumran, it does this not as a God-given arrangement for redemption but as a membership pledge to a secret society which had deviated into self-righteousness.

101. "Undoubtedly," TWNT, II:136.

102. Rudolf Bultmann denies, indeed, that the concepts either of sacrifice ("my blood of the testament," Mk. 14:24, Lk. 22:20) or of redemption ("poured out for many," Mk. 14:24) constituted an authentic part of the Lord's message; he considers them as later additions to the original idea of sacramental communion (*Theology of the New Testament* [New York: Scribners, 1951], I:146–51). Yet the New Testament's repeated references to the blood of Christ testify to the central significance of His sacrificial death.

103. Alan Richardson, *An Introduction to the Theology of the New Testament* (New York: Harper, 1958), p. 231.

104. *Ibid.*, p. 371, cf. p. 383. See also the constant allusions in Hebrews to ritual forgiveness under the Sinaitic testament (G. Vos, "Hebrews, the Epistle of the Diatheke," PTR, 14 (1916): 1–61.

105. Cf. the writer's presentation in BETS, 10 (1967): 3–14.

106. For relegating Deut. 28 to the 1st millennium *B.C.*, JBL, 86 (1967): 254–5.

107. A. R. Millard, "For He Is Good," TB 16, (1966): 115–17.

108. Edward J. Young, *My Servants the Prophets* (Grand Rapids: Eerdmans, 1952), ch. 2.

109. Hobart Freeman, *An Introduction to the Old Testament Prophets* (Chicago: Moody, 1969), ch. 1, esp. pp. 24–8.

110. As by G. Fohrer, *op. cit.*, p. 424, who insists that prior to Jeremiah the prophets were "unfamiliar with any covenant theology." Contrast the more current appreciation of the prophets as b'rith-centered, from their overall status within the movement of "covenant renewal," down to their specific threats *and promises*, references to the curses and blessings of the b'rith (see above, note 23).

111. See above, I:B; Weinfeld, *op. cit.*, p. 253.

112. Derek Kidner, *Genesis*, Tyndale Old Testament Commentaries (London: Tyndale; Chicago: Inter-Varsity; 1967), p. 125.

113. KD, *Pentateuch*, II:453.

114. Cf. the writer's "Eighth Century Israelitish Background of Isaiah 40–66," WTJ, 29 (1967): 179–90; 30 (1967–68): 50–8, 185–203.

115. So H. S. Gehman, "An Insight and a Realization," *Interpretation*, 9 (1955): 279–93; see also John Murray's description of the embodiment of the b'rith in the Messiah (*Covenant of Grace, op. cit.*, pp. 24–5).

116. Vos's statement, that through the Servant the b'rith will be realized, is true

but seem to do inadequate justice to the force of the words (*Biblical Theology*, p. 277).

117. But note RSV's conjectural emendation, "at Adam."

118. The writer has proposed eight: the Edenic, Noachian, Abrahamic, Levitical, Sinaitic, and Davidic—making up the older testament—and the New Testament and the Testament of Peace, making up the newer testament, though further variation is by no means impossible (Payne, *Theology*, summary p. 95).

119. Ryrie, *op. cit.*, p. 185.

120. A major correction in *The New Scofield Reference Bible*, pp. vii, 1124; cf. Scofield I (1917): 1115.

121. Cf. W. Vischer, *The Witness of the Old Testament to Christ* (London: Lutterworth, 1949), I:11.

122. J. Barton Payne, *An Outline of Hebrew History* (Grand Rapids: Baker, 1954), pp. 220–8; idem, *Theology*, ch. 6.

123. Meredith Kline, WTJ, 23 (1960): p. 13.

124. Vos, *Biblical Theology*, pp. 62–3.

125. See above, II:B, on Hos. 6:7.

126. Murray, *op. cit.*, p. 32.

127. John Murray, *Christian Baptism* (Philadelphia: Presbyterian and Reformed, 1962), p. 47; Meredith Kline, "Law Covenant," WTJ, 27 (1964): 17.

128. Ryrie, *op. cit.*, pp. 186–7.

129. Payne, *Theology*, pp. 92–3.

130. L. Alonso Schökel, "Sapiental and Covenant Themes in Genesis 2–3," *Biblica*, 43 (1962): 295–315.

131. Eichrodt, *op. cit.*, I:36–7.

132. Payne, *Theology*, p. 87.

133. Eichrodt, *op. cit.*, I:66.

134. Cf. Jocz, *op. cit.*, pp. 24–31.

135. Mendenhall, IDB, I:718; cf. Josephine M. Ford's description of the b'rith as "the way in which God and man drew themselves together" (*Wellsprings of Scripture* [New York: Sheed & Ward, 1968], p. 3).

136. *Scofield Reference Bible*, p. 20. Contrast, but also compare, p. 19 of the revised Scofield, and Ryrie's stated regret over the "impression given" that the law was a retrogression in God's purpose (Ryrie, *op. cit.*, p. 117).

137. *New Scofield Reference Bible*, p. 18; John F. Walvoord, *Bibliotheca Sacra*, 110:437 (1953), 3.

138. G. Ernest Wright, *The Old Testament Against Its Environment* (Chicago: Regnery, 1951), ch. 11. Cf. Ryrie's increased recognition of grace under the law (*op. cit.*, pp. 119–22).

139. As Ryrie defines "dispensation" (*op. cit.*, p. 29). Cf. P. Verhoef's discussion of this problem as the concluding chapter in the present symposium.

140. Ryrie, *op. cit.*, p. 123; Payne, *Theology*, pp. 351–2.

141. Ryrie, *op. cit.*, pp. 114, 131.

142. Jn. 1:18, I Pet. 2:21, I Jn. 2:6; cf. Jer. 31:34; Mk. 10:19, Rom. 13:9, cf. Mt. 5:17, 19.

143. Though the veil of ceremony was rent away (Mt. 27:51), some of the rituals were maintained, though in a transmuted form (Lk. 22:15–20; or Col. 2:11–12, "the circumcision made without hands . . . buried with Christ in baptism"), as seals of righteousness by faith (Rom. 4:11). Their performance therefore continues, as a commemoration of Christ's past work, as a witness of His present salvation, and as an anticipation of His future redemptive activity (I Cor. 11:23–26).

144. Meredith Kline, "Oath and Ordeal Signs," WTJ, 27 (1964): 115, 124.

145. Cf. *ibid.*, 28 (1965): 26, 28.

146. *Ibid.*, 27 (1964): 119.

147. So also in the other references alleged; *ibid.,* 27 (1964) : 136, 138, or 28 (1965) : 3–9; e.g., in Mt. 3:10, "the axe laid at the root of the trees" seems unrelated to a "judgment of circumcision" or to Lev. 19:23–25's mention of trees as "circumcised unto the Lord," since it is the *un*circumcised that are judged; in I Cor. 10:1–2, Israel's "baptism in the Red Sea" is not viewed as an ordeal (like Ps. 69:2, Isa. 43:1–3) but a blessing (cf. the following context) ; and in I Pet. 3:20–22 the comparison of baptism with Noah's ark is to illustrate how "souls were saved through water," not destroyed.

148. Deut. 30:6, Mk. 1:4, Tit. 3:5; contrast the unfitness and unyieldedness of un-circumcision—Ex. 6:12, Lev. 26:41, Col. 2:11. Kline's proposed explanation for the baptism of infants, as "placing them under the authority of His ministry" (*ibid.,* 28 [1965], 31) , thus seems correspondingly inadequate.

149. Payne, *Theology,* p. 463.

150. Richardson, *op. cit.,* p. 257.

151. J. Murray, "Covenant," *New Bible Dictionary* (New York: Eerdmans, 1962) , p. 267.

152. Charles C. Ryrie, *The Basis of Premillennial Faith* (New York: Loizeaux, 1953) , pp. 117–21.

153. *Ibid.,* p. 121; cf. Heb. 9:11.

154. Cf. B. Ramm, *Protestant Biblical Interpretation,* rev. ed. (Boston: Wilde, 1956) , p. 256.

155. Ryrie, *Basis, loc. cit.*

16

THE CORRELATION OF THE CONCEPTS
OF CANON AND COVENANT

Meredith G. Kline

Preoccupation with the critique of aberrant current reconstructions has forestalled the orthodox elaboration of a genuinely Biblico-historical version of the formation of the Old Testament canon. And since the modern approach to the Old Testament canon has concentrated narrowly on the aspect of a final, definitive "limitation" of the canon, the attention of all concerned has been directed for the most part to developments, whether actual or alleged, in the last pre-Christian and the earliest Christian centuries. Discovery of the relevant new evidence from this period in the library of the Qumran community has been regarded as the most significant new light on this subject and has engendered reassessments. However, no really radical revisions of the characteristically modern viewpoint have emerged. Accounts of the Old Testament canon in the latest editions of the standard Old Testament introductions produced by that school adhere to the same theological posture and the same general historical positions presented in the old handbooks on the canon from the end of the last century.

The familiar hypothesis that the Old Testament canon recognized in Alexandria was broader than that accepted by Palestinian Judaism has indeed been challenged from within the modern school. Not, however, on the grounds that the evidence for a broader Alexandrian-Septuagint canon is inadequate, but, on the contrary, that there is evidence for a similarly broad attitude in Palestine itself during the first Christian century, particularly in Judaism before A.D. 70.[1] The new theory contends that during the days of Jesus and his apostles no closed canon of Jewish scriptures had been defined, whether Palestinian or Alexandrian, and that the Western church accepted a broader collection while Judaism of the late first century settled for a narrower canon. The conclusion is then drawn that Roman Catholics and Protestants should be able to concur on the Christian (or ecclesiastical as versus Judaistic) Old Testament canon. This is certainly congenial to the ecumenical tide, but it may well sound startling to many Protestant ears. Nevertheless, this thesis too is only a variation on the usual theme, working as it does with the definition of canon in which human decision is decisive, and confining itself to the historical era centering around the activities at the school of Jabneh in the late first Christian century.[2]

A necessary service has been performed by the orthodox critics in the exposure of the false theological foundations of the modern approach to the canon and its misreading of the historical developments, as expressed particularly in the theory of a threefold "canonization" of the Old Testament.[3] In effect, this critique reveals that such treatments deal scarcely at all with the history of the formation of the Old Testament canon, as they purport to do, but almost entirely with its epilogue, that is, with the recognition of the boundaries of that canon in the post-formative period. The real history of the Old Testament canon's formation—a millennium-long history—largely antedates even the era relegated in these reconstructions to the "pre-history."

Moreover, the apologetic-critical concerns of orthodox scholarship have not entailed a total neglect of the positive historiographical task. There have, of course, been repeated, if unheeded, reminders that the formation of the canon, rather than being a matter of conciliar decision or a series of such decisions with respect to a pre-existing literature, was a divine work by which the authoritative words of God were through the mystery of inspiration inscripturated in book after book, the canon being formed by the very appearance of these books. In the positive orthodox efforts, however, concrete historical analysis has tended to yield to formulation of Scriptural authority in the dogmatic categories of the Bible's own objective self-authentication as Word of God and the Holy Spirit's internal testimony to the Word, and the relation of these to individual faith and the church's sealing attestation to the Word. But the more precise delineation of Biblical canonicity requires that it be perceived as fully as possible in its specific historical character.

It is then with the relatively neglected subject of the actual history of the formation of the Old Testament canon, particularly its beginnings and their formal Near Eastern background, that this paper is concerned. The attempt is made to arrive at a specifically and authentically historical conception of the matter, and thereby to make some contribution in the area of prolegomena to Old Testament canonics. It will emerge, we believe, that for purposes of reappraising the Old Testament canon the most significant development in the last two decades has not been the Dead Sea scroll finds but discoveries made concerning the covenants of the Old Testament in the light of ancient Near Eastern treaty diplomacy.[4]

I. Canon Inherent in Covenant

We take our start with the observation that the beginnings of canonical Scripture coincided with the legal constituting of Israel as the kingdom of God by the covenant-making at Sinai. In the treaty then and there given by Yahweh as Lord of the covenant to his servant people, Scripture as canon had its origin. For that document, the foundational Scripture, precisely in its nature as a covenant document possessed the formal characteristics essential to the concept of canon.

The covenant solemnized at Sinai was an administration of the lordship of Yahweh over Israel. In it the divine Lord spoke his authoritative words to his earthly vassals, the law of his kingdom, normative for their faith and practice. And these sovereign words of God, his covenant law, were inscripturated in treaty form on tables of stone. In due course provision was made according to Yahweh's direction for that treaty to be preserved inviolate in the holy ark of the covenant, this enshrinement of the treaty testifying to its abiding authority over Israel. Here then was everything essential to the canon concept properly conceived: a divinely authoritative revelation,[5] documentary in form, its content unalterable. It was the nuclear canon of the Old Testament.

Steadily increasing knowledge about the nature of covenants in the ancient world of the Bible has demonstrated that the Sinaitic and other divine covenants were formally analogous to the suzerain-vassal covenants by which international relationships were often governed in those days.[6] In these, an overlord addressed his vassals, sovereignly regulating their relations with him, with his other vassals, and other nations. The central role played by the treaty tablet in which the covenant was customarily inscripturated is attested by the fact that the disposition of these tablets was at times made the subject of a special document clause. Moreover, copies of the text, duplicates of which were prepared for all the parties concerned, were to be preserved in the presence of a god, carefully guarded, and periodically read publicly in the vassal kingdom.[7] In its formal features the canonical aspect of the Biblical covenants was thus already clearly present in these international treaties and it will, therefore, be instructive to refer to them along with the Biblical covenants as we seek to trace the historical sources of the Biblical canon idea.

Of particular importance for identifying the roots of canon in covenant is of course the practice that called for drawing up the suzerain's authoritative words in writing.[8] Besides the separate document clause cited above as indicative that the written text of the treaty was integral to covenant administration, there are occasionally found in the treaties special references to the tablets, descriptive of the tablets themselves or of significant details in their history. Thus, reference is made to the extraordinary material of a tablet: the tablet of silver that Hattusilis III made for Ramses II and the iron tablet inscribed by Tudhaliyas IV for Ulmi-Teshub. It is recorded that a treaty was written at such and such a place and in the presence of named witnesses. It is stated by a suzerain that he wrote the tablet and gave it to a vassal, just as, in the case of

God's covenant at Sinai, Israel's heavenly Sovereign inscribed for them the tables of stone. Mursilis II mentions the tablet made by his father for the vassal but later stolen, and relates his own writing, sealing, and delivering of a second tablet. According to the Hittite treaty with Sunassura the transferal of his allegiance from the Hurrians to the Hittites, that is, the abrogation of one covenant and making of another, was effected by destroying the old treaty tablet and preparing a new one.

A feature of the covenant tablets of peculiar significance for their canonical character is the inscriptional curse, or what we may call the canonical sanction. The tablet was protected against alteration or destruction by making such violations of it the object of specific curses. This protective documentary curse (not exclusively a feature of treaties, as will be noted further presently) wherever found has a somewhat stereotyped formulation. This is so both in respect to the techniques envisaged by which the text might be defaced or removed and with respect to the divine retribution threatened as a deterrent to any contemplating such transgression.

From the treaty of Tudhaliyas IV with Ulmi-Teshub comes the inscriptional imprecation: "Whoever . . . changes but one word of this tablet . . . may the thousand gods of this tablet root that man's descendants out of the land of Hatti."[9] Similarly in Suppiluliuma's treaty with Niqmad of Ugarit anyone who changes any of the treaty words is consigned to the thousand gods. The treaty of Suppiluliuma with Mattiwaza states that the vassal's duplicate of the tablet has been deposited before the deity and is to be read at regular intervals in the presence of the vassal king and his sons, then proceeds: "Whoever will remove this tablet from before Teshub . . . and put it in a hidden place, if he breaks it or causes anyone else to change the wording of the tablet—at the conclusion of this treaty we have called the gods to be assembled . . . to listen, and to serve as witnesses." The invocation of a lengthy list of gods follows, with a reiteration of the purpose of their presence, and finally the curses on violators of the treaty and blessings on those who observe its injunctions. The sanctions begin: "If you, Mattiwaza, . . . do not fulfill the words of this treaty, may the gods, the lords of the oath, blot you out . . ."[10] Continuing this tradition in the first millennium B.C., Esarhaddon stipulated concerning the tablet of the treaty-oath with its dynastic and divine seals: "You swear that you will not alter it, you will not consign it to the fire nor throw it into the water . . . and if you do, may Ashur . . . decree for you evil."[11] And Bar-ga'ayah cursed with death under torment anyone who boasted: "I have effaced these inscriptions from the *bethels*."[12]

The way in which the content of the treaties and the treaty tablet itself merge in the charge to guard it and in the conjoined curses against offenders reveals how closely identified with the idea of suzerainty covenant was its inscripturated form. And the inviolable authority of these written tablets, vividly attested to by the document clause and, especially, the document curse, sufficiently justifies our speaking of the canonicity of these treaties.

Along with the treaties there were other ancient documents that contained authority-laden directives and thus possessed in a broad sense a canonical quality. Even though the treaty form was the particular canonical genre adopted as nucleus for the Biblical revelation, it is well that we should be aware of this wider formal background of the Bible as canonical document. One such type of document was the professional prescription; examples would be the Egyptian medical papyri,[13] or magical incantations and cultic formulae. Another type would be the documents issuing from royal chancelleries, like edicts and law codes. There were also the royal land grants witnessed to by the *kudurru* stones, which in general concept and literary tradition have much in common with the state treaties.[14] Another category was the "letters of gods" addressed to Assyrian kings.[15] And as previously observed, the peculiarly significant document curse was employed in various kinds of texts such as commemorative and funerary inscriptions, votive inscriptions, like those on temple gate-sockets,[16] law codes, like those of Lipit-Ishtar and Hammurapi, and elaborately on the *kudurru's*.[17]

The formal correspondence of the canonical aspect of the Bible to that of other ancient writings is made strikingly clear by the appearance in the Bible, as in the extra-Biblical treaties and other documents, of the documentary clause and the inscriptional curse, the brand-mark of canonicity. They appear in the Mosaic covenantal documents which constituted the nuclear Old Testament canon. (See Ex. 25:16, 21; 40:20; Deut. 4:2; 10:2; 31:9–13; *cf.* Deut. 27 and Josh. 8:30 ff.) Noteworthy as a reflection of the literary tradition of the inscriptional curse is the account of Jehoiakim's destroying of the scroll that contained the words of covenant sanctions spoken by God through Jeremiah.[18] This account, like the inscriptional curses, concerns itself with the topics of the method employed to destroy the document and the curse visited on this offense. Moreover, the similarity extends to the use of fire in the act of destruction and to the pronouncing of curses on both the person and property of the king, and particularly to the specific curses of the cutting off of his descendants and the casting out and exposure of his corpse.[19] This tradition of the canonical imprecation continued down into the New Testament: "For I testify unto every man that heareth the words of the prophecy of this book, If any man shall add unto these things, God shall add unto him the plagues that are written in this book: And if any man shall take away from the words of the book of this prophecy, God shall take away his part out of the book of life" (Rev. 22:18 f.; *cf.* 1:3). Though referring to the Apocalypse, the appropriateness of these sanctions to canonical Scripture as a whole cannot fail to be appreciated.

To sum up thus far, the canonical document was the customary instrument of covenant administration in the world in which the Bible was produced. The formal structure of the canonicity of the Scriptures was, therefore, inherent in the covenant form as that had developed in the history of international relationships in the ancient Near East, needing only to be taken up and inspired by the breath of God to become altogether what the church has confessed as canon. And that is what happened when Yahweh adopted the legal-literary form of the suzerainty covenants for the administration of his kingdom in Israel.

Our conclusion in a word is then that canon is inherent in covenant. Hence it is to the covenant structure utilized in the historical covenants of the Bible and ancient international diplomacy that theology should turn for its perspective and model in order to articulate its doctrine of canon in terms historically concrete and authentic. It is the covenant form that will explain the particular historical-legal traits of the divine authority that comes to expression in the Scriptures.

II. Covenantal Structure of the Bible

Are we justified in extending the conclusions we have reached concerning the covenantal nature of the canonicity of the earliest Scriptures beyond the Mosaic documents that are clearly couched in the classic treaty form? Our answer will depend on our measurement of the influence that has been exerted on the literary form and content of the remainder of the Old Testament by the legal-literary tradition of the treaties, and on what we understand that to signify concerning the functional character of the Old Testament as a whole.

It was inevitable that the various parts of the Old Testament canon should bear the covenantal stamp, since the *Sitz im Leben* of them all was the thoroughly covenantalized life of Yahweh's holy nation. Israel's cult and culture (the latter in both the family-private and kingdom-public spheres) stood under the covenant rule of Yahweh. They derived their peculiar meaning from him as God-King, whose covenantal dominion, exercised from the nation's cultic center, the royal site of his theophanic presence, claimed Israel's life to its full circumference. And because Israel's cult and its cultural structures were thus covenantalized, the inspired literature deriving from and related to that cult (like ritual legislation and hymns) and associated with that culture (like civil law, national history, diplomatic messages of prophets, and instruction of sages) could not but display the basic and pervasive reality of the covenant.

To arrive at a covenantal identification of the various parts of the Old Testament, an identification suggested by their covenantalized provenance and supported by formal correspondences to the ancient covenants, is not to claim that all the literary forms of the Old Testament derived from the treaty form nor even that particular features common to, say, Old Testament prophetic or wisdom literature and the treaties were peculiar to the treaties outside the Scriptures or had their ultimate source in them. The relationships of these ancient genres, even in their employment within the Old Testament corpus, were intricately interdependent. But taking account of the origin of the Old Testament within a covenantally constituted kingdom and observing that the influence of the treaty traditions can be traced throughout the Old Testament literature, revealed there both by broad, general correspondences and by strikingly specific parallels to treaty form and features, we find ourselves persuaded that the primary purpose for which the various types of literature were utilized in the Old Testament was to serve as instruments of the covenantal administration of God's lordship over Israel. And we would maintain that thereby and in that sense a covenantal character was imparted to the entire Old Testament which comprised these several literary forms.[20]

It is the task of Old Testament canonics to display fully the covenantal orientation that is to be found throughout the several sections and individual books of the Old Testament. The effect of this would be to demonstrate that in the Bible God has created a literary organism, covenantal in its unity, while it would at the same time exhibit by form-critical exposition the rich literary variegation of the Scriptures. Indeed, it is by addressing itself to precisely this task that orthodox Biblical scholarship may hope to do something creatively instructive for the church which lives by those Scriptures, turning the trackless wasteland that usually goes under the name of Old Testament Introduction into a fruitful field.[21]

It is not possible in this paper to survey even briefly the salient data showing that the full range of Old Testament literary genres has been marshalled under the controlling interest and influence of Yahweh's covenant, consequential though the establishment of that point is for the central thesis of the paper.[22] We may, however, indicate here how the covenant reality and the pattern of its administrative on-going explains not alone the form and function of individual parts of the Old Testament—its law, history, prophets, psalms, and wisdom—but, beyond that, the overall form of Scripture as a whole. That is, covenant accounts for the larger literary relation of the Old and New Testaments to one another—something to be reckoned with when their canonicity is being analyzed.

The ancient treaties spoke of the alliances they founded and the terms they stipulated as valid down through following generations indefinitely.[23] Nevertheless, the treaty was under the sovereign disposition of the great king and subject to his revisions. By reason of changing circumstances in the development of the covenant relationship, treaty provisions might be altered,[24] and especially by reason of changing leadership on either side, great king or vassal king, renewal of covenants took place,[25] with new documents being prepared in witness to these changes.[26] The covenant renewals, in both the extra-Biblical and Biblical traditions, gave expression at once to the (at least theoretically) eternal character of these treaties and to the fact that the covenant order was not static but correlated to historical movement and change. The legal compatibility of these two aspects, the eternal and the changing, must have resided in a recognition of a distinction between the fundamental tributary allegiance of the vassal to the great king (or the peaceful mutual stance of the partners to a parity treaty), which was theoretically and ideally permanent, and the precise details, such as boundary definitions and tribute specifications, etc., which were subject to alteration.[27]

This kind of covenant administration with its renewal arrangements, especially with the documentation of these renewals in a succession of canonical treaties, supplied a most suitable model for the Scriptural revelation given in organic connection with redemptive history. For that history is characterized by a pattern of renewal in the unfolding of the eternal relationship established by God with his people. The dynamics of eschatological progress in this renewal movement of redemptive history are unique. Nevertheless, the comprehensive schema of this history as it is reflected in its Scriptural documentation, especially in the Scriptures' major divisions into old (pre-messianic) and new (messianic) revelations, clearly fits the formal ancient covenantal pattern of treaty-documented renewal.

It thus appears that the documentary nature of the Bible in its overall form is covenantal. Our traditional designation of the Bible in its major subdivisions as the "Old" and "New Testaments" has been all the while more appropriate than has been commonly realized. According to our usual understanding, this customary nomenclature merely reflects the close association of the Biblical books with the history of the covenants, or provides a succinct table of contents of the Bible. But this falls short of the truth of the matter. "Covenant," or "testament," denotes more than a prominent element in the contents of the Bible. The documents which combine to form the Bible are in their very nature—a legal sort of nature, it turns out—covenantal. In short, the Bible *is* the old and the new covenants.

Back of the common Christian designations, "Old Testament" and "New Testament," there is inner-Biblical precedent. For the designations "law" and "prophets," or together "the law and the prophets," were employed for parts or all of the Old Testament,[28] and it is demonstrable that these categories had definitely covenantal significance.[29] Clearer still is Paul's reference to the Israelites' reading of "the old covenant" (II Cor. 3:14). Whether he had in view there the Pentateuch only or the entire Old Testament,[30] he plainly identified Scripture and covenant closely.

If this interpretation of the nature of the Old and New Testaments as covenantal is valid, then (relating it to the central thesis of this paper) what has been noted concerning the relation of canonicity to the covenantal form may be applied to the whole Old Testament and to the total Biblical structure. The covenant words of Scripture are God's and, therefore, their canonical authority is in a class by itself. Yet at the formal literary level, Biblical canonicity is to be classified as belonging to the category of authoritative treaty words. And in this sense, Biblical canonicity in general is inherent in the fact that the Bible *is* the old and new covenants. Was it out of an awareness of this that *endiathēkos,* "covenantal,"[31] was used in the early church instead of *kanōn* to express the canonical character of Scripture?[32]

III. Old Testament and Church Canon

The identification of the Old-New Testament schema with the pattern of treaty documented renewal found in ancient covenant administration establishes the formal perspective for an approach to the intertwined questions of the discontinuity between the Old and New Testaments and of the place of the Old Testament in the canon of the Christian church. In a manner analogous to other ancient treaties, the Old Testament as canonical covenant was both "forever" and yet subject to change. The changes were determined according to the sovereign purpose of God who directed redemption's eschatological progress by His decisive interventions, initiating distinctive new eras and authoritatively redefining the mode of His kingdom.

Reluctance to accept the reality of God's sovereignty in history as expressed in this divine structuring of the redemptive process into distinctive eschatological epochs underlies the misguided modern analyses that view the discontinuity between Old and New Testaments in simplistically evolutional fashion and judge not a little in the Old Testament to be sub-Christian.[33] On the other extreme, interpretations of a dispensational brand, while quite insistent on the fact of divinely differentiated eras, misconstrue the discontinuity aspect of the redemptive process, positing such radical disjunctions between the successive eras that a genuine continuity between the Old and New Testaments becomes insolubly problematic. The actual covenantal continuity-discontinuity pattern of the Old and New Testaments does not come into its own in either evolutional or dispensational historiography; and, in the measure that that is so, the question of the authority of the Old Testament in the Christian church cannot be properly assessed. The danger of having our position misunderstood as fostering the errors of one or both of these viewpoints ought not deter us from drawing out its implications.

It follows from the covenantal character of Old and New Testament canonicity, at once "forever" and yet subject to revision, that Scripture is not a closed canon in some general, absolute sense. In fact, instead of speaking of the canon of Scripture it were better to speak of the Old and New Testament canons, or of the canonical covenants which constitute the Scripture. Each authoritative covenantal corpus is of fixed extent, but the historical order of which it is constitutional is not a perpetually closed system. The Old and New Testaments are discrete covenantal canons in series. Each is of divine authority in all its parts, but that does not imply the absolutizing of its norms in abstraction from the covenantally structured historical process. They share in that eschatological movement with its pattern of renewal, of promise and messianic fulfillment, the latter in semi-eschatological and consummate stages. Each inscripturated covenant is closed to vassal's alteration, subtraction, or addition (as the proscriptions of the treaty document clauses insist), yet each is open to revision by the Suzerain, revision that does not destroy but fulfills, as the history of God's kingdom proceeds from one epochal stage to the next, particularly, in the passage from the old covenant to the new. "Closed" as a general description of a canon would be suitable only in the eternal state of the consummation.

Another corollary of *covenantal* canonicity is that the Old Testament is not the canon of the Christian church. From a strictly legal standpoint, the Old Testament viewed in its identity as the historical treaty by which God ordered the life of pre-messianic Israel belongs to the church's historical archives rather than to its constitution. Covenant Theology is completely Biblical in its insistence on the Christological unity of the Covenant of Redemption as both law and gospel[34] in its old and new administrations; nevertheless, the old covenant is not the new covenant.

A distinction thus arises for the Christian church between canon and Scripture—that is, between the treaty-canon that governs the church of the new covenant as a formal community (*i.e.,* the New Testament) and the Scriptures, the broader entity—not really a book—consisting of the canonical oracles of God communicated to his people in the Mosaic and messianic eras (*i.e.,* the Old Testament and New Testament together). The character of all Scripture as equally the word of God and the thoroughgoing eschatological-spiritual unity of all God's redemptive administrations command for the old canon the place it has actually held along with the new canon in the faithful church from the beginning—profitable for doctrine, reproof, correction, and instruction in righteousness. And much more of like force could be said. But it is also necessary to distinguish from this general concept of the authority and truthfulness of all the Scriptures the more specific authority of the covenant canon that is currently normative.

In these terms, the Old Testament, though belonging to the church's Scriptures, is not the church's current canon. It works both ways, therefore; canon and covenant mutually determine one another. Canonical treaty defines the covenant and the bounds of the treaty's canonicity are in turn determined by the specific limitations of the covenant to which it pertains. Hence the church which acknowledges that the covenant defined by the Old Testament has now been superseded by being fulfilled in the new, may readily acknowledge also that the new canon has superseded the old canon.[35]

IV. Antiquity of Covenantal Canon and Anachronisms of Modern Criticism

As indicated in the introductory observations above, twentieth-century critical versions of the formation of the Old Testament canon adhere faithfully to the nineteenth-century evolutionistic reconstructions, the central assumption of which was the notion that the canon concept was late in dawning on the Israelite mind. The question must be faced whether these reconstructions are not exposed as modern fictions when their central assumption is scrutinized in the light of the ancient historical-literary data that reveal canon to have been the correlate of covenant.

In order to consider the antiquity of the canonical concept it is necessary to call attention again to the covenantal nature of the very oldest Scripture. The formal nature and disposition of the Decalogue, and of Deuteronomy too, laid up in or by the ark of the covenant from the time of Israel's Mosaic beginnings, accorded closely with the form and treatment of ancient treaties, not least with those documentary features of the treaties that were most significant for their canonical quality.

Thus, the duplicate tables of the covenant written at Sinai reflect the custom of preparing copies of the treaty for each covenant party.[36] The enshrinement of these two tables and of the Deuteronomic document to serve as witnesses to God's covenant followed the practice stipulated in the document clause of treaties, that clause itself being included in the Deuteronomic treaty (31:9 ff.).[37] And, of course, the standard documentary pattern of the treaties was followed in the Decalogue and Deuteronomy.[38] Even the element of covenant renewal and treaty revision that marks ancient covenant administration was present in these early Scriptures. It was present prophetically in the curses and blessings section of Deuteronomy, which speaks of the radical forgiving grace of God that would renew the covenant in the last days, beyond the threatened curse of exile.[39] More than that, Deuteronomy was itself a new covenant, formalizing the restoration in a new generation of the community which in its older generation had experienced covenant excommunication in the wilderness exile. In fact, the two Sinaitic tables that were kept in the ark of the covenant were themselves the documentary witnesses to a renewed covenant. They were the new covenant given by the Lord in mercy to the vassal community which had so soon broken his covenant— as his servant Moses had attested by shattering the first two treaty tablets.[40] The structure of the Bible as old and new covenant canons was thus already incipiently present in the Decalogue and Deuteronomy.

And the origin of these covenant documents which were a nuclear model of the covenantal-canonical Bible coincided with the origins of the nation Israel.

To be sure, modern Old Testament scholarship is for the most part unwilling to accept the Biblical record of the origins of the Decalogue and Deuteronomy in the days of Moses. Some also would oppose the acknowledgment generally made of the Hittite treaty pattern in the Decalogue. The picture is further complicated by those who would support von Rad's hypothesis that the Sinai-covenant tradition was not originally related to the exodus tradition.[41] But even the holding of such viewpoints has proved compatible with consent to the judgment of the great majority who have now been obliged to repudiate Wellhausen's arbitrary recasting of historical sequence by which the covenant idea was made out to be a late outgrowth of prophetic thinking. Very few now fail to recognize the presence of the covenant in the pre-prophetic history of Israel's life and thought, and the tendency is to respect the evidence that traces covenant as far back as Israel can be traced.

It is evident that an unrecognized tension has developed within the dominant type of Old Testament scholarship between its altered thinking about covenant and its unaltered, nineteenth-century thinking about canon. By the reversal of the Wellhausenian dogma of late covenant the rationale has been removed for the modern theory of late canonization. It will no longer do to assert that the concept of canonical Scripture was an innovation of the late prophetic era and at the same time admit that the covenant concept was a formative factor in Israel's literature in pre-prophetic times. For where there is divine covenant of the classic Old Testament kind there is divine canonical document.

It is to be expected that devotion to traditional critical doctrine will tend to prevent awareness that what the modern critics have been theorizing about the formation of the Old Testament canon has been rendered obsolete by what is now known and commonly acknowledged about covenant. That, however, is the case. The theory of a process of canonization beginning in the post-exilic era, if not considerably later— whether a threefold process or otherwise, whether assuming a broader

Alexandrian canon or following an approach like Sundberg's—is a grotesque distortion of the historical facts, a Wellhausenian anachronism on a millennial order of magnitude.

The origin of the Old Testament canon coincides with the founding of the Kingdom of Israel by covenant at Sinai. The very treaty that formally established the Israelite theocracy was itself the beginning of the Old Testament canon—and the nuclear covenant-canon model for the rest. The critical fiction that has been foisted on the church as a history of the formation of the canon should be unceremoniously scrapped and orthodox Old Testament scholarship should set to work on the Biblico-theological task of delineating the real history of that process. When that is done and the relevant historical realities of ancient covenant procedure are brought to bear, the formation of the Old Testament canon will be traced to its true origins in the covenantal mission of Moses in the third quarter of the second millennium B.C., providentially the classic age of treaty diplomacy in the ancient Near East.

Notes

1. Thus, Albert C. Sundberg, Jr., in *The Old Testament of the Early Church* (Cambridge: Harvard University Press, 1964) ; "The Protestant Old Testament Canon: Should It Be Re-examined?," CBQ, 28 (1966) : 194–203 (part of "A Symposium on the Canon of Scripture" (pp. 189–207) by Roman Catholic, Protestant, and Jewish scholars) ; and "The 'Old Testament'; A Christian Canon," CBQ, 30 (1968) : 143–55.

2. On the extreme exaggeration of the significance of these discussions see Jack Lewis, "What Do We Mean by Jabneh?," *Journal of Bible and Religion*, 32 (1964) : 125–32.

3. For a critique from quite a different viewpoint of the traditional modern notion of a successive "canonization" in three stages of law, prophets, and writings, conceived according to the Massoretic arrangement and with the law as the foundation and controlling perspective in the development, see J. C. H. Lebram, "Aspekte der alttestamentlichen Kanonbildung," VT, 18 (1968) : 173–89.

4. The present paper is a condensed version of an article scheduled for early publication in the *Westminster Theological Journal*, under the title, "Canon and Covenant" (hereafter referred to as: WTJ version) .

5. See WTJ version for a discussion of modern concessions to the early recognition of this authority.

6. The present writer has treated the matter at some length in *Treaty of the Great King* (Grand Rapids: Eerdmans, 1963; hereafter, TGK) and *By Oath Consigned* (Grand Rapids: Eerdmans, 1968; hereafter, BOC) .

7. Cf. F. Korošeç, *Hethitische Staatsverträge* (Leipzig, 1931) , pp. 100 f. For the corresponding treatment accorded the Sinaitic tables of the covenant, cf. TGK, pp. 19 f.

8. Cf. Walter Beyerlin, *Origins and History of the Oldest Sinaitic Traditions*, trans. S. Rudman (Oxford: Blackwell; New York: Humanities; 1965) , esp. pp. 55 ff. Note the combination of *kōṯeḇîm* with *kōreṯîm* in the covenant ratification of Neh. 10:1 (9:38) .

9. See D. J. McCarthy, *Treaty and Covenant* (Rome: Pontifical Biblical Institute, 1963) , p. 185.

10. See A. Goetze's translation in ANET, pp. 205 f.

11. See Donald J. Wiseman, *The Vassal-Treaties of Esarhaddon* (London: British School of Archaeology in Iraq, 1958), p. 60.

12. Sefireh II, C; cf. TGK, pp. 43 f.

13. The authority of a prescription was commonly traced to its derivation from a canonical exemplar, an ancient document, particularly one found in a temple. The prescription might then be described as "what was found in writing under the feet of [the deity]," i.e., under the immediate guardianship of the god's image. The concept and terminology here parallel the practice of enshrining copies of treaties as stipulated in their document clause. The remedy might even claim to be a divine revelation. Thus, one papyrus reads: "This remedy was found in the night, fallen into the court of the temple in *Koptos*, as a mystery of the goddess, by the lector-priest of this temple." For this translation and sample texts of these prescriptions, see J. A. Wilson's treatment of them in ANET, p. 495a.

14. For a further discussion of the *kudurru's* in relation to Biblical and extra-Biblical treaties, see WTJ version.

15. Cf. A. Leo Oppenheim, *Ancient Mesopotamia* (Chicago: University of Chicago Press, 1964), p. 280.

16. Cf. S. Gevirtz, "West-Semitic Curses and the Problem of the Origins of Hebrew Law," VT, 11 (1961): 137–58.

17. Cf. Delbert R. Hillers, *Treaty Curses and the Old Testament Prophets* (Rome: Pontifical Biblical Institute; Chicago: Argonaut, Inc.; 1964), pp. 11, 86; F. C. Fensham, "Common Trends in Curses of the Near Eastern Treaties and *Kudurru*-Inscriptions Compared with Maledictions of Amos and Isaiah," ZAW, 75 (1963): 155–75.

18. See Jer. 36.

19. For parallels in treaties and *kudurru's*, see Fensham, *op. cit.*, pp. 161 ff. and Hillers, *op. cit.*, pp. 68 f.

20. Cf. Ronald E. Clements, *Prophecy and Covenant* (Naperville, Ill.: Allenson, Inc., 1965), p. 24, where it is observed that the controlling factor in the development of various literary forms (law, psalms, wisdom, and prophecy), all of them developing side by side, intersecting and influencing each other, was Israel's knowledge of covenant relationship to Yahweh.

21. Cf. my programmatic comments to this effect in WTJ, 29 (1966): 61 f.

22. For some suggestions, see WTJ version.

23. So, for example, the copies of the Bar-ga'ayah treaty with Mati'el speak in various connections of its arrangements, sanctions, and the suzerain's authority as being "forever"; and both Egyptian and Hittite versions of the parity treaty between Ramses II and Hattusilis declare repeatedly that that treaty of peace and brotherhood was valid "forever."

24. For example, Tudhaliyas IV, preparing a new tablet definitive of his covenant relationship with Ulmi-Teshub, explains this revision as due to his having observed that the military-support requirement stipulated on an earlier treaty tablet had proved to be excessive.

25. See TGK, pp. 36 ff.

26. Cf. Klaus Baltzer's analysis of the causes of covenant renewal and reaffirmation in the Old Testament in his *Das Bundesformular*, 2nd ed. (Neukirchen: Neukirchener Verlag, 1964), pp. 59 ff., 71 ff. In the historical prologues of the Hittite treaties references are found to previous treaty relationships with the vassal or his predecessors, occasions being mentioned when renewal of the covenant had been called for by circumstances like change in the dynastic succession or restoration of the vassal after violation of the treaty.

27. Baltzer, *ibid.*, distinguishes in the treaty structure between a declaration of principle and the specific stipulations that follow it. The variations among the three

Sefireh steles, which describe the treaty relationship they record as "forever" valid, show how the concept of covenant permanence was compatible even with a degree of difference in detail in contemporary versions of the same treaty. (For discussion, see McCarthy, *op. cit.*, pp. 62 f.) . Such variations are of importance too for a study of scribal freedom, of interest to the Biblical scholar as a possible explanation of textual variations in parallel passages without recourse to easy assumptions of transmissional mutation.

28. For the comprehensive use of "law" to cover the entire Old Testament, cf. I Cor. 14:21 and Jn. 10:34; 12:34; 15:25. For the use of "the law and the prophets" in the New Testament and Qumran as a designation for the whole Old Testament, see R. Laird Harris, "Was the Law and the Prophets Two-Thirds of the Old Testament Canon?" BETS, 9 (1966) : 163–71.

29. On the virtual synonymity of "law" and "covenant," see TGK, p. 17. Cf. also note 3 above.

30. In the context (v. 15) , Paul uses "Moses" apparently as an equivalent of "the old covenant," but "Moses" here, like "law" elsewhere, possibly denotes the entire Old Testament.

31. Cf. G. W. H. Lampe, *A Patristic Greek Lexicon* (Oxford: Clarendon Press; New York: Oxford University Press; 1962) , II, 2, p. 468.

32. Note the usage of Origen and Eusebius in the latter's *Church History* III, 3, i and iii; III, 25, vi; VI, 25, i.

33. For a recent popular restatement of this viewpoint in connection with a discussion of the canon question and from an ecclesiastically significant source, see Floyd V. Filson, *Which Books Belong in the Bible?* (Philadelphia: Westminster, 1957) , pp. 52 ff.

34. Cf. BOC, ch. 2.

35. On the present approach to Biblical canonicity, the role of the community in relation to the canon needs reassessment. An attempt at this is made in the WTJ version.

36. Cf. TGK, pp. 17 ff.

37. *Ibid.*, pp. 19 f.

38. *Ibid.*, pp. 14 ff., 28 ff.

39. *Ibid.*, pp. 132 f.

40. *Ibid.*, p. 43.

41. For a helpful recent critique of this hypothesis, see H. H. Huffmon, "The Exodus, Sinai, and the Credo," CBQ, 27 (1965) : 101–13. The counter observations of P. B. Harner in "Exodus, Sinai, and Hittite Prologues," JBL, 85 (1966) : 233–6, do not meet the issue.

17

THE RELATIONSHIP BETWEEN THE OLD AND THE NEW TESTAMENTS

Pieter A. Verhoef

Church and Theology are continually confronted with the vast and actual problem of the relationship between Old and New Testament. The problem is as old as the Christian Church itself, and the whole of Christian Theology is concerned with its solution.[1] At the same time it is commonly agreed that the last word is not yet spoken, and that this problem is due to remain on the program of theological investigation.[2] This problem is of special interest to us as evangelical theologians, because it concerns the authority of the Bible and the significance of its message.

I. Basic Considerations

In assessing the relationship between Old and New Testament we have as point of departure the conviction that both Testaments are the canon of our life and faith, the infallible Word of God. We, therefore, reject every form of denial of this truth. The content of the Bible is not the product of human reflection or historical circumstances,[3] but of inspiration[4] and divine revelation.[5] It is quite obvious that this conviction will have a bearing upon our attitude towards the problem of the relationship between the Old and New Testaments.

II. Illegitimate Solutions

In defining the relationship between Old and New Testament there are two extreme positions with which we cannot agree.[6] Both are as old as the Christian Church itself.

A. Dichotomy

According to the one point of view the two Testaments are essentially different. In the course of history this point of view has found expression in two different ways. On the one hand the Old Testament was degraded by Marcion and other groups outside the church, but on the other hand it was considered by Judaism to be the only Bible.[7] In both cases the difference between Old and New Testament was stressed in such a way that the unity of the Bible was destroyed and the problem of the relationship between Old and New Testament had no relevance.[8] The Marcionite approach to the Old and New Testament in its relation to the New Testament is in modern times represented by men like Adolf von Harnack, Friedrich Delitzsch, A. Rosenberg, E. Hirsch and in a certain sense also Rudolf Bultmann.[9] We may add to this short list the names of the God-is-dead theologians, like J. A. T. Robinson and Paul van Buren,[10] because the Old Testament is entirely neglected in their writings.[11]

The Judaistic trend in dealing with the relationship between Old and New Testament is still represented by modern Jewish scholars,[12] and even by Reformed theologians, like A. A. van Ruler, whose dictum is well known: the Old Testament is the real Bible; the New Testament is merely the explanatory glossary at the back of the Old Testament.[13]

B. Identity

We cannot approve of any form of approach on the basis of the assumption that the two Testaments are essentially different. This is the first extreme position. The second one is inclined to do just the opposite. According to this point of view the unity of the two Testaments is expressed in terms of identity. Their differences and discontinuity are disregarded. They have the same content and message. The problem of their mutual relationship, therefore, is irrelevant.

This point of view is also as old as the Christian Church itself. In its struggle against Judaism on the one hand and the heretical views of Marcion, Mani (215–276), and others on the other hand, the Church maintained both the unity and the diversity of the Old and New Testament.[14] In their practical use of the Bible, however, the unity became identity.[15] The application of the *analogia fidei*, that is, the *analogia Scripturae*, caused the Reformers to conceive of the two Testaments as being dogmatically one.[16]

This tendency of eliminating the differences between Old and New Testament has its modern representatives in men like C. H. Dodd,[17] Karl Barth,[18] W. Vischer[19] and others.

In a certain sense we have an affinity to this point of view, because we regard both Testaments to be the Word of God; and this includes our appreciation for the Old Testament with its full and rich revelation.[20] The fact, however, remains that the problem of the relationship inevitably loses its point when the unity of the two Testaments is overstressed in such a way that it becomes identity. This is an illegitimate solution.

III. Legitimate Lines of Connection

The theological relationship of the Testaments can legitimately be conceived of in various ways. The point I would like to stress in this connection is that all of these formulations are to be taken into considera- tion. It is not a matter of choice between them, because every one of them has a certain validity and serves to indicate an aspect of the com- plex relationship between Old and New Testament. No one of them is alone entirely adequate to provide the sole solution to this problem. We, therefore, need all of them to furnish a comprehensive approach to the rich and varied legitimate lines of connection.

We know that the theological relationship of the two Testaments has been formulated in such a variety of ways that it is almost impossible to classify them.[21] At the same time we cannot approve of all the definitions that have been suggested.[22] We may, however, consider the following nine lines of connection between the two Testaments. They are: A) reference to Scripture (Scriptural proof) ; B) typology; C) words and their mean- ings; D) the relation of full parity within the unity of divine revelation; E) the relation in which the Old Testament is viewed as the historical and theological preparation for the gospel; F) the relation in which the Old Testament is understood as a propaedeutic to the gospel in terms of the dialectic of law and gospel; G) promise and fulfillment; H) unity of perspective (Heilshistories-Eskatologiese samehang), and I) continuity and discontinuity.

On account of present limitations, discussion is confined to a brief survey in each case.

A. *Reference to Scripture*

One of the connecting lines between Old and New Testament is the quotations in the New Testament from Old Testament texts. In German and Dutch it is called "Skrifbewys," which could best be rendered by Scriptural proof. The idea of proof[23] is of importance because the quo- tations are placed in the context of an argument and are referred to as part of the promulgation of the gospel.[24] In this treatment of the Old Testament its divine authority is presupposed. The fact and number of these quotations can easily be assessed by turning the pages of Nestlé's Greek New Testament.

We know that Scriptural proof as connecting link between the two Testaments has been criticized, especially on the following grounds: The New Testament quotations from Old Testament texts are mainly taken from the Septuagint, even where it deviates from the Hebrew text;[25] many of these quotations are not in accordance with the obvious meaning of the Old Testament texts, and for that matter with a sound exegetical method;[26] in a few instances Jesus and Paul contradict the purport of Old Testament statements.[27]

We inevitably have to admit the seriousness of these objections.[28] We may suggest that Old and New Testament scholars should combine their efforts in trying to solve especially the first two problems in an adequate way.

Some of the most conspicuous quotations taken from the deviating text of the Septuagint are Psalm 16:8-11 (Acts 2:26-29); Psalm 8 (Heb. 2); Amos 9:11-15 (Acts 15:15-17); Hosea 13:14 (I Cor. 15:54 f.). A close exegetical study of these quotations reveals the meaningful manner in which they functioned within the context of the proclamation of the gospel;[29] but at the same time we must admit that new elements were being introduced, and that these elements were taken from the Septuagint.[30]

The same conclusion would apply to the second objection against the Scriptural proof. Quite a number of Old Testament quotations are given a significance that does not follow from the obvious meaning of the Old Testament texts.[31] The promise to Abraham that by his descendants all the nations of the earth will be blessed (Gen. 22:18), was applied by Paul to one descendant—Christ (Gal. 3:16). The phrase "out of Egypt I called my son" in Hosea 11:1, is applied to Jesus in Matthew 2:15. The language of the heavens in Psalm 19:5 was made to bear in Romans 10:18 upon the worldwide spreading of the gospel. The point of comparison is, indeed, the universal aspect both of the psalm and of the gospel;[32] but at the same time it is interesting to note the manner in which this psalm was applied by Paul.

These and other instances indeed call for a thorough investigation and an evangelical solution. We reject the idea of an arbitrary Scriptural reference just for the sake of obtaining material for illustrations.[33] We do not agree with men like Bultmann[34] that this use of the Old Testament can be best explained as a projection of the convictions of the New Testament writers. We also reject the solution according to which this use of the Old Testament could adequately be explained in terms of the accommodation to the technique and method of the rabbinical exegesis.[35] This point of view does not distinguish between the purport and scope of the rabbinical and Qumran[36] exegesis on the one hand, and the unique perspective of the New Testament usage of the Old Testament on the other hand. The great variety of quotations from the Old Testament are all focused on the proclamation of the one gospel of Jesus Christ as the Messiah who was promised and who has come.[37]

The third objection against the relevance of the Scriptural proof, viz. that Christ and Paul had denied the canonical significance of some Old Testament statements, must be turned down as a matter of principle, but also as a matter of sound exegesis. Jesus, according to the Dutch scholar

Vriezen, because of His spiritual understanding of the law, again and again contradicts the Judaic theology of His days derived from the Old Testament ("them of old time"—Mt. 5, Mk. 7), and even repeatedly contradicts certain words of the law (Mt. 5:38 ff.; 19:1 ff.).[38] With Paul, he says, two lines become clearly visible. The former is that of absolute acceptance of the Old Testament as the revelation of God. The second is that God creates a new relationship with Himself by the revelation in Christ so that the Jewish way of salvation, the way of the law and its works, is superseded. "The Mosaic Law came to be regarded as intermediate in character, while Abraham's faith became the expression of true revelation. This meant a disintegration of the Torah," which is deemed to be subsequent, temporary and also inferior (Gal. 3:19). In this reversal of the order of the law and explanation of its temporary meaning and spiritually preparatory function, an internal, material, theological criticism of the Old Testament is implicit.[39]

The consequence of this point of view is that elements "of varying degrees of canonicity" are detected in the Old Testament,[40] and this in turn would affect the assessment of the true relationship of the two Testaments.

We agree that Jesus occasionally contradicted the theology of the Jews, but this does not imply His contradiction of the Old Testament as such. As a matter of fact, Jesus appealed to the Old Testament in His criticism of the Jewish theology (Mt. 12:7; Mk. 2:26). Vriezen rightly points out that Paul has contested the notion of law as a means of salvation,[41] but this was not meant to be a criticism of the law itself. Paul's concern was the legalistic way in which the law was conceived by the Jews, separating it from the covenant of grace.[42] Acknowledging the difficulties with respect to the Scriptural proof as line of connection between the two Testaments, we shall have to maintain its validity and its importance. It is true that the reference to the Old Testament was not conducted in a systematic manner and was rather done sporadically,[43] but this does not diminish the significance of an extensive procedure of quotation. Over and against critical views we maintain that the New Testament in citing the Old Testament nowhere presupposes a fundamental breach between the Testaments.[44] This is in full correspondence with the Church's acceptance of the Canon, consisting of both Old and New Testaments.

B. Types

A second line of connection between Old and New Testaments is found in typology.[45] Scholars differ in their opinion with respect to the relevance of typology in this connection. According to some scholars the typological approach to the Bible is the only legitimate way of connecting the persons, institutions and events in the Old Testament with their counterparts in the New Testament.[46] Others have pointed out that this procedure of finding references to Christ in every detail of the Old Testament tends to become an arbitrary method of exegesis, which cannot be approved of.[47]

It is impossible to touch on all the problems in connection with this subject.[48] It may be sufficient to say that we do not approve of the manner in which men like von Rad deal with this problem. The typological approach is indeed not the only legitimate way of connecting the Old and New Testaments. We do not agree with his notion of a history of traditions, with its analogies and prefigurations for which new reinterpretations are to be *substituted*.[49] An essential presupposition for the typological approach to the Bible is the recognition of the historical character of the revelation. This presupposition confronts us with one of the most significant theological problems of our day, viz. whether the Bible contains real history, or only the interpretation of the main events in accordance with the theological viewpoint of the Old and New Testament writers.[50] According to von Rad and his school, the object of Old Testament theology is not the actual history of Israel, but the interpretation of the decisive events as they were recorded by tradition and their significance applied to the different periods of Israel's history.[51] It is obvious that this viewpoint has an important bearing on our subject. Is it possible to maintain the historicity of a type when it is not based on actual history? We agree with von Rad's critics that his typological approach is in danger of breaking down just at this point.[52]

This having been said, we cannot deny the relevance of the typological approach within the scheme of redemptive history as a legitimate connecting line between the two Testaments.

The term "type" is derived from the Greek *tupos*, from the verb *tuptein*, meaning "to beat, to strike," *tupos*, therefore, is a *print* or *mark* which was caused by a blow. This word occurs in sixteen places in the New Testament, and is respectively translated in the RSV as "print," "mark," "figure," "pattern," "effect," "warning," "example," "model" and "type."[53]

In trying to discover the theological idea underlying this term, we shall have to consider its meaning in Romans 5:14. In this verse Adam is called "a type of the one who was to come." The Apostle stresses the likeness, the "Entsprechung" in the relationship between Christ and His members (Rom. 3:21–5:11), and between Christ and Adam, the last named being the head of mankind (Rom. 5:12–13). The likeness between Adam and Christ is essentially this, that they both are totally representative, the one of all humanity and the other of all believers. The significance of Adam is correlated with the significance of Christ and also points forward to Christ in the broad context of the history of redemption. The real significance of Adam can thus be fully understood only in relation to Christ.[54] According to Romans 5:14 a "type" can be defined only in terms of an essential correspondence between two historical persons (institutions and events) within the broad outline of the history of revelation, in such a way that the "lesser" one points forward to the one who is to come.

Attention is directed to the following considerations. In the first place, typological exegesis must never violate the sound hermeneutical principle that "the first meaning" of a text must always be taken seriously.[55] Secondly, the typological approach to the Bible must not be overrated: it represents a certain aspect of the scheme of redemptive history, but does not constitute the only legitimate pattern of connecting Old and New Testament.[56] Lastly, it will always remain a very difficult problem to define precisely the exact content and scope of the typological material in the Bible. The extent of the typological meaning of the Old Testament can only be appreciated when it is viewed in the light of the examples given in the New Testament.[57] In this connection we will find types in the spheres of the cult and of prophetic history,[58] which will concern persons, events and institutions.[59] We must, however, bear in mind that the writers of the New Testament did not make a clear distinction between typological and allegorical exegesis,[60] so that we are warned not to discern the typological significance of Old Testament material arbitrarily. We must remember, for instance, that the persons in the Old Testament are not to be regarded as types of Christ in every aspect of their personality and life.[61] The different aspects of the "types" must enter so plainly into the scheme of redemptive history that their prefigurative meaning is clear beyond doubt.

Within the scope of these and other reservations, we shall have to consider the typological approach as a legitimate line of connecting the two Testaments.

C. Words and Their Meanings

A third connecting line between Old and New Testament is to be found in the relation between *the Word* and the *words* of the Bible. The relevance of this important approach has been given a certain relief in the new hermeneutical approach to the problem of translation.[62] The understanding of a text is not only connected with the definition of the words concerned, but with the explanation of their message. We have in the Bible many words by various persons addressed to different individuals. But these words have their significance when we understand them in the light of the New Testament, as being the dialogue between God and man. This is the purport of the formula by which an Old Testament word or utterance is cited in the New Testament: ". . . have you not read . . . how God said . . ." (Mk. 12:26, cf. Mt. 19:4, 5).

This new hermeneutical approach, with its dialogical conception of the functioning of the word opens up a perspective on the Old Testament as the Word of God.[63] By the same token the words themselves are exposed to a new understanding. This manner of translating the message contained in the words presupposes the continuity of the Old and New Testaments. Old Testament words are cited in the New Testament, and the New Testament concepts are permeated with the meaning of their Old Testament counterparts.[64]

We have arrived at a crucial point in the theological discussion of our day. Do Old and New Testament words and concepts have a revelatory meaning,[65] which in its turn would serve as link for the message expressed in these words and concepts in both Testaments? This presupposition is affirmed by some scholars[66] and forms the basis of the monumental work of G. Kittel,[67] in which New Testament concepts are being studied against the background of the Old Testament meaning. At the same time we have to agree (even if reluctantly) with the criticism brought by James Barr,[68] that words in the Old and New Testaments cannot be forced into a fixed pattern of meaning; they must be studied in their functional and linguistic context. It would have been easier if words and concepts in the Bible were used in a technical sense. This, however, is not generally the case. One's method of approach, therefore, must always be to understand the meaning of a word in its linguistic, functional, and cultural context.[69] But at the same time we must try to discern the Word of God in the words of the sacred writers, and in doing so we will surely be able to apprehend the connecting line between the "Greek words and their Hebrew meanings,"[70] that is between Old and New Testaments.

The next three ways of conceiving the theological relationship of the Testaments are taken from John Bright's *The Authority of the Old Testament,* pp. 185–192. We may, therefore, confine ourselves to a brief survey.

D. Parity of the Old Testament

According to Bright it is legitimate to understand the relationship of Old Testament to New as one of *full parity within the unity of divine revelation.* This view implies the following:

> Since the Old Testament is the revelation of Israel's God, and since he is also the God who is revealed in Jesus Christ, the Old Testament remains for the Christian a revelation of *his* God and an authentic witness to the faith he claims as his own; as such, it is in all its parts useful for edification and for moral and doctrinal instruction.[71]

There is manifestly a profound truth in this. To say that the God of the New Testament is also the God of the Old and that both Testaments have as their subject His redemptive dealings with men is to make a theologically correct statement, and one insisted upon by the New Testament itself. But then Bright's criticism is that such a statement cannot without qualification be turned into a hermeneutical principle, for there is another side to the matter. The two Testaments do indeed have a unity; but there are also differences, and these must be taken into full consideration.[72]

We do agree with Bright that the emphasis on the essential unity of the Testaments is legitimate and necessary, but with certain reservations as we have pointed out in the beginning; as a one-sided formula we would rather regard it as an illegitimate assessment of the relationship between Old and New Testaments.[73]

E. The Old Testament as Preparation

The next relationship of the Testaments could, according to Bright, be defined in terms of continuity, in the sense that the Old Testament is viewed as *the historical and theological preparation for the Gospel.* The element of truth in this point of view is obvious. The Old Testament unquestionably provides both the historical background and the theological preparation for the rise of Christianity. Bright rightly warns against the danger of seeing the Old Testament as chiefly of historical interest, and thereby relegating it to a subordinate position within the canon of Scripture.[74] This legitimate line of connection must, therefore, be qualified in the sense that it must never imply a degrading of the Old Testament as a secondary phase in the process of revelation.

F. The Old Testament as Teacher

According to Bright the Old Testament can also be understood as a *propaedeutic to the Gospel in another* sense.[75] One can see its primary function in providing the subjective preparation for the gospel in the hearts of men. This understanding of the matter has its roots in the dialectic of law and gospel, which has played such an important role especially in the Lutheran tradition.[76] Bright then goes on to say: "In view of this, it is legitimate to ascribe to the Old Testament, with its strong element of 'Law,' the pedagogical function of preparing men for the reception of the Gospel." He correctly warns against the mistake of turning "Law-Gospel" into a formula for describing the theological relationship of the Testaments, as if the Old Testament were synonymous with law, the New with gospel. According to him scholars like Emanuel Hirsch, Rudolf Bultmann, Friedrich Baumgärtel as well as certain of their respective followers, albeit in different ways, all accord to the Old Testament a purely pedagogical function and stress its radical discontinuity with the New.[77]

Although this line of connection has an element of truth,[78] the Old Testament and especially the law being the *paidagogos,* the "schoolmaster" to Christ,[79] it represents only one aspect of the complex and varied relationship between the two Testaments. The danger in this formula would consist in the tendency to degrade the Old Testament as being *merely* a preparation for the gospel, thereby overstressing the discontinuity between the Testaments.[80]

G. Promise and Fulfillment

We must now turn our attention to one of the most important formulas in assessing the relationship of the Testaments, which is usually expressed in terms of *promise and fulfillment*,[81] but needs to be examined a little more closely.[82] We have the impression that a great amount of the criticism against this formula is unwarranted, because it is based on a misapprehension of the real significance of both terms "promise" and "fulfillment," as well as a certain understanding of the history of revelation.

We start with the latter. The pattern of promise and fulfillment is inconceivable without the idea of the progression of the history of revelation. This idea is rejected by some neo-orthodox theologians. According to them we do not have a progressive unfolding of redemptive history within the scheme of promise and fulfillment, but rather the encounter within the reality of Jesus Christ.[83] The history of revelation in the Old and New Testament does not represent a continuous line, even though it be a broken line,[84] but rather two semicircles around the same center, Jesus Christ.[85] According to Hellbardt it is of extreme importance to eliminate the idea of history from the dialectic of promise and fulfillment. The futurity of the realizing of events in connection with the Old Testament is not the historical futurity of the birth and life of Christ. The fact that Jesus has come after the time of the Old Testament is, theologically speaking, of secondary importance.[86]

The relationship between history and revelation lies at the center of this theological discussion.[87] We cannot enter into this problem, but must state as our opinion that the cyclic conception of time does not do justice to the Scriptural data. The Dutch scholar Bleeker thus criticizes this point of view.[88] From the annunciation of the birth of Christ and onwards the whole New Testament vibrates with a shout of joy for the reality of redemption which has *now* come to pass (see Lk. 2:10,11).

Criticism against this pattern of promise and fulfillment is, furthermore, directed against the terms themselves. In both cases we have a reduction of the meaning and scope of these terms.

Scholars like Friedrich Baumgärtel, Franz Hesse, and others distinguish between "Verheissung" and "Weissagung." "Verheissung" is connected with the absolute substance of the promise, which was expressed in the well-known dictum: "I am the Lord, your God." This "Verheissung" is fully realized in Christ. In this faith the Church participates in the Old Testament as the authoritative, decisive Word of God. The Church does not have any need for casual "Weissagungen" and typologies, which are supposed to be fulfilled in the New Testament.[89]

According to these scholars the real promise is limited to this central theme of both Old and New Testament, and everything else in the Old Testament is of secondary importance. Even the predictions of the prophets do not belong to this substance of the revelation.

We may admire Baumgärtel's earnest desire to return to the text of the Old Testament itself and to consider the problem of the discontinuity between the Testaments. At the same time we cannot accept his reduction of the element of promise or his arbitrary distinction between "Verheissung" and "Weissagung," especially when the last-named is equated with the predictions of the prophets.[90]

The term "promise" is restricted in yet another way. It is limited to the Messianic prophecies.[91] The consequence of this procedure is that the term "promise" has a bearing on only a minute part of the revelation in both Testaments. Against the background of this reduction, my colleague F. C. Fensham of the Semitic Language Department at the University of Stellenbosch refers to the pattern "promise and fulfillment" as "inadequate and unsatisfactory." According to him "it leads on the one hand to a rigorous search for Christ in the Old Testament . . . or on the other hand it leads to a vague idea without any real proof of its effectiveness . . . . There is much more to this unity of Testaments than the automatic fulfillment of Old Testament promises."[92]

We agree with his warning against a "rigorous search for Christ in the Old Testament," but we do not agree with this superficial restriction of the concept of promise. When the Church and its theology referred to promise and fulfillment, they included the whole of the Old Testament in its intimate relationship with the New Testament in the broad scope of the history of redemption.[93] This is not limited to some explicit Messianic prophecies, the number of which is still more being restricted by some scholars.[94] This relationship in the context of promise and fulfillment is extensive and comprehensive. Bright is in full agreement with this. He says:

> . . . the Old Testament's theology understands the whole course of Israel's history in terms of God's dealings with his people and his redemptive purpose for them and through them. It is a history that moves between promise and fulfillment. The story of Israel's origins from the call of Abraham, through the Exodus deliverance, to the entry into the land of Canaan, is cast in a framework of promise and fulfillment. Israel's history in the Promised Land—her exile from it and her ultimate return to it—is understood as a history guided by God's sovereign will, subject to the stipulations of his covenant, and interpreted through his prophetic word of summons and warning, judgment and promise. And through all the pages of that history, through tragedy and beyond it, we see—expressed in manifold forms—a continued reaching out, a continued straining toward history's ordained conclusion: "the triumph of God's rule in the earth."[95]

The substance of this lengthy quotation is indeed in accord with the comprehensiveness of the "promise." This is attested by the Old Testament itself (Josh. 21:45; 23:14; Ps. 105:8–11, etc.), but the scope of the promise is especially evident in the light of the New Testament. The promise links up with the history of Abraham and his descendants (Acts 7:17; Rom. 4:13), rests on grace (Rom. 4:16), is an essential aspect of Israel's spiritual inheritance, (Rom. 9:4 f.),[96] includes all believers even from the Gentiles (Rom. 15:8), has a perspective on new heavens and a new earth (II Pet. 3:13), and on eternal life (I Jn. 2:25). All the promises of God, not only the Messianic prophecies or predictions, find their Yes in Christ (II Cor. 1:20). We must not try to restrict these promises. Scholars like Berkouwer, Rowley, and others rightly point out that there are many forms of expectation in the Old Testament which move on to their realization in the New Testament and beyond.[97] When my colleague Fensham finds the pattern of promise and fulfillment "inadequate and unsatisfactory," and would rather substitute for it a thorough discussion of the covenant as a binding factor of both Testaments, he does not seem fully aware of the fact that no covenant in the Old Testament is without a promise.[98]

The comprehensiveness of the promise has as its corollary the comprehensiveness of the fulfillment. With respect to the fulfillment there is a misapprehension that presupposes the abandonment of the Old Testament altogether. According to this point of view, the promise becomes obsolete in the fulfillment. This is obviously incorrect, because it is a misrepresentation of the category of fulfillment in the New Testament.

The Greek words[99] in the New Testament designating fulfilling and fulfillment have significant meaning. Through its fulfillment something is given real content and meaning, it attains to its purpose and realizes itself. It is not annulled or left without any further meaning or purpose, but is rather confirmed and ratified. In the reality of its fulfillment it realizes itself and becomes an integral part of that reality, even when the fulfillment still points forward towards the consummation, the coming *pleroma* of God.[100]

It is surprising how many realities of the Old Testament are said to be fulfilled in the New.[101] Bijlsma finds occasion in this to restrict the promises to a separate category within these various realities,[102] but unjustly so. The spoken and written Word of God, all the components of the history of revelation in its bearing on the life of His people, are so many aspects of God's dealings with men and of His promises. All these realities are focused on Jesus Christ; He is the hinge of all fulfillments in the Bible.

We agree with Bijlsma, Herman Ridderbos and others that this fulfillment is a presence in which the future of the prophecy is taken up.[103] This presence, however, retains the aspect of the future both in the Old

and in the New Testament. With this concept of the process of fulfillment, the panoramic view of the redemptive purpose and saving deeds
of God is unfolded, and we are made spectators and collaborators of this
comprehensive movement towards the ultimate goal of the pleroma of the
eternal kingdom of God.

In the light of this significance of the concepts "promise" and "fulfillment," we cannot agree with Bright's criticism when he says:

> Certainly the whole of the Old Testament cannot neatly be classified as prom-
> ise, the whole of the New as fulfillment. If there is promise in the Old Testa-
> ment, there is also an element of fulfillment; and if there is fulfillment in the
> New Testament, there is also the promise of things yet to come.[104]

This, of course, is quite true, but irrelevant in the context of the real
meaning of these concepts. When Bright goes on to say that "the entire
Old Testament cannot readily be subsumed under the rubric of *Heilsgeschichte;* . . . it was a history that led on to Christ—and equally to
the rejection of Christ,"[105] then we are in need of a clarification of our
terms. We have in the Bible not only the revelation of God, but also
the reaction of men. The last-named is not normative and does not figure
in the whole scheme of the relationship between the Testaments. The
"history" which has led "to the rejection of Christ" could not have been
part of the history of revelation.[106] When our Savior reproached the men
of Emmaus because they did not understand the things which happened
the previous days, He interpreted to them in all the Scriptures the things
concerning Himself. They were not misled by the Scriptures, but they
were foolish men, and slow of heart to believe all that the prophets had
spoken (Lk. 24:25–27) .

The significance of the formula of promise and fulfillment cannot easily
be overstressed, especially when viewed in the light of the comprehensiveness of both terms.

At the same time we agree with Bright and others that this formula
needs to be supplemented by definitions which will express certain aspects
of the relationship more explicitly. This is done by the remaining two
formulas: the unity of perspective, and continuity and discontinuity.

H. Unity of Perspective

The message of both Testaments has but one and the same perspective
in connection with the coming of the kingdom of God. Vriezen puts it
this way:

> At the heart of the Old Testament message lies the expectation of the kingdom
> of God, and it is the initial fulfillment of this expectation in Jesus of Naza-
> reth . . . that underlies the message of the New Testament. *The true heart of
> both Old Testament and New Testament is, therefore, the eschatological per-
> spective.*[107]

In Vriezen's opinion Martin Buber is mistaken because he has not seen this common eschatological perspective of Old and New Testament clearly enough and has, therefore, arrived at an excessively one-sided notion of the Christian faith as the belief in something that has already been accomplished, thus neglecting the other aspect—the faith of Israel as faith in a God who will act in the future.[108]

Many eminent scholars are agreed on the significance of this definition as a sound theological expression of the interrelationship between the Testaments.[109] This is one of the most obvious and conspicuous aspects of the history of revelation, that it is directed towards the end of the ways and the works and the words of God. We have one continuous movement in the direction of the Eschaton, the coming of the Day of the Lord. The whole history of revelation is one pilgrimage, looking forward to the city which has foundations, whose builder and maker is God (Heb. 11:10). On this pilgrimage we have many stops, many initial fulfillments, but every one of them becomes a point of departure again. Koole rightly points out that in the eschatology of Paul, the predictions concerning the last days according to the synoptic Gospels, and the parables of the kingdom (Mt. 13), it is evident that the expectation of the Old Testament is continued in the New Testament.[110] Notwithstanding the seeming delay in the realization of the full salvation, the perspective on the day of the coming of the Lord remains open.

The secret of this unity of perspective is to be found in the revelation of God as the God of salvation through Christ, and as the Lord of history. The end of His works and ways is the consummation of all things in heaven and on earth. This is the pervasive theme of both Old and New Testaments.

I. Continuity and Discontinuity

Nearly all the above named formulations emphasize the unity and continuity in the relationship between the Testaments. The differences were implied or presupposed, but not explicitly expressed. Thus, we have need of still another definition which will stress not only the unity, but also the differences between Old and New Testament. The whole problem of the relationship can be conceived of as a problem of continuity *and* discontinuity.

This point has often been made. According to Bright the relationship of the Testaments is inevitably a dual one.

> The continuity lies in the obvious fact that Christianity is historically a development out of Judaism; the discontinuity in the equally obvious fact that Christianity is not a continuation, or even a radical reform, of Judaism, but an entirely separate religion. The continuity lies in the fact that the theological structure of the two Testaments is fundamentally the same, with the major themes of the theology of the Old carried over and resumed in the New; the

discontinuity lies in the fact that these themes receive radical reinterpretation in the New in the light of what Christ has done. Above all, continuity lies in the New Testament's affirmation that Jesus is the Christ (Messiah), who has fulfilled the law and the prophets; the discontinuity lies in the fact that this fulfillment, though foreshadowed in the Old Testament, is not necessarily deducible from the plain sense of the Old and was in fact so surprising that the majority of the Israelites could not see it as fulfillment. The New Testament, while unbreakably linked with the Old, announces the intrusion of something New and, therewith, the end of the Old. In a word, the two Testaments are continuous within the unity of God's redemptive purpose; but their discontinuity is the discontinuity of two aeons.[111]

This point of view is also stressed by men like Schweitzer.[112]

We may agree with the general thrust of Bright's definition.

There are, however, a few minor points of criticism. Theologically speaking, Christianity did not develop out of Judaism.[113] The discontinuity in this case is, therefore, not a discontinuity between Old and New Testament, but a radical breakdown between two different religions.[114] Furthermore, we would rather follow the terminology of Rowley and speak of "the texture of the revelation" than of the "theological structure."[115] Theology is the product of human reflection upon revelation, and this cannot be our guiding principle in discerning the sound relationship between the Testaments. The fact that the majority of the Israelites could not see the fulfillment of the Old Testament promises is hardly evidence of discontinuity between promise and fulfillment. In teaching His disciples, Christ did not speak of another, more spiritual reality but rather led them to understand the Scriptures.

We agree with Bright that neither aspect of this twofold relationship is for a moment to be lost from view.

> To ignore the continuity is to forget that the New Testament has claimed the Old. . . . To ignore the discontinuity is to forget the claim of the New Testament to be "New." . . . Both aspects are to be held in view in dealing with all parts of the Old Testament.[116]

This, indeed, is a major point in our discussion. The continuity must not be endangered by overstressing the discontinuity, by speaking of a primary (New Testament) and secondary (Old Testament) source of our Christian faith.[117] At the same time the discontinuity must not be eliminated by overemphasizing the continuity. We have not only a progression from the Old into the New Testament, but also the crossing of the boundary between two dispensations.[118] The Old Testament is not only a rosebud that opens up in the New, but it is also a fruit which casts off its peel in the New.

This discontinuity-in-continuity is expressed in many New Testament passages. In II Timothy 1:9–10 Paul admonishes Timothy "not to be ashamed of testifying to our Lord . . . who saved us . . . in virtue of his own purpose and the grace which He gave us in Christ Jesus ages ago, and now has manifested through the appearing of our Savior Christ Jesus." In both Testaments the saving grace was connected with Christ, and this spells out the continuity between Old and New Testament. But the difference is that it now has been manifested through Christ's appearance.

We have the same dual relationship in Hebrews 1:1 f: "In many and various ways God spoke of old to our fathers by the prophets; but in these last days he has spoken to us by his Son. . . ." In both Testaments it was the same God speaking; but the manner in which He did it in each aeon was different: in times of old He did it in many and various ways, sporadically and in a piecemeal fashion, but now He has revealed Himself in the Word that has become flesh.

In considering the discontinuity between the Testaments we must not use the scissors in an arbitrary way. Nothing in the Old Testament needs to be cut out. Everything functions within the context of the history of revelation. In crossing the boundary into the A.D. situation, however, things have changed in the outward scheme of the divine economy. According to J. Ridderbos[119] it concerns especially the earthly, nationalistic, particularistic, and legalistic character of the old dispensation. All these aspects had their meaning and function in the period covered by the Old Testament, but now they have been transcended in two different aspects: spiritually and universally.

According to Herman Bavinck[120] this process of transition from the Old to the New Testament is the casting off of the non-arbitrary, but nevertheless temporary, sensuous nationalistic forms in which one and the same grace has been revealed in the days of old. The new aeon commenced when the Old Testament promises were fulfilled in the birth of John the Baptist and of Jesus. The old aeon, nevertheless, remained in force until the death of Christ. But then the curtain was torn apart (Mt. 27:51), the Testator died on the cross (Heb. 9:15–17), and the new covenant was founded in His blood (Mt. 26:28), the bond which stood against us with its legal demands was canceled (Col. 2:14), and the dividing wall of hostility was broken down (Eph. 2:14). The old aeon may continue to exist, but legally it was abrogated; or to put it a better way, nothing was abolished, but the ripe fruit cast off its peel.

Summary

Summarizing our results, we may stress again the utmost importance and significance of our subject. We cannot study and understand our Bible without resolving this problem. Here we have the crossroads dividing the critical, Jewish, and evangelical exegesis. Proper awareness of the relationship of the Testaments is a prerequisite for studying Biblical theology. The results of our eschatology are affected by the way we conceive of the continuity and discontinuity of the Testaments. This is the crucial point in the discussion between millennialists and amillennialists. In our practical Church life our decisions need to be substantiated by a clear understanding of this relationship. Should we as ministers follow the custom in wearing official clothes like the high priests of old? Are we still under the obligation to bring "the full tithes into the storehouse," as was done under the Old Tesament dispensation? Every preacher amongst us would like to testify to the problem of preaching from the Old Testament in a responsible fashion. We are continually in danger of missing the point in two directions: either we neglect the historical context of our sermon, or we do not know how to relate it to Christ.[121]

The problem of the relationship between the Testaments will abide with us in all our labors in church and theology. This relationship is so varied and complex that we cannot define it in a single definition, but we need many definitions to do justice to its variety of aspects. In this paper we have tried to draw attention to some of these formulas, with the realization that we have only touched on some aspects of this complex problem.

Notes

In addition to the abbreviations listed elsewhere, the following are also used in this study:

NGTT *Nederduitse Gereformeerde Teologiese Tydskrif*
ZThK *Zeitschrift für Theologie und Kirche*

1. K. Schwarzwäller, *Das Alte Testament in Christus*, Theologische Studien, No. 84, ed. Karl Barth and Max Geiger, (1966), p. 5: "Die Frage nach dem Verhältnis der beiden Testamente zueinander steht wieterhin im Vordergrund der theologischen Debatte." See Nic. H. Ridderbos, "De Verhouding van het Oude Testament en het Nieuwe Testament," GTT, 68 (1968) : 97: "De verhouding van Oud en Nieuwe Testament: dat is zo ongeveer alles, daarin is het geheel van de theologie betrokken."

2. Gerhard von Rad, *Theologie des Alten Testaments* (Munich: Chr. Kaiser Verlag, 1960), II: 348: "Ja, es kann—überblickt man die gesamte Auslegungsgeschichte des Alten Testaments in der Kirche—die Vermutung aufkommen, es sei die Kirche über das Verhältnis der beiden Testamente zueinander in theologisch begrifflicher Hinsicht kaum je zu einer befriedigenden Klärung gekommen." See also Joh. de Groot and A. R. Hulst, *Macht en Wil* (Nijkerk: G. F. Callenbach), pp. 340 f.

3. Compare the remarks of G. C. Berkouwer on the origin of the Messianic prophecies in *De Persoon van Christus* (Kampen: J. H. Kok, 1952), pp. 113 ff.

4. Cf. J. Barton Payne, *The Theology of the Older Testament* (Grand Rapids: Zondervan, 1962), pp. 505–19.

5. We may refer to the relevant articles in Carl F. H. Henry, ed., *Revelation and the Bible* (Grand Rapids: Baker Book House, 1958). Cf. also G. C. Berkouwer and A. S. van der Woude, eds., *De Bijbel in het Geding* (Nijkerk: G. F. Callenbach, 1968); *The Book of Confessions* (The Constitution of the UP Church in the U.S.A., Philadelphia, 1967), pp. 9, 27, 28.

6. John Bright: *The Authority of the Old Testament* (Nashville: Abingdon, 1967), pp. 184 f., refers to "two opposing tendencies."

7. According to A. D. R. Polman, *Het Woord Gods bij Augustinus* (Kampen: J. H. Kok, 1955), pp. 75–83, Augustine had to defend the Bible as the Word of Christ against three groups of persons: the Manichaeans, the Jews, and the followers of Pelagius.

8. On Marcion see Bright, *op. cit.*, pp. 60–4, with relevant literature.

9. *Ibid.*, pp. 64–72. Bright gives a short but clear exposition of the relative points of view.

10. Cf. Ridderbos, *op. cit.*, p. 97.

11. They are reproached for not taking the Old Testament into consideration by Hans-Joachim Kraus, "Der lebendige Gott," *Evangelische Theologie*, 27 (1967) : 169–200.

12. Cf. H. J. Schoeps, *Jüdischer Glaube in dieser Zeit. Prolegomena zur Grundlegung einer syst. Theol. des Judentums*, (1932), p. 25: "The canon of the Old Testament belongs to Israel and does not need any Ergänzung und Uberhöhung mehr." See also H. J. Schoeps, *Paul: the Theology of the Apostle in the Light of Jewish Religious History* (London: Lutterworth Press; Philadelphia: Westminster; 1961) ; Theodorus C. Vriezen, *An Outline of Old Testament Theology* (Newton Center, Mass.: Charles T. Brantford; Oxford: Basil Blackwell; 1958), p. 98.

13. A. A. van Ruler, *Die Christliche Kirche und das Alte Testament* (Munich: Chr. Kaiser Verlag, 1955), p. 68, n. 125; cf. his *Religie en Politiek* (Nijkerk: G. F. Callenbach, 1945), pp. 128–48.

14. In different periods of the church's history this relationship was expressed in the following classical terms: "Novum Testamentum in Vetere Testamento latet, Vetus Testamentum in Novo Testamento patet" (Augustine) ; "de similitudine (vel potius unitate) Veteris et Novi Testamenti; de differentia unius Testamente ab altero" (Calvin) ; "opertum initio tenetur, quod deinde opertum cernitur" (J. A. Bengel).

15. Cf. G. F. Oehler, *Theology of the Old Testament*, trans. E. D. Smith (Edinburgh: T. & T. Clark, 1882) I:33; and Emond Jacob, *Theology of the Old Testament*, trans. A. W. Heathcote and Ph. J. Allcock (London: Hodder & Stoughton; New York: Harpers; 1958), p. 13; Hermann Diem, *Dogmatik* (Munich: Chr. Kaiser Verlag, 1955), II:196 ff.

16. Cf. Oehler, *op. cit.*, pp. 38, 41.

17. Cf. Wolfgang Schweitzer, *Schrift und Dogma in der Oekumene* (Gütersloh: C. Bertelsmann Verlag, 1953), p. 128: "Die Folge dieser Anschauung ist, dass bei Dodd der Unterschied zwischen dem Alten Testament und der Kirchengeschichte verblasst."

18. Cf. Schweitzer, *op. cit.*, p. 171 f., for a discussion of Barth; also Ridderbos, *op. cit.*, p. 100 f.

19. W. Vischer, *Das Christuszeugnis des Alten Testaments* (Munich: 1936), I:16, 19, 23.

20. Typical representatives of this point of view are the Dutch scholars A. A. van Ruler, and especially K. H. Miskotte in his interesting book, *Als de Goden Zwijgen*, 2nd ed. [When the Gods Are Silent] (Haarlem: D. M. Holland, 1965). He emphasizes the plus-aspects of the Old Testament revelation as compared with that of the New Testament, pp. 141–229.

21. Van Ruler lists ten ways of stating the relationship which according to him is being advocated (*Die Christliche Kirche, op. cit.*, pp. 9–12). Bright feels that van Ruler's categories do not all stand on the same footing and that one could logically reduce them to five or six—each of them, of course, with variations (Bright, *op. cit.*, p. 184, n. 17). Cf. also Vriezen, *op. cit.*, p. 111, who draws attention to *typology, preparation, similarity* and *contrast*.

22. For instance, the relationship of the Testaments is expressed by Hellbardt, *Das Alte Testament und des Evangelium* (1933) and his *Der verheiszene König. Das Christuszeugnis des Hosea* (1935), as a relationship of *truth* and *reality*. According

to him there is no *heilsgeschichtliche* difference between the Old and New Testaments, and we do not have any progression of the revelation. The only difference is that the Old Testament is witnessing to the reality of the gospel in terms of truth, and the New Testament in terms of the reality of salvation (*Das Alte Testament* p. 32 f.) .

Another "solution" of which we cannot approve is represented by the so-called *Motivforschung*, especially by men like Gustaf Aulén, *Christus Victor*, trans. A. G. Herbert (New York: Macmillan) , and Anders Nygren, *Agape and Eros* (Philadelphia: Westminster, 1953). See Schweitzer, *op. cit.,* pp. 187–92 for a thorough discussion.

23. Cf. G. C. Berkouwer, "Het bewijs in de theologie," *Interfac. Voordrachten,* 1959, p. 14 f., and his *De Heilige Schrift* (Kampen: J. H. Kok, 1967) , II:178.

24. This is evident from passages like the following: Mt. 4:4, 7, 10; 21:13; Mk. 11:17; Lk. 4:4, 8; 19:46; Acts 23:5; Rom. 12:19; 14:11; I Cor. 1:19; 3:19; 15:45; Gal. 3:10, 13; 4:22, 27; I Pet. 1:16. The authoritative character of the Old Testament quotations is also emphasized by the use of the Greek preposition *hina* (Mt. 1:22; 2:15; 4:14; 12:17; 21:4; 26:56; Mk. 14:49; Jn. 12:38; 13:18; 15:25; 17:12; 19:24, 28, 36) and *hopōs* Mt. 2:23; 13:35) .

25. Cf. R. H. Gundry, *The Use of the Old Testament in St. Matthew's Gospel, with special reference to the Messianic Hope* (Leiden: E. J. Brill, 1967) . According to him formal quotations which Matthew shares with Mark are almost purely Septuagintal— and this prevailing Septuagintal form of OT quotation is seen throughout the rest of the NT (abstract) . See, however, G. Howard, "Hebrews and the Old Testament Quotations," *Novum Testamentum,* X (1968) : 208–16. Also Simon Kistemaker, *The Psalms Citations in the Epistle to the Hebrews* (Amsterdam: 1961) .

26. Cf. Frederick F. Bruce, *Biblical Exegesis in the Qumran Texts* (Den Haag: Uitgeverij van Keulen, 1959) ; Geza Vermès, *Scripture and Tradition in Judaism* (New York: Humanities Press, 1961) ; see also J. L. Koole, *De overname van het Oude Testament door de Chr. Kerk* (1938) . According to J. Bonsirven, *Exégèse Rabbinique et Exégèse Paulinienne* (Paris: 1939) , p. 13, Paul's technique of Old Testament exegesis finds close parallels in Rabbinic sources.

27. Cf. J. Hänel, *Der Schriftbegriff Jesu* (Gütersloh: 1919) ; Vriezen, *op. cit.,* pp. 2–5, 79 ff.

28. See also J. L. Koole, *Hermeneutische Oriëntatie,* 1962, p. 14 f.

29. Cf. Berkouwer, *De Heilige Schrift* II, 168 f.

30. Cf. Berkouwer's discussion of these quotations, *ibid.,* p. 161 ff.

31. Cf. Calvin's statement in his commentary on the letter to the Hebrews, chapter 2: "Nunc videtur apostolum verba trahere in diversum sensum, quam intellexarit David. Nam 'brachu ti' videtur ad tempus referre." Cf. Berkouwer, *De Heilige Schrift* II, 168 ff.; Claus Westermann, "Prophetenzitate im Neuen Testament," *Evangelische Theologie,* 27 (1967) : 307–17; Otto Michel, "Das Alte Testament in Neuen Testament," *Das Alte Testaments in unserer Verkündigung,* Lehre und Leben, Bahnauer Hefte 5 (Stuttgart: Quell-Verlag) , pp. 41ff.; *"Die Schwierigkeit besteht in der Veränderung des Sinngehaltes,"* p. 41.

32. See Herman Ridderbos, *Romeinen,* Commentaar op het Nieuwe Testament (Kampen: J. H. Kok, 1959) , pp. 242 f.

33. As is done by Franz Hesse, *Das Alte Testament als Buch der Kirche* (1966) , p. 38: "Das Alte Testament bietet ihm [Paul] lediglich Illustrations material für seinen eigenen, ganz anderen Text."

34. Rudolf Bultmann, "Weissagung und Erfüllung," in *Probleme alttestamentlicher Hermeneutik,* ed. C. Westermann (Munich: Chr. Kaiser Verlag, 1960) , pp. 28–53.

35. Cf. E. Earle Ellis, *Paul's Use of the Old Testament* (1967) , pp. 138, 143: "Pauline exegesis employs a great deal of methodology found in rabbinical and other literature."

36. For the exegesis at Qumran, see Bruce, *op. cit.,* O. Betz, *Offenbarung und Schriftforschung in der Qumransecte* (1960) ; J. A. Fitzmijer, "The use of explicit Old

Testament quotations in Qumran and in the New Testament," New Testament Studies (1961), p. 297 ff.; Gundry, *op. cit.*, who points out the contrast between the non-atomizing "Matthaean" hermeneutics and Qumran and rabbinical literature.

37. See Berkouwer, *De Heilige Schrift*, p. 176 f.; S. Amsler, *L'ancien Testament dans l'Église* (1960), p. 65 f.; James Barr, *Old and New Interpretation: A Study of the Two Testaments* (New York: Harper & Row, 1966), p. 145. According to Kistemaker, *op. cit.*, p. 151, "Every psalm citation serves the purpose of communicating sacred history to the first recipients of the Epistle."

38. Vriezen, *op. cit.*, p. 2.

39. *Ibid.*, pp. 82, 83.

40. *Ibid.*, p. 6.

41. *Ibid.*, p. 2, n. 2; p. 81 f.

42. A thorough discussion of this point can be found in Herman Ridderbos, *Paulus, ontwerp van zijn Theologie* (Kampen: J. H. Kok, 1966), pp. 139 ff. especially pp. 165–70. Cf. William D. Davies, *Paul and Rabbinic Judaism* (London: SPCK; New York: Harper Torchbooks; 1962). He says: "We cannot too strongly insist that for Paul the acceptance of the Gospel was not so much the rejection of the old Judaism and the discovery of a new religion wholly antithetical to it . . . but the recognition of the advent of the true and final form of Judaism, in other words, the advent of the Messianic age of Jewish expectation. . . . Paul parted company with Judaism on this one point, viz. at the valuation of Jesus of Nazareth as the Messiah with all that this implied" (Davies, p. 324). See also Hermann Diem's *Dogmatik*, II: 137 ff. "Das Rabbinat weiss nichts mehr von dem Trost und der Verheissung des Gesetzes und von der Bedeutung der ganzen Schrift als dem 'Bundesbuch,' als dem Dokument für Gnadenbund Gottes" (p. 139).

43. Cf. Berkouwer, *De Heilige Schrift*, p. 175.

44. Cf. Berkouwer, *De Persoon van Christus*, p. 90. See also S. du Toit, *'n Nuwe fase in die stryd om die Oude Testament* (Pretoria: 1936), pp. 21 f.; Max. Meinertz, *Theologie des Neuen Testaments* (Bonn: Peter Hanstein Verlag, 1950) II: 53 f.

45. The literature on this topic is very extensive. In *Vox Theologica Interacademial Theologisch Tijdschrift* (Assen: 1961), pp. 150–1, a brief survey of the most important titles is given by Nic. H. Ridderbos. Since his article was written, the steady flow of books touching on this subject has continued. According to Berkouwer, *De Heilige Schrift, II*, p. 175, the "shares" of Typology are tending upward. For its history, see L. Goppelt; *Typos: Die typologische Deutung des Alten Testaments* (1939); Emil G. Kraeling, *The Old Testament Since the Reformation* (1955); H. J. Kraus, *Geschichte der historisch-kritischen Erforschung des Alten Testaments* (1956). See J. E. Wood, "Isaac Typology in the New Testament," *New Testament Studies*, 4 (1968): 583–9.

46. See Gerhard von Rad, "Typologische Auslegung des Alten Testaments," *Evangelische Theologie*, July/August, 1952.

47. See Moorehead, "Type," in *International Standard Bible Encyclopedia*, and Oswald T. Allis, *Prophecy and the Church* (Philadelphia: Presbyterian & Reformed, 1945), pp. 21 f.

48. See the present writer's article: "Some Notes on Typological Exegesis," *New Light on Some Old Testament Problems*, Papers read at 5th Meeting of Die Oude Testament Werkgemeenskap in Suid-Afrika (1962), pp. 58–63.

49. Von Rad, *Theologie des Alte Testament*, II; 329 ff.; see J. L. Koole, *Hermeneutische Oriëntatie*, p. 20. Cf. also the interesting discussion between Hans Conzelmann and von Rad, in *Evangelische Theologie*, 24 (1964): 113–25, 388–94.

50. With respect to the New Testament, see Paul Althaus, *Das sogenannte Kerygma und der historische Jesus;* Joachim Jeremias, *Das Problem des historischen Jesus,* (1960), published in English as *The Problem of the Historical Jesus* (Philadelphia: Fortress Press, 1964); and others.

51. See von Rad's article: "Typologische Anslegung des Alten Testaments," pp. 25–7; and *Theologie*, II, 329–424. This point of view has been criticized by Franz Hesse, *Zeitschrift für Theologie und Kirche* (1960), and Fr. Baumgärtel in *Theologische Literaturzeitung*. (Nov./Dec., 1961). On the other hand, it has been pointed out by von Rad's students that von Rad's *Theologie* testifies to the fact that he himself paid much attention to the historicity of the events and that his theory was vindicated by the soundness of his practice; cf. W. Pannenberg, "Kerugma und Geschichte," *Studien zur Theologie der alttestamentlicher Uberlieferungen*, ed. R. Rendtorff und K. Koch (Neukirchener Verlag, 1961), pp. 129–40.

52. Cf. J. L. Koole, *Hermeneutische Oriëntatie*, pp. 20 f., with literature.

53. Cf. Jn. 20:25; Acts 7:43, 44; 23:26; Rom. 5:14; I Cor. 10:6, 11; Phil. 3:17; I Thess. 1:7; II Thess. 3:9; I Tim. 4:12; Tit. 2:7; I Pet. 5:3; Heb. 8:5.

54. Cf. Herman N. Ridderbos, *Romeinen*, p. 116, and his *Paulus*, pp. 99 ff.

55. This in contrast to the point of view that a *type* does not have a real meaning in itself. See Moorehead, *op. cit.*; Georges Florovsky, "Revelation and Interpretation," *Biblical Authority for Today* (London: 1951), pp. 175 ff.: "a *type* is no more than a 'shadow' or 'image'": cf. L. Köhler, *Theologische Zeitschrift* (July/August, 1953), p. 252: "Typus ist eine gestalt, eine Begebenheit, ein Zusammenhang, der nicht um seiner selber willen gewicht und Bedeutung hat."

56. In this we agree with scholars like J. Ridderbos, "Over de uitlegging der H. S.," *Bijbelsch Handboek*, (Kampen: J. H. Kok, 1935), I: 404 f.; James D. Smart, *The Interpretation of Scripture* (London: SCM Press; Philadelphia: Westminster; 1961), pp. 129–33; C. van Leeuwen, "Hoe moeten wij het Oude Testament uitleggen?" *Op het spoor van Israël* ('S-Gravenhage: 1961), pp. 99–114; Bright, *op. cit.*, pp. 79 f., 83 ff., 91 ff.

57. Scholars like W. Vischer and even Gerhard von Rad, tend to an arbitrary application of this method, since they are convinced that the number of types in the Old Testament is unlimited, because every dealing of God with His people could be interpreted as a "shadow" of the "Christusgeschehen"; see von Rad, "Typologische Auslegung des Alten Testament," p. 31. On the other hand, scholars like Stuart maintain that "just so much of the Old Testament is to be accounted typical as the New Testament affirms to be so, and no more." Against this extreme point of view it has rightly been observed that the New Testament does not exhaust all cases of types which could be found in the Old Testament, but rather gives a few examples in an arbitrary way. Cf. Moorehead, *op. cit.*

58. Cf. Koole, *Hermeneutische Oriëntatie*, p. 19.

59. Cf. Moorehead, *op. cit.*, Milton S. Terry, *Biblical Hermeneutics*, 2nd ed. (Grand Rapids: Zondervan, 1956); Louis Berkhof, *Principles of Biblical Interpretation* (Grand Rapids: Baker, 1950).

60. Cf. Bright, *op. cit.*, pp. 91 f.

61. Cf. G. Ch. Aalders, "De Profetie," *Christus de Heiland* (Kampen: J. H. Kok, 1948), pp. 34–7.

62. I may refer to an article by E. P. Groenewald, "Krisis in die Interpretasie van die Heilige Skrif," which appeared in NGTT, January, 1969. Cf. G. C. Berkouwer, *De Heilige Schrift, II:* 143 f.; Koole, *Hermeneutische Oriëntatie*, pp. 24–8; Eduard Schweizer, *Recent Theological Literature in Switzerland*, Third Annual Bibliographical Lecture (Richmond, Va.: Union Theological Seminary, 1962), pp. 15 ff.

63. Cf. Koole, *Hermeneutische Oriëntatie*, p. 25.

64. A controversy will illustrate this point. According to Adolf Deissmann, *Licht vom Osten*, 4th ed. (Tubingen: 1923), p. 286 f., the New Testament word *diathēkē* derives its meaning from the Hellenistic word. This point of view was contradicted by H. A. Kennedy, "The Significance and Range of the Covenant-Conception in the New Testament," in Exp. Ser. 8—Vol. 10 (1915): He says: "When writers like Paul and the author of Hebrews used *diathēkē*, they very well knew that its content came from *berith*, the 'Covenant' made by God with their fathers, as this 'Covenant' was under-

stood, in the Old Testament." Cf. J. de Vuyst, *'Oud en Nieuw Verbond' in de Brief aan de Hebreeën,* (Kampen: J. H. Kok, 1964), pp. 57 f. An aspect of this problem is the question of the background of Paul's theology—was it Hellenistic, as affirmed by S. L. Knox, *St. Paul and the Church of the Gentiles,* (Cambridge: 1939), or Jewish (which is the general view)? Cf. D. E. H. Whitley, *The Theology of St. Paul* (Oxford: Basil Blackwell, 1964), W. C. von Unnik, *Tarsus or Jerusalem: The City of Paul's Youth.* (London: The Epworth Press, 1962); Davies, *op. cit.,* Ulrich Luz, "Der alte und der neue Bund bei Paulus und im Hebräerbrief," *Evangelische Theologie,* 27 (1967): 318–36.

65. Cf. Nic. H. Ridderbos, "Is het Hebreeuws één van de Bronnen van de Openbaring?" GTT, 64 (1964): 209–29, for a thorough discussion of James Barr's, *The Semantics of Biblical Language* (London and New York: Oxford University Press, 1961). Cf. the latter's "Hypostatisation of Linguistic Phenomena in Modern Theological Interpretation," JSS, 7 (1962): 85–94; David Hill, cf. note 70. Stephen Neill, *The Interpretation of the New Testament 1861–1961* (London and New York: Oxford Paperbacks, 1966), 329–35, quotes abundantly from Barr.

66. Cf. G. Sevenster, "Het Nieuwe Testament—§ 2 De Taal," *Het oudste Christendom en de antieke cultuur* II (Haarlem: 1951), II:38.

67. Gerhard Friedrich and G. Kittel, eds., *Theologisches Wörterbuch zum Neuen Testament;* English edition, *Theological Dictionary of the New Testament,* 4 Vols., trans. and ed. G. W. Bromiley (Grand Rapids: Eerdmans, 1964–68).

68. Barr, *op. cit.;* see also his *Biblical Words for Time* (London: SCM; Naperville, Ill.: Allenson, Inc.; 1962).

69. In this I agree with J. de Vuyst, *op. cit.,* pp. 58, 67 f.

70. Cf. David Hill, *Greek Words and Hebrew Meanings: Studies in the Semantics of Soteriological Terms* (Cambridge: University Press, 1967); cf. Also Norman W. Porteous, "Second Thoughts—II: The Present State of Old Testament Theology," *Evangelische Theologie,* 75 (Dec. 1963): 70–4.

71. Bright, *op. cit.,* p. 185.

72. *Ibid.,* p. 186, 187.

73. See above, pp. 280–81.

74. Bright, *op. cit.,* pp. 187, 188 f.

75. *Ibid.,* p. 189.

76. The concepts "Law" and "Gospel" were connected by Luther with the terms "written code" and "Spirit" (II Cor. 3:6), but then applied to both Old and New Testaments. See H. Bornkamm, *Luther und des Alte Testament* (Tübingen: 1948); E. Kamla, "Buchstabe und Geist," *Evangelische Theologie,* 1954, pp. 276 ff.

77. Bright, *op. cit.,* p. 190. Cf. also Geerhardus Vos, *Biblical Theology* (Grand Rapids: Eerdmans, 1948), p. 144.

78. Its Scriptural basis is found in texts like Lk. 16:16; Jn. 1:17; Rom. 4:16; 6:14, 15; II Cor. 3:1–18; Gal. 5:4.

79. Gal. 3:24, 25.

80. It is still interesting to read Calvin's *Institutes,* II, chapters X and XI, on these matters. According to him Law and Gospel are but two administrations of one and the same covenant of grace. Cf. M. Simon, "Die Beziehung zwischen Altem and Neuem Testament in der Schriftauslegung Calvins," *Reformierte Kirchenzeitung,* 82 (1932): 19 f.; and especially H. H. Wolf, *Die Einheit des Bundes, das Verhältnis von Altem und Neuem Testament bei Calvin* (Neukirchen: 1958), pp. 19–54.

81. Bright, *op. cit.,* pp. 192–6, 198 f.

82. An excellent exposition is to be found in Berkouwer, *De Persoon van Christus,* pp. 87–123. Cf. W. G. Kümmel, *Verheissung und Erfüllung, Untersuchungen zur eschatologische Verkündigung Jesu* (Basel: Heinrich Meyer, 1945; English trans., S.C.M., 1957). A *Festschrift* for N. S. Hooke bears the same title, *Promise and Fulfillment,* ed. Frederick F. Bruce (Edinburgh: 1963); Otto Weber, *Grundlagen der Dogmatik,*

(Neukirchen-Moes: Verlag der Buchhandlung des Erziehungsvereins, 1955), I: 336–40.

83. Cf. Berkouwer, *De Persoon,* pp. 98 f.; 104 f.; Payne, *op. cit.,* p. 18; W. Zimmerli, "Verheissung und Erfüllung," *Vergegenwärtigung, Aufsätze zur Auslegung des Alten Testaments* (Berlin: 1955), p. 13; C. Westermann, *Zur Auslegung des Alten Testaments,* pp. 88 ff.; Bright, *op. cit.,* pp. 130 ff.

84. Cf. Schweitzer, *op. cit.,* p. 267; F. C. Fensham, "Covenant, Promise and Expectation in the Bible," *Theologische Zeitschrift,* 23 (1967): 322.

85. This point of view is stressed by A. A. van Ruler, "De waarde van het Old Testament," *Religie en Politiek* (1945), pp. 127 f.

86. Hellbardt, *Das Alte Testament und das Evangelium* (1933), pp. 127 f. Cf. Hellbardt, *Theol. Blatter* (1937), and Berkouwer, *De Persoon,* p. 98.

87. See Th. C. Vriezen, *Hoofdlijnen der Theologie van het Oude Testament,* 3rd ed. (Wageningen: H. Veenman en Zonen, 1966), pp. 205 f. N.B.: The third Dutch edition is expanded by about a hundred pages. The discussion on the relationship between history and revelation to which we refer is not found in the English edition. See also Martin Noth, *Developing Lines of Theological Thought in Germany,* Fourth Annual Bibliographical Lecture (Richmond, Va.: Union Theological Seminary, 1963), pp. 5 ff.; Felix Christ, ed., *Oikonomia, Heilsgeschichte als Thema der Theologie* (Hamburg-Bergstedt: Herbert Reich Evang. Verlag, 1967).

88. L. H. K. Bleeker, *Hermeneutik van het Oude Testament* (Haarlem: 1948), p. 207, cf. pp. 190–207.

89. Cf. Friedrich Baumgärtel, "Das hermeneutische Problem des Alten Testaments," *Probleme Alttestamentlicher Hermeneutik, Aufsatze,* ed. Claus Westermann (Munich: Chr. Kaiser Verlag, 1960), pp. 114 ff.; and Franz Hesse, "Zur Frage der Wertung und der Geltung alttestamentlicher Texte," *ibid.,* pp. 266 ff.

90. Cf. Koole, *Hermeneutische Oriëntatie, ibid.,* pp. 22 f.

91. Cf. Berkouwer, *De Persoon,* pp. 89 f., 113 ff.

92. Fensham, *op. cit.,* pp. 305 f.

93. Cf. Berkouwer, *De Persoon,* pp. 90, 107.

94. Cf. especially G. Fohrer, "Messiasfrage und Bibelverständnis" (1957). He reduces the number of Messianic prophecies to the following: Isa. 9:1 ff.; 11:1 ff.; Jer. 23:4 f. = 33:15 f.; Ezk. 17:22 ff.; Mic. 5:1 ff.; Hag. 2:20 ff.; Zech. 4:1 ff.; 6:9 ff.; cf. Mal. 3:23 f.— this political figure, however, was not Jesus of Nazareth!

95. Bright, *op. cit.,* p. 198 f. According to G. Fohrer, "The Centre of a Theology of the Old Testament," NGTT, 7 (1966): 198–206, the connecting line between the Testaments is based upon the dual concepts of the rule of God and the communion between God and man; see especially p. 206.

96. According to some scholars (for instance, Korff, *Christologie,* II: 49), Rom. 9:4 shows that the promises are but a subsection of all the categories of the Old Testament. Berkouwer, rightly contradicts this line of thought *(De Persoon,* p. 107, n. 65).

97. Berkouwer, *De Persoon,* pp. 90 f., 101, 105, 107, 110, 118 f.; Harold H. Rowley, *The Unity of the Bible,* 2nd ed. (London: Carey Kingsgate; Philadelphia: Westminster; 1955), pp. 108 ff.; Zimmerli, *op. cit.,* p. 18; Schweitzer, *op. cit.,* 261 f.

98. This is endorsed by C. F. D. Moule, "Fulfilment—Words in the New Testament: Use and Abuse," *New Testament Studies,* 14 (1968): 293–320. The third and most important set of correlatives according to Moule is covenant-promise over against fulfillment proper. "The protasis in this pair . . . is no mere prediction, nor a mere beginning, nor even a promise or threat in general, but God's covenant-promise in particular; and by this is meant not any single, limited promise, but all the promise and hope attaching to all that is epitomized in the Bible by God's covenant with his people" (p. 294).

99. The Greek words are *pleroun, telein, teleioun* and *plethein;* they occur respectively 86, 28, 23, and 24 times in the NT.

100. Cf. R. Bijlsma, *Schriftuurlijk Schriftgezag* (Nijkerk: G. F. Callenbach, 1959), pp. 332 ff. Cf. also this statement by H. W. Obbink quoted by Vriezen in *Outline of Old Testament Theology*, pp. 100 f.: "Fulfilment does not mean here a replacement of the Old Testament message by something else. . . . Fulfilment does not mean that the promise comes to an end and is replaced by the very thing that was promised but it means that now the promise itself becomes completely unambiguous and consequently affective. . . ."

101. For an enumeration, see Bijlsma, *op. cit.*, p. 335 f. See also R. Schippers, o.v. "Fulle," *Theologisches Begriffslexikon zum Neue Testament* (Wurppertal: Theologischer Verlag Rolf Brockhaus, 1967), pp. 407 ff.

102. Bijlsma, *op. cit.*, p. 335.

103. *Ibid.*, p. 336; Herman Ridderbos, *De Komst van het Koninkrijk* (Kampen: J. H. Kok, 1950), p. 67.

104. Bright, *op. cit.*, p. 196.

105. *Ibid.*

106. Max. Meinertz (*op. cit.*, p. 54) puts it in the following words: "Dass das ungläubig gebliebene Judentum den Messias und sein Evangelium verworfen hat, entspringt nicht dem echten gottgewollten Alt Gedanken, sondern seiner verengten, unorganischen, nämentlich pharisäischen Interpretation."

107. Vriezen, *op. cit.*, p. 100; see Bijlsma, *op. cit.*, pp. 367–77.

108. *Ibid.*, n. 1. The reference is to Martin Buber's work *Two Types of Faith* (New York: Harper Torchbooks, 1951).

109. Among others Rowley, *op. cit.*, p. 110; Zimmerli, *op. cit.*, p. 26; Schweitzer, *op. cit.*, pp. 250, 261, 266; Bright, *op. cit.*, pp. 137 f.; Berkouwer, *De Persoon*, pp. 106 ff.; Bijlsma, *op. cit.*, pp. 338 ff.

110. Koole, *Hermeneutisch Oriëntatie*, p. 23.

111. Bright, *op. cit.* p. 201.

112. Schweitzer, *op. cit.*, p. 259.

113. Cf. also Vriezen, *op. cit.*, p. 98: "The Church must always be willing to admit that 'from the historical point of view the Talmud is just as legitimate a continuation of the Old Testament as the Gospel,' but the Church can never admit that, essentially and spiritually, the Talmud is the true continuation of the most profound elements of Old Testament preaching." See the excellent discussion of the relationship between Old Testament, New Testament, and Judaism in Harold H. Rowley's *Unity of the Bible* (Philadelphia: Westminster, 1955), pp. 94 f.; cf. Berkouwer, *De Persoon*, p. 89; Schweitzer, *op. cit.*, pp. 171 f.

114. See especially, Rowley, *op. cit.*, p. 94 f.

115. The former is Rowley's phrase (*ibid.*, p. 98). The latter is Bright's (*op. cit.*, pp. 126 f., 131 ff., 148 f.).

116. Bright, *op. cit.*, p. 202.

117. See Berkouwer, *De Heilige Schrift*, p. 107.

118. Cf. Schweitzer, *op. cit.*, pp. 261, 265; Rowley, *op. cit.*, pp. 97, 102; Berkouwer, *De Persoon*, pp. 106, 111 f.

119. J. Ridderbos, "Oud en Nieuw Verbond," *De Apostolische Kerk* (Kampen: J. H. Kok, 1954), pp. 32–8.

120. Herman Bavinck, *Gereformeerde Dogmatiek*, 4th ed. (Kampen: J. H. Kok, 1929), III:204 f.

121. For an excellent discussion on this point, see the chapters "The Old Testament in the Christian Pulpit" and "Preaching from the Old Testament: The Principles Illustrated" in Bright, *op. cit.*, pp. 161–212, 213–51. See also Gottfried Voigt, *Der helle Morgenstern, Homiletische Auslegung alttestamentlicher Texte* (Berlin: Evangelische Verlagsanstalt, 1956).

Notes about the contributors to *New Perspectives on the Old Testament,*
their educational backgrounds, publications, and present positions.

R. L. ALDEN
Ph.D., Hebrew Union College, Jewish Institute of Religion. Periodical
literature on the prophets. Assistant Professor of Old Testament, Conservative Baptist Theological Seminary, Denver, Colorado.

G. L. ARCHER, JR.
Ph.D., Harvard University. *Survey of Old Testament Introduction,*
Commentaries on Hebrews, Romans, Isaiah. Head of Old Testament
Department, Trinity Evangelical Divinity School, Deerfield, Illinois.

C. E. DeVRIES
Ph.D., University of Chicago. Excavation reports, The Oriental In-
stitute, University of Chicago, in Egypt. Research Associate (Associate
Professor of Egyptology), Oriental Institute, University of Chicago,
Chicago, Illinois.

R. L. HARRIS
Ph.D., Dropsie College for Hebrew Learning. *Introductory Hebrew
Grammar, Inspiration and Canonicity of the Bible.* Dean of the Faculty
and Professor of Old Testament, Covenant Theological Seminary, St.
Louis, Missouri.

W. C. KAISER, JR.
M.A., Brandeis University, Ph.D. candidate, Brandeis. Periodical liter-
ature on the Pentateuch. Associate Professor of Old Testament, Trinity
Evangelical Divinity School, Deerfield, Illinois.

F. D. KIDNER
M.A. Oxford University. Tyndale Commentaries: *Genesis, Proverbs.*
Warden, Tyndale House Theological Research Library, Cambridge,
England.

K. A. KITCHEN
B.A., University of Liverpool. *Ancient Orient and Old Testament.*
Lecturer, School of Archaeology and Oriental Studies, University of
Liverpool, England.

M. G. KLINE
Ph.D., Dropsie College of Hebrew and Cognate Languages. *Treaty of
the Great King. By Oath Consigned.* Professor of Old Testament,
Gordon Divinity School, Wenham, Massachusetts.

A. A. MacRAE
Ph.D., University of Pennsylvania. *Nuzi Personal Names.* President
and Professor of Old Testament, Faith Theological Seminary, Elkins
Park, Pennsylvania.

J. B. PAYNE
Th.D., Princeton Theological Seminary. *Outline of Hebrew History,
Imminent Appearing of Christ, Theology of the Older Testament.*

Professor of Old Testament, Wheaton College Graduate School of Theology, Wheaton, Illinois.

E. B. SMICK

Ph.D., Dropsie College for Hebrew Learning. *The Wycliffe Bible Commentary* (O.T. Books). Professor of Old Testament Language and Literature, Covenant Theological Seminary, St. Louis, Missouri.

P. A. VERHOEF

Th.D., Free University of Amsterdam. *The Apocrypha, a Translation; The Prophecies of Nahum and Habakkuk.* Professor of Old Testament, Stellenbosch Theological Seminary, South Africa.

B. K. WALTKE

Ph.D., Harvard University; Th.D., Dallas Theological Seminary. Periodical literature on textual criticism. Professor of Semitics and Old Testament, Dallas Theological Seminary, Dallas, Texas.

L. J. WOOD

Ph.D., Michigan State University. *Is the Rapture Next?* Periodical literature on Old Testament chronology. Dean and Professor of Old Testament, Grand Rapids Baptist Theological Seminary, Grand Rapids, Michigan.

M. H. WOUDSTRA

Th.D., Westminster Theological Seminary. *The Biblical Expositor, The Wycliffe Bible Commentary* (O.T. books). Professor of Old Testament, Calvin Theological Seminary, Grand Rapids, Michigan.

J. S. WRIGHT

M.A., Cambridge University. *Man in the Process of Time, The Date of Ezra's Coming to Jerusalem.* Principal of Tyndale, 1951–1970, Bristol, England.

E. M. YAMAUCHI

Ph.D., Brandeis University. *Greece and Babylon, Composition and Corroboration in Classical and Biblical Studies.* Associate Professor of History, Miami University, Oxford, Ohio.